# Oliver Hart and the Rise of Baptist America

# Oliver Hart and the Rise of Baptist America

ERIC C. SMITH

# OXFORD
UNIVERSITY PRESS

Oxford University Press is a department of the University of Oxford. It furthers the University's objective of excellence in research, scholarship, and education by publishing worldwide. Oxford is a registered trade mark of Oxford University Press in the UK and certain other countries.

Published in the United States of America by Oxford University Press
198 Madison Avenue, New York, NY 10016, United States of America.

© Oxford University Press 2020

First issued as an Oxford University Press paperback, 2024

All rights reserved. No part of this publication may be reproduced, stored in a retrieval system, or transmitted, in any form or by any means, without the prior permission in writing of Oxford University Press, or as expressly permitted by law, by license, or under terms agreed with the appropriate reproduction rights organization. Inquiries concerning reproduction outside the scope of the above should be sent to the Rights Department, Oxford University Press, at the address above.

You must not circulate this work in any other form
and you must impose this same condition on any acquirer.

Library of Congress Cataloging-in-Publication Data
Names: Smith, Eric C. (Eric Coleman), author.
Title: Oliver Hart and the rise of Baptist America / Eric Coleman Smith.
Description: New York, NY, United States of America : Oxford Universtity Press, 2020. | Includes bibliographical references and index.
Identifiers: LCCN 2020008348 (print) | LCCN 2020008349 (ebook) | ISBN 9780197506325 (hardback) | ISBN 9780197769836 (paperback) | ISBN 9780197506349 (epub)
Subjects: LCSH: Hart, Oliver, 1723–1795. | Regular Baptists—South Carolina—Charleston—Clergy—Biography. | Baptists—United States—History. | United States—Church history—To 1775.
Classification: LCC BX6495.H275 S645 2020 (print) | LCC BX6495.H275 (ebook) | DDC 286/.1092 [B]—dc23
LC record available at https://lccn.loc.gov/2020008348
LC ebook record available at https://lccn.loc.gov/2020008349

Paperback printed by Marquis Book Printing, Canada

*For my parents,*

*Gene and Ginger Smith*

Enlarge the place of thy tent, and let them stretch forth the curtains of thine habitations: spare not, lengthen thy cords, and strengthen thy stakes;

For thou shalt break forth on the right hand and on the left; and thy seed shall inherit the Gentiles, and make the desolate cities to be inhabited.

Isaiah 54:2–3
King James Version

# Contents

| | |
|---|---|
| *List of Abbreviations* | ix |
| Introduction | 1 |
| 1. "The humble Baptists": Oliver Hart's Baptist Community | 11 |
| 2. "The power of religion greatly displayed": Baptists and the Great Awakening | 33 |
| 3. "All things are become new": Moving to the South | 55 |
| 4. "Bringing many souls home to Jesus Christ": Moderate Revivalism in Charleston | 80 |
| 5. "A regular Confederation": Laying the Foundations of the Baptist South | 105 |
| 6. "Every day brings fresh wonders!": The 1754 Charleston Revival | 125 |
| 7. "Seals of my ministry": Training the Next Generation | 149 |
| 8. "Promoting so laudable a Design": Baptist Development in the 1760s | 172 |
| 9. "Comforts and mercies, losses and crosses": A Transitional Season | 199 |
| 10. "The rising glory of this continent": The American Revolution | 222 |
| 11. "Directed in the path of duty": Staying the Course | 249 |
| 12. "The Baptist Interest": A Respectable Denomination in a New Nation | 271 |
| 13. "All the Baptists on the Continent": A Dream Briefly Realized | 299 |
| *Bibliography* | 317 |
| *Index* | 331 |

# Abbreviations

| | |
|---|---|
| ANTS | Andover-Newton Theological Seminary Library at Yale Divinity School |
| HSP | Historical Society of Pennsylvania |
| JBDML | James B. Duke Memorial Library, Furman University |
| JHL | John Hay Library, Brown University |
| SCL | South Caroliniana Library, University of South Carolina |

# Introduction

It being the Lord's Day, Oliver Hart ordinarily would have been preaching at the Charleston Baptist Church, where he had pastored for thirty years. But on April 12, 1780, Hart found himself instead at the home of his son-in-law, Thomas Screven, in St. Thomas Parish, South Carolina, tensely awaiting news of the impending British occupation of Charleston. The fifty-seven-year-old Baptist minister had been convalescing at Screven's home for the past two months, having suffered at least one mild stroke and several bouts with fever over the past year. From his bed, Hart wrote, "Nothing was heard but the hideous roar of cannon by day and night." Too old and sick for combat, all Hart could do was pray. "Often did I petition God with prayers and tears that poor Charles Town might be spared, and not suffered to fall into the enemy's hands," Hart recalled in his diary. "Never could I give it up until I heard of its surrender."[1]

Ever since Sir Henry Clinton and his British forces had first threatened Charleston, Hart's friends and his doctor had insisted that Hart leave the city. Not only was he physically weak; he was a marked man. From the first rumblings of revolution in colonial Charleston, Hart had used his position as the South's most revered Baptist to promote liberty for the colonies. In addition to lobbying for religious liberty under the new state constitution, Hart had served on a special commission from the South Carolina Council of Safety. Along with a Presbyterian minister, William Tennent III, and a lawyer, William Henry Drayton, Hart had undertaken a mission to persuade the loyalist Carolina backcountry to join the colonials. Now the Red Coats were at the gates, and Hart's outspoken patriotism put him in line for enemy reprisals. It is possible that, like his fellow Baptist Richard Furman, Hart had a bounty on his head.

---

[1] Oliver Hart, *A Copy of the Original Diary of Rev. Oliver Hart of Charlestown, Pastor of the Baptist Church of Charlestown*, mimeographed copy, James P. Boyce Centennial Library, Southern Baptist Theological Seminary, Louisville, Kentucky, 13.

*Oliver Hart and the Rise of Baptist America.* Eric C. Smith, Oxford University Press (2020). © Oxford University Press.
DOI: 10.1093/oso/9780197506325.001.0001

## 2 · OLIVER HART AND THE RISE OF BAPTIST AMERICA

So when Hart learned on this Sunday morning that a strong detachment of the British army was a few miles from Screven's home, flight seemed his only option. "I packed a few clothes in haste, and about 12 o'clock took leave of my dear wife and the family," he wrote, calling it "the most affecting parting I ever experienced." With tears on every face in the household, he mounted his horse. Echoing the biblical story of Abraham, he added, "I set off, but whither was I going or when I should return I did not know." Like the Old Testament patriarch, Hart would be sustained on the journey by his faith in the personal care of an invisible God. On his part, he could only "endeavor to leave my connections and place myself in the hands of the great and wise Disposer of all events."[2]

But as his horse carried him steadily northward over the next few months, Hart found that the Almighty had seen fit to place him in the hands of a great many Baptists. Everywhere he traveled, it seemed, he met Baptists of one stripe or another. In every hollow of the Carolina backcountry was a gang of roughhewn Separate Baptists. They had migrated to the South in 1755 out of New England's radical Separate movement, and there experienced "a happy revival of religion."[3] In Virginia, Hart lodged for a few days with John Leland, an eccentric evangelist and defender of religious liberty. Leland introduced Hart to John Waller, William Dawson, and David Thomas, all grizzled survivors of a brutal Anglican suppression of the growing Baptist movement during the 1760s and 1770s that had brought on them ridicule, physical abuse, and jail time. Hart remarked that he and the Virginia Baptists were all "very happy together."[4] He would ultimately land in Philadelphia, the cradle of Baptist denominationalism in America, the center from which his refined Particular Baptist friends had been exporting Calvinistic Baptist doctrine for decades, publishing confessions of faith, sending missionaries and planting churches, and even helping found Rhode Island College (today Brown University) in the 1760s. Further north still, in New England, where the American Baptist story had begun, Baptists like Isaac Backus of Middleborough, Massachusetts, were still chafing under the church-state standing order of Puritan Congregationalism. But they were now growing numerous and respectable enough to make their voices heard; Backus had even published the first of a three-volume history of New England Baptists in 1777. Hart had many contacts among these Baptists, too, corresponding

[2] Hart, *Original Diary*, 13–14.
[3] Oliver Hart to Samuel Jones, June 30, 1769, McKesson MSS, HSP.
[4] Hart, *Original Diary*, 14.

INTRODUCTION 3

regularly with Backus, Hezekiah Smith of Haverhill, and James Manning of Providence.

Hart had begun his flight from Charleston in fear, but at some point it must have hit him: Baptists were now everywhere in the British American colonies. "It would seem as if trees had become men, and them men Baptists. This is the Lord's doing, and it is marvelous in our eyes," Hart would write in 1789.[5] And Baptists were growing more numerous all the time. Hart preached to a group of Presbyterians on his way through North Carolina in a display of evangelical camaraderie, only to have a prominent member come to him by night, Nicodemus-like, to request immersion. What could Hart do but baptize him? Hart's flight further revealed that all these Baptists, diverse in their cultural contexts, worship styles, and secondary doctrinal beliefs, and separated by hundreds of miles, were more connected now than ever before. Not many years after Hart's hasty retreat from Clinton's forces, these Baptists would come together to form a national denomination in the young American republic.

*

Fifty years earlier, a horseback ride along Hart's route to Philadelphia would have discovered a very different picture. Over the course of the "long" eighteenth century, Hart's American Baptists underwent a remarkable transformation. At the end of the 1600s, colonial Baptists were a small, disorganized, marginal sect in a sea of more powerful religious groups. In colonies with a strong religious establishment, like Massachusetts, Baptists were harassed and persecuted; in more pluralistic colonies like Pennsylvania and South Carolina, Baptists scrapped and competed with a dizzying variety of religious options; in still other corners of British colonial America, like Virginia, Baptists were too few and too weak to make much of a difference. By the beginning of the 1800s, their position had changed completely. Baptists entered the nineteenth century a large, rapidly growing, increasingly sophisticated, and relatively unified denomination. They were ready not only to take their place among the other respectable religious groups in America but to make a run at becoming the largest and most influential denomination in the country. In the South, at least, they would succeed in this.

How did it happen? The eighteenth-century American Baptist story can be understood as unfolding in a series of several overlapping stages. First was

---

[5] Oliver Hart to Richard Furman, September 28, 1789, Hart MSS, JBDML.

a period of Baptist stabilization, extending from the late seventeenth century until the Great Awakening. Here, Baptists focused on staking out their beliefs and practices in the New World, surviving both persecution and pluralism and making their earliest efforts at organizing beyond the level of local churches. The second stage was one of dramatic multiplication. Beginning with George Whitefield's evangelical revivals in 1739, colonial American Baptists experienced a growth surge, through both the revitalization of the existing Particular Baptists and the birth of an entirely new Baptist subgroup, the Separate Baptists. Both sets of revivalist Baptists, the moderate Particulars and the radical Separates, continued to increase numerically all the way through the American Revolution, the Separates at an unprecedented clip. By the early 1780s, a whole new and rapidly growing Baptist movement would emerge in New England, the Free Will Baptists, led by the visionary Benjamin Randall. By at least that same time, American Baptist groups had begun spilling out of what would be the contiguous Unites States, to Nova Scotia to the north and Jamaica to the south. The third stage of Baptist development involved increasing sophistication and unification. Starting in the late 1760s, America's Baptists gave more serious thought to larger-scale organization, communicating between regional associations, adopting official documents, founding institutions, educating ministers, reaching into new areas, and keeping track of growth through statistics. Seizing the opportunity to obtain religious freedom during the Revolutionary War, the Particular (by this time known as Regular) Baptists and the Separate Baptists began to lay aside their numerous stylistic differences to unite as one Baptist body (ultimately smoothing out the radical edges of the Separates). During this stage of continued growth and increased sophistication, many Baptist leaders began to dream of uniting "all the Baptists on the Continent" into a single, powerful, national denomination. They finally achieved this goal at the founding of the Triennial Convention in 1814, when distinguished Baptists from all over America banded together to support foreign missionaries, leading to a host of other cooperative efforts. By the 1840s, however, American Baptists would enter a fourth stage: fragmentation. Already diverse by nature, Baptists in 1845 were pulled apart by the same sectional forces that would eventually plunge the American Union into Civil War, never to unite again. The rise of Baptist America had been breathtaking to watch; its sudden rending was just as spectacular.

*

INTRODUCTION 5

This book attempts to tell the story of America's Baptists in the long eighteenth century through the life of Oliver Hart. Hart, it seems to me, is particularly well-suited for understanding the development of early American Baptists. Born in 1723, he died in 1795, his life spanning the most critical years of development in the American Baptist story, which he experienced in a variety of important Baptist contexts. He spent the first twenty-six years of his life in Warminster, Pennsylvania, home of the enormously influential Philadelphia Association and a hotbed of revival activity during the peak years of the Great Awakening. Both of these forces—the denominationalism of the Philadelphia Association and the revivalism of George Whitefield—would make a decisive impact on Hart and his compatriots who shaped Baptist America. At the end of 1749, Hart moved to Charleston, South Carolina, where he would spend thirty years blazing new trails for the South's Baptists as a revivalist pastor, denominational architect, educator and mentor of young ministers, and missions advocate. Later he would participate in the events of the American Revolution as a patriot and religious liberty lobbyist. When the British drove Hart from Charleston in 1780, he returned to the middle colonies, where he spent his final fifteen years as a pastor in Hopewell, New Jersey, continuing to promote the Baptist interest in a new republic as a leader in the Philadelphia Association. Throughout his adult life, Hart maintained an extensive personal correspondence with Baptists all over America, as well as across the Atlantic. There were, in fact, few major events or influential figures in the eighteenth-century Baptist story to which Hart was not somehow connected.

Hart was self-conscious about his participation in the ascendancy of American Baptists. Like many of his Baptist contemporaries, he was passionate about promoting what he termed "the Baptist interest." He invested his most fruitful years in the South, where he became, as the twentieth-century Baptist historian Loulie Latimer Owens called him, Southern Baptists' "most important pioneer."[6] I intend to demonstrate in the pages that follow that Owens was exactly right on this, but also that Hart's impact extended far beyond the Baptist South. Hart dreamed of uniting "all the Baptists on the Continent," a phrase repeated often in his personal writings. He wanted to connect Baptists across the colonies—from Salisbury, New

---

[6] Loulie Latimer Owens, *Oliver Hart, 1723–1795: A Biography* (Greenville: South Carolina Baptist Historical Society, 1966), 1.

Hampshire, to Savannah, Georgia—in a well-coordinated network of communication and ministry activity. He worked to unify the buttoned-down, moderate revivalist Particular Baptists of whom he was a part with the rowdy, radical Separate Baptists who were taking the colonial American frontier by storm. He wished to improve the image of Baptists on a national scale, yearning for them to be known for something other than "meanness" and "ignorance" and to become a respectable denomination with their own theological schools, missions organizations, and everything else that mainstream denominations had, without losing their commitment to the "primitive" and "ancient" paths of New Testament religion to which Baptists had always tenaciously clung. Hart desired Baptists to have a voice in the government, banding together with each other and with other Dissenters to obtain religious freedom in the new republic. Most of all, he wanted Baptists to be instruments of widespread spiritual awakening, "bringing many souls home to Jesus Christ" through the moderate revivalism he had learned during the Great Awakening. Hart was an ambitious American Baptist. He did not believe, as will be seen, that Baptists had found the only way. His warm catholicity toward evangelicals of other denominations is in fact one of the most striking elements of his ministry. But Hart believed unapologetically that Baptists had found the best way. He spent his life advancing their cause in America.

Hart is also a good selection to study the early development of America's Baptists because of his role in the most controversial aspect of their history: slavery. As much as any white eighteenth-century Baptist could, Hart took a journey regarding race. Born into a family of former Quakers, he began his life exposed to antislavery ideas in southeastern Pennsylvania. Upon moving to Charleston, he adopted the classic evangelical proslavery position of the times, ministering to many Africans while buying and selling numerous slaves himself. Finally, he ended his life as a pastor in New Jersey by endorsing abolition as a member of the Philadelphia Association in the 1780s and 1790s. Hart thus provides a unique vantage point from which to view the key issue that prevented his dream of "all the Baptists on the Continent" from remaining a reality beyond 1845.

*

In his landmark 2002 book *America's God: From Jonathan Edwards to Abraham Lincoln*, Mark Noll lamented, "The history of the Baptists in the eighteenth and nineteenth centuries is a subject as scandalously neglected as had been, until very recently, the history of early American Methodism."[7] Noll did note William G. McLoughlin's magisterial *New England Dissent*[8] as an important historiographical exception to this assessment, to which I would also add Gregory A. Wills's superb study of the antebellum Baptist South, *Democratic Religion*[9] and Susan Juster's *Disorderly Women.*[10] Thankfully, a number of works treating Baptists in this era have also appeared in the years since *America's God*, including Janet Moore Lindman's *Bodies of Belief: Baptist Community in Early America*,[11] Thomas S. Kidd and Barry Hankins's *Baptists in America*,[12] Joshua Guthman's *Strangers Below*,[13] and my own *Order and Ardor*.[14] Added to these are a number of fine studies that help place Baptists in the context of early American evangelicalism, including Kidd's *The Great Awakening*[15] and Thomas J. Little's *Origins of Southern Evangelicalism*.[16] Each of these excellent resources has been immensely helpful, but much work remains to be done for understanding American Baptists as a whole. This is particularly the case for the long eighteenth century, the period of their decisive transformation. This book attempts to make a contribution toward filling that gap by providing the most thorough account to date of the institutional development of Baptists in the South and mid-Atlantic, while also providing the first modern biography of Oliver Hart, arguably the most important evangelical leader in the Revolutionary-era South.

In the following pages, I will argue that Oliver Hart played a pivotal role in the rise of Baptist America in the second half of the eighteenth century by practicing a singular and understated style of religious leadership. Hart was a good preacher, but not nearly the orator his mentor George Whitefield

[7] Mark Noll, *America's God: From Jonathan Edwards to Abraham Lincoln* (New York: Oxford University Press, 2002), 149.

[8] William G. McLoughlin, *New England Dissent, 1630–1833: The Baptists and the Separation of Church and State*, 2 vols. (Cambridge, MA: Harvard University Press, 1971).

[9] Gregory A. Wills, *Democratic Religion: Freedom, Authority, and Church Discipline in the Baptist South, 1785–1900* (New York: Oxford University Press, 1998).

[10] Susan Juster, *Disorderly Women: Sexual Politics and Evangelicalism in Revolutionary New England* (Ithaca, NY: Cornell University Press, 1994).

[11] Janet Moore Lindman, *Bodies of Belief: Baptist Community in Early America* (Philadelphia: University of Pennsylvania Press, 2008).

[12] Thomas S. Kidd and Barry Hankins, *Baptists in America: A History* (New York: Oxford University Press, 2015).

[13] Joshua Guthman, *Strangers Below: Primitive Baptists and American Culture* (Chapel Hill: University Press of North Carolina, 2015).

[14] Eric C. Smith, *Order and Ardor: The Revival Spirituality of Oliver Hart and the Regular Baptists of Eighteenth-Century South Carolina* (Columbia: University of South Carolina Press, 2018).

[15] Thomas S. Kidd, *The Great Awakening: The Roots of Evangelical Christianity in Colonial America* (New Haven, CT: Yale University Press, 2007).

[16] Thomas J. Little, *Origins of Southern Evangelicalism: Religious Revivalism in the South Carolina Lowcountry, 1670–1760* (Columbia: University of South Carolina Press, 2013).

## 8 OLIVER HART AND THE RISE OF BAPTIST AMERICA

was or his Baptist peer John Gano. He made no groundbreaking insights as a creative theologian but plodded on steadily and predictably in the old paths of Particular Baptist Calvinism. Though he testified to some deep spiritual experiences, he was not a charismatic visionary, like the Free Will Baptist leader Benjamin Randall. Nor did Hart possess the forceful personality of his Separate Baptist counterpart Shubal Stearns; Hart was in fact quite introspective and often insecure about his ministry talents. How, then, are we to account for Hart's almost unmatched influence as a Baptist leader?

As Hart's story unfolds, three strengths especially stand out. First, he practiced an earnest Christian piety that virtually everyone he met recognized and respected. "We recommend to you all to pray fervently; believe firmly; wait patiently; work abundantly; live holily; die daily; watch your hearts; guide your senses; redeem your time; love Christ; long for glory," he wrote in 1778. By all accounts, he appears to have pursued this all-consuming spiritual program in both public and private throughout his adult life.[17] After one meal together, Hart impressed the Methodist Joseph Pilmoor as "truly evangelical, and very devout." His longtime friend Richard Furman, with allowances for the context of a laudatory funeral address, nevertheless paid a striking tribute to Hart's well-known piety:

> But as a Christian and divine, his character was most conspicuous; no person who heard his pious, experimental discourses, or his affectionate, fervent addresses to God in prayer; who beheld the zeal and constancy he manifested in the public exercises of religion, of the disinterestedness, humility, benevolence, charity, devotion, and equanimity of temper he discovered on all occasions in the private walks of life; could for a moment doubt of his being not only *truly*, but *eminently*, religious.[18]

Hart was not a perfect man, and he knew it; his own Calvinistic theology attested that perfection was unattainable in this life. Yet Hart's failure to maintain consistency in practical holiness continually frustrated and disappointed him and always moved him to strive afresh for that lofty standard of godliness he desired. He appears to have won over his contemporaries, both within and outside of the Baptist fold, by his sheer sincerity and spiritual zeal.

---

[17] Charleston Association, *Minutes of the Charlestown Association, October 19, 1778* (Charleston, SC, 1778), 4.

[18] Richard Furman, *Rewards of Grace Conferred on Christ's Faithful People: A Sermon, Occasioned by the Decease of the Rev. Oliver Hart, A.M.* (Charleston, SC, 1796), 24.

INTRODUCTION 9

Hart's second great strength as a leader was his remarkable ability to make friends. He was simply unsurpassed at forming and cultivating relationships, which inevitably developed into important ministry partnerships. These included the Particular Baptist ministers of South Carolina he coaxed into forming the Charleston Association, the young men he closely mentored and sent out to the Baptist churches of the South, the suspicious frontier Separate Baptists whom he drew into the larger Baptist fellowship, and the numerous evangelical friendships he formed outside the Baptist fold, among Anglicans, Presbyterians, and Methodists. Furman would comment that Hart "had a mind formed for friendship," and he was right; time and again, Hart's relational skills proved instrumental in advancing his Baptist cause.[19]

Hart's third great strength was his ability to integrate tested ministry practices he had observed in other places and among other denominations, another prominent theme in this book. He transplanted the Baptist denominational model of the Philadelphia Association to Charleston in 1751, successfully implementing their institutional structure, adapting their confessional documents, and adopting their cooperative ministry methods among the Baptists in the South. But Hart also brought to Charleston many of the evangelical revival practices he had observed in Great Awakening Pennsylvania, including itinerant evangelism, organizing and addressing small inquirers' groups in homes, and cooperation with other denominations to promote wide-scale conversions and holiness. Hart's potent combination of Baptist precisionism and evangelical revivalism proved to be instrumental in Baptist expansion in the South in the mid-eighteenth century.

Hart's unique brand of religious leadership ultimately elevated him to the status of Southern Baptists' most important pioneer. He of course would not have viewed himself as a "Southern Baptist" in today's technical sense, as a member of the Southern Baptist Convention. This body did not form until half a century after his death. He did, however, view himself as doing important work in the fledgling Baptist South from 1750 to 1780, and his legacy— for good and for ill—did indeed endure in the Southern Baptist Convention, today America's largest Protestant denomination.

In this book, I will interact with a number of important themes in the story of American Baptist development: the doctrines and worship practices that defined the early Baptists; how Baptists viewed other denominations (and how others viewed the Baptists); to what degree the tumultuous events of

---

[19] Furman, *Rewards of Grace*, 24.

the Great Awakening and the American Revolution impacted Baptist development; how Baptists served as a prophetic counterculture in eighteenth-century society in some ways and capitulated to prevailing cultural trends in others; how Baptists self-consciously transformed themselves into a respectable denomination by the dawn of the nineteenth century; and more. I am grateful for the numerous historians in the fields of Baptist and early American religious history who have shaped my own ideas on these matters, and references to their works will appear in the notes of this study. I hope, however, by tracing the ascendancy of "all the Baptists on the Continent" through the life of one of early America's seminal but understudied religious leaders, to offer something illuminating and worthwhile of my own.

# 1

## "The humble Baptists"

### Oliver Hart's Baptist Community

When Oliver Hart was fifty-eight years old, an elegant society lady's reluctance to receive baptism prompted him to reflect on his own, long association with the Baptist people. Writing from Charleston, South Carolina, Hart's friend Richard Furman (1755–1825) had related the conversion of a young woman in town whom they both knew. While Hart was happy to learn that the young lady had found grace, he held out little hope that she would make her profession public by submitting to immersion in the Ashley River. Hart had been well acquainted with her parents. They too had agreed with Baptist principles, but when Hart had urged them to enter the waters, they balked. "They were Baptists in judgment, sober and well behaved, but never made profession," Hart recalled. "Hope they were pious, but diffident; and could not come forward." There was no getting around it: baptism was undignified. To be publicly plunged underwater required a crucifixion of pride and relinquishment of control that many adults, even born-again folk, were unwilling to make. It was for good reason that Baptists viewed their initiation rite as a symbolic death to self. Hart admitted that he would be surprised if Furman's young friend ever moved beyond the commitment level her parents had shown a generation earlier. "Their daughter is perhaps raised too high to associate with the humble Baptists," he sighed. "It is a pity that grandeur should have so much influence on the minds of those who would be deem'd followers of that humble Jesus, who had no where to lay his head."[1]

As Hart wrote these lines, it had been fifty years since he had himself identified with "the humble Baptists." This designation of his denomination certainly reflected the broader cultural perception of the Baptist people throughout Hart's life; Baptists occupied a decidedly lower rung on the social ladder than at least Anglicans, Congregationalists, and Presbyterians in the eighteenth century. The self-portrait of "humble Baptists" also undoubtedly

---

[1] Oliver Hart to Richard Furman, November 9, 1791, Hart MSS, JBDML.

*Oliver Hart and the Rise of Baptist America.* Eric C. Smith, Oxford University Press (2020). © Oxford University Press.
DOI: 10.1093/oso/9780197506325.001.0001

served Hart's own desire to identify his people with the character of the Savior. At the same time, Hart had done as much as anyone in the second half of the eighteenth century to transform Baptists from a marginal sect to a respectable denomination in the mainstream of American culture.

*

Oliver Hart came to Baptist convictions by way of the meandering spiritual journey of his paternal grandfather. John Hart was born November 16, 1651, in Whitney, Oxfordshire, in England. The Harts were prosperous, educated people; they were also among the earliest adherents of a radical religious sect called the Society of Friends, or Quakers. The Friends arose in the 1640s as a result of George Fox's (1624–1691) disillusionment with the English religious scene. As a young spiritual seeker, Fox could find neither an Established nor a Dissenting minister who could adequately care for his soul. Ultimately, Fox found relief only when he stopped listening to outward religious voices and heard a voice within. "There is one, even Jesus Christ, that can speak to thy condition," the voice said. It was a life-altering experience for Fox, who began to pursue "the pure knowledge of God, and of Christ alone, without the help of any man, book, or writing." Fox developed from this quest his distinguishing doctrine, the "Light within," the idea that God's presence is found in all people, regardless of social rank, gender, or even traditional Christian belief. As Fox promoted his new ideas, he found multitudes of English people hungry for the same immediate, personal access to God. One of his most famous followers, William Penn (1644–1718), recalled that Fox's message "reached the conscience and broke the heart, and brought many to a sense and search, so what people had been vainly seeking *without*, with much pains and cost, they by this ministry found *within*; where it was they wanted what they sought for, viz., the right way to peace with God. For they were directed to the Light of Jesus Christ within them." Fox's inner voice had spoken to the spiritual desires of a nation.[2]

The Quaker movement stirred considerable controversy among traditional English Protestants. When Fox claimed, "The Lord God opened to me by his invisible power, 'that every man was enlightened by the divine light of Christ,'" he denied the foundational Protestant doctrines of original sin and divine regeneration. Furthermore, whereas Protestants historically located

[2] Wilson Armistead, *Journal of George Fox* (London, 1852), 1:55–56, 11. For a recent study, see Hilary Hinds, *George Fox and Early Quaker Culture* (Manchester, England: Manchester University Press, 2011).

"THE HUMBLE BAPTISTS" 13

God's supreme revelation in the Bible, Fox urged his followers to experience God by "looking within," listening for still, small voices, and seeking mystical encounters. (The Quaker name came from the group's reputation for shaking under the Spirit's influence.) Quaker teaching also generated major social waves. Fox preached a radically individual faith, urging his listeners to "look unto Christ in them, and not unto men; for it is Christ that sanctifies." He rejected all the offices, sacraments, and rituals of the Anglican Church, telling crowds that "all their preaching, baptism, and sacrifices, would never sanctify them." Fox encouraged women to teach and recognized no social or clerical rank. He claimed that the Lord forbade him "to put off my hat to any, high or low; and I was required to Thee and Thou all men and women, without any respect to rich or poor, great or small." This provocative egalitarian message inspired a flood of polemical pamphlets and sermons from both Established and Dissenting ministers, and he and his followers regularly landed in jail. In spite of this, John Hart and thousands more found such power and liberty in Fox's message that they overcame the social and religious stigma and aligned themselves with Quakerism. By 1680, the Friends boasted some sixty thousand adherents in England and Wales.[3]

It was John Hart's Quaker connections that led him to America. In 1681, his friend William Penn received a land grant in the New World from King Charles II by virtue of a debt that the Crown owed Penn's family. Penn intended his proprietary colony to be more than a real estate venture: it would be a "holy experiment." He envisioned Pennsylvania ("Penn's woods") as a place of religious freedom and tolerance for people of all faiths, "a free colony for all mankind that should go thither, more especially those of my own profession, not that I would lessen the civil liberties of others because of their persuasion," Penn wrote.[4] Such religious pluralism was unusual for the time, even in the New World. By the early eighteenth century, Pennsylvania had attracted Quakers, Anglicans, Presbyterians, Baptists, German Reformed, Pietists, Mennonites, Lutherans, Independents, Roman Catholics, Jews, as well as a variety of short-lived, "experimental" religious societies. As one Welsh immigrant to Pennsylvania wrote, "We all agree and are at peace with one another and worship God in his own way." The reality was a bit more

---

[3] Armistead, *Journal of George Fox*, 1:70, 44, 80, 72.

[4] Article 1 of the Pennsylvania Charter of Privileges, signed in 1701, established "that no Person inhabiting in this Province or Territories, who shall confess and acknowledge One almighty God, the Creator, Upholder and Ruler of the World; and profess to live quietly under Civil Government, shall be molested or prejudiced because of his Conscientious Persuasion or Practice, nor be compelled to maintain any religious Worship, contrary to his Mind."

14   OLIVER HART AND THE RISE OF BAPTIST AMERICA

complex, of course. As John Hart would soon discover, Pennsylvania's multiplicity of religious options created an environment of fierce competition between the sects.[5]

John Hart purchased one thousand acres in Pennsylvania and sailed for America with his sister Mary in the fall of 1681. Over the next three years, four thousand others would join them. Hart settled near the Poquessing River, where he devoted himself to farming and married a Quaker girl named Susannah Rush (1656–1725). The Harts were integrally involved in the new community. When Penn drew up the charter of government in the fall of 1682, he named John Hart a member of the assembly of Philadelphia County. John also provided spiritual leadership among his neighbors, hosting meetings of the Friends in his home, visiting the poor and sick, and even preaching. John also participated in some of the earliest Quaker conversations about the impropriety of slavery. In 1688 he reported to his local Quaker meeting on the concerns of a group of German Quakers about the institution. Afterward he wrote that his meeting found the Germans' objections "so weighty that we think it is not expedient for us to meddle with it here, but do rather commit it to ye consideration of ye quarterly meeting: ye tenor of it being related to ye truth." It would be another hundred years before these recommendations began to gain traction throughout Pennsylvania.[6]

John's peaceful association with the Pennsylvania Quakers abruptly ended in 1691, however, in a controversy centered on the reforming efforts of the Scottish preacher George Keith (1638/39–1718).[7] Keith had accepted William Penn's invitation to come to America in 1684, after repeated imprisonments in England for his religious beliefs. There he helped organize Penn's land interests in East and West Jersey, tilted publicly against the Quakers' New England Puritan opponents Increase (1639–1723) and Cotton (1663–1728)

---

[5] Janet Moore Lindman, *Bodies of Belief: Baptist Community in Early America* (Philadelphia: University of Pennsylvania Press, 2008), 11. On the religious pluralism of early Pennsylvania, see Michael Zuckerman, "Introduction: Puritans, Cavaliers, and the Motley Middle," in *Friends and Neighbors: Group Life in America's First Plural Society*, edited by Michael Zuckerman (Philadelphia, PA: Temple University Press, 1982); Sally Schwartz, *"A Mixed Multitude": The Struggle for Toleration in Colonial Pennsylvania* (New York: New York University Press, 1982); and Martin E. Lodge, "The Crisis of the Churches in the Middle Colonies, 1720–1750," *PMHB* 95 (April 1971): 195–220.

[6] W. W. H. Davis, *History of the Hart Family of Warminster, Bucks County, Pennsylvania* (Doylestown, PA: W. W. H. Davis, 1876), 15–18; W. W. H. Davis, *History of Bucks County, Pennsylvania, From the Discovery of the Delaware to the Present Time* (Doylestown, PA: Democrat Book and Job, 1876), 215.

[7] See Jon Butler, "Gospel Order Improved: The Keithian Schism and the Exercise of Quaker Ministerial Authority," *William & Mary Quarterly* 31, no. 3 (July 1974): 431–52.

Mather, and taught in a Quaker Latin school. However, Keith soon disturbed his Quaker neighbors by rejecting that key tenet of Quakerism, "their Notion of the Sufficiency of the Light within every man to Salvation without anything else." Keith exhorted the Friends to look upon themselves as sinners who could not find salvation within, but only in the objective work of Jesus Christ on the cross. In this, Keith was simply articulating what would become the standard evangelical critique of Quaker doctrine.[8] Keith also criticized the Quakers for their low views of Scripture and what he considered to be their unbiblical form of church government. When Quaker leaders tried to shut down Keith's meetings, he accused them of abusing their spiritual authority like little popes in the Church of Rome; when Keith refused to back down, the Friends expelled him from their fellowship. He returned to England in 1694, where he later became an Anglican missionary to Quakers, but he left behind some five hundred "Keithians," composing fourteen or fifteen separate meetings. To the dismay of the Friends, John Hart joined the exodus. Though William Penn himself pleaded with John by letter to reconsider his decision, John's mind was fixed. He even signed his name to a published confession of faith on behalf of the new sect.[9]

*

In search of a new faith community, several Keithians applied for membership at the nearby Pennepek Baptist Church, just outside Philadelphia in Lower Dublin Township.[10] Like the Quakers, Baptists had been religious outsiders in England, having formed out of the English Separate movement in the early seventeenth century. They too had endured persecution for their convictions and had migrated to Pennsylvania seeking religious freedom. The Pennepek Church was one of the earliest Baptist congregations to form across the Delaware Valley in the late seventeenth century, comprised of Welsh, English, and Irish immigrants. They did not greet the Keithians warmly. Shortly into Pennsylvania's "holy experiment," all denominations

---

[8] George Whitefield voiced the same concern two generations later, after attending a Quaker meeting in Philadelphia. "I heartily wish that he would talk of an outward as well as an inward Christ," Whitefield would complain, "for otherwise, we may make our own holiness, and not the righteousness of Jesus Christ the cause of our being accepted by God. From such doctrine may I always turn away." George Whitefield, *Journals* (Edinburgh: Banner of Truth Trust, 1960), 341.

[9] Davis, *History of Bucks County*, 215.

[10] Pennepek is sometimes spelled "Pennypack"; the congregation was also known as the Lower Dublin Baptist Church.

16    OLIVER HART AND THE RISE OF BAPTIST AMERICA

were learning to guard their fellowships from the corrupting influences of other faiths.[11]

Admitting strangers into the fold had burned the Pennepek Baptists before. Their founding pastor, Elias Keach (1665–1699), was a charlatan, neither ordained nor converted when he began his work among them. Keach had passed himself off as a minister by trading on the reputation of his famous father, English Baptist Benjamin Keach (1640–1704). Parroting his father's preaching style, Keach convinced everyone of his sincerity. The charade continued until, to his shock, Keach cracked with conviction during one of his own sermons. He confessed his fraudulence to the church and professed a sincere faith in Christ for the first time. When he later announced a legitimate call to ministry, the Pennepek Baptists recognized him as their pastor again. Keach then arose as one of the leading American Baptist ministers of the late seventeenth century, planting churches throughout the region, including one in Philadelphia in 1698. By the time the Keithians applied for membership at Pennepek, however, Keach had returned to England, leaving the church without a minister. The members wrote to Keach for advice, and he counseled against receiving the Keithians. As the Pennepek meeting book noted, "We found them still too much of Quakerism, Reuben-like, unstable as water,[12] too ready to give ear to any notion or new opinion." All religious groups were seeking stability in Pennsylvania's volatile religious climate; receiving the Keithians with all their strange and shifting ideas was a risk the fragile Baptist community could not afford to take.[13]

John Hart responded to this rejection by assembling a Keithian remnant in his home, to whom he preached for the next several years. In time, however, he grew as disillusioned with Keithianism as he had with the Quakers. Increasingly, Baptist emphasis on New Testament church order attracted him, until, in 1702, he submitted to immersion by one Thomas Ritter. It was not long after this that the Pennepek Baptist pastor died, and the church invited John's Keithian house church to join them. As the eighteenth-century Baptist historian Morgan Edwards (1722–1795) observed, these Keithians transformed into a kind of hybrid group that was becoming typical of pluralist Pennsylvania. Some called them "keithian Baptists" and others "quaker

---

[11] Ernest Hawkins, *Historical Notices of the Missions of the Church of England* (London, 1845), 26; Lindman, *Bodies of Belief*, 15–18.

[12] See Genesis 49:4.

[13] Lindman, *Bodies of Belief*, 15. See also R. E. E. Harkness, "Early Relations of Baptists and Quakers," *Church History* 2 (December 1933): 227–42.

Baptists" because they "retained the language, dress, and manners of the quakers," Edwards wrote.[14] John Hart's lingering habits from his years as a Friend did not deter the Pennepek Baptists from appointing him an assistant minister in the church, a position he held until his death twelve years later. Though never ordained, John Hart was "esteemed a good preacher, and considered a pious and exemplary Christian." When he died in 1714 at the age of sixty-three, his last words were "Now I know to a demonstration that Christ has saved me."[15] After a long religious odyssey, John Hart had found a home among the Baptist people. His story illustrates how volatile religious life in the middle colonies could be in the late seventeenth century; far from the stability they hoped to one day achieve in America, the "humble Baptists" John Hart had joined were simply struggling to survive.

*

Baptist churches in colonial Pennsylvania formed close-knit communities defined by deeply held beliefs and cherished ritual practices. Their most distinctive rite, believer baptism, set them apart from virtually all their Protestant neighbors. To outsiders, adult immersion was "an obsolete, unfashionable, odious ceremony" that made Baptists "differ[ent from] all the rest of the Christian world," rendering them "contemptible" and "odious" to all.[16] Outside broadminded Pennsylvania, Baptists in the Old and New Worlds paid a steep price for their commitment to immersion, but they remained unmoved by both ridicule and violence. Baptists believed that only the complete submergence in water was "agreeable to the ancient practice of John the Baptist and the apostles of our Lord Jesus Christ."[17] In the act of immersion, Baptists preserved the symbolism of the individual believer's faith-union with Jesus Christ in his death, burial, and resurrection, and expressed the individual's total separation from the world and consecration to God. This was the step that John Hart Sr.'s oldest son, John Hart Jr., took in 1706, four years after his father had joined the Pennepek Baptist Church. Born July

---

[14] Morgan Edwards, *Materials towards a History of the Baptists*, 2 vols., edited by Eve. B. Weeks and Mary Bondurant Warren (Danielsville, GA: Heritage Papers, 1984), 1:55. If Oliver Hart's parents continued the Quaker practice of plain speech (addressing one another with "Thee" and "Thou") and plain dress in their home, as many former Keithian Baptists did, it does not show up in any of Oliver Hart's adult letters home to his father and brothers.

[15] Davis, *History of the Hart Family*, 24–28.

[16] David Thomas, *The Virginian Baptist, or, A view and defence of the Christian religion as it is professed by the Baptists of Virginia* (Baltimore, MD: Enoch Story, 1774), 50.

[17] Charleston Baptist Association, *A Summary of Church Discipline. Shewing the qualifications and duties, of the officers and members of a Gospel-church* (Charleston, 1794), 17.

16, 1684, John Jr. had observed his father's evolving religious convictions and experienced the tumult it caused at close range. He had been seven years old when John Sr. joined the Keithian schism and was dis-fellowshipped by the Quakers, and eighteen when his father joined the Pennepek Baptists. At age twenty-two, John Jr. was also persuaded of Baptist principles, confessed his faith, and received immersion.

Baptists believed that immersing only confessing believers proclaimed a vital message about the nature of the church. In most other Protestant traditions, sprinkled infants entered the church on the basis of their parents' faith. As the Baptists often pointed out, since all these infants did not subsequently experience conversion for themselves, Pedobaptist churches quickly filled with nominal Christians with hearts un-renewed by God's grace. Baptists believed that Pedobaptism contributed to individuals going to hell from the comfort of a church roll and created "mixed multitude" congregations that did not reflect the holy character of Christ to the world. Pedobaptists defended their practice by pointing to Old Covenant Israel, in which all the infant males of God's people received the sign of the covenant community, regardless of personal faith. They frequently accused Baptists of "criminal neglect of their duty towards their offspring," and their unchristened children were labeled by their opponents as "poor heathen."[18] But Baptists argued that Jesus Christ had established a different model for his New Covenant church: a community made entirely of regenerated men and women, separated from the world. After all, had the Old Covenant model been so successful in establishing a holy people for God in the world, what need would there be for a New Covenant? Only a pure, "believer's church" realized the New Testament ideal of the church as a "spiritual house" built with "living stones," a temple in which were offered "spiritual sacrifices" through Jesus Christ (1 Peter 2:5). Thus, before receiving his baptism, John Hart Jr. would have related his conversion story to the church's membership for their approval. Baptists saw the establishment of a believers' church as the key issue wherein their Protestant brethren had failed to carry out the full, biblical implications of the sixteenth-century Protestant Reformation. But they intended to go all the way, even if it meant standing apart from the majority.

Baptists maintained their ideal of a believers' church through the use of covenants and the practice of discipline. The church covenant, which had

---

[18] David Benedict, *Fifty Years among the Baptists* (New York, 1860), 93.

been used by Scottish Presbyterians and English Dissenters throughout the seventeenth century, was a formal agreement to live a holy life separated from the world, which all church members made with one another and with God himself.[19] It was this voluntary commitment to walk together in holiness that held Baptist churches together, rather than the mere geographical boundaries of a parish. Baptists' separation from the world included the avoidance of sinful activities such as "defaming speeches; revealing church secrets, or any thing that may grieve or trouble one another." The covenant also involved positive commitments, as in the pledge to "exhort and stir up one another to a diligent attendance on the means of grace, [and] stir up one another to zeal in holy living and in supporting the gospel."[20] Baptists enforced these covenant commitments through the practice of church discipline. As all Baptists understood when they submitted to immersion, church members were liable to public censure if they failed to uphold their covenant obligations. Mild rebukes could be issued in private, according to the practice of Matthew 18; more serious matters would come before the entire church at monthly business meetings, following the pattern of 1 Corinthians 5. At these meetings, offending members could be charged with a variety of crimes, from drunkenness and tale-bearing to sexual impropriety. The accused would have the opportunity to repent or experience censure. Joining the Baptists meant entrance into a community in which one's personal holiness was everyone's business.[21] The ritual sent a clear message that Baptists were serious about living as Christ's New Covenant people in the world. It also provided more material for Baptist critics, who considered the Baptist communion "the most rigid and uncharitable sect in the land."[22]

Along these lines, John Hart Jr. may have felt some pressure from his Baptist community when he married Eleanor Crispin (1687–1754) in 1708. Eleanor came from a reputable Pennsylvania family, her grandfather Thomas Holme (1624–1695) having served as William Penn's surveyor general. But as the Pennepek Baptist Church Minute Book pointed out, she was "no church member." Eleanor was a Quaker.[23] Interfaith marriages were a serious concern for all denominations in the middle colonies, and the Baptists

---

[19] Gregory A. Wills, *Democratic Religion: Freedom, Authority, and Church Discipline in the Baptist South, 1785–1900* (New York: Oxford University Press, 1996), 20–21.
[20] Lindman, *Bodies of Belief*, 90–91.
[21] Wills, *Democratic Religion*, 11–25.
[22] Benedict, *Fifty Years among the Baptists*, 33.
[23] Pennepek Baptist Church Minutes, HSP.

20 OLIVER HART AND THE RISE OF BAPTIST AMERICA

discouraged them as best they could.[24] Church officers expected members to notify them of their plans to marry and insisted that their people marry only converted individuals, ideally other Baptists. In 1726 the Pennepek congregation would discipline Ruth Brock for "hastly and rashly contracting marriage with one Robert Brower upon two or three days acquaintance," a "very vain, profane, swearing, wicked Church of England man." The two had eloped one night and were seen the next day, "sailing up and down the river with firing of guns on the shore in a vain manner."[25] Perhaps some of the Pennepek Baptists feared that John Hart Jr.'s relationship with Eleanor would result in similar trouble. Though the marriage went through, Eleanor remained outside the covenant community for another six years, apparently while continuing to practice the Quaker piety of her childhood. It was not until November 6, 1714, that Eleanor was baptized and received into full communion.

*

John and Eleanor settled in Warminster Township in southeastern Pennsylvania, where John farmed four hundred acres. Contemporaries considered the region to be "the best poor man's country" in the world. Wheat was the most lucrative crop, but local farmers grew a variety of produce on the same land, including rye, barley, oats, buckwheat, Indian corn, and potatoes. By the middle of the eighteenth century, the greater Delaware Valley and the southern Susquehanna Valley formed the breadbasket of America, the largest exporter of flour and wheat in the British colonies. John enjoyed enough success as a farmer to be considered "a man of wealth" in the community. He likely made the largest portion of his wealth by selling wheat to Philadelphia millers, who then exported flour throughout the colonies.[26] John's agricultural and business achievements opened the door for a number of civil service positions, including sheriff, justice of the peace, and coroner.[27]

John and Eleanor had ten children, though six preceded them in death. Oliver was the seventh, born July 5, 1723. No details of Oliver Hart's

[24] See Lodge, "The Crisis of the Churches."

[25] Lindman, *Bodies of Belief*, 102. For marriage in early Pennsylvania, see Merril D. Smith, *Breaking the Bonds: Marital Discord in Pennsylvania, 1730–1830* (New York: New York University Press, 1991).

[26] For farming in colonial Pennsylvania, see Pennsylvania Historical and Museum Commission, "Southeastern Pennsylvania Historic Agricultural Region, c. 1750–1960," 4–26, http://www.phmc.state.pa.us/portal/communities/agriculture/files/context/southeastern_pennsylvania.pdf, accessed 8 November 2017. Also James T. Lemon, *The Best Poor Man's Country: A Geographical Study of Early Southeastern Pennsylvania* (New York: Norton, 1976).

[27] Davis, *Hart Family*, 30–33.

childhood remain on record, but he would have spent much time working on the farm alongside his father and three brothers, John, Joseph, and Silas. The boys' responsibilities would have included fencing, haying, ditching, tending the animals, as well as working in the orchards and garden. Since there was always plenty of work to do, Oliver and his brothers may have labored alongside one of the many indentured servants who immigrated to Pennsylvania in these days. It is also possible that the Hart family owned an African slave or two. Black men and women made up a relatively small portion of Pennsylvania's population in the early eighteenth century, since the economy revolved around small family farms and manufacturing rather than the large plantations of the southern colonies. Slavery was also generally unpopular with Pennsylvania's large Quaker population. Historians estimate between 2,500 and 5,000 Africans in the colony in 1721, and still only 11,000 by 1751. But the highest concentration of Pennsylvania's slaves was in and around the Harts' home in Bucks County.[28] Slaves in this area of colonial Pennsylvania could not only provide permanent, cheap labor on some of the larger farms but also served as an important status symbol for white landowners in the young society.[29]

The strong Quaker background of both John and Eleanor Hart suggests that they would have resisted employing slave labor, as does John's former association with the Keithians. In 1693 George Keith had published one of the earliest American antislavery tracts, *An Exhortation and caution to Friends Concerning Buying or Keeping of Negroes.* "Blacks and Tawnies are a real part of mankind," Keith wrote, "for whom Christ hath shed his precious blood, and are capable of salvation, as well as White Men." Keith emphasized the incompatibility of slavery with the Golden Rule, condemned the slave trade as the sin of "manstealing," and called professing Christians to fight for both the "inward and outward" liberty of all people.[30] John Hart Sr.'s earlier testimony implies that he would have approved of Keith's position, but it is unknown what John Jr. thought. As a child Oliver would have been exposed to both sides of the early slavery debate, as he observed both free and enslaved Africans performing a variety of tasks all around him, especially when the Harts visited Philadelphia. There he would have seen black men working as

[28] Edward Raymond Turner, *The Negro in Pennsylvania: Slavery—Servitude—Freedom 1639–1861* (Washington, DC, 1911), 11–12.

[29] See Alan Tully, "Patterns of Slaveholding in Colonial Pennsylvania: Chester and Lancaster Counties 1729–1758," *Journal of Social History* 6, no. 3 (Spring 1973): 284–305.

[30] George Keith, *An Exhortation and caution to Friends Concerning Buying or Keeping of Negroes,* edited by George Moore (New York, 1693), 1–2.

22 OLIVER HART AND THE RISE OF BAPTIST AMERICA

bakers, blacksmiths, bricklayers, sailmakers, tailors, and tanners, along with black women cooking, sewing, keeping house, and nursing white babies. He also would have noticed the many advertisements in Benjamin Franklin's *Pennsylvania Gazette* and other newspapers, offering rewards for the return of runaway slaves. Oliver would have known fellow Baptists who owned slaves, as records from several New Jersey churches at this time indicate, though before the American Revolution black men and women made up less than 1% of Baptist church membership in Pennsylvania and New Jersey.[31] As a man in South Carolina Oliver would be forced to make many personal decisions regarding race and slavery, and those decisions would carry many lingering consequences for the Baptist people.

*

Baptists were frequently accused of neglecting their children's souls by refusing to sprinkle them in infancy. They "were all strong for plunging, and let their poor ignorant children run wild, and never had the seal of the covenant put on them," according to one critic.[32] But in fact, like all other religious groups in colonial Pennsylvania, Baptists placed a strong emphasis on developing piety in the home and expected Baptist men, as heads of their households, to take the lead.[33] Throughout the eighteenth century Baptist churches disciplined male members for negligence in this area, including failure to bring the family to church meetings, working on Sundays, neglecting family prayer, and abusing or deserting one's wife. John Hart Jr. took his spiritual duties seriously and was widely recognized for his piety. He and his family attended the Pennepek Baptist Church faithfully until 1743, when he and his Southampton neighbors formed a church closer to their home. The group immediately elected John as their first deacon. He also served for many years as church clerk and was responsible for providing for the Lord's Table. Oliver perhaps drew from his own childhood experience in 1775 when he admonished the fathers of the Charleston Baptist Association,

[31] Norman H. Maring, *Baptists in New Jersey: A Study in Transition* (Valley Forge, PA: Judson Press, 1964), 39; Travis Glasson, *Mastering Christianity: Missionary Anglicanism and Slavery in the Atlantic World* (New York: Oxford University Press, 2011), 52.

[32] Benedict, *Fifty Years among the Baptists*, 94.

[33] The Quaker background of John and Eleanor Hart reinforces the idea that they would have cared very much for the nurture of their children. Levy suggests that one reason the large tracts of land in Pennsylvania appealed to Quaker immigrants is the opportunity to insulate their children from the corrupting influences of the world and engage them in "holy conversation." See Barry Levy, "'Tender Plants': Quaker Families and Children in the Delaware Valley, 1681–1735," *Journal of Family History* 3 (Summer 1978): 116–35.

"Maintain the Worship of God in your Families; pray with and for them, instruct them in the Principles of Religion, and enforce your precepts by the best Examples." Oliver never failed to express deep affection for John in their correspondence, addressing him as "Honoured Father," discussing spiritual matters with him freely and confiding in him details about his ministry. Oliver's brothers Silas and Joseph also became active leaders in their respective Baptist churches. (Brother John died at an early age.)[34]

Outside his own home, the weekly meetings of the Pennepek Baptist Church made the most profound religious impact on Oliver's mind and heart. There he experienced a swirl of symbolic actions that subtly but powerfully formed his understanding of the Christian faith and of the world. The most important was the weekly sermon, which for more than twenty years of his life he heard from a Welsh Baptist preacher named Jenkin Jones (1686–1760). Welsh Baptists wielded a significant influence on Baptists in the Delaware Valley, where fifteen of the twenty-one first-generation Pennsylvania Baptist ministers came from Welsh descent. These Welsh Baptists were Calvinistic in theology, called "Particular Baptists" for their belief that Christ died "particularly" to save God's elect people. This distinguished them from the "General Baptists," who held that Christ died in the same way for all people and stressed that people were saved by their choosing God, not by God choosing them. Through sermons marked by "erudition, clarity, and common sense," Jones and his fellow Particular Baptists sought to nurture their congregations in the sturdy Calvinistic doctrines of the *Second London Confession* of 1689, a Baptist version of the more famous *Westminster Confession of Faith*.[35]

From the Pennepek pulpit, Jones proclaimed a big, transcendent God, who ruled with absolute, kingly power over all things great and small, having "decreed in himself, from all eternity . . . all things, whatsoever comes to pass."[36] Nothing troubled, threatened, or frustrated the God of the Pennepek Baptists. Imposing as such a sovereign sounds, Jones also declared that God was not cold and distant but eternally existed in a warm and happy community of three persons, "the ever adorable Trinity," as Oliver would later style it. This Triune God was near and knowable, having created man in his

[34] Charleston Association, *Minutes of the Charles Town Baptist Association, February 6* (Charleston, SC, 1775), 4.

[35] On the Welsh Baptists, see Geraint Jenkins, *Literature, Religion, and Society in Wales, 1660–1773* (Cardiff: University of Wales Press, 1978), 193–99, and Hywel M. Davies, *Transatlantic Brethren: Rev. Samuel Jones (1735–1814) and His Friends: Baptists in Wales, Pennsylvania, and Beyond* (Bethlehem, PA: Lehigh University Press, 1995).

[36] *Second London Confession* 5.1, available at https://www.the1689confession.com.

image to share with him a personal relationship of love. Oliver learned as a boy that the purpose of his life was, in harmony with the *Westminster Shorter Catechism*, to glorify God and enjoy him forever.[37]

Yet Oliver also learned from Jones that his relationship with God had been fractured by sin, his own, willful heart-resistance to God's rule. Rooted in the Augustinian tradition, Jones preached that the anti-God bent of the human soul had been inherited in the "fall of Adam," the original representative of the human race. Through Adam, man had "contracted a contrariety of soul to the perfections of the Deity, and a horrid enmity against God," as Hart later put it. There was no "light within" to draw from, only darkness. Yet sin was not the final word for the human race. Foreseeing the rebellion of their creatures before the world began, the members of the Trinity had made a covenant to redeem an elect people for themselves. God the Father was the author of this plan; God the Son accomplished it through his substitutionary life, death, and resurrection; and God the Holy Spirit would apply the work of salvation to the individual by enabling him or her to repent and believe in Jesus Christ. In later years Hart learned to delight in this "covenant of grace," calling it "the foundation of all our happiness." Despite their robust affirmation of God's determining will, the Pennepek Baptists viewed themselves not as fatalists but as "evangelical Calvinists." They believed that God accomplished his predetermined will through the responsible actions of people. Thus, while the recipients of God's saving grace were "a certain, select number, out of the race of mankind," Hart and the rest of the congregation were exhorted to trust in Jesus Christ, for God chose to save his elect through the means of gospel preaching. If Oliver could be personally united to Christ through faith, he could walk through life with assurance that his sins were forgiven, that he was reconciled to God, and his entire life was ruled by the hand of Providence. Oliver Hart never departed from this received tradition. In the course of his seventy-two years, he would pass through days of considerable theological innovation in the American religious scene. But at the end of his life, friends still described him as "an uniform advocate, both in public and in private, for the doctrines of free and sovereign grace," and as "an orthodox divine." Hart would make many new paths in Baptist life as a

---

[37] Oliver Hart, Sermon on 1 Timothy 4:16, Hart MSS, SCL.

"THE HUMBLE BAPTISTS" 25

denominational organizer, missions advocate, and educational activist. But doctrinally he remained content to follow the old paths of his fathers.[38]

*

Beyond the sermon, a variety of other Baptist rituals shaped Oliver's early life, many of which bore a distinctly Welsh flavor because of the ethnic background of the Pennepek church.[39] One gets a sense of this when reading Morgan Edwards's *The Customs of the Primitive Churches* (1767), which describes the worship practices of Particular Baptists in the middle colonies. William Lloyd Allen has drawn attention to the "intensely physical nature" of the Welsh spirituality recounted in these pages, what he called an "acutely earthed piety."[40] This included the practice of laying hands on newly baptized believers, symbolizing the indwelling of the Holy Spirit, and the new spiritual bond between the members of the congregation. Following this rite, the minister extended to the candidate the right hand of fellowship and kiss of charity, visible displays of welcome into the fellowship of God's people. Welsh Baptists also loved the hearty singing of the psalms, and the Baptist churches of the Delaware Valley even added an article to the *Second London Confession* to highlight that it is "injoined on the churches of Christ to sing psalms, hymns, and spiritual songs; and that the whole church in their public assemblies, as well as private Christians, ought to sing God's praises according to the best light they have received." This too left its mark on Oliver. As an old man he would insist that "no part of divine service so much resembles heaven" as "harmoniously singing the praises of God, with united voice."[41]

Between four to six times a year, Oliver watched Jenkin Jones tear a loaf of bread into pieces, pour a cup of red wine, and serve the baptized members of the Pennepek Church a special meal called the Lord's Supper. Through this ceremony Baptists memorialized the death of Jesus Christ, and also underscored their unity as the family of Jesus. Many Baptists observed the Lord's Supper at night, by candlelight, recalling the original setting on the

---

[38] Oliver Hart, *Of Christ the Mediator*, in A. D. Gillette, ed., *Minutes of the Philadelphia Baptist Association, from A.D. 1707, to A.D. 1807* (Philadelphia, PA: American Baptist Publication Society, 1851), 181; Oliver Hart, Sermon on 1 Timothy 4:16, Hart MSS, SCL.

[39] See Wayland F. Dunaway, "Early Welsh Settlers of Pennsylvania," *Pennsylvania History* 12, no. 4 (October 1945): 251–69.

[40] Wm. Lloyd Allen, "The Peculiar Welsh Piety of *The Customs of the Primitive Churches*," in *Distinctively Baptist: A Festschrift in Honor of Walter B. Shurden*, edited by Marc A. Jolley (Macon, GA: Mercer University Press, 2005), 181–82.

[41] Oliver Hart, *A Gospel Church Portrayed, and Her Orderly Service Pointed Out* (Trenton, NJ: Isaac Collins, 1791), 24.

26    OLIVER HART AND THE RISE OF BAPTIST AMERICA

night Christ was betrayed. Baptists distanced themselves from the Roman Catholic view that the communion elements physically became the body and blood of Jesus, but they still believed that they partook in a profound spiritual reality at the table. There they did "inwardly by faith, really and indeed, yet not carnally, and corporeally, feed upon Christ crucified, and all the benefits of his death; the body and blood of Christ, being then not corporally, or carnally, but spiritually present to the faith of believers, in that ordinance, as the elements themselves are to their outward senses."[42] After the meal they parted by singing hymn lyrics like these from Isaac Watts: "Sitting around our father's board, we raise our tuneful breath; Our faith beholds her dying Lord, and dooms our sins to death. We see the blood of Jesus shed, Whence all our comforts rise; The sinner views th' atonement made; And loves the sacrifice."[43] Occasionally, Welsh-influenced Baptists also ate together in homes for a special "love feast." A church member would host a small number of fellow believers for a "chearful" meal, accompanied by prayer, singing, foot-washing, the exchange of a kiss of charity, the right hand of fellowship, and a collection for the poor.[44] Long before Oliver could articulate in a doctrinal formula what it meant to belong to the church, the worship rituals of Pennepek Baptist church had trained him to know intuitively: the church was to be a consecrated, disciplined people; a happy, singing people; a nourished, feasting people; a loved and loving people.

*

The Delaware Valley Baptists did not have to fear state-sponsored persecution, as did their New England brethren. Yet they did find their faith constantly threatened by the crowd of other denominations around them.

---

[42] *Second London Confession* 30.7.

[43] Morgan Edwards, *The Customs of Primitive Churches* (Philadelphia, PA: Andrew Stuart, 1768), 89–90. Edwards specifically cites these Watts lyrics in 1768, but it is unknown when Pennsylvania Baptist first adopted Watts's hymns. Watts's *Hymns and Spiritual Songs* (1707) and *The Psalms of David Imitated in the Language of the New Testament* (s1719) sparked a revolution among all sorts of English-speaking worshippers, who until that point were characterized by their commitment to exclusive psalm-singing. As early as 1733, one observer noted that "some Baptist demand in and around Philadelphia helped to encourage [Benjamin Franklin" to issue a reprint of Watts. Though the acceptance of Watts and other modern hymn writers often stirred controversy among psalms-only Baptists during this period, by 1782, the Philadelphia Association recommended an edition of Watts's psalms published in the city the previous year. See David W. Music and Paul Akes Richardson, *"I Will Sing the Wondrous Story": A History of Baptist Hymnody in North America* (Macon, GA: Mercer University Press, 2008), 79–87.

[44] For the early American Methodist practice of the love feast, see John H. Wigger, *Taking Heaven by Storm: Methodism and the Rise of Popular Christianity in America* (New York: Oxford University Press, 1998), 87–89.

Pluralistic Pennsylvania is sometimes remembered as a kind of tolerant utopia in which religious groups mutually appreciated and encouraged one another's diversity. In reality, one historian has called the middle colonies "a veritable battleground of warring religions," with all denominations "inflamed with a lust for proselytes."[45] Zealous adherents employed a variety of methods to discourage their neighbors' faiths, including ridicule and insult. One Quaker, learning of his neighbor's recent baptism, reportedly jeered, "Why didn't thee desire the Minister rather to piss upon thy Head. . . . That would have been of more effect."[46] It was not the kind of respectful interfaith dialogue William Penn had envisioned.

Baptists learned how tricky Pennsylvania ecumenism could be when a group of Philadelphia Baptists attempted to share meetings with their Presbyterian neighbors in the late 1690s. For several years the two groups worshipped together at the Barbados storehouse. Sometimes the Baptist John Watts would pray and preach, and other times the New England Presbyterian Jedediah Andrews (1674–1747). Andrews is the same Presbyterian minister who would often visit Benjamin Franklin (1706–1790), admonishing him to attend church. After attending for five straight Sundays, Franklin found Andrews's polemical and doctrinal messages to be "very dry, uninteresting, and unedifying," designed more "to make us Presbyterians than good citizens."[47] Not surprisingly, Andrews disliked the arrangement with the Baptists and worked to dislodge them from the house through means both subtle and otherwise. Finally the Baptists appealed to the Presbyterians by letter. Citing their "duties of love to and bearing with one another," and remembering that "peace and unity tend much to the honor of Christ and Christianity," the Baptists insisted that they were "desirous of your company heavenward as far as may be" and wished to "heal the breach betwixt us, occasioned by our difference in judgment (none being yet perfect in judgment)." They proposed that both parties agree to welcome in their assemblies "all approved ministers, who are fitly qualified and sound in the faith, and of holy lives," whether Presbyterian or Baptist. Wishing to avoid any "further disputes and vain janglings," they called for "plain and direct answer." Andrews offered to meet in person, asking the Baptists to set the time and place. But on the appointed

---

[45] Lodge, "The Crisis of the Churches," 212. See also Patricia U. Bonomi, *Under the Cope of Heaven: Religion, Society, and Politics in Colonial America* (New York: Oxford University Press, 2003), 72–84; and Jon Butler, *Awash in a Sea of Faith: Christianizing the American People* (Cambridge, MA: Harvard University Press, 1990), 174–76).

[46] Lodge, "The Crisis of the Churches," 214.

[47] Benjamin Franklin, *Autobiography* (Boston: Houghton and Mifflin, 1906), 84.

28    OLIVER HART AND THE RISE OF BAPTIST AMERICA

day, he and the Presbyterians refused to show. Dejected, the Baptists resigned themselves "to meet apart from you until such time as we receive an answer, and we are assured that you can own us so as we do you." Andrews's plan had succeeded.[48]

This, however, was not the end of the interdenominational "janglings" for the Philadelphia Baptists. Hearing about their trouble, Rev. Thomas Clayton (d. 1699), rector of Christ Church in Philadelphia, seized an opportunity to increase his Anglican flock. He sent a letter to the Baptists in 1699, urging them to unite with the Church of England, that they might gather in a convenient house of worship. If they refused, Clayton requested that they state their reasons. The Baptist response was courteous but straightforward: they would happily unite with the Church of England if they did not find them so thoroughly unbiblical. Objectionable points of Anglican practice included the "mixed multitude" of the church's membership, the union of the church with the state, the hierarchical government and unscriptural multiplicity of church offices, the ostentatious apparel of the priests, the use of instruments in worship, the practice of infant baptism, the mode of pouring and sprinkling for baptism, and the signing of the cross in the administration of baptism. Their message was clear: a Baptist-Anglican reconciliation was not going to happen, not even in pluralist Pennsylvania.[49] With or without a comfortable meetinghouse, Baptists would continue to fight to preserve their distinctive faith community.

In addition to competing with mainstream Protestant denominations, Baptists contended with a host of more radical sects in Pennsylvania. The Swiss settler Esther Werndtlin complained in 1736, "The religions and nations are innumerable, this land is an asylum house for all expelled sects, a refuge for all delinquents of Europe, a confused Babel, a receptacle for all unclean spirits, a shelter of devils, a first world, a Sodom."[50] Among the more colorful of these groups was the mystical Ephrata Cloister, founded by a German immigrant, Conrad Beissel (1690–1768). Beissel had joined the German Baptists when he arrived in Pennsylvania in 1720, but then borrowed from a variety of mystical sources, including Gnosticism, to develop his own religion. In 1730 he established Ephrata Cloister on 180 acres in Lancaster County. There he and his followers sought to commune with God through an

[48] David Spencer, *The Early Baptists of Philadelphia* (Philadelphia, PA, 1877), 31–35.
[49] Spencer, *Early Baptists of Philadelphia*, 35–38.
[50] Quoted in Thomas S. Kidd, *Colonial American History: Clashing Cultures and Faiths* (New Haven, CT: Yale University Press, 2016), 234.

austere lifestyle of self-denial, dressing in white monastic robes, practicing celibacy (even in marriage), and fasting regularly. Another Ephrata trademark was their mystical singing, which they believed lifted them to a higher spiritual plane. With heads bowed solemnly and mouths barely open, the Ephrata singers lifted their "sweet, shrill, and small voices" to make "ethereal" sounds in an attempt to reproduce angelic music and enter the harmony of the divine. Despite his eccentricities, Beissel proved to be an effective evangelist in the Delaware Valley. He awed listeners with his otherworldly delivery, speaking with closed eyes and closed Bible, as if receiving direct messages from God. He also disseminated his ideas through an active printing press at Ephrata. By 1750 some three hundred people called Ephrata home.[51]

Baptists feared the corrupting influences of aggressive fringe groups like the Ephrata mystics and charismatic leaders like Beissel. In addition, occultic practices and "fantastic notions of witchcraft and Satanic arts" remained widespread enough in Pennsylvania deep into the eighteenth century that the Lutheran Henry Melchior Muhlenberg (1711–1787) could claim there were "more Necromancers . . . than Christians."[52] In many "dark corners" of the frontier, total irreligion seemed to reign. The Anglican missionary John Talbot (1645–1727) wrote in 1703, "It is a sad thing to consider the years that are past; how some that were born of the English never heard of the name of Christ; how many others were baptized in his name, and [have] fallen away to Heathenism, Quakerism, and Atheism, for want of Confirmation."[53] If Baptists were to survive in Pennsylvania, it was imperative that they stake out the boundaries of their beliefs and practices.

Looking for models from the Old World, Baptists took a major step toward denominational stability in 1707 by forming the Philadelphia Baptist Association, the first organized body of Baptist churches in America. This regional network joined together five Particular Baptist churches across the Delaware Valley: the Pennepek and Welsh Tract churches of Pennsylvania, and the Middletown, Piscataway, and Cohansey churches in New Jersey. In principle, Baptists were committed to the autonomy of each congregation and instinctively resisted any infringement on the independence of local churches. Since the seventeenth century, however, Baptists in Great Britain

---

[51] Robert P. Sutton, *Communal Utopias and the American Experience: Religious Communities, 1732–2000* (Westport, CT: Praeger, 2003), 1–9.

[52] Butler, *Awash in a Sea of Faith*, 87.

[53] C. F. Pascoe, *Two Hundred Years of the S.P.G.: An Historical Account of the Society for the Propagation of the Gospel in Foreign Parts, 1701–1900* (London, 1901), 11.

# 30 OLIVER HART AND THE RISE OF BAPTIST AMERICA

had acknowledged the benefits of formal, voluntary associations of churches. In his 1749 essay, "Respecting the Power and Duty of an Association," one Philadelphia Association minister, Benjamin Griffith (1688–1768), wrote, "Several such independent churches, where Providence gives them their situation convenient, may, and ought, for their mutual strength, counsel, and other valuable advantages, by their voluntary and free consent, to enter into an agreement and confederation." The Association convened annually, publishing a circular letter relating its activities, and sought to keep Baptists connected throughout the year.[54] By forming a centralized denomination, Baptists followed a general trend of American religious groups between the years 1680 and 1760 to attain stability.[55]

The Philadelphia Association prioritized grounding its member churches in Baptist doctrine. In 1737, for example, the Association delivered a "warm and loving exhortation" to "maintain the great and necessary doctrines of the Christian religion, and, in particular, to be steadfast against errors," highlighting the doctrines of the Trinity, man's creation, fall, and restoration by grace through Christ, and the real divine and human nature in union in the person of Christ.[56] The association looked to the *Second London Confession* as its doctrinal standard, frequently settling questions and disputes in its minutes by merely referencing the appropriate article. In 1742 the Association officially adopted the confession as its own, adding two Welsh-influenced articles on psalm singing and the laying on of hands. They called it the *Philadelphia Confession*, and it set the tone for Baptist theology in America for the next century. The *Philadelphia Confession* provided a theological rule to unify Baptist churches, its basic content serving as a test of fellowship in the Association. The *Philadelphia Confession* also became a vital teaching tool to educate the Baptist people. Beginning in 1773 the Association published an essay expounding one article of the confession in its annual circular letter. Missionaries sent out by the Association used the *Philadelphia Confession* on the frontier, whether instructing new believers for the first time or reforming the doctrine of dying General Baptist congregations.

In addition to pure doctrine, the Philadelphia Association was concerned with establishing orderly church practice for its Baptist congregations. Each year at the annual meeting, churches submitted questions, as in 1724, when

---

[54] Gillette, *Minutes*, 61.
[55] Butler, *Awash in a Sea of Faith*, 98–128.
[56] Kidd, *Colonial American History*, 234; Gillette, *Minutes*, 38.

"THE HUMBLE BAPTISTS" 31

one asked whether a believer might marry an unbeliever without coming under church censure. The church at Hopewell, New Jersey, inquired in 1728 how to go about selecting a new ruling elder in the church. In 1732 the Association fielded a question about the validity of a private baptism administered by an unbaptized individual. (The Association ruled in the negative.) By delivering judgments on so many matters, the Association verged on "imposing its sentiments on the churches," thus violating local church autonomy and making many Baptists nervous. This concern inspired Benjamin Griffith's 1749 essay, which carefully defined the authority of churches and associations. When following its intended function, the Association served in an advisory capacity only, embodying the biblical principle that "in a multitude of counselors, there is safety." Still, the Association intended its rulings to be taken seriously.[57]

One of the Association's most important functions was vetting ministers. At its first meeting in 1707, the Association announced, "A person that is a stranger, and has neither letter of recommendation, nor is known to be a person gifted, and of good conversation, shall not be admitted to preach, nor be entertained as a member in any of the baptized congregations in communion with each other."[58] The earlier story of Elias Keach illustrates how a man of dubious beliefs or behavior could pass himself off as legitimate, and the Association was serious about protecting churches from their influence. One infamous example is Desolate Baker (1694–1778), an English immigrant who came to America under the assumed name "Henry Loveall." The Association advised the Piscataway congregation against ordaining Baker, but the church ignored the warning. In time the Piscataway Baptists learned that Baker had adopted the alias to hide his checkered past: he had run away from his master, committed bigamy, and engaged in sexual relations with black and Indian women, contracting syphilis. Nathaniel Jenkins (1678–1754) of the Cohansey Baptist Church scolded the Piscataway Baptists because they "neither minded my advice nor that of our Association."[59] Jenkins also commented that the "Loveall" moniker was "a very suitable name agreeable to his properties who loves so well the black, the swarthy, and the white so as to lie with them." Jenkins's remark indicates that, however progressive the Quaker-influenced Pennsylvania Baptists may or may not have been

---

[57] Gillette, *Minutes*, 27, 29, 33, 38, 60–62.
[58] Gillette, *Minutes*, 25.
[59] See Lindman, *Bodies of Belief*, 24–25.

## 32   OLIVER HART AND THE RISE OF BAPTIST AMERICA

in regard to slavery, they clearly believed Baker to be guilty of having committed a serious social taboo through his interracial dalliances.

*

By the time Oliver Hart was coming of age in the late 1730s, the Philadelphia Association had succeeded in stabilizing Baptist life in the middle colonies. As the eighteenth century progressed, the Association would look to expand the Baptist influence beyond the Delaware Valley. No longer preoccupied with mere survival on the Pennsylvania frontier, the churches of the Philadelphia Association would cooperate to relieve destitute churches in distant regions, send missionaries to evangelize the western frontier, and help establish educational institutions. They earned the reputation of "an emporium of Baptist influence" and took their place among other growing denominations of the American colonies. The Philadelphia Association provided a model of denominationalism that Baptists would copy in other areas all over America during the course of the eighteenth century, most significantly by Oliver Hart himself in the Lower South.[60]

---

[60] Benedict, *Fifty Years among the Baptists*, 46–47.

# 2

# "The power of religion greatly displayed"

## Baptists and the Great Awakening

Despite his extensive nurture in the Baptist community of faith, Oliver Hart looked back on his early years with a dim view of his spiritual condition. "My youth was spent in vanity and a listlessness to all that was good," he asserted in 1791.[1] Hart's negative evaluation of his adolescent self reflected his convictions about the doctrine of original sin. Affirming a tradition that stretched back through the Puritans to St. Augustine and the Apostle Paul, Hart believed that human beings entered the world not in a state of innocence but alienated from and hostile to God. This condition stemmed from the primal rebellion of Adam in the Garden of Eden, who had acted as humanity's federal representative when he attempted to cast off God's rule. Adam's descendants now shared his sinful destiny (physical death, followed by eternal punishment) and his sinful disposition (what Hart once called "a contrariety of soul to the perfections of the Deity, and a horrid enmity against God").[2] Hart believed original sin manifested differently in different persons. The "poor sensual sinner" broke all the rules in a reckless quest to gratify the appetites of the flesh, while the self-righteous sinner prided himself on his moral rectitude and religious activity. Yet according to Hart's Calvinistic tradition, both were profoundly separated from God at the level of the heart. The poison of original sin coursed through the veins of every son and daughter of Adam, including teenage Oliver Hart in the pews of Pennepek Baptist Church.[3]

Particular Baptists believed that no external measures were sufficient to save one from sin: not the reformation of one's morals, not the scrupulous practice of good deeds, not participation in the church's liturgy and sacraments. God alone could intervene to provide the transformation of the

[1] Oliver Hart to Richard Furman, June 1, 1791, Hart MSS, JBDML.
[2] Gillette, *Minutes*, 181.
[3] Hart, Sermon on 1 Timothy 1:15, Hart MSS, SCL.

*Oliver Hart and the Rise of Baptist America.* Eric C. Smith, Oxford University Press (2020). © Oxford University Press.
DOI: 10.1093/oso/9780197506325.001.0001

heart necessary to rescue sinners in the momentous personal experience of conversion. This conviction placed Hart's Philadelphia Association Baptists within the broad boundaries of an energetic new movement of Protestant Pietism emerging in the North Atlantic world in the 1730s we now know as modern evangelicalism. Evangelicals arose from a variety of denominational contexts: Anglicans, Congregationalists, Presbyterians, Baptists, and more. Yet all sounded the same, unrelenting call to seek God's saving grace through conversion, or the "new birth." "The rising evangelical movement," writes D. Bruce Hindmarsh in a recent study of evangelicalism, "was distinguished first and foremost by its appeal to men and women to be true and earnest Christians rather than nominal believers."[4] Evangelicals did not claim to have discovered the concept of conversion; after all, they viewed the doctrine as the throbbing center of New Testament Christianity, summed up in Jesus's own terse declaration, "You must be born again." In the seventeen centuries since Jesus uttered those words, Christians from Augustine to Patrick of Ireland, Bernard of Clairvaux, and Martin Luther had testified to powerful conversion experiences, and no movement had so painstakingly analyzed the conversion process as the seventeenth-century Puritans. Yet evangelicals accented the new birth in a fresh way. The literature of the period— including such famous pieces as Jonathan Edwards's sermon "A Divine and Supernatural Light Immediately Imparted to the Soul by the Spirit of God" and Charles Wesley's hymn "And Can It Be?" and the private journals of ordinary women like Sarah Osborne and Hannah Heaton—attests that the new birth experience was to the early evangelicals a source of bottomless fascination and delight.[5]

So at age sixteen, though Oliver Hart participated faithfully in the church's worship, he knew that he remained on the outside of things in the most important sense. Meanwhile, both inside and outside the church, the new birth seemed to be the subject of every conversation around him. The year 1739 would prove pivotal in the epochal series of revivals in both Europe and the American colonies that birthed the evangelical movement, known today as

---

[4] D. Bruce Hindmarsh, *The Spirit of Early Evangelicalism: True Religion in a Modern World* (New York: Oxford University Press, 2018), 9.

[5] For an introduction to the early evangelicals and their beliefs, see especially Hindmarsh, *The Spirit of Early Evangelicalism*; Mark A. Noll, *The Rise of Evangelicalism: The Age of Edwards, Whitefield, and the Wesleys* (Downer's Grove, IL: IVP Academic, 2015); Jonathan M. Yeager, ed., *Early Evangelicalism: A Reader* (New York: Oxford University Press, 2013); Thomas S. Kidd, *The Great Awakening: The Roots of Evangelical Christianity in America* (New Haven, CT: Yale University Press, 2008); and D. W. Bebbington, *Evangelicalism in Modern Britain: A History from the 1730s to the 1980s* (New York: Routledge, 2003).

the First Great Awakening. A young Church of England itinerant named George Whitefield (1714–1770), already touted by many as the most powerful evangelist since the apostles, was set to visit Philadelphia that fall. Both the *Pennsylvania Gazette* and the *American Weekly Mercury* in Philadelphia covered his departure from England, and Philadelphia printers were turning out copies of his printed sermons and journals.[6] In anticipation of his arrival, many of Hart's neighbors were setting aside ordinary concerns to wrestle with the paramount issue of their conversion.

The Great Awakening had a profound affect on Hart's spiritual development. Richard Furman drew attention to this in his memorial sermon for Hart, noting that he was converted when "the power of religion was greatly displayed in various parts of this continent."[7] The revivals of the late 1730s and 1740s would also infuse new life into Hart's Particular Baptists, in Pennsylvania and throughout the American colonies. Historians have tended to overlook the Particular Baptists' participation in the Great Awakening, focusing instead on the radical Separate Baptist movement, which the revival created. But as Hart's contemporary Isaac Backus (1724–1806) noted, "the word was powerful among the Baptists in New Jersey and Pennsylvania" too in those days.[8] Only the American Revolution would so decisively shape the fortunes of Oliver Hart and the Baptists of America as the Great Awakening.

*

The springs of revival had been bubbling up in the middle colonies twenty years before Whitefield preached his first sermon in Philadelphia. It is well documented by now that three distinct, revival-oriented streams formed across the region during the 1720s and 1730s.[9] First was German Pietism, associated with the seventeenth-century German Lutheran Philip Jacob Spener (1635–1705).[10] Troubled by the cold intellectualism of the Lutheran Church, Spener had sounded a call for spiritual renewal in his small book *Pia Desideria* (Pious Desires) in 1675. Spener lamented that few church

---

[6] Kidd, *The Great Awakening*, 46–47.

[7] Richard Furman, *Rewards of Grace Conferred on Christ's Faithful People* (Charleston, SC: J. McIver, 1796), 21.

[8] Isaac Backus, *A History of New England, with particular reference to the Denomination of Christians called Baptists* (Boston: Edward Draper, 1777), 2:41.

[9] See Charles Hartshorn Maxson, *The Great Awakening in the Middle Colonies* (Chicago: University of Chicago Press, 1920); and Kidd, *The Great Awakening*, 24–39.

[10] For Spener and his influence on the early evangelicals, see William R. Ward, *Early Evangelicalism: A Global Intellectual History, 1670–1789* (New York: Cambridge University Press, 2006), 24–39.

36 OLIVER HART AND THE RISE OF BAPTIST AMERICA

members "really understand and practice true Christianity (which consists of more than avoiding manifest vices and living an outwardly moral life)." Despite possessing religious knowledge, many were "altogether unacquainted with the true, heavenly, light and life of faith." As opposed to the prevailing German model of dry scholasticism, the heart of Pietism was the heart, renewed by the Spirit of God, aflame with love for Jesus Christ, and devoted to a life of practical holiness. Spener offered "several simple Christian proposals" for promoting vital godliness in the church, including personal Bible reading and the formation of *collegia pietatis*, private Christian societies outside the church's regular services. He developed an enormous following in Germany at the end of the seventeenth century, leading to the founding of the University of Halle in 1694 as a center of Pietistic influence. Many German Pietists relocated to Pennsylvania at the beginning of the eighteenth century. Some were radical, such as Conrad Beissel's Ephrata Cloister. Other Pietist leaders simply promoted the ideals of heart religion within a variety of more traditional German religious groups in Pennsylvania, including Lutherans, Mennonites, German Quakers, Schwenkfelders, and Dunkers. Hart would have rubbed shoulders with many of these German Pietists in Warminster Township.[11]

The second stream of revivalism in the middle colonies flowed from the Dutch Reformed Church tradition in Holland, which fused a passion for theological precision with a hunger for godly living. The man most credited with bringing Dutch Reformed Pietism to the American colonies is Theodorus Jacobus Frelinghuysen (1691–1747). After graduating from the University of Lingren, Frelinghuysen sailed for the New World to pastor a church in the Raritan River Valley of central New Jersey. Once in New Brunswick, however, he was dismayed to find the wealthy and refined people of his new charge formally religious but utterly clueless about "living Christianity," as he called it. As Frelinghuysen's friend William Tennent Jr. recalled the situation, "Family prayer was unpracticed by all, a very few excepted; ignorance so overshadowed their minds that the doctrines of the new birth when clearly explained, and powerfully pressed upon them, as absolutely necessary to salvation . . . was made a common game of." When Frelinghuysen preached the new birth, he was suspected of promoting "some new false doctrine." The confrontational (and often abrasive) Frelinghuysen quickly launched a

---

[11] Philip Jacob Spener, *Pia Desidera*, translated by Theodore G. Tappert (Philadelphia, PA: Fortress Press, 1964), 45, 46; Maxson, *Great Awakening in the Middle Colonies*, 1–10.

crusade against lifeless formalism. He traveled the region preaching hard, searching messages and did not shrink from accusing church members and ministers alike of being unconverted. This latter habit would become commonplace during the Great Awakening, to the utter enragement of the guardians of religious establishments everywhere.[12]

Not surprisingly, Frelinghuysen's aggressive ministry offended many. In 1725 two Dutch Reformed ministers published a complaint against him for his "bitter denunciations ... to the effect that we were, all of us, unconverted; and we were discouraged from approaching the Lord's Table."[13] At the same time, many listeners melted under the red-hot passion of Frelinghuysen's sermons, resulting in hundreds of conversions under his preaching in the 1720s and 1730s. Frelinghuysen utilized many classic Pietistic vehicles for revival, including the *collegia pietatis*, the appointment of lay exhorters, and published sermons aimed at awakening sinners. His activity played a vital role in preparing for the later revival in the middle colonies. When Whitefield met Frelinghuysen in 1739, he judged him to be "a worthy old soldier of Jesus Christ ... the beginner of the great work which I trust the Lord is carrying on in these parts."[14]

The third revival tributary in the middle colonies was composed of the Scots Irish Presbyterians of the New Brunswick Presbytery. From the founding of the first presbytery in Pennsylvania in 1706, tens of thousands of Ulster Scots had poured into William Penn's colony. The most significant for the revival was William Tennent (1673–1746), a graduate of the University of Glasgow and an ordained priest of the Church of Ireland. Dissatisfied with the Anglican Church's Arminian doctrine and hierarchical government, Tennent emigrated to America and applied for ordination with the Presbyterian Synod of Philadelphia in 1718. For the next several years he zealously preached an evangelical message throughout Pennsylvania and New York. In 1726 he settled his family at Neshaminy, Pennsylvania, just a few miles from Oliver Hart's home in Bucks County. Tennent opened a seminary there, housed in a rustic cabin he built with his own hands. His opponents would deride the backwoods school as a mere

---

[12] The disruptive nature of the "Whitefieldian" evangelists in colonial New England is highlighted in Douglas Winiarski's recent work, *Darkness Falls on the Land of Light: Experiencing Religious Awakenings in Eighteenth-Century New England* (Chapel Hill: University of North Carolina Press, 2017), especially 287–310.

[13] Hugh Hastings, ed., *Ecclesiastical Records, State of New York* (Albany, NY, 1901), 4:2318.

[14] Archibald Alexander, *Biographical Sketches of the Founder, and Principal Alumni of the Log College* (Princeton, NJ: J. T. Robinson, 1845), 255; Whitefield, *Journals*, 352.

38    OLIVER HART AND THE RISE OF BAPTIST AMERICA

"Log College," a name that would become hallowed in evangelical circles. Tennent trained young ministers not only to exegete the Greek and Hebrew Scriptures but to preach passionate, invasive messages aimed at awakening spiritual sleepers. The nineteen students whom Tennent graduated constituted a new generation of revivalists who would change the religious face of the middle colonies. His pupils included Samuel Blair (1714–1751), Samuel Finley (1715–1766), and John Rowland (d. 1745) and his four sons, Gilbert (1703–1764), William Jr. (1705–1777), John (1707–1732), and Charles (1711–1771). Oliver Hart later recalled, "[I] frequently heard most of [the Tennents] preach with great pleasure, and, I hope, some profit." He fondly remembered them as "a race of men, devoted to the service of the sanctuary; who, for their abilities, zeal and usefulness, need not give any place to any family, that ever graced the American continent . . . the happy instruments of converting thousands of souls."[15]

All the Tennents experienced revival in their ministries, but Gilbert stole the headlines. In 1727 he was ordained and assigned to a new Presbyterian church in New Brunswick, Frelinghuysen's parish. The first six months of Tennent's ministry were relatively quiet, with no one professing conversion under his ministry. But Frelinghuysen reached out to the younger man, exhorting him to follow his more aggressive methods at awakening souls while preaching. "[The letter] excited me to greater earnestness in ministerial labours," Tennent recalled. As soon as Tennent joined Frelinghuysen in attacking nominal Christianity, he began experiencing similar results. The two took to the road, partnering to spread revival across the region in spite of their different denominational affiliations. They held meetings across the middle colonies in both Dutch and English. As one attendee recalled, "Frelinghuysen preaches and Tennent prays and baptizes; and then together they administer the Holy Supper."[16] Enormous crowds flocked to have their consciences flayed open by the blood-earnest revivalists.

No matter where it manifested, revival always disrupted established religious institutions. The Great Awakening rocked the Presbyterian Synod with the same violence as it had the Dutch Reformed Church.[17] The Synod voted in 1738 to establish a new presbytery in New Brunswick, consisting

---

[15] Oliver Hart, *The Character of a Truly Great Man Delineated* (Charleston, SC: David Bruce, 1777), 24.

[16] Kidd, *Great Awakening*, 30.

[17] For a summary of the Presbyterian experience of the Great Awakening in the middle colonies, see John Fea, *The Way of Improvement Leads Home: Philip Vickers Fithian and the Rural Enlightenment in America* (Philadelphia: University of Pennsylvania Press, 2008), 34–57.

"THE POWER OF RELIGION GREATLY DISPLAYED" 39

entirely of churches led by revivalist ministers. At the same time, the Synod voted to test all ministers without a degree from Harvard, Yale, or a reputable European university. The objective was clear: New Brunswick ministers with a Log College degree would have to pass through the Synod's appointed committees before receiving ordination. Gilbert Tennent protested that the Synod was attempting "to prevent his father from training gracious men for the ministry."[18] The New Brunswick Presbytery promptly tested the new ruling, bypassing the synod by licensing the Log College graduate John Rowland. When the Synod revoked Rowland's license, the New Brunswick Presbytery doubled down, ordaining Rowland to preach in the New Jersey communities of Hopewell, Maidenhead, and Amwell.

Established ministers closed their pulpits to Rowland, but local residents gathered in barns and outdoor settings to hear his fiery evangelical sermons. For six months he sought to plow up the fallow ground of his hearers' hearts with a strict message of "conviction and conversion," earning him the nickname "Hell-fire" Rowland. His critics accused him of stirring up carnal "enthusiasm" by his lurid descriptions of judgment for the unconverted. Even Gilbert Tennent admitted that his friend could take it too far: "Being young in years and of a warm temper, he was thereby led into some indiscretions in his honest and earnest attempts to do good," Tennent surmised. Once, when preaching to a small group of fifteen people, Rowland stopped his address because of the incessant cries of his listeners; they told Rowland "that they saw hell opening before them, and themselves ready to fall into it."[19] By May 1739 Rowland perceived that his listeners had been sufficiently awakened to their sinful condition, and he changed his tone to "inviting and encouraging subjects." In the course of the next year he led a significant revival in southwest New Jersey. Oliver Hart experienced his oratorical powers firsthand, when Jenkin Jones invited Rowland and Gilbert Tennent to preach at the Philadelphia Baptist meetinghouse in 1740. In these peak years of the Great Awakening, Jones would do his best to keep his Particular Baptists in the middle of revival excitement.

*

[18] Maxson, *Great Awakening in the Middle Colonies*, 35; Presbyterian Board of Publication, *Records of the Presbyterian Church in the United States of America* (Philadelphia, PA, 1904), 185.

[19] Gilbert Tennent, *A funeral sermon occasion'd by the death of the Reverend Mr. John Rowland* (Philadelphia, PA, 1745), 42; Maxson, *Great Awakening in the Middle Colonies*, 36.

The early streams of revivalism in the middle colonies converged into a single, surging river when George Whitefield arrived in Philadelphia on November 2, 1739. Passionate and endlessly energetic, immensely talented and deceptively savvy, Whitefield more than any other person embodied the evangelical revival; he would also wield an incalculable influence on Oliver Hart. At twenty-five, Whitefield had already achieved international fame as the "Grand Itinerant" of the transatlantic world. Born in an inn in Gloucester, England, in 1714 and raised within the Church of England, Whitefield grew up torn between the allure of Gloucester's bawdy theater culture and seriously seeking after God. While a student at Oxford University, he came into the circle of spiritually intense friends called the Oxford Holy Club. The club included future revival leaders John (1703–1791) and Charles (1707–1788) Wesley, though they, like Whitefield, would later consider themselves unconverted at the time. The Holy Club followed a strict regimen of spiritual discipline, study, and service, earning them derisive names from classmates, such as "Methodists," and "Bible moths." Through the Holy Club, Whitefield read various Pietistic manuals for Christian living, most notably Henry Scougal's *The Life of God in the Soul of Man* (1677). Whitefield would claim afterward that he "never knew what true religion was" until he read this book and began fervently seeking the new birth. After a protracted period of agonized searching, he finally "found and felt in myself that I was delivered from the burden that had so heavily oppressed me." It was then, at the age of twenty, that "the Spirit of God [took] possession of my soul." Having experienced the new birth, Whitefield now had a message to preach.[20]

Whitefield was ordained as a deacon in the Anglican Church in 1736 and immediately began filling pulpits across Bristol and London. His sermons, focusing on the necessity of the new birth and delivered with the flair of a trained actor, were enormously effective. As his reputation grew, he drew larger and larger crowds; then, in 1738, at the urging of the Wesleys, he sailed for the colony of Georgia for a brief stint of missionary work. In three months there he saw tremendous opportunity for future ministry, both through evangelism and in the orphanage that he founded in Savannah, Bethesda House. Multitudes awaited Whitefield when he returned to England. After receiving ordination as a priest, he determined to try the innovative method

---

[20] Whitefield, *Journals*, 58. For an introduction to Whitefield, see Thomas S. Kidd, *George Whitefield: America's Spiritual Founding Father* (New Haven, CT: Yale University Press, 2014), and Harry S. Stout, *The Divine Dramatist: George Whitefield and the Rise of Modern Evangelicalism* (Grand Rapids, MI: Eerdmans, 1991).

of field preaching at the beginning of 1739. The results were spectacular. At the mining community of Kingswood in February he drew ten thousand; in London that spring the crowds swelled to fifty and sixty thousand. By August Whitefield was ready to take his field preaching to America. He shrewdly utilized the mass media of his day to hype his upcoming visit: newspaper articles, printed sermons, and his published journals set Philadelphia abuzz long before he arrived. The journals made for especially racy reading, as Whitefield recorded not only the record-breaking crowds he preached to and his soaring spiritual experiences but many unguarded assessments of Anglican clergy whom he deemed to be without grace. He was the biggest celebrity in the English-speaking world, and his visit to Philadelphia the event of the year for its citizens. Oliver Hart was caught up in the furor.[21]

*

Arriving in Philadelphia on November 2, Whitefield immediately contacted the city's religious leaders. On his first Sunday he read prayers at the Anglican Church in the morning and attended a Quaker meeting that night. On Monday, November 5, he met Hart's pastor, Jenkin Jones, who at this time served Baptist churches at both Pennepek Creek and Philadelphia. The two men bonded almost immediately. "I was visited in the afternoon by the Presbyterian minister, and went afterward to see the Baptist teacher who seems to be a spiritual man," Whitefield recorded in his diary.[22] As Whitefield would repeatedly state, he believed that the shared "spiritual" realities of the new birth formed a far more significant bond among Christians than did denominational affiliations.[23] The next night Jones exhibited the same catholicity by going to hear Whitefield in the Anglican Church, where he was reportedly "much rejoiced to hear Jesus Christ preached." Protestant denominations had been suspicious of and competitive with one another since Pennsylvania's founding, but Whitefield seemed able to transcend those

---

[21] For the role media played in spreading revival, see especially Frank Lambert, *"Pedlar in Divinity": George Whitefield and the Transatlantic Revivals, 1737-1770* (Princeton, NJ: Princeton University Press, 1994), and *Inventing the "Great Awakening"* (Princeton, NJ: Princeton University Press, 1999).

[22] The Presbyterian ministers were the redoubtable Jedidiah Andrews (the same who appeared in the previous chapter, strong-arming the Baptists out of their meeting house), and Robert Cross, a junior minister ordained in 1739. Both would eventually oppose Whitefield's revivals in Philadelphia. See Maxson, *Great Awakening in the Middle Colonies*, 46-47.

[23] See Eric C. Smith, *Order and Ardor: The Revival Spirituality of Oliver Hart and the Regular Baptists of Eighteenth-Century South Carolina* (Columbia: University of South Carolina Press, 2018), 100-116.

42    OLIVER HART AND THE RISE OF BAPTIST AMERICA

old rivalries. The Great Awakening was creating an international and inter-denominational network of evangelicals who were willing to set aside their traditional differences to promote what they perceived to be a once-in-a-generation work of God. Though not all American Baptists looked favorably upon this trend, Jones and the majority of his Particular Baptist compatriots of the Philadelphia Association were happy to join this new evangelical alliance. At least at first.

With preliminary matters in Philadelphia settled, Whitefield finally preached in the open air, to a tremendous response. The crowds amazed even Benjamin Franklin, Philadelphia's most notorious religious skeptic. So amazed was Franklin, in fact, that the curious polymath even staged an experiment to test whether or not the evangelist's Philadelphia numbers could stand up to the reports from England. One night as Whitefield preached from the Court House steps, Franklin estimated that he could be heard by thirty thousand people. The experience "reconciled me to the newspaper accounts of his having preached to 25,000 people in the fields," Franklin wrote.[24] Whitefield's American audiences seemed unusually open to the democratic rhetorical setting of field preaching. In England, Whitefield reflected, "the generality of people think a sermon cannot be preached well without; here, they do not like it so well if delivered within church walls." Over the next week in Philadelphia he drew crowds of six and eight thousand. (The population of Philadelphia was about thirteen thousand at this time.) Hart was likely among this number on more than one occasion. With enthusiasm in Philadelphia now raised to a fever pitch, Whitefield left for New York on November 12.[25]

On the way, Whitefield continued to build his evangelical coalition, connecting with many established revival leaders in the region. Passing through New Brunswick, New Jersey, he met Gilbert Tennent, whom he called "a son of thunder, who does not fear the faces of men." Tennent accompanied Whitefield to New York, where the duo preached from the pulpit of the Presbyterian Ebenezer Pemberton (1705–1777), soon to become a key evangelical leader in his own rite. After five days in New York, the pair returned to New Jersey, where Tennent introduced Whitefield to Rowland and Frelinghuysen. Crossing back into Pennsylvania, Whitefield came to

---

[24] Thomas S. Kidd, *Benjamin Franklin: The Religious Life of a Founding Father* (New Haven, CT: Yale University Press, 2017), 126–27. Kidd explores Franklin's complex relationship with both Whitefield and the Christian faith throughout this work.

[25] Whitefield, *Journals*, 342–43.

"THE POWER OF RELIGION GREATLY DISPLAYED" 43

Neshaminy Creek and preached to three thousand in the churchyard of William Tennent Sr. The revival work of Tennent and the Log College men thrilled him. He admired the elder Tennent as "an old grey-headed disciple of Jesus Christ" and thought that his rustic seminary "resembled the school of the old prophets." He sympathized with the Tennents' being "secretly despised by the generality of the Synod," as all zealous promoters of revival must be. "Though we are but few, and stand alone, as it were like Elijah, yet I doubt not, but the Lord will appear for us as he did for that prophet, and make us more than conquerors," he wrote. The image of the lonely but fearless, truth-telling prophet was fast becoming one of the evangelical's favorite self-portraits. Outsiders viewed it as a pious cloak for irresponsible, attention-seeking, and trouble-making behavior. Whitefield preached in the Philadelphia area for five more days, attracting crowds upward of ten thousand, which again likely included Oliver Hart. On November 29 Whitefield headed for Georgia.[26]

Whitefield's tour of the middle colonies had unleashed the floodgates of revival. Over the next five months numerous local awakenings broke out, including in Aaron Burr's (1716–1757) congregation in Newark, New Jersey; William Tennent Jr.'s and James Davenport's (1716–1757) in Long Island, New York; Samuel Blair's church at Fagg's Manor, Pennsylvania; John Rowland's New Jersey circuit; and Jenkin Jones's Baptist congregations at Pennepek and Philadelphia. When Whitefield returned to Philadelphia on April 14, 1740, Jones delivered a breathless report of all that had transpired. Whitefield wrote, "It is impossible to express the joy many felt when they saw my face again. O how did they comfort my heart with the account of what God had done for their own and many other people's souls. The Baptist minister in particular, who has been instrumental in watering what God has planted, recounted to me many noble instances of God's power of free grace shown in the conviction and conversion of some ministers as well as common people." Like many local pastors, Jones had seized upon the moment Whitefield had created to call his own Baptist people to "close with Christ." According to Whitefield, Jones was himself no mean revival preacher; he "preached the truth as it is in Jesus" and was "the only preacher that I know of in Philadelphia, who speaks feelingly and with authority. The poor people are much refreshed by him, and I trust the Lord will bless him more and more." On May 9 Jones asked Whitefield to preach at the Pennepek

---

[26] Whitefield, *Journals*, 344, 354.

44  OLIVER HART AND THE RISE OF BAPTIST AMERICA

Baptist meetinghouse. Over two thousand gathered to hear Whitefield that day.[27] His revival was already proving to be a great boon for the Baptists of America, but that story was only just beginning.

\*

Outside the middle colonies, other Particular Baptists also embraced the Great Awakening, resulting in significant growth. This was especially true in the Lower South. Traveling through Charleston, South Carolina, in the summer of 1740, Whitefield received an invitation to stay in the home of Isaac Chanler (1701–1749), pastor of a Particular Baptist church at Ashley Ferry, about fourteen miles outside the city. Chanler immediately struck Whitefield as "a gracious Baptist minister," and he accepted the invitation. Whitefield preached at the Ashley Ferry Baptist meetinghouse on July 7, 1740, "to the conviction of some and the comfort of others," he reported in his diary. The sultry South Carolina summer took a toll, however, and he afterward collapsed from "the violent heat of the weather, and great expense of sweat." But by the next day he had recovered sufficiently to preach twice at the Independent Presbyterian Church before staying with Chanler again, still feeling "very weak." On the morning of July 9 he preached again for Chanler, though this time the Baptist meetinghouse could not contain the crowd. Whitefield moved the meeting outdoors, standing under a tree. "People seemed to come from all parts, and the Word came with convincing power," he wrote.

By July 20 Whitefield's preaching had made its desired effect on the Ashley Ferry Baptists and other residents of Charleston. "Though the heat of the weather, and frequency of preaching, have perhaps given an irrevocable stroke to the health of my body; yet I rejoice, knowing it has been for the conviction, and I believe conversion of many souls," a gratified Whitefield recorded. "Numbers are seeking after Jesus."[28] Before leaving town he advised Chanler and the other revival-friendly pastors in the Charleston areas to establish a weekly, interdenominational religious meeting for new converts and seekers. Chanler delivered the first address, published as *New Converts Instructed to Cleave to the Lord* (1740). Addressing the mixed crowd, he lauded Whitefield, calling his listeners to imitate the evangelist's piety,

---

[27] Whitefield, *Journals*, 406, 310, 420.
[28] Whitefield, *Journals*, 440–44.

"THE POWER OF RELIGION GREATLY DISPLAYED" 45

particularly his catholic spirit. "Let our love like his be catholic, breathing in a free and open air, abstracted from all bigotry and party zeal, loving the image of God on whomever we may see it impressed ... that is to say, all the regenerate sons and daughters of God, howsoever they may be distinguished by different denominations amongst men," Chanler implored.[29] In his instruction to the new converts that followed, Chanler conspicuously avoided any mention of distinctively Baptist church orders, including the need to be immersed. After years of carefully guarding their fellowships from other denominations, revival seemed to make the Baptists more open to becoming broadly evangelical.

Later that month Whitefield received an equally warm reception from the Particular Baptist minister William Tilly (1698–1744). Tilly joined a group of friends in visiting Whitefield at his Bethesda orphanage in Savannah on July 31, 1740. They found the evangelist in poor health. His incessant activity under the southern sun left him feeling, "I was struck, as I thought, with death." On Sunday several guests had come to the orphanage to hear Whitefield, but he was so weak that he asked Tilly to preach for him instead. Not eager to stand in for Whitefield, Tilly refused. Whitefield recorded that Tilly urged him to believe that "God would strengthen me if I began." So Whitefield began. As he opened in prayer, one guest fell to the ground, "as though shot with a gun." That was all it took; from there "the influence spread." As the congregation listened, "tears trickled down apace, and God manifested himself much amongst us at the Sacrament." Even more impressive to Whitefield, Tilly and the other guests afterward shared communion in the Anglican style, kneeling to receive the bread and the cup. Baptists typically repudiated this practice as a Roman Catholic veneration of the communion elements. For a Baptist to overcome this deep aversion speaks to the powerful effect that the revival was having on Tilly. The significance of this was not lost on Whitefield, who wrote the next week, "The word runs like lightning in Charles-Town. A serious lively Baptist minister, named *Tilly*, is

---

[29] Isaac Chanler, *New Converts Exhorted to Cleave to the Lord* (Boston: D. Fowle for S. Kneeland and T. Green, 1740), 1–2, 4–5, 38–42. Whitefield wrote to Chanler the following year, sending his love to the flock at Ashley Ferry; see George Whitefield to Isaac Chanler, February 17, 1741, in George Whitefield, *Works of the Reverend George Whitefield*, 4 vols. (London: Edward and Charles Dilly, 1771), 1:237–38. For a helpful treatment of Chanler and the spread of evangelicalism in the Lower South at this time, see Thomas J. Little, *Origins of Southern Evangelicalism: Religious Revivalism in the South Carolina Lowcountry, 1670–1760* (Columbia: University of South Carolina Press, 2013), 111–13, 146–47, 154–57, 174–75.

46 OLIVER HART AND THE RISE OF BAPTIST AMERICA

here also; he has preached often for me, and last Sunday received the sacrament in our way—O bigotry, thou art tumbling down a-pace!"[30]

Though their story is often overlooked, the Particular Baptists of the Lower South, like those in the middle colonies, generally celebrated both Whitefield and the Great Awakening and experienced significant numeric growth and spiritual renewal in the 1740s as a result. Baptist leaders like Isaac Chanler and William Tilly were so enthused about the evangelical awakening that they set aside traditional Baptist agendas in order to promote the revival. The Great Awakening had opened an important new chapter for the Baptist movement in America, but as in other denominations, revival would also bring Baptists their share of controversy.

\*

In later years, Oliver Hart could still recall the spectacle of hearing Whitefield, the Tennents, John Rowland, and the itinerating Baptist revivalist Abel Morgan Jr. (1713–1785). At the height of their powers, these evangelists could elicit intense emotional and physical responses from the men and women who came under their spell. Weeping, moaning, crying out, trembling, and falling on the ground were all common occurrences in these heady days of revival.

Hart may have witnessed one remarkable episode in a special service at the Philadelphia Baptist meetinghouse, where Jones had invited Morgan to preach. It involved an unnamed African American woman who later related her experience to Whitefield. As Morgan spoke, the woman recalled, "the word came with such power on her heart, that at last she was obliged to cry out." Morgan asked the woman to be quiet. Ordinarily the public rebuke of a white male religious leader would have instantly silenced a black woman. Yet filled with the Spirit, the woman believed herself to be operating under a far greater authority than Morgan possessed; she claimed she could not be quiet. "The glory of the LORD shone so brightly round about her, that she could not help blessing and praising God, and telling how God was revealing himself to her soul," Whitefield reported. The woman was removed from the meetinghouse, but her raptures continued in the streets, as she fell to her knees, shouted, and worshipped God. It was a disturbing episode for many

---

[30] Leah Townsend, *South Carolina Baptists, 1670–1805* (Baltimore, MD: Clearfield, 2003), 38; David Benedict, *A General History of the Baptist Denomination in America, and Other Parts of the World*, 2 vols. (Boston: Lincoln and Edmonds, 1813), 2:127–28; Whitefield, *Journals*, 447; George Whitefield to Mr. N., August 15, 1740, in *Works*, 1:203.

of the meeting's attendees, not least for Morgan. But Whitefield clearly had no problem with it. He assessed the woman to be "rational and solid" and her response to conversion to be entirely appropriate in a revival context. "When an extraordinary work is carrying on," he wrote, "God generally manifests himself to some souls in this extraordinary manner." In this case, God had manifested himself through a layperson, not a member of the clergy; through an emotional outburst, not a prepared sermon; through a black woman, not a white man. In 1740 this was extraordinary.[31]

The presumably white Baptist men who escorted the black woman out into the Philadelphia streets that night were encountering a decidedly uncomfortable side of the evangelical revival. Embedded in the new birth message that the evangelicals celebrated was the implication that every individual, including women and people of color, could be directly and personally indwelt with the Holy Spirit, who might even empower some of those individuals to speak to others on behalf of God. Evangelicalism carried within it seeds of radical egalitarianism every bit as explosive as Quakerism had in seventeenth-century England. (Numerous critics of Whitefield in fact compared him to George Fox.) It threatened to topple all the prevailing social structures of the day, including those related to religion, gender, and race. As Thomas Kidd has noted, it was the issue of just how radical the movement would become that constituted "the most interesting question in the first generation of American evangelicalism."[32]

As Kidd has further noted, observers responded to the more controversial aspects of the revival along a spectrum. On the radical end, some evangelicals welcomed the physical outbursts and egalitarianism as proofs that God's liberating Spirit was doing a new thing in their midst. As his remarks suggest, Whitefield was quite radical in the earliest years of the revival, though he moderated his position by the mid-1740s. On the other end of the spectrum, opponents of the revival seized upon episodes like the one among the Philadelphia Baptists, with its signs of wild "enthusiasm" and spiritual delusion, as reason to reject the revival altogether. When the arch-antirevivalist Charles Chauncy (1705–1787) wanted to discredit the Awakening, he sneered, "Women and Girls; yes, Negroes, have taken upon them to do the Business of Preachers."[33] Many evangelicals, like Abel Morgan Jr. and the

[31] Whitefield, *Journals*, 419–20.
[32] Kidd, *Great Awakening*, xv.
[33] Charles Chauncy, *Seasonable Thoughts on the State of Religion in New England* (Boston: Rogers and Fowle, 1743), 226.

48 OLIVER HART AND THE RISE OF BAPTIST AMERICA

troubled ushers at the Baptist meetinghouse, attempted a moderating position. Firmly in favor of the revival, they nervously sought to control its more unsettling elements without quenching the Spirit entirely.[34]

Oliver Hart had ample opportunity to witness this spectrum within his own Particular Baptist community. By the middle of 1740 Jenkin Jones was taking every possible opportunity to assemble his Baptist people (and whoever else would come) for revival meetings, without regard for the preacher's non-Baptist background or unorthodox methods. A star-studded cast of revivalists paraded through Jones's Baptist meetinghouse throughout 1740, including Whitefield, Morgan, and the Presbyterians Rowland and Gilbert Tennent. The passions in these meetings often ran high, as they did one night when both Tennent and Rowland visited. Rowland's impassioned oratory brought the people to such desperation over the state of sinners that Tennent was compelled to run to the pulpit stairs and cry out, "Oh Brother Rowland, is there no balm in Gilead?" Startled by Tennent's intervention, Rowland shifted his message to "unfold the way of recovery."[35] It was an unforgettable night, but the excitement was just getting started for the Baptist church.

While most of Jones's congregation shared his enthusiasm for revivalism, his assistant minister, Ebeneezer Kinnersley (1711–1778), did not. Kinnersley was a Baptist minister with an intellectual bend, who would later teach English at the University of Pennsylvania and assist Benjamin Franklin in his research of electricity. The emotionalism of the Awakening had long disgusted Kinnersley, and Rowland's histrionics from the Baptist pulpit finally provoked him to speak out. He selected Franklin's *Pennsylvania Gazette* as the forum to air his grievances, skewering the out-of-control passions stirred by the revivalists. Under these irresponsible leaders, listeners were "filled brim-full of enthusiatical raptures and ecstasies, pretending to have large communications from God; to have seen ravishing visions; to have been encompassed, as it were, with flames of lightning, and there to have beheld our blessed Savior nailed to the cross, and bleeding before their eyes in particular for them! These and such like enthusiastic extravagancies some of our bigoted young zealots (who are not as yet distracted) have run into." An associate opposing his own senior minister in the local newspaper indicated that the Baptists had now entered fully into the religious tumult of the Great Awakening.

---

[34] Kidd develops this spectrum throughout *The Great Awakening*.
[35] Maxson, *Great Awakening in the Middle Colonies*, 62.

## "THE POWER OF RELIGION GREATLY DISPLAYED" 49

Remarkably, Jones still asked Kinnersley to fill his Philadelphia pulpit after this. Still bristling, Kinnersley took the occasion to again criticize the revival, its leaders, and even Jones himself. Several offended church members walked out on Kinnersley's sermon, many of them women and African Americans. For Kinnersley, the demographics of the demonstrators simply confirmed his suspicions about the revival's disorderly character. Later the church brought charges against him for undermining Jones's leadership. When Kinnersley refused to apologize, the church excluded him from the Lord's Table. Matters turned uglier still when Kinnersley blasted the congregation in the *Pennsylvania Gazette.* He accused Jones of lying and showing ungodly favoritism toward Rowland, a fellow Welshman. Incensed, the church fired off its own public letter, exonerating Jones and demanding that Kinnersley repent. Kinnerseley responded in print once more before the controversy died out. Refused communion at the Philadelphia Baptist Church, Kinnersley departed for the Episcopal church, though he would eventually return to the Baptists as a faithful member until his death. In a display of solidarity with Jones, the Philadelphia Association asked the embattled revivalist to deliver the annual message the following year. Jones and the Philadelphia Baptists had weathered the initial storm of revival divisions, but these events must have made a deep impression on Hart.[36]

Most Particular Baptists in the middle colonies and the Lower South celebrated the revival, but Baptist churches in New England sharply disagreed over it. Rather than growing during the Great Awakening years, older New England Baptist churches generally experienced division and setback.[37] Isaac Backus later suggested that New England's religious context was a key factor in Baptist suspicion of the Great Awakening. Unlike their brethren in Pennsylvania, Rhode Island, or South Carolina, Baptists in New England had suffered fines, imprisonment, corporal punishment, and social exclusion at the hands of the established Congregational Church for more than one

[36] Maxson, *Great Awakening in the Middle Colonies,* 62; Thomas Ray, "Jenkin Jones (c. 1686–1760)," in *A Noble Company: Biographical Essays on Notable Particular-Regular Baptists in America,* edited by Terry Wolever (Springfield, MO: Particular Baptist Press, 2006), 200–210; Spencer, *Early Baptists of Philadelphia,* 68. Kinnserly would go on to make his mark as the master demonstrator "of electricity in British America. See James Delbourgo, *Most Amazing Scene of Wonders* (Cambridge, MA: Harvard University Press, 2006), 93–108.

[37] Thomas S. Kidd and Barry Hankins, *Baptists in America: A History* (New York: Oxford University Press, 2015), 19–24.

50 OLIVER HART AND THE RISE OF BAPTIST AMERICA

hundred years.[38] When these Baptists heard their Pedobaptist antagonists promoting the revival, many wanted no part of it. As Backus put it, "As the work has begun and carried on almost wholly by Pedobaptusts, from which denomination their fathers had suffered much, most of the Baptists were prejudiced against the work, and against the Calvinian doctrine it promoted."[39] Evangelical ecumenism was simply a harder sell for Baptists in New England.

Some New England Baptists also shared Kinnersley's disdain for the Great Awakening's emotionalism. John Callender (1706–1748), pastor of the First Baptist Church in Newport, Rhode Island, sneered at Whitefield as "a second George Fox."[40] Joining Callender in scorning the revival was Jeremiah Condy (d. 1768), pastor of Boston's First Baptist Church. A refined graduate of Harvard College, "there was little difference between Jeremiah Condy and the typical eastern Congregational minister of his time accept that he had been immersed," according to one historian.[41] Condy openly opposed the revival, claiming, "Christians cannot know or distinguish the operation of the Spirit of God upon their souls, from the operation of their own minds." Many of Condy's flock were deeply offended by their pastor's position. His comments exhibited to them "the most dangerous tendency; a striking at the root and main evidence of the Christian consolation and hope." One faction in his church left altogether. They formed their own, revival-friendly Baptist fellowship in 1743, citing Condy's opposition to the revival and his Arminian doctrine as the reasons for their leaving.[42] The group sent a copy of their principles to the renowned London pastor John Gill (1697–1771), the godfather of all Calvinistic Baptists in the English-speaking world. Gill approved of the new church's position, sending back fifty dollars' worth of books, as well as a beautiful communion set and seven baptismal garments.[43] Within five years the Second Baptist Church had grown to 125 members. Condy, now in the unenviable position of opposing George Whitefield *and* John Gill, watched his church decline throughout the 1740s, as did most New England Baptist churches that rejected the revival. First Baptist Boston would not rebound

---

[38] The best treatment of the New England Baptist experience is still William G. McLoughlin's magisterial *New England Dissent, 1630–1833: Baptists and the Separation of Church and State*, 2 vols. (Cambridge, MA: Harvard University Press, 1971).

[39] Backus, *History of New England*, 2:41.

[40] Backus, *History of New England*, 2:505.

[41] C. C. Goen, *Revivalism and Separatism in New England, 1740–1800* (Middletown, CT: Wesleyan University Press, 1987), 237.

[42] Backus, *History of New England*, 2:420.

[43] Backus, *History of New England*, 2:422.

until the 1760s, when a revival-minded pastor trained by Oliver Hart would assume leadership.

Boston's Second Baptist Church was one of many new congregations in New England created by the revival tumult of the Great Awakening. Most of these new churches initially split from revival-resistant Congregationalist churches and formed "Separate" Congregational churches that practiced radical revivalism.[44] As these new Separate churches continued to question their traditional beliefs, over one hundred of them eventually embraced Baptist principles about the church and sacraments, earning them the name "Separate Baptists." Hart would one day recall Whitefield remarking of this phenomenon, "These Anabaptists are stealing Sheep, they wash my sheep and they fleece my Sheep."[45] In the ensuing decades these Separate Baptists would come to represent the most dynamic and most radical wing of the new evangelical movement. They would experience their most explosive growth in the southern colonies, during the same years Hart would occupy the Charleston Baptist Church. Helping unite the vibrant Separate Baptist movement with his Particular Baptists to form a single Baptist denomination in America would constitute one of Hart's greatest works. But in 1740 all this lay well in the future; at this point Hart himself still needed to be born again.

*

In 1740, at the peak foment of the Great Awakening, Oliver Hart experienced an evangelical conversion. "My youth was spent in vanity and listlessness to all that was good," he remembered of his preconversion days. It is impossible to know exactly what he had in mind by this statement. Most likely he recalled with sensitive conscience the typical struggles of adolescence, including sexual lust, pride, resistance to authority, and an indifference to the spiritual things he later came to prize. Such a sweeping, negative self-assessment of life before meeting Christ was typical of evangelical autobiography, which aimed to magnify the change wrought by the new birth. But though Hart left no first-person account of the event, he ever after looked back on it as the defining event of his life. He described it as undergoing "a saving change," wrought by "the powerful, inscrutable operations of the Spirit." At the core

---

[44] For a recent treatment of the Separate movement, see Winiarski, *Darkness Falls on the Land of Light,* especially 288–519.

[45] Oliver Hart to Richard Furman, November 9, 1791, Hart MSS, JBDML.

52  OLIVER HART AND THE RISE OF BAPTIST AMERICA

of this experience was the creation of a personal faith in Jesus Christ, as Hart once reflected in poetry:

Faith! 'tis a precious grace,
Wherein it is bestow'd
It boasts of a celestial birth
and is the gift of God!
Jesus it owns a King,
An all-atoning Priest
It claims no merit of its own,
But looks for all in Christ
To him it leads the soul
When fill'd with deep distress,
Flies to the fountain of his Blood,
and trusts his righteousness.
Since 'tis thy work alone,
And that divinely free;
Lord, send the Spirit of thy Son
to work this faith in me.[46]

In Baptist history Hart and the so-called Charleston Tradition he established in the Baptist South would come to be identified with strict church order, confessionalism, and a formal approach to worship and piety. These were important elements in his piety, to be sure, but are often highlighted in order to draw a sharp contrast between Hart's Particular Baptist stream and the revival-oriented Separate Baptists.[47] In fact the revival spirituality Hart imbibed in the years of his earliest development never left him. For the rest of his life he maintained a passion for the centrality of conversion, energetic activism, evangelical catholicity, and a longing for revival.[48]

*

[46] Oliver Hart to Richard Furman, May 8, 1790, Hart MSS, Furman; Hart, Sermon on 2 Timothy 1:9, Hart MSS, SCL; the poem can be found in Hart MSS, SCL.
[47] For this very influential interpretation, see especially William L. Lumpkin, *Baptist Foundations in the South: Tracing through the Separates the Influence of the Great Awakening, 1754–1787* (Nashville, TN: Broadman Press, 1961); and Walter B. Shurden, "The Southern Baptist Synthesis: Is It Cracking?," *Baptist History and Heritage* 16, no. 2 (April 1981): 2–11.
[48] This is the major thesis of my earlier work, *Order and Ardor*.

The Great Awakening was a defining moment for Hart and the Baptist movement in America he would help shape in the second half of the eighteenth century. Most obviously, the revivals that began in the late 1730s and continued periodically into the nineteenth century contributed to a significant numerical increase among American Baptists during the same period. There were 60 known Baptist churches in the colonies in 1740; there would be 979 in America by 1790. Numerous historians have considered Baptists the greatest beneficiaries of the First Great Awakening in America.[49] Baptists, and by the end of the century Methodists, would ultimately outgrow all other American denominations because they proved most adept at tapping into the new, popular, individualist religious ethos unleashed by the evangelical revivals.[50]

The revivals also magnified the diversity that already existed among Baptists before 1740, as well as introducing new diversities. There were antirevivalist Baptists, like Ebenezer Kinnersley and Jeremiah Condy; the small collection of Particular Baptists of Virginia would also develop a reputation for resisting revival during the 1750s and 1760s. At the other end of the spectrum the new Separate Baptists, who would soon outgrow all other Baptist groups, were among the most radical evangelicals of the eighteenth century. But the majority of Particular Baptists in the Philadelphia Association and in the Lower South warmly embraced the Great Awakening, while attempting to guard against the perceived excesses of the movement. As the eighteenth century progressed, Baptists realized that, to forge a powerful and respectable denomination, they had to unify all these diverse groups into a single body of American Baptists. Hart would invest considerable time and energy in doing just that.

The Great Awakening also brought Baptists into conversation with the broader group of Protestant Christians forming in Europe and North America in these years. This unofficial network was united not by denominational affiliation but by a shared commitment to the basic principles of the revival: the authority of the Bible, the atoning death of Jesus on the cross, the necessity of the new birth, the dynamic activity of the Holy Spirit, and the call for energetic activism. The Great Awakening gave birth to what we today recognize as the modern evangelical movement. The wholehearted endorsement

---

[49] See Noll, *The Rise of Evangelicalism*, 180–83.

[50] Leon H. McBeth, *The Baptist Heritage: Four Centuries of Baptist Witness* (Nashville, TN: Broadman Press, 1987), 206.

54   OLIVER HART AND THE RISE OF BAPTIST AMERICA

of interdenominational evangelical activity by Jones and Chanler shows just how open Baptists could be to the new movement, and Hart would show the same openness in the following decades. At the same time, the new evangelical currents would raise important questions about how they would maintain a distinctively Baptist identity, holding onto those beliefs and ritual practices they treasured, which almost none of their fellow evangelicals shared. Could Baptists be "evangelicals" in the broader sense and still be Baptists?[51] It was a question that Baptists would wrestle with throughout the 1740s, and beyond.

---

[51] For a helpful survey of the Baptists' relationship with broader evangelicals, see Barry Hankins, *Uneasy in Babylon: Southern Baptist Conservatives and American Culture* (Tuscaloosa: University of Alabama Press, 2002), 14–40.

# 3

# "All things are become new"

## Moving to the South

On April 3, 1741, Oliver Hart stepped into the chilly waters of Pennepek Creek with Jenkin Jones. On the bank stood his mother and father, along with the rest of the Pennepek Baptists. They had watched Oliver wrestle through the ordeal of conversion over the past year and had accepted his public testimony of experiencing God's grace. A handful of curious non-Baptists could have been present, too, to observe the spectacle of public immersion. After exhorting his young charge with Scripture's solemn words about baptism's significance, Jones led Hart out into sufficiently deep water. Taking hold of Hart's thumbs with his right hand and the back of his baptismal garment with his left, Jones dipped Hart backward into the water until he was completely submerged, announcing, "In the name of the Lord Jesus, and by the authority of our office, we baptize you in the name of the Father, in the name of the Son, and in the name of the Holy Ghost. Amen." Reemerging into the sunlight, Hart would have felt Jones's hands resting on his head and shoulders, symbolic of his receiving the Holy Spirit.

Hart's baptism meant that he had finally entered the Baptist church as a full, communing, covenant member. When he waded back to the bank, the waiting church members greeted him with the right hand of fellowship and kiss of charity. Before departing for home, Hart would have heard Jones say:

> You who have been baptized in the likeness of Christ's death are now risen in the likeness of his resurrection. I congratulate you on this first resurrection after a death to sin and watery burial. Welcome to the newness of life, and this open profession of Christianity before men! This your birth of water bids me rejoice over you; hold this day as your birth day; and this place as Antioch where the disciples were first called Christians, and had that better name given them. And as old things are done away and all things are become new, let us pray in the newness of the spirit, and sing a new song; for as soon as Jesus was baptized, he prayed.

*Oliver Hart and the Rise of Baptist America.* Eric C. Smith, Oxford University Press (2020). © Oxford University Press.
DOI: 10.1093/oso/9780197506325.001.0001

56    OLIVER HART AND THE RISE OF BAPTIST AMERICA

Dripping wet, eighteen-year-old Oliver Hart joined in the prayers and songs of the church. He may well have been overwhelmed by the sense that a whole new life had begun for him.[1]

*

The Baptist commitment to immersion of professing believers only, and the requirement of immersion as a prerequisite for church membership and communion, set them apart from virtually every other Christian tradition. Since the sixteenth century, Baptist men and women in America and Europe had been ostracized, harassed, imprisoned, and even killed for refusing to follow the rest of Christendom's accepted practice of sprinkling their infant children. But Baptists were convinced that Christ intended baptism to be the immersion of a repentant and believing disciple, a powerful symbol of the inward change wrought by the Spirit in conversion, and a visible, physical "putting on of Christ." Baptists would continue immersing as a matter of obedience to their Lord, even if it meant alienation from the broader church.

Yet with the dawn of the Great Awakening, Particular Baptists found their distinctive beliefs and practices challenged by the rise of what we today recognize as the modern evangelical movement. Promoters of the Great Awakening had deliberately de-emphasized the issues that had historically separated Protestants, stressing instead a core of issues that they all agreed upon, namely the authority of the Bible, the atoning death of Christ, and the necessity of the new birth. By following this strategy, early evangelicals formed the broadest possible alliance in order to promote what they believed to be a once-in-a-lifetime move of God. This had been the ecumenical policy of George Whitefield, the person most responsible for creating the international evangelical coalition. "Though I profess myself a minister of the Church of England, I am of a catholic spirit; and, if I see any man who loves the Lord Jesus in sincerity, I am not very solicitous to what outward communion he belongs," Whitefield declared.[2] As we have seen, many staunch Particular Baptists, like Jenkin Jones in Philadelphia and Isaac Chanler in South Carolina, embraced the catholicity of the Great Awakening during the revival's peak years. After all, Baptists were benefiting from the mass conversions of the Awakening more than anyone.

---

[1] Details of the baptism ceremony are drawn from Edwards, *Customs of Primitive Churches*, 81–83.
[2] George Whitefield to Ralph Erskine, January 16, 1740, in Whitefield, *Works*, 1:140.

"ALL THINGS ARE BECOME NEW"    57

Yet as they entered the 1740s Baptists discovered that revival could not long mask the differences that separated them from other denominations. This became evident in a public dispute between the Baptist Abel Morgan Jr. and the Log College Presbyterian Samuel Finley, in Cape May, New Jersey. After preaching the same conversion-centered message as itinerant evangelists throughout the Delaware Valley hinterlands, Morgan and Finley found themselves opposed on what to do with these new converts. Morgan, of course, urged them all (regardless of their previous church background) to be immersed. When many of Finley's converts followed Morgan into the water, the Presbyterian was incensed. In his view, Morgan had "earnestly persuaded the People to renounce their former Baptism and be dipt." Finley had no intentions of standing idle while his sheep were "misled in such a point as adult baptism." The conflict sparked a pamphlet war between the two revivalists on baptism and the nature of the church. It is an important though understudied episode, revealing how the evangelical ecumenism of the Great Awakening quickly gave way to interdenominational wrangling as various evangelical groups diverged on how the invisibly born-again should enter the visible church.[3]

*

The minutes of the Philadelphia Association during the 1740s reveal a movement at once flush with excitement over numerical growth and nervously scrambling to maintain their cherished Baptist church order. In 1740 the Association proudly announced in its circular letter that 111 baptisms had been recorded among their churches that year. Yet two churches also submitted questions indicating that revival was coming at a price for the orderly Baptists. The first request, from Cohansey, New Jersey: "Whether a pious person, of the number of Pedo-Baptists, who forbears to have his own children sprinkled, may be admitted in to our communion without being baptized? And doth not the refusing admittance to such an one, discover want of charity in a church so refusing?"[4] All evangelicals agreed on what made

[3] John Fea, "Samuel Finley versus Abel Morgan: Revivalism, Denominational Identity, and an Eighteenth-Century Sacramental Debate in Cape May, New Jersey," *New Jersey History* 117, nos. 3–4 (Fall–Winter 1999): 24–45. See also Bryan F. Lebeau, "The Acrimonious, Controversial Spirit among Baptists and Presbyterians in the Middle Colonies during the Great Awakening," *American Baptist Quarterly* 9 (September 1990): 167–83; and Ned Landsman, "Revivalism and Nativism in the Middle Colonies: The Great Awakening and the Scots Community in East New Jersey," *American Quarterly* 34 (1982): 149–64; Butler, *Awash in a Sea of Faith*, 164–93.

[4] Gillette, *Minutes*, 42

one a Christian: the experience of the new birth, resulting in a lively faith in Jesus Christ. What these born-again believers did next, especially how they entered church fellowship, is where sharp differences arose. The Cohansey Baptists were feeling the tension of recognizing a Pedobaptist as a brother or sister in Christ, while refusing him or her access to the Lord's Table in their church as an unbaptized believer. Whitefield had raised this very issue with Jones, his most ardent supporter in Philadelphia. "Oh admit of a *mixed communion*," Whitefield pleaded with Jones by letter. "I think the glory of God requires this at your hands. May the Lord give you a right understanding in all things."[5] Clearly, some Philadelphia Association Baptists were feeling the force of Whitefield's appeal; the revival caused them to question whether or not their most cherished ritual made them religious bigots.

But the Association responded firmly in the negative to Cohansey's query and took time to defend from Scripture both their doctrine and their charitable spirit. In short, they still found the Bible to be clear on the meaning of baptism, and sentimental appeals for unity could not change that. Further, admitting individuals who differed on issues as important as baptism to the same membership was a recipe not for unity but for confusion and strife. The Massachusetts Baptist Isaac Backus has left a detailed account of his personal experience on this issue. After he and several members of the Congregational church in Norwich formed a Separate congregation in 1745 as a result of the Great Awakening, Backus and several others became convinced of the necessity of the immersion of believers only. Backus himself received immersion, but for some time attempted to accommodate both Pedobaptist and Baptistic sentiments within the church, performing whichever rite each individual requested. This well-intentioned arrangement ultimately proved unsatisfactory to all parties involved, leading to much heartache for Backus. The two groups finally agreed to part ways, with Backus overseeing the Separate Baptists in Middleborough.[6] It seemed that focusing on evangelical essentials worked fine at a field meeting, but local congregations simply could not function without agreement on baptism.

The second query, coming from the Piscataqua, New Jersey, church, also indicated new currents of thought associated with the Great Awakening. They asked, "Whether it is regular to baptize persons proposing for baptism, upon the plea that they may be at liberty to communicate where they please?"

---

[5] George Whitefield to Jenkin Jones, May 12, 1740, in Whitefield, *Works*, 1:175.
[6] Kidd and Hankins, *Baptists in America*, 30–34. For a detailed account of Backus's spiritual journey, see Alvah Hovey, *A Memoir of the Life and Times of Isaac Backus* (Boston, 1858), 82–128.

In other words, some individuals wished to be immersed upon their conversion, but without making the covenant commitment to a congregation that had held Baptist communities together since its beginnings. The individualism inherent in the request had already become a hallmark of evangelical piety. The revival had taught thousands of listeners in the colonies and Great Britain that when it came to being right with God, all that mattered was the personal experience of the new birth. Traditional gauges of spirituality, such as church membership, were unreliable; to many evangelicals, they were downright unimportant. Evangelical individualism had already caused much havoc in established churches during the Great Awakening, as men and women in many places chose to neglect the ongoing ministry of their respective parish churches (whether they judged the minister to be unconverted or not warm enough toward the revival or simply not as captivating as the visiting revivalist) to go hear itinerants like Whitefield. The revivalists, particularly in the early years, had encouraged this practice, telling the crowds it was their duty to attend the ministry that most benefited their souls. This striking individualism revealed one of the many curious ways in which modern evangelicalism had imbibed the spirit of the Enlightenment, even as it appeared to stand as a conservative bastion against it.[7] With the Great Awakening, a decisive shift took place to the centrality of the individual as opposed to the community; the Piscataqua query indicated that Baptists would not be immune to these new trends.

Again the Association responded decisively. In his great commission of Matthew 28, Jesus ordered his church not only to baptize but to "teach and observe all things" he commanded, including how to structure the local church. The freewheeling individualism desired by these anonymous baptismal candidates did not reflect the practice of the apostles in the New Testament, who always connected baptism with participation in the life of the church (citing Acts 2:41–42). Morgan Edwards put it most succinctly: "No believers are at liberty to be, or not to be of a church."[8] Furthermore, in the practice of "churchless" baptisms, the Baptist leaders foresaw the total breakdown of the Baptist community they had practiced for so long: "Such a practice is directly destructive to all gospel rule, order, and discipline; for by such way all

---

[7] Much helpful work has been done on the interplay between the Enlightenment and evangelicalism, including Bebbington, *Evangelicalism in Modern Britain*; Catherine A. Brekus, *Sarah Osborne's World: The Rise of Evangelical Christianity in Early America* (New Haven, CT: Yale University Press, 2013); and Hindmarsh, *The Spirit of Early Evangelicalism*.

[8] Edwards, *Customs of Primitive Churches*, 6.

# 60 OLIVER HART AND THE RISE OF BAPTIST AMERICA

offences and irregularities, yea, even the most scandalous immoralities and fundamental errors must escape without proper censures, according to the gospel rule, Matt 18:17; Rom 16:17; Phil 3:16, 17; 1 Cor 5:5, 11:16, and 14:32, 33." From here forward, Baptists in America would find their older, church-centered piety existing in tension with the individual-centered approach to Christianity that the Great Awakening accelerated. It was one of many areas in which the Particular Baptists felt constrained to push back against the very revival whose conversions they so enthusiastically celebrated.[9]

\*

The Great Awakening also forced Baptists to grapple with the question of women's roles in the church. The revival had emboldened Baptist women across the Philadelphia Association. It was an African American woman's public testifying that had broken up Abel Morgan's meeting at the Philadelphia Baptist Church, and a group of women who had led the protest against Ebeneezer Kinnersley in the same church. Other Baptist women were also now publicly voicing their faith at an unprecedented rate, whether crying out in meetings, relating their conversion experiences to ministers, or advising others how to receive the new birth. Baptists had to decide how far these female liberties should be tolerated. In 1746 the Philadelphia Association addressed the question "whether women may or ought to have their votes in the church, in such matters as the church shall agree to be decided by votes?"[10] The Association's leaders knew they could not address this issue without a "mature consideration" of the Apostle Paul's strong statements about women "keeping silent in the churches," as in 1 Corinthians 14:34–35. They agreed that even an interpretation requiring absolute silence must still allow Baptist women "liberty to give a mute voice, by standing or lifting up the hands, or the contrary, to signify their assent or dissent to the thing proposed." Outlandish as the idea of a "mute voice" may sound today, it underscored a Baptist commitment that set them apart from many other denominations: whether male or female, all baptized members of the local church possessed the right and responsibility of expressing their conscience in church decisions.[11]

---

[9] For early Baptists in the South pushing back against rampant individualism in their church practices, see Wills, *Democratic Religion*, 4, 33.

[10] Gillette, *Minutes*, 53.

[11] See Wills, *Democratic Religion*, 51–54. Susan Juster has provided a thorough analysis of the suppression of the public roles of New England Baptist women after the Great Awakening in *Disorderly*

The Association ultimately rejected the absolute silence position for Baptist women, believing that it would hinder them from carrying out numerous Scriptural responsibilities. For instance, a woman must be allowed to offer public confession of her faith for the church's consideration. Baptists admitted women into the church as individuals, on the same basis as men, without regard to their marital status. This distinguished them, for instance, from their fellow Congregationalists in New England, who had prospective female members submit their profession of faith in writing, to be read aloud by the minister.[12] Baptists also called regularly upon women to testify during cases of church discipline; to cut off valuable female witnesses, and so force the church to "grope along in the dark" in resolving church problems seemed unwise. The Association further found it to be inhumane to forbid a woman from defending herself if accused in a church discipline trial. Thus they concluded, "There must be times and ways in and by which women, as members of the body, may discharge their conscience and duty towards God and men, as in the cases above said and the like." And if a woman had a "singular" contribution to make in a church decision, "her reasons ought to be called for, heard, and maturely considered, without contempt." In many ways, the power that Baptists accorded to women in their congregations was remarkably progressive for the times.[13] Yet in other ways, Particular Baptists took a conservative stance on gender issues. They maintained that Scripture forbade women, born again or not, from "teaching, ruling, governing, dictating, and leading in the church of God." Even in situations when it was permissible for women to speak, their privilege must be strictly limited, for "ought not they to open the floodgate of speech in an imperious, tumultuous, masterly manner."[14] Particular Baptists settled on an approach to women's involvement in church that in some ways progressed beyond the culture and in other ways followed it.

During this same period, the emerging Separate Baptists of New England and later in the South would embrace a more radically egalitarian approach to women in the church, akin to that of the Quakers.[15] Separate Baptists

---

*Women: Sexual Politics and Evangelicalism in Revolutionary New England* (Ithaca, NY: Cornell University Press, 1994), esp. 145–79.

[12] See, for instance, the experience of Sarah Osborne at Newport, Rhode Island's First Church of Christ in 1737, in Brekus, *Sarah Osborne's World*, 114.

[13] Gillette, *Minutes*, 53. See also Lindman, *Bodies of Belief*, 125–30.

[14] Gillette, *Minutes*, 53.

[15] See especially Juster, *Disorderly Women*, 1–107.

62    OLIVER HART AND THE RISE OF BAPTIST AMERICA

recognized women in official capacities, including as deaconesses and eldresses. These female offices were elected by "choice of the church" and set apart to serve pastoral functions among the women of the congregation. Morgan Edwards described deaconesses as caring "for the sick, miserable, and distressed poor."[16] Eldresses performed many pastoral tasks among women: "praying, and teaching at their separate assemblies; presiding there for maintenance of rules and government; consulting with the sisters about matters of the church which concern them, and representing their sense thereof to the elders, attending at the unction of sick sisters; and at the baptism of women, that all may be done orderly." There are also reports of Separate Baptist eldresses publicly addressing mixed audiences, though some allowances were made for their gender. Morgan Edwards noted that they must "be veiled when they preach or pray, especially if men be sent to their assemblies," in an effort to obey the Apostle Paul's injunction in 1 Corinthians 11:2–16.[17] Some Separate Baptist women apparently communicated with great power. Martha Marshall (1726–1754), wife of the important Separate Baptist pioneer Daniel Marshall (1706–1784), "in countless instances melted a whole concourse into tears by her prayers and exhortations."[18] Daniel Marshall's sister Eunice proved even bolder. It is said that she "took it upon herself to exhort and preach Baptist doctrines" and "was ordered to desist, but not obeying, was (although pregnant at the time) thrown into jail." The Separate Baptists' radical stance on female spiritual authority caused some of their Particular Baptist neighbors to hold them at arm's length early on. One Particular Baptist minister in the South would refuse to assist Shubal Stearns in the ordination of Daniel Marshall because they belonged to "a disorderly sect, suffering women to pray in public." Compared to the Separate Baptists, the Philadelphia Association appeared mired in traditionalism regarding women. As in most areas, they attempted to strike a balance between primitive church order and Great Awakening ardor.[19]

*

Another pressing issue confronting Particular Baptists in the 1740s was the question of what constituted a "regular ministry." Establishing who was and

---

[16] Edwards, *Materials towards a History of the Baptists*, 2:91.

[17] Edwards, *Customs of Primitive Churches*, 41.

[18] Robert Baylor Semple, *A History of the Rise and Progress of the Baptists in Virginia* (Richmond, VA: Pitt and Dickinson, 1894), 374.

[19] Catherine A. Brekus, *Strangers and Pilgrims: Female Preaching in America, 1740–1845* (Chapel Hill: University of North Carolina Press, 1998), 61–67.

"ALL THINGS ARE BECOME NEW" 63

who was not a legitimate minister had been one of the Association's central concerns since its founding, but the Great Awakening seemed to blur these categories as never before. Ordination processes seemed insignificant in the heat of revival, when anyone under the Spirit's influence could apparently speak for God. While countless unordained men informally testified and exhorted their neighbors, some also preached, baptized, and served communion apart from any church sanctions. These developments posed a significant concern for an association that professed to fear "self-made preachers" as much as they would "quack doctors" and "petti-fogging lawyers."[20] The Association advised Baptist churches gathering without an ordained minister to read a chapter of the Bible, sing, and pray. Lay preaching was not permitted, a strict policy that would later set them apart from the equally popular American Methodists.[21] Leaders in the Association were therefore troubled by the 1744 query about recognizing baptisms performed by an individual without a "regular call," insisting that the baptism was of no effect.[22] In 1747 another church inquired if they should allow a "gifted brother" to preach the gospel who refused to communicate with them "unless they comply with his own terms." (Answer: absolutely not.) The church followed up by asking if such a headstrong brother forfeited his right to communion and to preaching the gospel altogether. (Answer: absolutely yes.)[23] For the orderly Particular Baptists, it may have seemed as though evangelical individualism was threatening to topple the denomination they had worked so hard to stabilize over the past forty years.

In 1746 the Association gave its most detailed response to these developments, when a church asked "whether it be lawful or regular for any person to preach the gospel publicly without ordination?" In a lengthy reply the Association made a number of priorities clear for calling ministers. First, young ministers must not be ordained hastily. Instead "gifted brothers" should be given an opportunity to preach on a trial basis, allowing the church to evaluate their gifting. (Baptists would come to refer to this probationary status as being "licensed to preach.") Each congregation, rather than the prospective preacher, should determine when or if the individual should be ordained. Particular Baptists believed that this was how Christ intended to

---

[20] Lindman, *Bodies of Belief*, 24.
[21] Spencer, *Early Baptists of Philadelphia*, 57.
[22] Gillette, *Minutes*, 49.
[23] Gillette, *Minutes*, 53–54.

64  OLIVER HART AND THE RISE OF BAPTIST AMERICA

preserve his church from heretical or even just immature preachers.[24] Any man unwilling to submit to this examination simply proved that he was not ready to bear the weight of the call:

> It is an indication of a heavy, self-willed, obstinate, and ungovernable temper in any gifted brother to refuse to exercise his gifts as the church shall be inclined to call him; and a specimen sufficient to foreshow what may be expected from such a one if preferred. It is therefore running an imprudent risk, to ordain to office in the church of God men of such fluctuating temper, who, if in any wise offended, will behave strangely, and leave the assemblings of the church, and frequent other assemblies. Though they may have fine endowments, yet they can hardly be deemed faithful men. How the steady, sound, and orthodox principles and regular behavior of men shall be found without considerable time of trial, none can tell.[25]

It was another example of Particular Baptists attempting to walk the path of moderate revivalism. In the following generation, their radical Separate Baptist counterparts would largely reject these formal processes, emphasizing the individual's direct call from God. As the Separate Baptist (and arch-individualist) John Leland articulated it, "Christ called unto him *whom he would*, for the work of preaching, either fishermen, herdsmen, or men of science; and when he called and ordained them, if they neglected the work, and conferred with flesh and blood, they would be disobedient to the heavenly vision."[26] It is the question of the regular call that brings Oliver Hart back to the center of this story; in the mid-1740s no other issue so occupied his thoughts.

*

In forming a picture of Oliver Hart, the only surviving physical description comes from Richard Furman. According to Furman's memory, Hart cut an impressive figure, being "somewhat tall, well proportioned, and of a graceful

---

[24] Heyrman devotes a whole chapter in her *Southern Cross* to how the youthfulness and immaturity of many evangelical preachers in the movement's first couple of generations turned off many in the southern society. Particular Baptists were thus seeking to avoid this common slur against evangelical preachers. See Christine Leigh Heyrman, *Southern Cross: The Beginnings of the Bible Belt* (New York: Knopf, 1997), 77–116.

[25] Gillette, *Minutes*, 52.

[26] See John Leland, *The Writings of the Late Elder John Leland*, ed. L. F. Greene (New York: G. W. Wood, 1845), 105, 16.

"ALL THINGS ARE BECOME NEW" 65

appearance," paired with an "open and manly" countenance and "active, vigorous constitution."[27] With due allowances for Furman's celebratory language, we know that Hart had enough strength, energy, and coordination to work as a carpenter for the first ten years of his adulthood.[28] The precision required to accurately measure, cut, and join wood into a sturdy house or handsome piece of furniture also suited his methodical personality well. As his personal writings quickly reveal, Hart paid meticulous attention to detail, keeping careful records of everything from the condition of his soul to the weather, the distances he traveled on horseback, books he purchased, and sermon texts preached, Revolutionary War battles, and states that ratified the Constitution. His unwavering devotion to the Calvinistic theological system likely reflects a deep desire to understand his often apparently random and chaotic experience as in fact being perfectly ordered under the sovereign rule of God.

In his spare time Hart loved to read. He received little formal education growing up, but he had a bright and inquisitive mind. Through extensive self-study, he accrued "a useful fund of knowledge" on a range of subjects, including theology, spirituality, history, and the sciences.[29] He also enjoyed poetry and eventually developed a love for writing his own verse. After the British siege of Charleston, he would mourn the loss of "a large book of poems" he had written. A few of his poems remain, all giving voice to his evangelical piety. This undated selection is typical:

> Foreboding thoughts and gloomy fears
> Crowd thick into my breast;
> Perplexing doubts and anxious cares
> Forbid my soul to rest.
> Happy ye saints, above the skies,
> Beyond the reach of woe;
> Dear Lord, command my soul to rise,
> With joyful haste I'll go.
> The world in sackcloth and distress
> I'd leave beneath my feet;

[27] Furman, *Rewards of Grace*, 23.

[28] Public records on December 31, 1748, report, "Oliver Hart, carpenter, of Warminster, and Sarah his wife giving a mortgage to his brother Joseph on a tract of 50 acres in Warminster, 'to secure the payment of one hundred pounds.'" See Loulie Latimer Owens, *Oliver Hart, 1723–1795: A Biography* (Greenville: South Carolina Baptist Historical Society, 1966), 7.

[29] Furman, *Rewards of Grace*, 23.

# 66 OLIVER HART AND THE RISE OF BAPTIST AMERICA

> And mounting in a heavenly dress,
> I would my Saviour meet.

Throughout his adult years, composing poetry provided an important outlet for the introspective man to give voice to his often perplexing inner life. Though generally serious and focused, Hart also loved to be with friends. He "had a mind formed for friendship," according to Furman, making friends easily and investing considerable time and energy into maintaining these relationships, as his voluminous correspondence attests.[30]

There is an undated note in his personal papers that—whether original to him or a quote from elsewhere that he identified with enough to write down and keep for future reference—seemed to serve as a kind of guiding light for him: "But it is not the striking, dazzling qualities in men and women that make us happy. Good sense, and solid judgment, a natural complacency of temper, a desire of Obliging, and an easiness to be obliged, procure the silent, the serene happiness, to which the flattering tumultuous, impetuous fervors of passion can never contribute. Nothing violent can be lasting. Do nothing-Rashly-reflect.-then-act." Hart did not, in fact, possess a great many "striking, dazzling qualities," and apparently realized this. He was careful and thoughtful and steady in his pursuit of the "quiet, the serene happiness" described in the quote.

Hart continued to worship with the Pennepek Baptist Church as a young man, where his family traveled more than five miles from their home in Southampton every week. But through the growth of revival, enough worshippers were making this trip by 1746 to justify starting a new congregation in Southampton. Forty-three members petitioned the rest of the congregation for permission to form the new church: "We your brethren and sisters, in church fellowship and commission, living at and about Southampton, the county of Bucks, having always labored under great difficulties by reason of the remoteness of our habitations from you, and having signified our desire to be separated from you (not from any dislike or want of love to any of you) but that we may be constituted a church distinct from you."[31] Hart signed his name alongside those of both his parents. It was agreed that Jenkin Jones would temporarily serve both churches until a pastor could be secured at Southampton. Baptists marked the constitution of new churches with a

---

[30] Smith, *Order and Ardor*, 49–51.
[31] Davis, *Hart Family*, 32.

solemn ceremony akin to their baptismal practice, celebrating the occasion as a sign of God's kingdom advancing. The Baptist historian David Spencer describes members of the new congregation being instructed to "take one another by the hand, in token of their union, declaring at the same time that as they had given themselves to God, so they did give themselves also to one another by the will of God (2 Corinthians 8:5), to be a church according to the gospel."[32] The presiding minister's prayers at the ceremony further marked the solemnity of the moment: "One family more, O Lord, is now added to the families of faith! One temple more raised to Jesus! One church more prepared as a bride for the Lamb of God!" Oliver would serve in the new Southampton church with his father, John, who was elected as its first deacon.[33]

While Particular Baptists were concerned abut unauthorized preachers "running unsent" during the Great Awakening years, they also remained eager to raise up new ministers in an orderly fashion. In these years of rapid expansion, and with so much of the colonial frontier destitute of regular ministers, Baptists knew that they must funnel as many trustworthy young men into their ordination process as quickly as possible. They thus kept their eyes open for young men who possessed a desire to preach and who also possessed the right abilities, temperament, and moral reputation for the job. In this environment it was perhaps inevitable that a tall, intelligent, spiritually serious young man like Oliver Hart would be tapped sooner or later. On December 20, 1746, the Southampton Church set apart Hart and Isaac Eaton (1725?–1772) "to be on trial for the work of the ministry."[34] During their probation Hart and Eaton would be permitted "to exercise at the meetings of preparations; or in private meetings that might for that purpose be appointed." The church expressed its dependence on God to discern the truth regarding the calling of the young men: "Will it please the king of saints to be in the midst of us now? And at this time reign over us in a special manner? ... Is our brother—the man? Is he really fitted for ministry, who appeareth so to be? ... Shall we encourage him to a probation in the ministry, or shall we forbear? Thou Lord, which knowest the hearts of all men, show us

[32] Spencer, *Early Baptists of Philadelphia*, 53.

[33] Morgan Edwards provides a detailed discussion of the constitution of a new church in *Customs of Primitive Churches*, 4–10.

[34] Eaton's career would parallel Hart's in many ways. See Walter E. Johnson, "Isaac Eaton (1725?–1772)," in *A Noble Company: Biographical Essays on Notable Particular-Regular Baptists in America*, edited by Terry Wolever (Springfield, MO: Particular Baptist Press, 2013), 3:217–34.

68    OLIVER HART AND THE RISE OF BAPTIST AMERICA

these things!" For both prospective preacher and church, this discernment process was the most serious of matters.[35]

For Hart, licensure for ministry meant accepting a call to rigorous study. Particular Baptists wanted more from their ministers than a warm heart for God and personal charisma in the pulpit. They expected a pastor to prepare substantive, clearly organized expositions of Scripture, informed by extensive personal study of the Bible and appropriate works of theology. For instance, when Timothy Brooks, described by Morgan Edwards as "not eminent for either part of learning," served the Baptist church at Cohansey, New Jersey, he inspired association leaders, particularly the Welsh brethren, to "labour to instruct him in the ways of the Lord more perfectly."[36] The ideal of a learned pulpit ministry within the Philadelphia Association was in fact not much different from that of the cerebral New England Congregationalists, and Particular Baptists came to resent the public perception of Baptists as a rude, unlearned sect among the other American denominations.[37] But since Baptists had no Harvard or Yale to send their ministers to in the 1740s, their training came from guided mentorships with established pastors. Hart likely began reading under Jones. At various points in his writings Hart mentions a variety of works in the Reformed tradition, including those of Augustine, Herman Witsius, Matthew Poole, Matthew Henry, Joseph Caryl, Richard Baxter, and John Gill. As the Baptist historian Tom Nettles has observed, Hart had also memorized large portions of the *Baptist Catechism*.[38]

On February 21, 1748, Joshua Potts, whom Southampton Church had called as its first minister, came down with measles. His illness thrust Hart into one of his first opportunities to preach at a regular gathering of the church. Along with general study, he had been practicing the composition of sermons according to the typical Puritan method. First, a text was selected, invariably a single Bible verse upon which the whole "exposition" would be based. "Taking a text" ensured that the sermon carried God's own authority rather than simply the preacher's. "Let every thing you deliver be backed with Scripture, and be careful to advance nothing, but what you can confirm with

---

[35] Southampton Church Book, in Davis, *Hart Family*, 102; Tom J. Nettles, *The Baptists: Key People Involved in Forming a Baptist Identity. Beginnings in America* (Fearn, Scotland: Christian Focus, 2005), 459n68.

[36] Edwards, *Materials towards a History of the Baptists*, 1:35.

[37] For a thorough study of New England clergy and their approach to preaching in the early eighteenth century, see Harry S. Stout, *The New England Soul: Preaching and Religious Culture in Colonial New England* (New York: Oxford University Press, 1986), esp. 13–190.

[38] Nettles, *The Baptists*, 459n68.

a *'Thus saith the Lord,'*" Hart would later insist.[39] In the sermon's introduction, the preacher would set the verse in its broader context for the listeners, indicate something of its enduring relevance, and often introduce a kind of thesis sentence of what the message would be about. Usually it was the statement of some particular doctrine the preacher wished to emphasize. For instance, in a 1755 sermon from 2 Timothy 1:9, "and called us with an Holy Calling," Hart expounded on the effectual call of the Holy Spirit in the new birth. Moving to the body of the message, the preacher would carefully unpack the doctrine under several explanatory headings and subheadings. Hart structured his sermon on the effectual call according to the following outline:

I. What is meant by this call
   a. An external call
   b. An internal call
II. What kind of call this is
   a. An all powerful, efficatious [*sic*] call
   b. An holy calling
   c. Not according to our works
   d. But according to his purpose
   e. According to his grace
   f. This grace was given to us in Christ before the world began

In the sermon's final movement, Hart "improved" the doctrine, making practical application to various categories of listeners. In this particular message he offered two improvements. First, the doctrine refuted all those who dared to deny "the powerful, inscrutable operations of the Spirit in conversion." Second, the doctrine begged the preacher to press the question of personal experience on the audience: "Have you experienced this inward call?" Whatever his text or subject, Hart usually landed on the necessity of conversion in the end.[40]

Hart followed this identical sermonizing practice for the next forty-five years, keeping meticulous record of the texts he preached, along with the date and setting, in a special notebook. Sometimes he carried a complete manuscript into the pulpit with him, at other times a scrap of paper with a simple outline of the message, but he was always prepared. For the rest of his

---

[39] Oliver Hart, Sermon on 1 Timothy 4:16, SCL, emphasis in original.
[40] Hart, Sermon on 2 Timothy 1:9, Hart MSS, SCL.

life he would expend an enormous amount of time and energy in preparing, delivering, and evaluating sermons. He considered preaching "the most important service that ever demanded the attention of man."[41]

After Hart stood in for the ailing Joshua Potts, the church minute book reported that he had "performed to satisfaction."[42] Two months later the church extended both Hart and Eaton "a full call." The young men now possessed the church's blessing to "preach in any place where Providence might cast their lotts, or need required." All that remained was for that Providence to reveal itself. Until then Hart would continue to work as a carpenter; he now had a growing young family to look after. He had married nineteen-year-old Sarah Brees on February 25, and nine months later Sarah gave birth to Seth, the first of their eight children together. It had been an eventful year.[43]

*

Hart's future remained uncertain the following September, when he attended the 1749 meeting of the Philadelphia Association as a messenger for the Southampton Church.[44] In his first time as a messenger, he heard the annual sermon, listened to the reports from each of the Association's churches, and observed Association leaders fielding questions regarding church discipline and baptism. He also participated in adopting Benjamin Griffith's significant essay outlining "the power and duty of an association." But for Hart, these events were destined to become mere footnotes to the night's main event, when Jones read a letter from the Charleston Baptist Church in South Carolina, pleading for "any minister sound in the faith" to come fill their vacant pulpit.

*

The Charleston Church was the oldest Baptist congregation in the South. It was originally gathered in 1682 in the New England town of Kittery, in the Maine territory owned at that time by Massachusetts Bay. The church had been founded by an English immigrant named William Screven (1629–1713).[45] Praised at his ordination for possessing "the spirit of veterans," Screven would

---

[41] Hart, *Gospel Church*, 23.

[42] Davis, *Hart Family*, 103.

[43] Davis, *Hart Family*, 103; Hart, *Original Diary*, 6.

[44] Minutes from this meeting can be found in Gillette, *Minutes*, 59–64.

[45] For Screven, see Little, *Origins of Southern Evangelicalism* 27–39; and Robert A. Baker, Paul J. Cravens, and Marshall A. Blalock, *History of the First Baptist Church of Charleston, South Carolina, 1682–2007* (Springfield, MO: Particular Baptist Press, 2007), 33–95.

"ALL THINGS ARE BECOME NEW"     71

carry out his ministry with a sustained energy and grit that would make him one of the most remarkable Baptist leaders in American history. He had come to Kittery from Somerton in Somersetshire, England, in 1668. In Kittery he learned the trade of shipwright and joined the nearest Particular Baptist church—more than fifty miles away in Boston. But whether in Massachusetts or Maine, Screven would soon learn that seventeenth-century New England was a difficult time and place in which to be a Baptist.

The Puritan fathers who founded the Massachusetts Bay Colony in 1630, despairing of ever reforming the hopelessly compromised Church of England, envisioned a "Bible Commonwealth," a colony in which both the church and the state were strictly ordered according to Scripture. Their vision left no room for radicals and heretics who disagreed with their interpretation of Scripture on these matters. When, shortly into the experiment, the Puritan teacher Roger Williams (1603–1683) began questioning infant baptism, a state-established church, and other key tenets of the New England way, the colony banished him in 1636. Just south of Massachusetts, Williams helped found the colony of Rhode Island on principles of religious freedom that allowed Baptists to flourish in towns like Providence and Newport. In response to this unsettling Baptist growth, Massachusetts officially banned Baptists in 1645, condemning them as "the incendiaries of commonwealths and the infectors of persons in main matters of religion, and the troublers of churches in all places."[46] Yet Baptist sentiments continued to gain ground in Massachusetts over the next thirty years, in spite of several episodes of violent persecution from the state. Finally, in 1674, a Charlestown, Massachusetts, wagon maker named Thomas Goold (1607–1695) gathered a group of Baptists in a private home in Boston, beginning the First Baptist Church. By 1679 these Baptists had built their own meetinghouse, and by 1680 the congregation boasted eighty baptized members. In 1681 Baptists gained the begrudging approval of the Massachusetts General Court to meet publicly. These were the Baptists that William Screven joined.[47]

Back home in Kittery, Screven began preaching to his neighbors, and by September 1682 had gathered enough Baptist disciples in the region for the Boston Baptist Church to constitute them a new "Church of Christ in ye faith and order of ye Gospel." But since Maine operated under Massachusetts law,

---

[46] William G. McLoughlin, *New England Dissent, 1630–1833: The Baptists and the Separation of Church and State* (Cambridge, MA: Harvard University Press, 1971), 1:23.

[47] See McLoughlin, *New England Dissent,* 1:3–112.

Screven met there with the same resistance that New England Baptists had been facing for the past fifty years. In August 1682 the General Assembly of the province tried Screven for preaching in public, citing his "turbulent" and "contentious behavior." To the court, Screven's Baptist community was a "heretical sect"; his Baptist message constituted "offensive speech" and so many "rash and inconsiderate words tending to blasphemy." When Screven refused to stop preaching, he was fined ten pounds and barred from conducting "any private exercise at his house or elsewhere" in the province of Maine. Yet Screven had no intention of keeping quiet. As he put it, the Kittery Baptists had formed out of "a desire to the service of Christ . . . and the propagating of his glorious gospel of peace and salvation." He considered leaving New England altogether. At the same time that religious persecution was heating up against the Baptists, a spike in Indian attacks and the depletion of available timber for ships' masts made a move southward all the more attractive. Screven identified the colony of South Carolina, with its policy of religious pluralism, as the best site for relocation. Though already in his sixties, he elected to transplant the whole church. He and approximately thirty members made the nine-hundred-mile voyage down the east coast, perhaps in a ship built by Screven's own hands. (He continued to work as a shipwright until the end of his life.) On the banks of the Cooper River just outside Charleston, he and his flock settled an area he called Somerton. It was a memorable display of the "spirit of veterans" the Boston Baptists had spotted at Screven's ordination.[48]

Screven immediately established an aggressive evangelical presence in Low Country South Carolina, preaching across a wide circuit in the region. As in Massachusetts, his efforts often irritated other area ministers. An Anglican commissary named Gideon Johnston (1671–1716) reported a conflict involving "a ship carpenter, the Anabaptist teacher at Charleston . . . concerning some of the town Presbyterians seduced by him." Joseph Lord (1672–1748), a Harvard-trained Congregationalist minister, also complained to the governor of Massachusetts about "a certain Anabaptist teacher (named Scriven), who came from New England." While Lord was out of town, Screven "had taken advantage of my absence to insinuate into some of the people about us, and to endeavor to make proselytes."

---

[48] Baker, Craven, and Blalock, *History of the First Baptist Church*, 33–71; Henry S. Burrage, *History of the Baptists in Maine* (Portland, ME: Marks, 1904), 18–19, 13–14. Historians debate whether the year of the church's migration was 1682 or not until 1696.

"ALL THINGS ARE BECOME NEW" 73

Screven had scheduled for two women to join the church "by plunging," but Lord convinced one of the prospects "of the error of that way."[49]

Screven was joined in his labors at this time by another energetic Baptist revivalist, Gilbert Ashley (d. 1699), who partnered with him in winning new converts and planting new Baptist works across the Lower South. The Congregationalist John Cotton Jr. also griped against Ashley. When a ship's captain named Mr. Cocks abandoned Cotton's Independent Meetinghouse in Charleston for Ashley's Baptists, he grumbled, "Mr Cocks, who brought me hither, is a rotten Anabaptist [and] never comes to our meeting [but] to heare Gilbert Ashley, little did I thinke he would have prooved soe unworthy a fellow." By 1703 an Anglican missionary to the Charleston areas could report back to London, "We are very much infected with the sect of the Anabaptists." In 1708 the Charleston church had ninety members.[50]

From its inception the Charleston Baptist Church comprised a theologically diverse body, as Screven's Particular Baptist congregation from Kittery had united with a small group of General Baptists already in the area. While Screven succeeded in holding them together, he realized that their union was fragile. Near the end of his life, he urged the church to "as speedily as possible, supply yourselves with an able and faithful minister." Thinking of the General Baptist presence in the congregation, he specified that the next leader should be rooted in the Particular Baptist tradition. "Be sure you take care that the person be orthodox in faith, and of blameless life, and does own the confession of faith put forth by our brethren in London in 1689, etc."[51] Filling the leadership void left by Screven would bedevil the Charleston Baptists for the next thirty years. Morgan Edwards would later comment, "Had they attended to this counsel, the distractions, and almost destruction of the Church, which happened twenty-six years afterward, would have been prevented."[52] Little is known about Screven's two immediate successors beyond what Edwards reports from his conversations with Hart. Their names were Sanford, who served from 1713 to 1718, and William Peart, who served

[49] Arthur Henry Hirsch, *The Huguenots of South Carolina* (Durham, NC: Duke University Press, 1928), 309; H. A. Tupper, ed., *Two Centuries of the First Baptist Church of South Carolina, 1683–1883* (Baltimore, MD: R. H. Woodward, 1889), 58; Roy Talbert Jr. and Meggan A. Farrish, *The Antipedo Baptists of Georgetown, South Carolina, 1710–2010* (Columbia: University of South Carolina Press, 2013), 12.

[50] Little, *Origins of Southern Evangelicalism*, 42.

[51] The quotation from Screven is from *An Ornament for Church Members*, printed after his death and cited in Basil Manly, *Mercy and Judgment: A Discourse, Containing Some Fragments of the History of the Baptist Church in Charleston, S.C.* (Providence, RI: Knowles, Vose, 1837), 16.

[52] Edwards, *Materials toward a History of the Baptists*, 2:123.

from 1718 to 1722; both died shortly into their tenures. It was under the next pastor, Thomas Simmons (d. 1747), when the long-standing tensions in the church would erupt into open conflict.[53]

A period of steep decline in the Charleston congregation began in 1736, when two distinct groups broke away from the church. The first comprised Particular Baptists, weary of Simmons's Arminian leanings and miffed that he had jettisoned their treasured rite of laying hands on the newly baptized. They formed a new church at Ashley Ferry and soon found the Particular Baptist pastor they wanted in Isaac Chanler. Chanler was exactly the kind of pastor Screven had wished for his Charleston flock: a gifted preacher, an articulate defender of Calvinistic theology, and a spirited revivalist. It was Chanler who invited George Whitefield to preach in his church in 1740 and later defended the itinerant's ministry in print. He too itinerated all over the region himself, evangelizing destitute areas and supplying empty Baptist pulpits. Under Chanler the Ashley Ferry Baptists experienced significant numeric growth and spiritual renewal. The second group to separate from the Charleston Baptist Church in 1736 was made up of General Baptists, who had already built a meetinghouse on the Stono River for occasional worship back in 1728. According to Basil Manly Sr., the Stono group contained a strain of the Arian heresy, which denied the full deity of Jesus as the Son of God, from its inception. Like many General Baptist churches that followed this doctrinal trajectory in the eighteenth century, the Stono church would be extinct by 1791.[54]

After seeing its numbers dramatically reduced by these departures, the Charleston congregation entered a period of major turmoil, centering on pastor Thomas Simmons. Simmons identified himself as a Calvinist, but his doctrine was far too moderate for the taste of the Particular Baptists in the church. From Manly's perspective a century later, Simmons was "generally esteemed a good man," but his leadership was defective in that he "surrendered his judgment and feelings too much to the influence of others." Manly had in mind the corrupting influence of Simmons's son-in-law, who was a close friend of Stono's General Baptist minister Henry Haywood. For years Simmons had sufficiently ridden the theological fence to satisfy both the General and the Particular Baptist factions in his church. But his son-in-law convinced him to own his Arminian proclivities and declare himself

---

[53] Baker, Craven, and Blalock, *First Baptist Church*, 101–103.
[54] Manly, *Mercy and Judgment*, 20–21.

an outright General Baptist. Simmons finally did, to the scandal of his majority Particular Baptist congregation. Simmons then added to his troubles by publicly opposing the wildly popular Calvinistic evangelist Whitefield and the evangelical revival, openly clashing with Chanler and the Ashley Ferry Baptists in the process. The Anglican commissary Alexander Garden (c. 1685–1756), Whitefield's most notorious American antagonist, would publicly praise Simmons for his stance against the revival, but the unpopular Garden's endorsement hardly aided Simmons's cause among the Charleston Baptists.[55]

By 1744 the Particular Baptists in Charleston were fed up with Simmons and voted to suspend him as minister. But their troubles were far from over. The vote split the church, and the General Baptist faction initiated a lawsuit over rights to the meetinghouse property. Shockingly, the court ruled in their favor, and the Particular Baptists who considered themselves the true heirs of William Screven suddenly found themselves with neither minister nor meeting place. Then, in 1746, a group from the Edisto Island area broke away from this remnant to form the Euhaw Baptist Church. Manly believed that the Charleston church was reduced to three communicants at this time, dragging morale down to an all-time low. For the next two years the little group limped along, supported by the occasional preaching of Chanler. It was in this desperate condition that they wrote a letter to the Philadelphia Association in the fall of 1749, pleading for "any minister sound in the faith."[56]

*

The Charleston Baptists' plea indicates the kinship that colonial Baptists felt with one another, even when separated by vast distances. The communication network that these Baptists developed would be essential to the developing Baptist story in America. Baptists throughout the eighteenth century would correspond not only across the colonies but across the Atlantic Ocean, seeking ministers, strategizing about educational and missionary endeavors, expressing financial and spiritual support in times of need, and sharing news

[55] Little, *Origins of Southern Evangelicalism*, 112. Garden called Whitefield, among other things, "young George Fox." For an introduction to Garden and his role in the early development of South Carolina, see Fred E. Witzig, *Sanctifying Slavery and Politics in South Carolina: The Life of the Reverend Alexander Garden* (Columbia: University of South Carolina Press, 2018).

[56] Manly, *Mercy and Judgment*, 23–28; Townsend, *South Carolina Baptists*, 36–38; Baker, Craven, and Blalock, *First Baptist Church*, 115–19.

of revival with their British counterparts.[57] Few such communications would prove as significant for American Baptists as this 1749 letter from Charleston to Philadelphia. It would forge a vital link between the thriving Baptist center of the Philadelphia Association and a southern region where Baptists were barely hanging on.

After the meeting's conclusion, Jones and the other Philadelphia Association leaders approached Hart. The Charleston letter, they believed, was the call of God Hart had been waiting for. Hart did not take long to agree. One month later, on October 18, the Southampton Church called a service of prayer and fasting to ordain Hart for the work, with local ministers Joshua Potts and Peter Peterson Van Horne (1719–1789) presiding over the ceremony. Years later Hart would recall the "vows, and engagements" he had made that day:

> You are now to engage more immediately in a design which hath employ'd all ye zeal of Prophets, and apostles, and evangelists, and all ye preachers of Righteousness in every age, a design, for the promoting which, the Son of God came down, lived a painful life, dy'd a cursed death, and is now interceding at the Father's Right Hand. When the Lord Jesus Christ, the great Shepherd, ascended upon high, leading captivity captive, he received gifts for men, and set some in the Church; first Apostles, then Prophets, Teachers, and the like, who were design'd for the edification of the Body, and the building up of the Saints in love, that God ye Lord might dwell amongst them. Neither did the Ministry of the Word terminate with those primitive ages of the Church, for it is according to the divine appointment that there should be a standing Gospel ministry in the World, even to the End of it.[58]

In Hart's mind, he was stepping forward to take his place in a line of divinely sent messengers that stretched back through the ages. Having begun the 1740s by receiving baptism, he ended the decade with another momentous act of public consecration.

On November 13 Hart traveled to Philadelphia and boarded the *St. Andrew*, bound for South Carolina. Sarah, now expecting their second child, stayed behind with one-year-old Seth.[59] Hart sent ahead no word to

---

[57] On the extensive Baptist communication network of the eighteenth century, see especially Davies, *Transatlantic Brethren*.

[58] Hart, Sermon on 1 Timothy 4:16, Hart MSS, SCL.

[59] Hart, *Original Diary*, 2.

the Charleston Church. As the Philadelphia port disappeared from view, he saw his departure for South Carolina as an act of faith, trusting that this was where Providence had "cast his lott."

*

He arrived on December 2, 1749. As Charleston's harbor came into focus, Hart must have been struck, as eighteenth-century travelers invariably were, by the "handsome appearance" of the South's major port city. Located at the tip of a narrow peninsula and bounded on either side by two major inland waterways, the Ashley and Cooper rivers, Charleston was strategically positioned to connect Low Country South Carolina's booming rice and indigo plantations to the rest of the Atlantic world. After decades of industrious adaptation to the swampy Low Country, Carolina planters and their staggering slave force had sufficiently mastered rice harvesting to produce a crop that was praised in Europe as the finest in the world. Rice had made South Carolina the wealthiest city in colonial North America and helped shape a unique "planter culture" in which gentlemen farmers relished nothing more than making, discussing, and displaying material wealth.[60] As Hart would soon learn, Charleston's materialism often posed a challenge to the cultivation of piety. He would write to his father, "We have had a very Wet and fruitful season.—the planters, or farmers here go much upon Indico, which proves a very profitable Commodity; if peace was to Continue, in all probability this would be the richest province upon the Continent by far: Oh that it may be Rich in good Works!"[61]

As the *St. Andrew* docked, Hart would have seen what one contemporary described as a "fine fertile looking country, well wooded with noble lofty pines and oaks forming a prospect upon the whole strikingly beautiful."[62] The city of Charleston itself was a "neat, pretty place," its streets lined with distinctively narrow houses known as the "Charleston single," designed for maximum air circulation. Hart could not have known it on this winter day, but Charleston summers could be so brutal that he would one day stagger under the task of holding two services on a Sunday.[63] As Eliza Pinckney (1722–1793) described the climate to a friend, "The winters here are very fine

---

[60] See S. Max Edelson, *Plantation Enterprise in Colonial South Carolina* (Cambridge, MA: Harvard University Press, 2006), 126–99.

[61] Oliver Hart to John Hart, September 1755, SCL.

[62] Quotation from an English traveler sometime between 1772 and 1774, in "South Carolina Just before the Revolution," *Southern Literary Messenger* 11 (1845): 139.

[63] Oliver Hart to Samuel Jones, July 1765, Hart MSS, SCL.

and pleasant, but 4 months in the year is extreamly disagreeable, excessive hot, much thunder and lightening, and muskatoes and sand flies in abundance."[64] Charlestonians, in the words of one French visitor, would "vie with one another, not who shall have the finest, but who the coolest house."[65]

Above the lapping of the surf and the creaking of ships, a cacophony of accents and languages would have filled Hart's ears as he stepped ashore, including the heavy burr of the Scots, the musical French of the large Huguenot population, and the inimitable Gullah dialect of the West African slaves. Over the decades of the 1700s these sounds would converge into a distinct accent that Charleston's wealthiest sons would struggle to unlearn in their European schools.[66] One prominent reason for Charleston's diversity was its early policy of religious tolerance. Eager to populate the colony with Protestant dissenters, the colony's proprietors required in the Fundamental Constitutions (1669) that citizens affirm only that "there is a god," that "God is publickely to be worshipped," and that "it is lawfull & the duty of every man being thereunto called by those that Governe to beare wittnesse to truth." Citizens could worship freely as long as they did not "speak any thing in their Religeous Assembly Irreverently or Seditiously of the Government," and religious persecution was forbidden. These liberal terms succeeded in attracting a large influx of Dissenters beginning in the 1680s, including English Puritans, French Huguenots, Scots Presbyterians, Quakers from Barbados, and William Screven's Particular Baptists from Kittery, Maine.[67] Even after Anglicans attained establishment at the beginning of the eighteenth century, dissenters continued to enjoy a large degree of freedom and a relatively cordial relationship with Anglicans and with one another. One visitor observed in 1772 that, "although the city was divided into two parishes, there were six meeting houses, an Independent, a Presbyterian, a French, a German, and two Baptist, as well as Quaker and Jewish assemblages." Although the congregations differed in religious principles and "in the knowledge of salvation," there was no disorder, for the city since "its beginning [had been] renound for concord, compleasance, courteousness, and tenderness towards

[64] Elise Pinckney, ed., *The Letterbook of Eliza Lucas Pinckney, 1739–1762* (Columbia: University of South Carolina Press, 1997), 39–40.

[65] Walter J. Fraser, *Patriots, Pistols and Petticoats: "Poor Sinful Charles Town" during the American Revolution* (Columbia: University of South Carolina Press, 1993), 17; for colonial Charleston, see also George C. Rogers, *Charleston in the Age of the Pinckneys* (Columbia: University of South Carolina Press, 1980); and Frederick Patten Bowes, *The Culture of Early Charleston* (Chapel Hill: University of North Carolina Press, 1942).

[66] Rogers, *Culture of Early Charleston,* 76–77.

[67] See Little, *Origins of Southern Evangelicalism,* 1–32.

"ALL THINGS ARE BECOME NEW" 79

each other, and more so towards foreigners, without regard or respect of nation or religion."[68]

Ironically, when Hart inquired that day about the Charleston Baptists, he learned that they were burying Chanler, the de facto Baptist bishop of the Lower South for the past fifteen years and the last ordained Baptist preacher in the area. When Hart introduced himself to the church, he was "believed to have been directed by a special providence in their favor." Across the embattled congregation there spread a collective sense that an old era of frustration and futility had passed and a new day of hope had dawned. In later generations Hart's dramatic arrival became fairly embedded in Charleston Baptist lore. Manly offered the providential interpretation of the event in 1832: "But while God's dispensations are mysterious, they are all wise; and while it is the rule of his administration to interpose with seasonable aid in the hour of his people's extremity, he sometimes brings them into the greatest straits, that they may better appreciate and improve the blessings he bestows. The Lord had provided an instrument by which he designed greatly to promote the cause of truth and piety in the province, in the person of Rev. Oliver Hart."[69] In the minds of the Charleston Baptists, the prayers of William Screven had finally been answered; they extended the official call to Hart as pastor on February 16, 1750. The Baptist struggle during the 1740s to embrace the evangelical revival while holding fast to their confessional Baptist identity would prove vital in the ministry Hart would undertake in Charleston for the next thirty years.

[68] Rogers, *Charleston in the Age of the Pinckneys*, 94. Further insight into the religious scene of colonial South Carolina can be found throughout Witzig, *Sanctifying Slavery and Politics in South Carolina*.
[69] Manly, *Mercy and Judgment*, 31.

# 4

# "Bringing many souls home to Jesus Christ"

## Moderate Revivalism in Charleston

When Hart arrived in Charleston at the midpoint of the eighteenth century, the Baptists he had left behind in the middle colonies were in a thriving condition. The Baptists he was coming to were struggling to establish a presence in the South, where only about eleven churches existed by 1740. The smattering of General Baptists in the region were slowly traveling a trajectory toward Arianism and would largely cease to exist by century's end. The South's Particular Baptists had experienced significant gains during the peak Great Awakening years under leaders like Ashley Ferry's Isaac Chanler. But by 1750 those revival leaders were gone, and Particular Baptist churches remained few, scattered, and, in the case of the Charleston Baptists, badly fractured. The few Particular Baptist churches in Virginia fared little better. The dynamic Separate Baptists, who would eventually redraw the South's religious map, would not arrive until 1755. By accepting the pastorate of the Charleston Baptist Church, Oliver Hart purposed to establish a strategic beachhead for Baptist life in the South, importing the model of moderate revivalism and Baptist denominational order he had experienced in the Philadelphia Association in the 1740s.

*

Hart's first order of business was to establish a consistent pattern of weekly ministry at the Charleston Baptist Church. As a Particular Baptist, he modeled his pastoral work on the English Puritan tradition, which promoted a piety and public ministry that revolved around the Bible.[1] The pastor was responsible for catechizing and counseling, providing Bible readings and

---

[1] There are numerous resources for understanding the spiritual and pastoral priorities of English Puritanism, including Patrick Collison, *The Elizabethan Puritan Movement* (Oxford: Clarendon Press, 1967); Charles E. Hambrick-Stowe, *The Practice of Piety: Puritan Devotional Disciplines in Seventeenth-Century New England* (Chapel Hill: University of North Carolina Press, 1982); Charles Cohen, *God's Caress: The Psychology of Puritan Religious Experience* (New York: Oxford University

*Oliver Hart and the Rise of Baptist America.* Eric C. Smith, Oxford University Press (2020). © Oxford University Press.
DOI: 10.1093/oso/9780197506325.001.0001

"BRINGING MANY SOULS HOME TO JESUS CHRIST" 81

lectures, and above all for delivering the Sunday sermon. The sermon was the focal point of every Baptist worship service. Like other subgroups within the Puritan spiritual tradition, Particular Baptists jettisoned the "sensual worship" and ornate sanctuaries of Anglicanism for a simpler service in a deliberately stripped-down meetinghouse, where light streamed in through clear glass onto the pages of the listeners' open Bibles.[2] Hart normally preached for about an hour at both the morning and afternoon services each Sunday and often finished the Lord's Day with a devotional message in either his own home or that of a church member's. Not long into his tenure at Charleston, he also held a weekday lecture series up to three times a week to address doctrinal issues in a more didactic fashion. By remaining so "occupied with the Word," Hart followed the same basic pattern one would find in any colonial minister in the broadly Reformed tradition; it is striking how closely his basic pastoral routine followed Harry Stout's profile of the New England Congregationalist minister, for instance.[3]

Hart regularly addressed specifically Baptist issues from the pulpit, but the majority of his messages dealt with the major evangelical themes of salvation: the person and work of Jesus Christ, the character and attributes of God, the necessity of conversion, the power of the indwelling Holy Spirit, and the call to holy living. Like all preachers, Hart had his favorite texts to which he returned repeatedly. Among them were Deuteronomy 33:27, "The eternal God is thy refuge, and underneath are the everlasting arms"; Psalm 110:3, "Thy people shall be willing in the day of thy power"; and 1 Timothy 1:15, "This is a faithful saying, and worthy of all acceptation, that Christ Jesus came into the world to save sinners; of whom I am chief." Hart usually connected his morning and afternoon messages by either taking a new angle on the same text or preaching from consecutive verses. Sometimes he extended his exposition of a particular verse or chapter over several weeks, in a kind of sermon series. In 1774, for instance, Hart preached a mini-series from Psalm 9, covering Psalm 9:7–8 on January 9; Psalm 9:9 in the morning of January 16, and Psalm 9:11 that afternoon. In March he took up verses

Press, 1986). For less critical but thoroughly researched perspectives, see Leland Ryken, *Worldly Saints: The Puritans as They Really Were* (Grand Rapids, MI: Zondervan, 1986); and J. I. Packer, *A Quest for Godliness: The Puritan Vision of the Christian Life* (Wheaton, IL: Crossway, 1991).

[2] See Brekus, *Sarah Osborne's World*, 104–8.
[3] See Stout, *New England Soul*, 32–49; Bonomi, *Under the Cope of Heaven*, 67–72.

12–14, and in April, verses 15–20. In October he took several Sundays to work through Psalm 10.[4]

Particular Baptist sermons were designed to appeal to the mind, but they also aimed at transforming the heart. Hart apparently delivered his messages with great pathos. His friend William Rogers (1751–1824) praised Hart's passionate sermon delivery: "His manner was pleasing and his delivery animated; speaking from the heart, it was his aim that the hearts of those who heard him might always be benefitted."[5] Not theatrical like Whitefield, Hart the preacher was "peculiarly serious," compelling his audience to listen through his sheer earnestness in the pulpit.[6] In keeping with the Puritan preaching tradition, Hart shunned the idea of performance and self-display in the pulpit, asserting, "A plain and simple stile, seems best to comport with the simplicity of the gospel." But he did not disregard all rhetorical concerns. He believed preaching must not be "low, or groveling. However plain; it ought to be manly and striking." As he saw it, preachers should speak "with so much life and energy as to evince that their whole soul is engaged in the work. Their language should be plain, yet masculine; their reasoning clear, yet nervous; their countenance, open and free; their action, easy and graceful."[7] Hart accentuated the momentousness of the preaching event by wearing a black gown and bands in the pulpit. This tradition, followed by his successors for the next one hundred years, helped identify the Charleston Baptists as a respectable and dignified religious body in the cosmopolitan city.[8]

Like any good evangelical preacher, Hart believed that no degree of rhetorical skill could replace the supernatural ministry of the Holy Spirit. "Does success depend on the minister?" He once asked. "No. Were he possessed of the wisdom of Solomon, the firmness of Elijah and the zeal of Phineas, united with the sanctity of John, the engagedness of Paul and the eloquence of Apollos, he would be unequal to the task. A divine energy, only, can render his labours successful."[9] He filled his diaries with prayers that the Spirit

---

[4] Oliver Hart, Sermon Record, Hart papers, SCL.

[5] William Rogers, *A Sermon Occasioned by the Death of the Rev. Oliver Hart* (Philadelphia, PA: Lang and Ustick, 1796), 22.

[6] Furman, *Rewards of Grace*, 24.

[7] Hart, Sermon on 1 Timothy 4:16, SCL; Hart, diary, August 25, 1754, Hart MSS, JBDML.

[8] In 1868 James. P. Boyce recalled his pastor, Basil Manly Sr.'s, appropriation of this tradition. Boyce remembered "the very spot in the house, where the bands which he was accustomed to wear with his gown were laid on a certain Thanksgiving Day on which he dined with us." John A. Broadus, *Memoir of James Petigru Boyce* (Louisville, KY, 1893), 17.

[9] Oliver Hart, *A Gospel Church Portrayed, and Her Orderly Service Pointed Out* (Trenton, NJ: Isaac Collins, 1791), 23.

would enable him to "feel his subject" and preach with "power," "warmth," and "freedom." As Hart called on the Spirit's help, he sometimes employed violent language, petitioning God to "smite their hearts powerfully, and may they not rest, till they find rest in thee." On other occasions he favored gentler terminology, speaking of the Spirit falling on his listeners with "sweetness" and "light." By contrast, the absence of the Spirit's felt presence in the pulpit left Hart feeling "dull," "empty," and "straitened." Hart is never more miserable in his diaries than after delivering what he perceived to have been a Spirit-less sermon.[10]

Again echoing the Puritan tradition, Hart believed that his public ministry demanded fervent personal piety. He often made this point by drawing from an obscure text in Ezekiel: "Then the spirit entered into me, and set me upon my feet, and spake with me, and said unto me, Go, shut thyself within thine house" (Ezekiel 3:24). It was there, behind closed doors, alone with the Spirit and his Bible, that Hart did his most important work: "labouring [a favorite spiritual image] to be continually making advances in ye divine life." As a pastor, Hart believed he was responsible for setting the spiritual pace for the rest of the church. "It is not enough that you are upon a level with the bulk of Christians," he once cautioned fellow pastors, "more is expected of you than of others; and that justly too: for your every employ will lead you to a more constant converse with God, and to a greater intimacy with divine things."[11]

A record of Hart's quest for godliness can be found in his daily diary, where page after page is taken up with self-examination, perhaps the quintessential Puritan spiritual discipline.[12] "Turn into your own hearts, and labour after the most intimate and extensive acquaintance with your own souls," Hart advised. His robust doctrine of sin taught him of his own boundless capacity for self-deception; it was possible even for a busy minister to proclaim "an unknown Christ" on his way to hell. So Hart insisted that "continual self-examination" must be carried out "with all that holy severity, which ye nature, and importance of ye thing calls for." His sensitive, introspective nature ensured that he would do a thorough job. He rarely questioned the

---

[10] Oliver Hart, diary, August 24, 1754, Hart papers, James B. Duke Memorial Library, Furman University, Greenville, SC.

[11] Hart, Sermon on 1 Timothy 4:16, Hart papers, SCL.

[12] For a detailed discussion of the practice of evangelical diary-keeping, see Peter N. Moore, *Archibald Simpson's Unpeaceable Kingdom: The Ordeal of Evangelicalism in the Colonial South* (London: Lexington Books, 2018), xi–xxvii. See also the example of the New England Puritan Thomas Shepard in Stout, *The New England Soul*, 35–38; or Sarah Osborne throughout Brekus, *Sarah Osborne's World*.

84    OLIVER HART AND THE RISE OF BAPTIST AMERICA

authenticity of his salvation (though even this was up for debate in a few melancholic episodes), but he regularly lamented his low spirituality. Hart aimed at an extraordinary level of devotion, striving to "maintain that grace [the grace received at conversion] in its vigorous exercise," to be "lively, and active for God in the constant exercise of every Christian grace and virtue." He preached, "Let your faith be strong, your hope firm, your love fervent, your repentance sincere. In a word, imitate your Divine Exemplar in Patience, Meekness, humility, self-denyal, and ye like." Working from this standard, it is unsurprising that Hart was basically never satisfied with himself. He often vented his frustration in his diary over his spiritual "listlessness," "deadness," "barrenness," and "leanness of soul." Hart's constant self-inspection may strike the modern reader as a bit neurotic, but he believed that regular self-examination bore much good fruit, including humility before God and, ultimately, a more settled assurance of his salvation.[13]

Along with self-examination, Bible reading and prayer formed the pillars of Hart's private devotional life. He believed the Bible to be "the very mouth of God" and reverently read, studied, memorized, meditated on, and even sang its words. His interaction with a verse in his daily Bible-reading plan, John 10:11, indicates his typical use of Scripture. In the verse, Jesus declares, "I am the good shepherd: the good shepherd giveth his life for the sheep." As Hart reflected on the meaning and application of the words to his own life, he was prompted to pray, "Oh that Jesus may be my Shepherd, and that I may by him be led to green pastures. Blessed Jesus! Wilt thou take me into the number of thy sheep, and lead me in and out; and may I be enabled to follow thee withersoever thou goest."[14] Reading the Bible was for Hart the first half of a holy conversation in which God addressed him personally; prayer represented Hart's response of faith. He kept a set time for private prayers each morning, believing that "keeping close to God in prayer" was essential for maintaining "the life and power of godliness in your souls." Conversely, neglecting prayer tended to "coldness in religion, and renders the soul more unfit for communion with God."[15] As Hart saw it, his private piety built up a kind of spiritual "treasury" from which he could then make withdrawals in his public preaching ministry.[16]

---

[13] Hart, Sermon on 1 Timothy 4:16, Hart MSS, SCL.
[14] Hart, diary, August 11, 1754, Hart MSS, JBDML.
[15] Charleston Association, *Minutes of the Charleston Baptist Association, February 6, 1775*, 4.
[16] Hart, *Gospel Church*, 27. For a more detailed analysis of Hart's personal piety, see Smith, *Order and Ardor*, 29–51.

"BRINGING MANY SOULS HOME TO JESUS CHRIST"    85

*

Though most of Hart's pastoral work mirrored that of any Reformed evangelical minister, his serving of the sacraments of baptism and the Lord's Supper were, of course, distinctively Baptist. He always relished the opportunity to perform a baptism in one of Charleston's ubiquitous creeks and rivers, as it represented the culmination of the long ordeal of conversion. In the typical pattern, the conversion process began when Hart's preaching would suddenly alarm a formerly complacent pew-sitter over his or her condemned state before God. Next, the awakened sinner would often frantically attempt to restore inner peace through various self-help strategies, such as increased church attendance, Bible reading and prayer, or the renouncing of bad habits. Only after these human efforts failed to quiet the conscience would the now desperate individual finally approach Hart for relief. Hart fondly referred to this stage as "enquiring after Zion." In these private meetings Hart drew from his personal and pastoral experience to lead the seeker to despair of self and to rely entirely on Christ. At this critical stage only God could relieve the tormented soul by revealing His love to the individual's heart. When this occurred, Hart rejoiced to learn his subject had "got comfortable," "found hope," or "believed Christ loved [him or her]." Few ministerial duties thrilled Hart more than serving as spiritual midwife in the new birth process. After one Mary Sexton had obtained this peace with Christ, Hart preached from Psalm 66:16 at her baptism: "Come and hear, all ye who fear God, and I will tell what he has done for my soul."[17] The entire Baptist community shared in her sense of relief and gratitude.

Since all the church's communicant members had presumably experienced conversion and baptism, serving the Lord's Supper to the church was for Hart a deeply meaningful ritual of spiritual kinship. By the nineteenth century, Baptists in America and Great Britain would gravitate toward a strictly "memorial" view of communion.[18] Concerned to distance themselves from the Roman Catholic position of transubstantiation, these Baptists insisted that they were merely recalling the past work of Christ, not encountering his "real presence," at the table. But Hart and the eighteenth-century Particular Baptists embraced a more classically Reformed understanding of the Lord's Table, affirming the spiritual presence of Jesus in the sacrament. (Hart was

[17] Hart, Sermon Record, Hart papers, SCL.
[18] See Michael A. G. Haykin, "'His Soul-Refreshing Presence': The Lord's Supper in Calvinistic Baptist Thought and Experience in the 'Long' Eighteenth Century," in *Baptist Sacramentalism*, edited by Anthony R. Cross and Philip E. Thompson (Waynesboro, GA: Paternoster Press, 2003), 177–93.

also untroubled by any Roman Catholic connotations in this term and used it often.) He affirmed that Christ met with his believing people in a unique and powerful way during the communion hour, nourishing them spiritually as they looked to him in faith. He approvingly quoted the Dutch Reformed theologian Herman Witsius (1636–1708) in describing the Christian's experience at the Table, where "the promises of the New Testament and enlivening communion with Christ, made perfect by sufferings, both in grace and glory, are signified and sealed" to the hearts of believers. Hart's goal when serving the Lord's Supper was to "raise the faith and affections of the communicants to a crucified Savior." He set aside six Sundays each year to observe the Lord's Supper and typically gathered the church the day before for a "preparation day." In these Saturday meetings Hart preached a focused message on Christ's atonement in anticipation of the next day's communion. Receiving communion together was a high point for the baptized community.[19]

*

Beyond the church's public meetings, Hart attended to a variety of spiritual needs across his congregation. Life was fragile in colonial Charleston, a city notorious for "air so unhealthful" that its residents "had fevers all year long from which those attacked seldom recover." The Anglican commissary Alexander Garden had to recruit an assistant to help him conduct the "4 to 12 funerals of a day" required during a 1739 yellow fever epidemic in Charleston; his assistant died the next week.[20] One yellow fever season in 1757 was so deadly that Governor William Henry Lyttleton (1724–1808) called for a public fast to seek God's intervention in the plague.[21] Without warning, strong men and women could find themselves on a sickbed struggling for life. In these precarious moments, Hart made house calls to care for the soul. "Visiting the sick and dying persons, is not the least difficult part of your work," he admitted. "To flatter a dying man is little better than

---

[19] Oliver Hart, *An Humble Attempt to Repair the Christian Temple, Shewing The Business of Officers and Private Members in the Church of Christ, and How Their Work Should Be Performed; with Some Motives to Excite Professors Ardently to Engage in It* (Philadelphia, PA: Aitken, 1785), 17–18; Hart, *Gospel Church*, 27; Hart, diary, January 20, 1781, Hart MSS, SCL.

[20] Witzig, *Sanctifying Slavery and Politics in South Carolina*, n.p. Witzig provides many helpful insights regarding life in colonial Charleston and the requirements of church ministry there throughout this work.

[21] Walter B. Edgar, *South Carolina: A History* (Columbia: University of South Carolina Press, 1998), 156.

"BRINGING MANY SOULS HOME TO JESUS CHRIST" 87

Soul Murder; and yet such when penitent are by no means to be discouraged. You will endeavor therefore to act a tender, but withal a faithful part."[22]

On other occasions Hart was called to provide comfort after tragedy had already struck. In 1750 church member Mary Evans's joyful anticipation of a new baby was shattered when she delivered a child so severely disfigured that it was scarcely recognizable. The scene shook Hart: parents mourning over a newborn he could only describe as "ghastly to behold." Holes gaped in the child's face where nose and ears should have been. The eyes "appeared to be lumps of coagulated blood." The back of the child's head was "much open." As the parents cradled the crumpled, hardened limbs of their baby, the child "made a strange kind of noise, very low, which I cannot describe," Hart recalled. The baby would be dead within forty-eight hours. Hart's records reveal that he preached many funerals for children through the years and maintained a stock of comforting texts for the occasion, including 2 Samuel 12:23: "But now he is dead, wherefore should I fast? can I bring him back again? I shall go to him, but he shall not return to me." Outside the calm, controlled environs of his study, pastoral ministry was often conducted against a dark backdrop of confusion and heartbreak.[23]

*

In addition to the ongoing duties within his own congregation, Hart sought to promote the revivalism of the Great Awakening with the same vigor he had witnessed in his childhood minister, Jenkin Jones. Hart regularly embarked on itinerant preaching missions, often making short excursions to nearby island communities and to rural South Carolina settlements without regular ministers. On other occasions he pressed out further, for more extended periods. In 1756, for instance, he left Charleston for Philadelphia on January 19 and did not return home until November 4. He preached throughout the middle colonies on this journey, apparently with some success. He afterward confided to his father by post, "I believe the Lord hath owned my poor labors while in Pennsylvania, and the Jerseys: I have received several letters, giving me some encouraging accounts of something being done by such an unworthy instrument while there; may all the praise be to him to whom alone it is due."[24] Travel in the mid-eighteenth century was

[22] Hart, Sermon on 1 Timothy 4:16, Hart MSS, SCL.
[23] Hart, *Original Diary*, 3.
[24] Oliver Hart to John Hart, March 10, 1757, SCL

88　OLIVER HART AND THE RISE OF BAPTIST AMERICA

challenging under the best of conditions, but itinerant preachers needed the grit to endure the worst. Sometimes baking under the burning Carolina sun, other times soaked by a drenching rain, Hart and his horse plodded across poor roads, slogged through muddy forests, and waded swollen creeks to make preaching appointments. Sleeping conditions rarely approximated the comforts of home, whether in a roadside tavern, on a straw bed offered by some hospitable stranger, or outside under the stars. With Whitefield as his ideal, the itinerant's willingness to endure hardship to spread the gospel came to characterize the evangelical spirit in the eighteenth century. In a typical prayer from his diaries, Hart wrote, "Oh, may I be Enabled to lay out myself for God! I think I am willing to spend, and be spent, in his Service."[25]

Hart's zeal for itinerant evangelism aligned him with many non-Baptist evangelical leaders in Charleston. He was committed to the Philadelphia Association's brand of Baptist church order and was passionate about expanding the Baptist denomination, but he believed that the transdenominational Great Awakening was a genuine work of God in his time. As Jones had done, Hart went out of his way to partner with evangelicals of other denominations, developing a reputation as an irenic and unifying religious leader in Charleston. While praising his Presbyterian friend William Tennent III (1740–1777), Hart described his own philosophy of principled ecumenism. "It may not be amiss to observe, that his religious sentiments were open, free and generous, built upon principles of true catholocism [sic]; not influenced by bigotry or party spirit," Hart said. "He thought that religion should be left entirely free, and that there should be no manner of constraint upon the conscience. He was of opinion, that there was a wise providence in permitting people to think differently about modes of worship, and therefore valued good men of every denomination."[26] Hart's passion to spread the gospel, his amiable personality, and his experience of revival in Pennsylvania enabled him to cross many denominational boundaries while maintaining his Baptist convictions.

One of Hart's most valued evangelical allies was the Presbyterian William Hutson (1720–1761), a former New York stage player converted under Whitefield in 1740. Hutson went on to teach in a slave school on the South

---

[25] Lindman, *Bodies of Belief*, 169–72; Hart, *Original Diary*, 5, 14–15. Itinerant ministry was common among revivalists of all types, but it was an institution among early American Methodists. For a detailed treatment of the American Methodist itinerants, see Wigger, *Taking Heaven by Storm*, 48–79.
[26] Kidd and Hankins, *Baptists in America*, 28–29; Hart, *Great Man*, 26.

"BRINGING MANY SOULS HOME TO JESUS CHRIST"   89

Carolina estate of Hugh Bryan, served a brief stint at Whitefield's Bethesda Orphan House, and then helped pastor two Independent Presbyterian churches in the Charleston area. Hart mentioned being "much refreshed" by Hutson's visits. He invited Hutson to preach from the Charleston Baptist pulpit on several occasions and supported Hutson when he stood against Charleston's public vices. Hart also befriended the Swiss-born minister John J. Zubly (1724–1781) of the Independent Presbyterian Church. Zubly later gained infamy for switching to the Loyalist position during the Revolution, but Hart for years leaned on Zubly as a partner for revival in Charleston. In August 1754 Hart spent a week at Zubly's home "very agreeably." He commented, "Oh how pleasant it is for Brethren to dwell in Unity!" The next month Zubly returned the favor, staying with Hart and preaching several times, as "the Lord owned it for Comfort to many Souls."[27]

The Methodists would one day emerge as Baptists' fiercest religious competitors in America, but Hart also supported their ministers when Methodism was still a fledgling movement. Joseph Pilmoor (1739–1825), one of John Wesley's first Methodist missionaries to America, came to Charleston in 1772 to "preach the everlasting gospel and do all possible good to mankind."[28] He immediately offered his preaching services to the local General Baptists, who shared his Arminian theology. Only a small crowd gathered to hear Pilmoor the following Sunday, but it included "two ministers" whom Pilmoor thought "behaved very well." Pilmoor reported that one of these visitors was "the Baptist minister, Mr. Hart," who "returned me thanks for my sermon and invited me to preach in his pulpit." Hart's unexpected invitation encouraged Pilmoor to think that God had work prepared for him in the city. The next Sunday, Pilmoor preached to the Regular Baptists on a pair of classic evangelical subjects: the salvation of God from Psalm 18 in the afternoon, and the indwelling Holy Spirit from Romans 8:14 that night. Pilmoor remarked that the Baptist meetinghouse was "as full as it could hold" and that "the Lord was remarkably present." He preached several more times there before leaving Charleston, and even stayed in the home of a Baptist church member. Given Hart's commitment to both Baptist church order and

[27] Hart, diary, October 16, 18, 1754, Hart MSS, JBDML; see Randall M. Miller, "A Warm & Zealous Spirit": John J. Zubly and the American Revolution. A Selection of His Writings (Macon, GA: Mercer University Press, 1982); Hart, diary, August 17, 30, September 17–18, October 17–18, 1764, Hart MSS, JBDML.

[28] For more on Pilmoor (whose name is also sometimes spelled Pilmore), see Wigger, Taking Heaven by Storm, 99, 112–13; and Frank Baker, From Wesley to Asbury: Studies in Early American Methodism (Durham, NC: Duke University Press, 1976), 86–93.

90 OLIVER HART AND THE RISE OF BAPTIST AMERICA

a Calvinist view of salvation, his acceptance of the Methodist Pilmoor into his pulpit is a striking example of the priority he placed on the evangelical revival. Pilmoor would leave Charleston remembering Hart as "not only sensible, but truly evangelical, and very devout."[29]

Hart's catholicity extended even to the Anglicans. A brief walk up Church Street from the humble Baptist meetinghouse stood the towering St. Philip's cathedral, one of the most stunning religious structures in the colonial South. In the previous generation, Alexander Garden had excoriated Whitefield and the Great Awakening's supporters from the pulpit of this distinguished church. But from 1753 to 1759 an evangelical named Richard Clarke (1723–1802) occupied St. Philip's. Clarke eventually gained notoriety in the city as a radical, known especially for his wild, public prophecies regarding the end of the world.[30] For the majority of his tenure in Charleston, however, he was a popular preacher who wielded a significant evangelical influence among the city's upper crust. He also personally befriended Hart. With some surprise, Hart recorded in his diary, "[I] waited, this Afternoon, on the Rev. Mr. Clark, Rector of this place, who Receiv'd me with all possible Expressions of kindness; and after we had spent some time Agreeably together, he took me in his Chair to a funeral. I am heartily pleas'd to see the Catholic Spirit of which this man is possess'd; and I hope, and believe, he will be a Blessing to this Town." For the rector of St. Philip's to invite the Baptist to ride in his carriage was noteworthy enough, but Clarke later outdid even this gesture. On October 27, 1754, Clarke asked Hart to conduct a funeral service for him, in his "own way." Hart marveled in his diary:

> In the Evening I Buried a Child in the Church Burying Ground, and Spoke Extempore, perhaps the first Instance of this Nature ever known in this Province. The Church Minister was sick and could not attend himself; therefore, gave me free Liberty to speak in my own way; which discovered an Extraordinary Catholick Spirit. Oh that all Bigotry was rooted out of the earth; then would there subsist a greater Harmony between persons,

[29] Albert Micajah Shipp, *The History of Methodism in South Carolina* (Nashville, TN: Southern Methodist Publishing House, 1834), 123–24, 127–34.

[30] For Clarke, see especially Little, *Origins of Evangelicalism*, 149–50. In 1759 the governor of South Carolina William Henry Lyttleton reported to the Board of Trade, "In the month of February last the Reverend Mr. Clarke . . . preached some sermons in which he asserted that the world wou'd very soon be at an end, and that in this month of September some great calamity wou'd befall this province." Lyttelton continued, "At length this enthusiasm rose to such a height that he let his beard grow and ran about the streets crying, Repent, Repent for the Kingdom of Heaven is at hand, but on the 25th of March he resigned his Benefice and embarked for England."

## "BRINGING MANY SOULS HOME TO JESUS CHRIST" 91

than what does; it is indeed a pity that our little outward Differences should cause such a shyness between us.[31]

The high points of Hart's ecumenical revival activity, however, were the occasions in which he worked alongside his evangelical hero, George Whitefield. As we have seen, Whitefield relied heavily on local pastors in his campaigns, and Hart served as a key ally in Charleston until the revivalist's death in 1770. During this time Whitefield preached in Hart's pulpit and worshipped alongside him in the Baptist meetinghouse whenever he passed through the city. One evidence of their partnership comes from the diary of the young Baptist preacher John Gano (1727–1804). In the spring of 1755, when Gano arrived in Charleston on a missionary tour, Hart offered the pulpit to his guest. Gano accepted the invitation, though he admitted to being self-conscious about his "tattered garb." But when he rose to preach, Gano found further reason to be intimidated. He recalled, "The sight of so numerous and brilliant an audience (among whom were twelve ministers, and one of whom was Mr. Whitefield), for a moment, brought the fear of man on me."[32] Whitefield also heard Hart preach during these years, with approval. When a female correspondent in Charleston, Mrs. C., solicited Whitefield for spiritual counsel in 1755, he commended Hart's ministry to her. "I would have you write to Mr. H[ar]t by the bearer, who is an experimental Baptist preacher from the northward," Whitefield wrote her. "O that he may say something, that may do my dear family some good." For Hart, who owed his own conversion in large part to the preaching of Whitefield, there could be no higher praise than to receive his endorsement.[33]

In his ecumenical revivalism, Hart oversaw a unique moment in the history of America's Baptists. As we saw in the example of Abel Morgan and Samuel Finley, Baptists could move very quickly from cooperating with other denominations for revival to competing with them for members. By the early nineteenth century Baptists were known more for their insularity and separatist stance toward other denominations than for their catholicity. This was especially true in the South, where Baptists would often engage in a cutthroat race with Methodists and Presbyterians for souls of the frontier; later they would colorfully clash on the pages of denominational newspapers

[31] Hart, diary, October 27, 1754, Hart MSS, JBDML.
[32] Terry Wolever, *The Life and Ministry of John Gano, 1727–1804* (Springfield, MO: Particular Baptist Press, 1998), 60.
[33] Whitefield, *Works*, 2:116.

# 92 OLIVER HART AND THE RISE OF BAPTIST AMERICA

over the proper use of the ordinances.[34] One branch of the Southern Baptist family tree, the Landmark movement, would gain remarkable popularity beginning in the 1840s by trumpeting that Baptists constituted the only true church, stridently opposing the notion of sharing pulpits with a non-Baptist as Hart had once done.[35] Even into the twentieth century, the Southern Baptist Convention would grow so large, organizationally sophisticated, and self-sufficient that most of its leaders felt neither the need nor the desire to cooperate with non-Baptist evangelicals for missions, education, or benevolent causes.[36] But Hart explicitly promoted both denominational confessionalism and broader evangelical cooperation; it was a combination that would mark his entire ministry.

\*

Hart enjoyed wide acceptance among non-Baptists in part because of the care he took maintaining his public image. In a 1757 ordination sermon he addressed the importance of a minister's conduct in society, emphasizing the need to "walk circumspectly, not as fools, but as wise," because ministers lived "in the midst of a censorious world." Outsiders scrutinized a preacher's behavior, looking for a reason to condemn him and his message. Echoing the words of Jesus, Hart called his fellow ministers to exercise "the wisdom of the serpent, tempered with the innocence of the dove," that they might give the world "no just occasion for offense." He extended this code to secular business dealings, advising his fellow pastors to "act a just and upright part, doing to all, as you would they should do to you." Even casual conversation should be regulated in order to commend the gospel to outsiders:

> Let your speech at all times be seasoned, as that it may minister grace to the hearers. Be neither too open, nor too reserved in conversation, but labour to find out the happy medium. A loquacious disposition is attended with many disadvantages; therefore be more ready to hear than to give the sacrifice of fools. And yet, when you can speak to advantage, especially if an opportunity offers to speak for God; by no means be silent.[37]

---

[34] On evangelical competition on the frontier, see Philip N. Mulder, *A Controversial Spirit: Evangelical Awakenings in the South* (New York: Oxford University Press, 2002).

[35] For an introduction to the Landmark movement, see James A. Patterson, *James Robinson Graves: Staking the Boundaries of Baptist Identity* (Nashville, TN: B&H Academic, 2012).

[36] See Hankins, *Uneasy in Babylon*, 14–21.

[37] Hart, Sermon on 1 Timothy 4:16, Hart papers, SCL.

The theme running through Hart's presentation is a concern for social respectability. "Labour after a uniformity of conduct, that you may be always yourselves: yet not so as not to suit your temper, and conduct, to time, place, and circumstances. You may be grave, but not sullen, or morose; you may be cheerful, but not light or vain. You will be happy if you can so conduct as to be respected, and yet rever'd," he advised.[38] The biblical texts Hart emphasized in his sermon formed a ministerial ideal that contrasts noticeably with that of the more radical evangelicals, including the Separate Baptists, who certainly cared about their ethical conduct but did not express the same concern for a "respectable" social image that Hart did. If anything, they went out of their way to reject the polite norms of Southern society, so much that Virginia Anglicans feared they would overturn their social order altogether.[39] But while Hart sharply critiqued certain aspects of Charleston society, he seemed more concerned with maintaining his witness within that society than standing outside of it. This was characteristic of the moderate revivalists; this policy would wield a significant influence among American Baptists for the rest of the eighteenth century.

Hart likely knew that in the decade before his arrival, evangelicalism's radical side had scandalized Charleston. Hugh Bryan (1689–1753) was a wealthy Anglican planter in St. Helena's Parish and an ardent Whitefield supporter. In a surge of evangelical zeal and following Whitefield's suggestion, Bryan and his brother Jonathan (1708–1788) opened a school for slaves from a number of surrounding plantations with the goal of converting them. It was an edgy move in Low Country South Carolina, where the entire way of life depended on the massive slave force remaining submissive to the planter aristocracy. So when revival came to the slave school, local authorities investigated. In 1742 the Commons House of Assembly concluded, "However commendable it may be for any Master, or other Person having Care of Slaves, to instruct them in the Principle of Religion or Morality, in their own Plantations; it may prove of the most dangerous Consequence . . . if great Numbers of Negroes should be encouraged to meet together from different Plantations." They further concluded that white persons "who shall be so important as to excite, encourage or countenance them to meet and assemble, in [the] manner aforesaid, may be justly deemed guilty of a public Nuisance."[40]

[38] Hart, Sermon on 1 Timothy 4:16, Hart papers, SCL.
[39] See Rhys Isaac, *The Transformation of Virginia, 1740–1790* (Chapel Hill: University of North Carolina Press, 1982), 161–80.
[40] Little, *Origins of Southern Evangelicalism*, 159.

But Bryan would not be silenced. He now saw himself as God's prophet, authorized to bring spiritual liberation to the slaves and endowed with power to perform signs and wonders. Spending several days "in the woods barefoot and alone," he scribbled down prophecies of Charleston's destruction in a fiery slave insurrection if the city's leaders opposed the slave revivals. When Bryan presented his written prophecies to the House, its members were terrified that it would spark a slave insurrection, and they called for Bryan's arrest. But Bryan renounced his prophetic career only when, like a new Moses, he "went with a wan[d] to divide the waters" of a local river but could not perform the miracle. This embarrassment seemed to snap him back to reality. Afterward he publicly apologized for falling "into a Delusion of Satan" and "adhering to the Impressions of [his] Mind." He claimed that he had enjoyed for many days "an intimate converse with an invisible Spirit" he believed to have been from heaven yet turned out to be "the Father of Lies." Bryan humbly confessed, "[It] much abased my Soul with bitter Reflections on the Dishonour I've done to God, as well as the Disquiet which I may have occasioned to my Country."[41]

Bryan's erratic behavior seemed to confirm the worst suspicions of the Low Country's antirevivalists, and also embarrassed those who sympathized with evangelical heart religion. The devout Anglican plantation mistress Eliza Pinckney, for one, feared that Bryan had tarnished Christianity's reputation by his hysterics. She wrote, "With what anguish must he reflect on making the spirrit [sic] of God the author of his weaknesses, and of disturbing the whole community, who tho' they knew him to be no prophet dreaded the consequence of his prophecys coming to the ears of the African Hosts, as he calls them." Unlike the radical evangelicals, Pinckney believed that one's piety must be guided by Scripture and reason:

I hope he will be a warning to all pious minds not to reject reason and revelation and set up in their stead their own wild notions. He fancied indeed he was soported in his oppinions by the sacred Oracles, and (as a father of our church observes) so did all the broachers of herisey in the primitive church. But why should we not expect to be deluded when we refuse that assistance which the bountiful Author of our being has naturally revealed to us and set up in every mans mind, without which 'tis impossible to understand his will supernaturally revealed. For tho' their [sic] may be things in the Xtian

---

[41] Little, *Origins of Southern Evangelicalism*, 159–61.

"BRINGING MANY SOULS HOME TO JESUS CHRIST" 95

system above reason such as the incarnation of our Saviour, etc., yet surely they highly dishonor our religion who affirm there is any thing in it contrary to reason.[42]

With some exceptions, Pinckney's desire for a reasonable, moderate evangelicalism reflected the general consensus in Charleston. In Hart's three decades there he appears to have walked the line between evangelical fervor and cultural respectability with considerable skill, rejecting Charleston's culture in some significant ways, yet embracing it in others. He scraped his soul in intense personal examination, preached total depravity and the need for supernatural conversion, celebrated emotional revivalism within his own congregation, took itinerant mission journeys, harangued against dancing and theatergoing, and, as a Baptist, insisted on the public immersion of confessing believers. Still, Hart also maintained an image of respectability that kept him from being pushed to the margins of society by delivering polished sermons in a black preaching gown, establishing institutions for education and benevolence, participating in local politics, and maintaining relationships with non-Baptist public figures (including such leading lights in Charleston as Henry Laurens, Thomas Heyward Jr., Daniel Legare, William Henry Drayton, and John Rutledge). Hart's was a reasonable evangelical piety that Eliza Lucas Pinckney could have approved. Even the uppity Anglican itinerant Charles Woodmason (1720?–1789), who enjoyed nothing more than lambasting the rusticity of the South's Separate Baptists, seemed to hold Hart in esteem. Woodmason mentions in his diary delivering a parcel of letters and books to the Baptist minister in 1766, referring to him as "the Reverend Mr. Hart."[43] The remainder of the acerbic Anglican's diary leaves little doubt that no Separate Baptist could elicit such a respectful reference from him.

In her provocative work *Southern Cross*, Christine Heyrman argues that the earliest evangelicals of the mid-eighteenth century tended to repulse Southern society with their radical positions on a host of issues, including supernaturalism, family dynamics, masculinity, and race. Only as later evangelicals moderated their message to fit the prevailing expectations of Southern culture, she suggests, did they ascend to the dominant position

[42] Pinckney, *The Letterbook*, 29.
[43] Charles Woodmason, *The Carolina Backcountry on the Eve of the Revolution: The Journal and Other Writings of Charles Woodmason, Anglican Itinerant*, edited by Richard J. Hooker (Chapel Hill: University of North Carolina Press, 1953), 6.

## 96  OLIVER HART AND THE RISE OF BAPTIST AMERICA

they would enjoy in the South through most of the nineteenth and twentieth centuries.[44] The degree to which Hart consciously altered his persona to match Charleston's cultural expectations cannot be known; his acceptance there may well have had more to do with his own personality and the dignified ethos of the Philadelphia Association than any deliberate strategy. But there is no question that Hart's brand of respectable, moderate evangelicalism made him a better fit for Charleston than any Separate Baptist. It certainly established a precedent for future generations of Charleston Baptist ministers like Richard Furman and Basil Manly Sr., both of whom stood at the center of Charleston society even while proclaiming an evangelical message.[45] But of all the arenas in which Hart blended into Charleston society, none was so consequential as that of slavery.

*

Slavery was central to daily life in colonial Charleston. The booming rice and indigo industries that had established South Carolina as Britain's wealthiest North American colony were made possible only by the importation of thousands upon thousands of West African slaves. From 1735 to 1775, 1,108 shiploads of enslaved Africans arrived in Charleston; nearly eight thousand slaves entered the city in 1765 alone.[46] The population of Charleston remained roughly half white and half black throughout the pre-Revolutionary period, prompting one visitor to remark that colonial South Carolina "looked more like a negro country."[47] Hart would have been familiar with the sight of slave ships docking at Sullivan's Island just out from Charleston Harbor, where for ten days the ship and its inhabitants were cleansed before proceeding up the Ashley or the Cooper River to the plantations there. He would also have witnessed countless slave auctions at various locations in the city. As one Charleston contemporary recalled, "They are exposed on a sort of stage, turned about and exhibited, put up and adjudged to the highest bidder." Most of these slaves would end up in what Peter H. Wood has called the "labor camps" of the rice plantations of inland South Carolina, where the working

---

[44] Heyrman, *Southern Cross*, 3–27.

[45] For the development of this theme in the generation following Hart, see E. Brooks Holifield, *The Gentleman Theologians: American Theology in Southern Culture 1795–1860* (Durham, NC: Duke University Press, 1978).

[46] Rogers, *Charleston in the Age of the Pinckneys*, 42.

[47] Peter H. Wood, *Black Majority: Negroes in Colonial South Carolina from 1670 through the Stono Rebellion* (New York: Norton, 1996), 132.

"BRINGING MANY SOULS HOME TO JESUS CHRIST" 97

conditions to raise Carolina's staple crop were truly brutal.[48] Other slaves stayed behind in the city to perform a host of tasks for Charleston's white citizens: women who served as wet nurses, men who worked in Charleston shops as skilled laborers, and others. A visiting Jerseyman was struck by the number of personal black servants attending the gentry, exclaiming, "Every child has one accompanying it."[49]

Though the massive black labor force made Charleston's leisure culture possible, whites lived in constant dread of slave rebellion. The bloodiest slave revolt in colonial American history had taken place twenty miles outside Charleston on September 9, 1739, at the Stono River Bridge. There, in the words of South Carolina's lieutenant governor William Bull (1683–1755), "a great number of Negroes arose in rebellion, broke upon a Store where they got Arms[,] killed twenty one White Persons, and were marching the next morning in a Daring manner out of the province, killing all they met."[50] The grisly Stono Rebellion haunted Charleston for the rest of the eighteenth century, with sporadic episodes of slaves poisoning whites or committing arson keeping the city always on edge. In 1749, the year Hart arrived in Charleston, the *South Carolina Gazette* reported, "The horrid practice of poisoning white People, by the Negroes, has lately become so common, that with a few Days past, several Executions have taken Place in different Parts of the Country by burning, gibbeting, hanging, &c." In 1769 two slaves named Dolly and Liverpoole were "burnt on the Workhouse Green" for poisoning an infant.[51] Hart shared his neighbors' fears of slave rebellion, periodically voicing his own anxieties in his diaries. In one visit to a home, for instance, Hart learned of the murder of four adults committed there by "a negro fellow" a few years earlier; he shuddered when "[he] saw some of the Blood still remaining on the Door."[52]

It is unsurprising that many white South Carolina masters feared religious work among their slaves. But during the Great Awakening white evangelicals rejoiced to see many "Ethiopians" "stretching out their hands" to Jesus Christ,

[48] Peter H. Wood, "Slave Labor Camps in Early America: Overcoming Denial and Discovering the Gulag," in *Inequality in Early America*, edited by Carla Gardina Pestana and Sharon V. Salinger (Hanover, NH: University Presses of New England, 1999), 227. For a thorough study of the slave labor camps in colonial South Carolina, see S. Max Edelson, *Plantation Enterprise in Colonial South Carolina* (Cambridge, MA: Harvard University Press, 2006), esp. 92–179.

[49] Fraser, *Patriots, Pistols, and Petticoats*, 9–11.

[50] Robert Olwell, *Masters, Slaves and Subjects: The Culture of Power in the South Carolina Lowcountry, 1740–1790* (Ithaca, NY: Cornell University Press, 1998), 20–25.

[51] Rogers, *Charleston in the Age of Pinckneys*, 22–23.

[52] Hart, diary, December 9, 1769, Hart MSS, SCL.

98   OLIVER HART AND THE RISE OF BAPTIST AMERICA

which to them authenticated the Great Awakening as a true work of God.[53] Oliver Hart shared this excitement and ministered to the black citizens of Charleston with enthusiasm. He could listen intently as a female slave related to him her experience of converting grace, and then encourage her to share her testimony with a group of white females seeking evangelical assurance.[54] He thought nothing of entering the home of a free black man, taking him by the hand, and kneeling at his bedside to plead with God to save his soul.[55] Like his fellow Regular Baptist ministers in the Low Country, Hart presumably preached to a substantial crowd of African men and women every Sunday at the Charleston Baptist meetinghouse. He also knew some of the most important black preachers who emerged from the Great Awakening in the Low Country, men who along with him would rewrite the eighteenth-century Baptist story.

Of all the black preachers produced by the revival, few would equal the extensive influence of George Liele (c. 1750–1828). Liele was born a slave in Virginia, belonging to a Baptist named Henry Sharp. He received religious instruction from his father, a devout man whom Liele remembered as "the only black person who knew the Lord in a spiritual way in that country." Under his father's spiritual guidance, Liele would later comment, "I always had a natural fear of God from my youth, and was often checked in conscience with thoughts of death." But it was sometime in the early 1770s that Liele experienced his evangelical crisis. Henry Sharp had taken him to Georgia, where Liele heard the preaching of a Baptist minister named Matthew Moore. After six months of conviction, Liele received the new birth, and Moore baptized him, sometime around 1773. It was not long afterward that Liele "began to discover his love to other negroes, on the same plantation with himself, by reading hymns among them, encouraging them to sing, and sometimes by explaining the most striking parts of them." Recognizing his gifts, Liele's Baptist church licensed him as a probationer, allowing him to preach to fellow blacks on numerous plantations. He received full ordination to gospel ministry on May 20, 1775, and three months later started the First African Church of Savannah, Georgia. His experience reflected something of the Baptist paradox when it came to slavery: to a far greater extent than most

[53] Kidd, *Great Awakening*, 213–33.
[54] Hart, diary, August 26, 1754, Hart MSS, Furman.
[55] John Marrant and William Aldridge, *A Narrative of the Lord's Wonderful Dealings with John Marrant, a Black, now Going to Preach the Gospel in Nova-Scotia, born in New-York, in North America* (London: Gilbert and Plummer, 1785), 12–13.

# "BRINGING MANY SOULS HOME TO JESUS CHRIST" 99

denominations, the Baptists not only allowed but encouraged Liele to take on major roles of spiritual leadership; at the same time, he accomplished all of this while still enslaved to his fellow Baptist Sharp. It was not until August 17, 1777, that Sharp freed Liele.[56]

Liele's ministry touched the lives of many Low Country blacks in the late 1770s, among them David George (1742–1810). Born into slavery in Essex County, Virginia, George's childhood was filled with such violence that when a teenager he took the risk of running away from his master. Unfortunately he was taken captive by Creek Indians and later sold to another slave master in Silver Bluff, located near the Savannah River in western South Carolina. There he encountered two Baptist preachers who would redirect his future: a white pastor named Wait Palmer, and George Liele. One day George heard Liele preach from Matthew 11:28, "Come unto me, all ye that labour and are heavy laden, and I will give you rest." He afterward told Liele, "His whole discourse seemed for me . . . that I was weary and heavy laden, and that the grace of God had given me rest." Moved to the point of conversion, George offered himself for baptism and was immersed by Palmer. Like Liele, George soon began to preach to his fellow blacks and in 1773 was appointed elder over a new Baptist congregation, the Silver Bluff Church. It was the first continually operating African American church in the country. Both George and Liele bear witness to the crucial role that black converts played in the spread of evangelical Christianity among African Americans in the late eighteenth century.[57]

It is virtually certain that Oliver Hart would have known David Margarett (n.d.; sometimes spelled "Margate"), who during his brief stay in Charleston attended worship at Hart's church and lodged with one of Hart's church members. Margarett was the era's most controversial black preacher. A graduate of the famed evangelical preachers' school Trevecca College in Wales, Margarett came to Charleston in January 1775, intending to preach to the slaves at George Whitefield's Bethesda Orphan House in Savannah. While Margarett initially impressed his white hosts as being "pious and devoted," he also raised concerns that he "should speak imprudently to the black people."

[56] See Sylvia R. Frey and Betty Wood, *Come Shouting to Zion: African American Protestantism in American South and British Caribbean to 1830* (Chapel Hill: University of North Carolina Press, 1998), 115–16.

[57] For George, see Frey and Wood, *Come Shouting to Zion*, 116–17; Kidd and Hankins, *Baptists in America*, 46–47; and "An Account of the Life of Mr. David George," in John Asplund, *The Annual Register of the Baptist Denominations, in North America* (Southampton Co., VA: Thomas Dobson, 1792), 474–75.

Margarett spoke with a discomforting voice of spiritual authority, claiming that "the Lord had told him that he should take a Negro woman in [the] house to be his wife that was already wife to one of [the] slaves." Far more disturbing to his white listeners was Margarett's claim (like Hugh Bryan's) to be a second Moses, "called to deliver his people from slavery." News of Margarett's "imprudent" and "alarming conduct" spread all over the Low Country, with many white Georgians "under a continual apprehension" that Margarett would place himself at the head of an "insurrection among the slaves." The Rev. William Piercey speculated that Margarett's "wicked conduct" sprang from "his pride.... His pride seems so great, that he can't bear to think of any of his color being slaves." There was, Piercey concluded, "no making him sensible of the state of the blacks in this country." According to Margarett's fellow missionary John Cosson, who heard him preach, Margarett "not only severely reflected against the Laws of the Province respect[ing] slaves but even against the thing itself: he also compared their state to that of the Israelites during their Egyptian Bondade [sic]." As a result, some white Georgians apparently intended to "send a party of men to George & take David & should they lay hold of Him he will certainly be hanged for what he has designed, as all the laws are all against him." Piercy managed to hustle Margarett onto a ship ahead of his pursuers, allowing him to barely "get off with his life." George Liele and David George had discovered how to navigate the treacherous waters of black evangelical ministry in the colonial South, but David Margarett had transgressed all boundaries by his radical message of liberation. After less than seven months in the Low Country, Margarett had "render'd himself . . . odious, to the whites."[58]

Beyond promoting the new birth among the slaves, both black and white evangelicals differed widely on what to do and say about slavery. The most radical wing denounced the institution entirely, speaking out against the hypocrisy of proclaiming spiritual liberty to Africans while continuing to hold them in physical bondage. But especially after the Bryan debacle, radical evangelicals preaching abolition found a hard way to go in the South. Most evangelicals opted instead for an approach to slave ministry first pioneered in the South by the Anglican bishop William Fleetwood (1656–1723) in 1711. In what became a famous address to the Society for the

---

[58] Frey and Wood, Come Shouting to Zion, 112–13; Tim Lockley, "David Margrett: A Black Missionary in the Revolutionary Atlantic," Journal of American Studies 46, no. 3 (2012): 729–45; Vincent Carretta, ed., Unchained Voices: An Anthology of Black Authors in the South Carolina Low Country, 1690–1990 (Tuscaloosa: University Press of Kentucky, 1996), 325–50.

"BRINGING MANY SOULS HOME TO JESUS CHRIST" 101

Propagation of the Gospel, Fleetwood attempted to soothe the fears associated with slave evangelism by emphasizing the master's call to a benevolent
patriarchy over his slaves. In Fleetwood's telling, God intended to use slave
owners as instruments of his grace, having transported slaves from the paganism of Africa into an environment of enlightened Christianity. He urged
masters to view themselves as heads over a household of both white and
black members, with a spiritual duty to their slaves, and he stressed that the
"Liberty of Christianity" was "entirely Spiritual," granting blacks the freedom
that mattered most: "Freedom from their Sins, Freedom from the Fears of
Death, and everlasting Misery, and not from any State of Life." Thus, rather
than overturning the slave system, Fleetwood stressed how the gospel produced both better slaves and better masters.[59]

This was the same essential message Whitefield would sound forth in the
1740s in his famous *Letter to the Inhabitants of Maryland, Virginia, North
and South-Carolina*. Whitefield insisted on the evangelism of slaves and
rebuked masters for cruel mistreatment, but stressed the spiritual nature of
gospel liberty and never broached the subject of emancipation. By the time
Hart came to Charleston at the start of the 1750s, "sanctifying slavery" had
become the standard approach for moderate evangelicals in the South. In
fact by 1751 Whitefield himself would introduce the institution of slavery
to the colony of Georgia.[60] Slavery turned out to be one of the few issues that
Whitefield and his antirevivalist sparring partner in Charleston, Alexander
Garden, agreed on. Garden was instrumental in baptizing slavery by overseeing slave Christianization and education. In an ironic twist, the unwit-
ting partners Garden and Whitefield helped create the Old South culture that
would persist beyond the Civil War.[61]

Hart followed exactly Whitefield's moderate evangelical approach to
slavery. By the end of his ministry in Charleston, the First Baptist Church
was filled with both slaves and slave owners. As just one example, David
Williams, a prominent member who helped Hart tutor young ministers,
owned two plantations and more than seventy slaves.[62] But Hart not only left

[59] William Fleetwood, *A Sermon Preached before the Society for the Propagation of the Gospel
in Foreign Parts, at the Parish Church of St. Mary-le-Bow, on Friday the 16th of February, 1710/11*
(London: Joseph Downing, 1711); Little, *Origins of Southern Evangelicalism*, 72–73, 124–26.

[60] Kidd, *George Whitefield*, 209–16.

[61] See Witzig, *Sanctifying Slavery and Politics in South Carolina*, passim.

[62] Andrew Lee Feight, "Edmund Botsford and Richard Furman: Slavery in the South Carolina
Lowcountry, 1766–1825," *Journal of the South Carolina Baptist Historical Society* 19 (November
1993): 7.

# 102 OLIVER HART AND THE RISE OF BAPTIST AMERICA

his slaveholding parishioners undisturbed; he purchased a number of slaves for himself. As early as 1754 he was referring to Margaret Mageay as "a Young Woman who hath liv'd in my House almost two years." On April 9, 1771, he recorded the purchase of a twenty-year-old slave named Dinah and her son Friday for 356 pounds. The following August he reported that "Dinah was delivered of a daughter." After Hart's first wife died, his second wife, the wealthy Charleston native Anne Marie Sealy Grimball, brought several more slaves into his household. Hart likely justified his actions in terms similar to those used in later years by one of his young protégés, Edmund Botsford, who would write, "Providence has cast my lot where slavery is introduced and practice[d]. . . . Servants I want; it is lawful for me to have them; but hired ones I cannot obtain, and therefore I have purchased some: I use them as servants; I feed them; clothe them, instruct them, etc."[63] Indeed Hart strove to regulate his behavior as a master according to New Testament precepts, conscientious about his material and spiritual responsibilities to his slaves. As he said of his friend Francis Pelot (a fellow evangelical Regular Baptist), "He not only endeavored to train up his children in the paths of virtue and religion, but he also took much pains with his servants to teach them the fear of the Lord and the way of eternal happiness."[64] William Rogers, himself a Baptist abolitionist, commended Hart as a "mild and provident master," and Hart's wife once wrote to tell Hart that "the poor black members [of the household] hang about me and wish for Master," their love for him such that they "sometimes make me drop a tear."[65] Such expressions of family affection surely comforted Hart as he considered the state of his household, yet as Eugene Genovese and others have extensively documented, the complex reality of paternalism served to reinforce racism, even as it endued slaves with humanity as members of a household.[66]

It is possible that the Harts could have owned slaves back in Pennsylvania, though it would have required a break from their extensive background in antislavery Quakerism and Keithianism, and they do not appear to have traveled to South Carolina with any slaves. It is more likely that Hart did not embrace the evangelical slaveholding position until he arrived in Charleston, where, as one contemporary informed a Philadelphia, "persons coming from

---

[63] David Benedict, *A General History of the Baptist Denomination in America and Other Parts of the World* (Boston: Lincoln and Edmonds, 1813), 2:210.

[64] Hart, diary, August 26, 1754, Hart MSS, JBDML; Hart, *Original Diary*, 6, 8.

[65] Rogers, *A Sermon*, 23; Anne Hart to Oliver Hart, July 19, 1781, Hart MSS, SCL.

[66] Eugene Genovese, *Roll, Jordan, Roll: The World the Slaves Made* (New York: Pantheon Books, 1974), 1–7; see also Butler, *Awash in a Sea of Faith*, 144–51.

the Northward received a polish."[67] As Heyrman has perceptively noted, evangelicals' capitulation to Southern slavery contributed largely to their ascendancy in the South in the nineteenth century.[68] Hart's stance on slavery charted the course for the next hundred years of ministers at the Charleston Baptist Church, the South's most influential Baptist congregation during the nineteenth century. His successors Richard Furman and Basil Manly Sr. would both publish strong defenses of slavery in the following generations, and also held prominent places in Southern society. Though Hart would rethink his proslavery ideas later in life, his Charleston policies would have dramatic repercussions on subsequent generations of American Baptists.[69]

*

Not long into his tenure at Charleston, Hart wrote a letter to his father, expressing his desire to be an instrument of revival. "I am still trying to Labour for God as enabled, but find I come Short of that engagedness which I could Desire," he confessed. "Souls are precious Otherwise the Lord would not have done so much for their Salvation as he has done: and can I Trifle with them? God forbid! I would fain be made Instrumental in bringing many Souls home to Jesus Christ."[70] The Charleston Baptist Church flourished under Hart's moderate evangelical leadership. Precise records of the church's membership during Hart's tenure no longer exist, but Morgan Edwards spoke of over two hundred communicants there in 1772, meaning that many more nonmembers would have attended Sunday worship. By this same year the church had accumulated about fifteen thousand pounds through legacies and gifts of several sorts.[71] Hart's pastorate marked the end of the church's downward trajectory and the beginning of a century of prosperity and influence. Hart would not only right the ship of the once-foundering Charleston Baptists, but he would lead them to become the hub of Baptist life in the South, training ministers, planting churches, and uniting other Baptist congregations in the region into an organized and active denomination; today Charleston's First Baptist Church is recognized as the "mother church

---

[67] Fraser, *Patriots, Pistols, and Petticoats*, 29.

[68] Heyrman, *Southern Cross*, 155, 206–52.

[69] For an introduction to Furman, see James A. Rogers, *Richard Furman: Life and Legacy* (Macon, GA: Mercer University Press, 2001); for Manly, see James A. Fuller, *Chaplain to the Confederacy: Basil Manly and Baptist Life in the Old South* (Baton Rouge: Louisiana State University Press, 2000), esp. 212–27.

[70] Oliver Hart to John Hart, March 10, 1757, Hart MSS, SCL.

[71] Edwards, *Materials towards a History of the Baptists*, 1:98.

104  OLIVER HART AND THE RISE OF BAPTIST AMERICA

of Southern Baptists." Hart's thirty-year ministry in Charleston changed the face of the Baptist South and would prove critical for the development of the broader American Baptist story.[72]

In an influential twentieth-century lecture explaining the predominant shaping influences on contemporary Southern Baptists, the Baptist historian Walter Shurden drew attention to what he called the "Charleston Tradition." By this he meant the particular religious culture formed at the Charleston Baptist Church under Hart's tenure as pastor, subsequently developed by his successors Furman, Manly Sr., and William T. Brantly. For Shurden, the defining mark of the Charleston Tradition was a commitment to "order" in the areas of doctrinal confessions, church practice, liturgical worship, and a regular ministry. Shurden's analysis was accurate as far as it went, but he proceeded to contrast Hart's Charleston Tradition with what he called the Sandy Creek Tradition of the Separate Baptist movement. Following the earlier Baptist historian William Lumpkin, Shurden credited the Sandy Creek Tradition entirely for bringing the spiritual "ardor" of Great Awakening revivalism to the South's Baptists.[73] Shurden's presentation captured many true elements about both Baptist groups, but it failed to account for the vital role that revivalism played in the Charleston Tradition. Hart did not subscribe to the order-over-ardor spirituality of Baptists like Jeremiah Condy, Ebeneezer Kinnersley, or the revival-resistant Regular Baptists in Virginia.[74] Instead it was Hart's ability to apply a respectable, moderate revivalism in Charleston that began the period of flourishing for Baptist life in the South, and in fact paved the way for the later unification with the more radical Separate Baptists in the South later in the eighteenth century.[75]

---

[72] See Baker, Craven, and Blalock, *A History of the First Baptist Church of Charleston*.

[73] Shurden, "The Southern Baptist Synthesis," 2–11.

[74] Lumpkin profiles these Virginia Regular Baptists in contrast to the Separate Baptists in William L. Lumpkin, *Baptist Foundations in the South: Tracing through the Separates the Influence of the Great Awakening* (Nashville, TN: Broadman Press, 1961).

[75] I develop this argument in Smith, *Order and Ardor*.

# 5

# "A regular Confederation"

## Laying the Foundations of the Baptist South

On the morning of October 21, 1751, Oliver Hart stood outside the Charleston Baptist meetinghouse, anticipating the arrival of several Particular Baptist brethren from around the region. Hart had invited them to consider a proposal for uniting their congregations in a formal body modeled after the Philadelphia Baptist Association. The ministers of three other Baptist churches had agreed to come. John Stephens would travel in from Ashley River, Philip James and John Brown would represent the Welsh Neck Church, and Francis Pelot would bring delegates from Euhaw. Though floodwaters would force the last group to turn back home, the historic meeting took place. It was the first denominational meeting among Baptist churches of the South. Before many years had elapsed, the fledgling organization would adopt the name of their annual meeting place, calling themselves the Charleston Association.

Hart's initiative in forming the Charleston Association was part of a much larger religious movement within pre-Revolutionary American society. As we have seen, the New World was a place of remarkable pluralism, including not only a variety of traditional religious options but more mystical fringe sects, as well as "dark corners" in which operated extensive magic and occultism.[1] In this chaotic spiritual context, both Established and Dissenting churches alike took deliberate steps to establish a presence and extend their influence between the years 1680 and 1760. Essential to their strategy was "institutional proliferation," in which American religious groups duplicated the Old World patterns of erecting centralized denominational structures that met regularly to exercise ecclesiastical authority. These bodies administered discipline, regulated ministries, and launched a variety of voluntary

---

[1] Jon Butler goes to great lengths to expose the "dark corners" that existed in the early colonial landscape, arguing that magic and occultism persisted much longer into the supposedly "Enlightened" eighteenth century than scholars have generally recognized. See Butler, *Awash in a Sea of Faith*, 67–97.

*Oliver Hart and the Rise of Baptist America*. Eric C. Smith, Oxford University Press (2020). © Oxford University Press.
DOI: 10.1093/oso/9780197506325.001.0001

106 OLIVER HART AND THE RISE OF BAPTIST AMERICA

organizations. The establishment of these new denominational institutions shaped the American religious scene in significant ways that are still evident in the twenty-first century.[2]

The Church of England launched its own program of denominational resurgence by appointing James Blair (1656–1743) its first commissary of Virginia in 1689, to organize the colony's many Anglican parishes into an efficient state church. Blair helped Anglicanism keep pace with Virginia's expanding population, establishing a new church in every county formed in the colony between 1690 and 1740. Through Blair's efforts, Anglican churches in Virginia increased from about thirty-five in 1680 to about sixty-one in 1724. In 1693 Blair also helped found the College of William and Mary, to promote Anglican spiritual renewal and local clerical training. In addition to Blair's work, the Anglican Church launched a pair of important voluntary societies at this time. The Society for Promoting Christian Knowledge furnished Anglican ministers with theological libraries, and their congregations with tracts and pamphlets. The Society for the Propagation of the Gospel (SPG) recruited and sent trained ministers into the colonies. By 1720 the SPG had sent more than sixty Anglican priests to previously unserviced settlements. Hart would have witnessed the signs of the reenergized Anglican Church in South Carolina every day, as he looked up to the majestic steeple of St. Philip's Church, constructed in 1711. After 1752 St. Philip's would be joined in Charleston by the equally elegant St. Michael's Cathedral in 1752. The steady rise of Anglican church buildings across the colonial American horizon, where there had previously been no Christian buildings, signaled sweeping changes taking place in American society that Butler has called the "sacralization of the landscape."[3]

For all the Anglican advances in the first half of the eighteenth century, it was American Dissenters who led the way in fashioning "sophisticated, complex, and authoritative denominational institutions." Quakers were among the first of these groups to move toward centralizing church authority, establishing the Philadelphia Yearly Meeting in 1684. This gathered body exercised power across all Quaker meetings in Pennsylvania and East and West New Jersey. These annual meetings were small affairs of seven to ten representatives, almost invariably "Public Friends," or preachers. This centralization of Quaker ministerial authority had been among the complaints

[2] Butler, *Awash in a Sea of Faith*, 98–99.
[3] Butler, *Awash in a Sea of Faith*, 98–110.

"A REGULAR CONFEDERATION" 107

George Keith lodged during the Keithian controversy of the early 1690s, and the Quakers responded to that schism by investing nonministering Friends with more authority by the end of the decade. At the Yearly Meeting representatives began making public statements regarding slaveholding, dress, public pipe-smoking, and other social behaviors.[4]

Presbyterians developed their own institutional center in 1716 by founding the Synod of Philadelphia. The Synod regulated the work of Presbyterian ministers by assuming control of the ordination process. Each candidate for ordination was required to pass the inspection of the Synod in theological orthodoxy, education, and spirituality. (It was the Philadelphia Synod that had attempted to block the ordination of radical revivalists educated at the Log College in the late 1730s.) The Synod also received calls from churches seeking pastors and connected them to their pool of ordained men—if the church recognized the Synod's authority. The Synod became the arena for the most important discussions regarding Presbyterian life in the eighteenth century, hosting disputes over issues such as the adoption of the *Westminster Confession of Faith*, ordination standards, and the necessity of ministers sharing personal experiences of grace. The consolidation of Presbyterian authority seems to have contributed to the denomination's considerable growth in the mid-eighteenth century. Upon its creation in 1716, the Philadelphia Synod contained 27 ministers and 30 congregations; by 1740 the synod had six presbyteries and 50 ministers. By 1770 it counted nine presbyteries and more than 120 ministers, now spread from northern Virginia to New York.[5] "The English Presbyterian Church is growing so rapidly among the English in America that in a few years it will spread and surpass the Episcopal and all the rest," observed the German Lutheran Henry Melchior Muhlenberg in 1765. "The *progress* is due to the fact that they have established ministers, keep strict discipline, and tolerate no ministers except those who have good moral character and the ability to speak, and who are content with small salaries and able to endure hard work. Those denominations here which do not have these characteristics, just the opposite, are consequently decreasing and making room for the Presbyterians."[6] Clearly, establishing denominational order would be essential to success in the New World.

---

[4] Butler, *Awash in a Sea of Faith*, 118–21.
[5] Butler, *Awash in a Sea of Faith*, 124–25.
[6] *The Journals of Henry Melchior Muhlenberg*, translated by Theodore G. Tappert and John W. Dobberstein, 3 vols. (Philadelphia, PA: Muhlenberg Press, 1945), 2:181.

108   OLIVER HART AND THE RISE OF BAPTIST AMERICA

American Baptists followed a similar path toward institutionalism. They began simply, as we have seen, with scattered congregations in Pennsylvania and New Jersey forming informal connections to share ministers in the 1690s. Over the next decade various ecclesiastical disputes arising among the increasingly diverse Baptist people further prompted a move to consolidation. By 1707 the Delaware Valley Baptists agreed to meet annually to "consult about such things as were wanting in the Church and set them in order," resulting in the Philadelphia Baptist Association.[7] The Association's annual meetings were attended mostly by ordained ministers, and its first official act was to lay down rules for examining and approving new ministers in the area. Baptist organizations grew more sophisticated from there. Each year, the Philadelphia Association's messengers answered questions from churches and settled disputes and eventually began collecting funds to educate aspiring pastors and appoint missionaries to destitute regions. Though its leaders stridently denied the charge, the Philadelphia Association became a centralized, authoritative body in American Baptist life. It was in resistance to this conclusion that the association adopted Benjamin Griffith's 1749 essay on "the power and duties of an association." In it, Griffith upheld the traditional Baptist doctrine of the autonomy of the local church, denying any institution the role of "supreme judicature," over "independent churches," which had "complete power and authority from Jesus Christ."[8] Hart, present at this meeting, affixed his signature to the document in approval. In a phrase he would himself repeat ad infinitum, associations functioned strictly in an "advisory capacity," to autonomous, local churches, and nothing more. Yet despite these protests, the Philadelphia Association in fact wielded tremendous and far-reaching influence, contributing to impressive Baptist growth across the eighteenth century.

By the mid-1700s each of these Protestant denominations was gradually turning its attention to the South. When Hart reached Charleston in 1749, it seems he was already planning to establish a Baptist institution there similar to the Philadelphia Association. It is possible that some leaders in the Philadelphia Association had urged him to do so.

For the most part, the South's Particular Baptist churches were fighting for survival at midcentury. The Charleston congregation had struggled along for ten years preceding Hart's tenure. The Ashley River Baptists had

---

[7] Gillette, *Minutes*, 25.
[8] Gillette, *Minutes*, 60–61.

been the region's strongest Baptist church in the 1740s. Their pastor, Isaac Chanler, had been the face of the Baptist cause in the area since the late 1730s through his itinerant preaching, published writings, passion for starting new works, and support of weaker sister churches. His untimely death at the end of 1749 had impacted all the Particular Baptists in the South.[9] The Euhaw Baptist Church had subsisted without a regular minister for six years. Like the Charleston Baptists, the Euhaw Baptists had relied heavily on Chanler's occasional preaching, though they supplemented this by the sermons of a young lay preacher in the congregation named Francis Pelot (1720–1774). Pelot was a gifted preacher, but had balked at ordination, stalling the church's progress. The most stable church in the region was probably in Welsh Neck, founded in 1738, so called for its predominantly Welsh membership. Chanler had ordained their pastor, Philip James, assisted by a younger preacher named John Brown. Yet the inland location of the Welsh Neck Church left them disconnected from the other Baptists of the area.[10] As Hart looked at this handful of weak, scattered churches, he saw the makings of a Southern Philadelphia Association, but it would require a good bit of work to bring this vision about.

Hart began quietly. His first task was simply to connect every congregation with a competent minister, drawing on his extensive Baptist contacts in the North. He influenced a young preacher named John Stephens to come to Ashley River just months after his own arrival in Charleston. Originally from Staten Island, New York, Stephens, like Hart, had been converted under George Whitefield. After his ordination in 1747, Stephens had gathered a small Particular Baptist church at Horseneck, Connecticut, which then became part of the Philadelphia Association. But Hart persuaded Stephens to join his pioneering efforts in the South, and on May 12, 1750, Hart recorded in his diary, "The Rev. John Stephens arrived at Charles Town from Philadelphia." The next month, on June 1, Hart delivered the charge at Stephens's installation service. Hart now had an ally in his cause. Stephens preached "with a good degree of Warmth, and Freedom" and had experienced the benefits of associational life in the North.[11] By 1755 he had baptized or received thirty-nine adults, thirty-five at Ashley River and eight at

[9] For the Ashley River Baptist Church, see Sarah E. Kegley and Thomas J. Little, "The Record of the Ashley River Baptist Church, 1736–1769," *Journal of the South Carolina Baptist Historical Society* 27 (November 2001): 3–32.

[10] For the Euhaw Baptist Church, see Townsend, *South Carolina Baptists*, 36–50, and Little, *Origins of Southern Evangelicalism*, 174–78.

[11] Hart, *Original Diary*, 2; Townsend, *South Carolina Baptists*, 35.

the church's branch on the Black River.[12] His name would appear regularly thereafter in Hart's notes about revitalization efforts across the region.

Hart next moved to the Euhaw Church, where he met Pelot, who had immigrated to South Carolina in 1734 at the age of fifteen as part of a larger Swiss relocation to the Carolina backcountry. Industrious and business-savvy, Pelot became a wealthy planter and by 1772 owned "three islands, and about 3789 acres on the continent, with slaves and stock in abundance."[13] After Pelot's conversion under Isaac Chanler and his baptism into the Euhaw Church, it was "discovered that he was endowed with ministerial gifts," and the church prevailed upon him to "make tryal" of them. According to Hart, Pelot had been "blest with a pretty good education, whereby a foundation was laid, for the great improvement he made, by reading, study, and conversation." But while he agreed to preach occasionally, Pelot resisted all solicitations toward ordination. This was presumably out of "modesty and self diffidence," in Hart's words. Pelot's financial interests possibly also delayed his commitment to full-time ministry. As Pelot related it, Hart's persuasive powers finally overcame his reluctance. Hart and Stephens ordained Pelot on January 13, 1752, with Hart preaching on Christ's words from Matthew 10:16, "Behold, I send you forth as sheep in the midst of wolves. Be ye therefore wise as serpents and harmless as doves," and reported that "many attended the solemnity and in general they were much affected." His wealth, refinement, and status as a slaveholding planter also meant that Pelot fit the moderate revivalist profile even better than Hart did. Sharing a common commitment to Baptist order and evangelical ardor, Pelot and Hart became the closest of friends in the ensuing years.[14]

Hart was still positioning these pieces in 1751 when he proposed his association plan. No report of the meeting remains, but Hart left a written address outlining the benefits of an association that historian Robert Baker has plausibly argued is his message to this early gathering. Whenever Hart may have delivered this speech, its contents clearly delineate his vision for early Baptist denominational life in the South.[15]

---

[12] Kegley and Little, "Record of the Ashley River Baptist Church," 5.

[13] Morgan Edwards mentioned this, he claimed, "not to flatter my friend Pelot, but in hope that his conduct may influence other rich planters to preach the gospel among the poor baptists when God inclines their hearts to do it" (*Materials towards a History of the Baptists*, 2:133).

[14] Hart, *Original Diary*, 2, 8.

[15] Owens, *Oliver Hart, 1723–1795*, 10; Baker, Craven, and Blalock, *First Baptist Church*, 150–52; Smith, *Order and Ardor*, 77–79. All quotations from this speech come from Oliver Hart, Sermon on Associations, Hart papers, SCL.

"A REGULAR CONFEDERATION" 111

Hart introduced the address by underscoring the necessity of distinctively Baptist belief and practice for membership in the association. "Several Churches there must be, agreeing in Doctrine, & Practice, and Independent in their Authority, or Church Order, before they can enter into a regular Confederation," he insisted. He envisioned area Baptist churches appointing messengers to represent them in the association's meetings, thinking primarily of ordained men. He reasoned, "As Ministers are commonly suppos'd to be Men of Superior Abilities; being generally more fluent in Conversation, Solid & penetrating in their Judgments, & candid in their disquisitions, than others; it is necessary they should be concerned as Helps: not to mention their Right by Office, to act, and even preside in all Councils where Church Matters are to be considered." Consolidating power among a few professional clergy may have stirred anxiety among some Baptists, but Hart had witnessed firsthand in the Philadelphia Association the denominational efficiency that resulted when a group of gifted leaders were invested with decision-making authority.[16] Further, Hart believed he had a New Testament precedent for his proposal: throughout his speech he referenced the activities of the Jerusalem Council in Acts 15, in which first-century church leaders gathered to settle an early doctrinal dispute. Baptists always felt they were on safe ground when they could cite a biblical example of their activities.

As Hart laid out the responsibilities of the association, he focused on the same issues that had been so important in the Philadelphia Association: mediating Baptist disputes, opposing false doctrine, identifying false preachers, and answering "difficult cases of conscience" within the churches. He closed by urging the association to consider "affairs in general which relate to the welfare of Zion." It was in these final remarks that Hart revealed his expansive vision for an energetic Baptist denomination. He foresaw an active association as the most powerful and efficient vehicle for advancing Baptist life in the region. An association could unify the scattered Baptist people for a variety of causes, including collective prayer on special days for humiliation or thanksgiving. The association could also accelerate the process of calling and training a new generation of Baptist preachers. The scarcity of ministers in the rapidly growing American colonies was a major concern for all denominations in this period. The South's frontier was grossly underserviced by ordained clergy, leaving the population to drift into the fold of whichever

[16] For the development of associational authority over local churches in the antebellum South, see Wills, *Democratic Authority*, 98–102.

denomination offered the nearest worship opportunity. From the Baptists' perspective, this led to an erroneous mixture of beliefs and sometimes, when settlers gave up attending worship altogether, devolved into sheer paganism.[17] Quickly turning out ministers to these unchurched areas was thus a top priority for all denominations at this time, and Hart urged the association to "conclude upon some methods for educating, and trying the gifts, and honorably calling out persons to the great work of the ministry." Training young Baptist ministers would become an abiding passion of Hart's life. He also believed that the association should actively connect needy churches with capable pastors, as he himself had been doing. This could even mean, at times, that the association might ask a pastor to leave his church to itinerate in a destitute area for a season, "when there is a greater prospect of usefulness in that way than in their own charge."

As the Baptist presence spread across the South, Hart wished the association to provide Baptist churches a sense of connectedness. In addition to hosting an annual meeting for this purpose, the association should also attempt to keep Baptists informed by publishing "circular letters," an idea also taken from the Jerusalem Council of Acts 15, by way of the Philadelphia Association. These yearly missives would brief Baptist churches "of their proceedings, and determinations, and to give such advice with regard to their moral and religious conduct as is necessary." As in the Philadelphia Association, Hart intended the Charleston Association to have an important voice in every Baptist congregation in the South.

Hart closed by urging the association to conduct its business with godly decorum, cautioning the ministers "to be instant and fervent in prayer, and to conduct with a gravity becoming those who are working for God and transacting business for eternity." They must "guard against a clamorous, contentious disposition; and by no means to give way to a sprit of anger or revenge; but to adhere to their contrary virtues, of meekness, patience, humility and the like." Once more Hart looked to the Jerusalem Council as his model. "While Peter is speaking all is hush'd. When he had finished speaking, the same attention is paid to the speech of James," he said. "After this, tho' these seem to have been the chief speakers, what they had offered was weighed, and judiciously considered by the whole body, and the conclusion drawn accordingly. A pattern well worthy of imitation!" As American Baptists became known for their interdenominational squabbles across the nineteenth and

---

[17] See Bonomi, *Under the Cope of Heaven*, 54–61.

"A REGULAR CONFEDERATION" 113

twentieth centuries, Hart's warnings of civility took on a certain irony. As one recent Baptist monograph has pointed out, "Baptists are notorious for two things—evangelism and schism."[18]

At meeting's end, the attendees accepted Hart's proposal. They committed to meet annually, on the Saturday before the second Sunday in November. The meeting's first two days would be devoted to public worship, and the business of the association would commence with an introductory sermon on Monday morning at 10 o'clock. These decisions were ratified at the next year's meeting, signed by Hart, Stephens, Pelot, Brown, and Joshua Edwards, along with eight lay messengers. Hart would serve as the association's moderator in the years 1759, 1764, 1769, 1773, 1775, and 1778, and as clerk from 1752 to 1757 and in 1777.[19]

One of the chief concerns for all the American denominations by the mid-eighteenth century was reaching out from their established urban religious centers to the unchurched frontier. The problem was particularly acute in South Carolina, where vast stretches of territory were being quickly populated yet remained unserviced by regular clergy of any kind. In the late 1720s South Carolina's governor Robert Johnson (1682–1735) had created eleven townships in the territory that became known as the "backcountry," more than one hundred miles inland from the coast. Beginning at the fall line of the Sand Hills, this western frontier rose into the Piedmont, a land of dense forests crisscrossed with countless creeks and rivers. From Johnson's perspective, a well-populated backcountry would create a convenient buffer for the Low Country from Indian, French, and Spanish attacks, as well as from slave uprisings. Through land concessions and generous offers of material aid, Johnson successfully recruited a variety of Protestant Dissenters from Europe to fill the new backcountry in the 1730s and 1740s.[20] Swiss, German, French, and Dutch Reformed, German Lutherans, Moravians, sectarian groups from Continental Europe, Welsh Baptists and Scottish and Scots Irish Presbyterians all poured into the new settlements. After the French and Indian War in the 1760s, immigrants from northern colonies swelled the frontier population further.

---

[18] Kidd and Hankins, *Baptists in America*, 251. For further study on Baptist contentiousness, see Nancy Tatom Ammerman, *Baptist Battles: Social Change and Religious Conflict in the Southern Baptist Convention* (New Brunswick, NJ: Rutgers University Press, 1990); and Walter B. Shurden, *Not a Silent People: Controversies That Have Shaped Southern Baptists* (Macon, GA: Smyth & Helwys, 1972).

[19] Baker, Craven, and Blalock, *History of the First Baptist Church*, 147.

[20] Little, *Origins of Southern Evangelicalism*, 82–83.

114   OLIVER HART AND THE RISE OF BAPTIST AMERICA

Each denomination scrambled to keep pace. The Anglican SPG had already begun sacralizing the Carolina wilderness with a number of tidy church buildings in the early eighteenth century, such as St. Andrews (1706), St. James Goose Creek (1708), and Strawberry Chapel (1725), but they struggled to get enough trained ministers out to the people. The rector of St. James Parish, Goochland, in South Carolina, reported a typical experience. In addition to serving three churches, he had seven congregations up in the mountains, besides preaching in twelve other places twice a year, "which I reckon better than 400 miles backwards and forwards and foard 19 times the South and North Rivers." Traveling through the Carolinas in 1755, the Presbyterian Hugh McAden also commented on the challenges of serving on the frontier, noting in his diary, "Alone in the wilderness. Sometimes a house in ten miles, and sometimes not that." Without many settled pastors, frontier settlers were prone to simply attend whichever form of worship was most convenient. One South Carolina rector commented that these settlers "must have one [religious] leader or another," and, "wanting a true and faithfull one, they'd rather follow an Anabaptist, a Presbyterian, or a Quaker than be without one."[21] Other backcountry inhabitants sloughed off into total irreligion. In North Carolina, McAden claimed that he preached "to a number of those poor baptized infidels, many of whom I was told had never heard a sermon in all their lives before, and yet several of them had families." He also related a story of an older man in South Carolina Indian territory who claimed he "had never seen a shirt, been in a fair, heard a sermon, or seen a minister, in all his life." The SPG responded by commissioning itinerants to the region, like Charles Woodmason in the 1760s.[22] Other denominations followed. The Virginia Presbyterian William Robinson traveled a circuit through several North Carolina settlements in 1742 and 1743. There are records of Presbyterian settlers petitioning the Synod of Philadelphia as early as 1744, claiming that "many people" there desired a settled ministry. It would be the early 1750s before Presbyterian Synods in Philadelphia and New York began sending missionaries there.[23]

Those ministers who visited the Southern frontier found a world very different from the wealthy and sophisticated societies of Charleston or Philadelphia. Charles Woodmason judged many of his listeners to be a "vile

[21] Bonomi, *Under the Cope of Heaven*, 58.
[22] See Woodmason, *Carolina Backcountry on the Eve of the Revolution*, xi–xxxvi.
[23] William Henry Foote, *Sketches of North Carolina, Historical and Biographical* (New York, 1846), 158.

"A REGULAR CONFEDERATION" 115

disorderly Crew" rather than a "serious Moral Community." "How hard the Lot of any Gentleman in this Part of the World! . . . As for Society and Converse—I have not yet met with one literate, or travel'd Person—No ingenious Mind," he complained. There was nothing polished about backcountry society to be sure, and Woodmason also found frontier spirituality to fall woefully beneath his standards. He reported after one service that his congregation dispersed for "Revelling Drinking Singing Dancing and Whoring."[24] Woodmason was not alone in his dim estimation of the backcountry. In 1768 the Baptist Jeremiah Dargan called it a "wild, wild place, a wicked, wicked neighborhood," where he preached to "no purpose except provoking them to outrage."[25] The Presbyterian Hugh MacAden found a similar reception among a group of North Carolina immigrants from the Scottish Highlands, who "scarcely knew one word that I said" and were "the poorest singers I ever heard in all my life." Another group of Highlanders praised his message, but McAden feared it was "all feigned and hypocritical" because they stayed around the house afterward drinking and swearing, ignoring his protests and keeping him from sleep.[26]

The violence and volatility of frontier life also made it difficult to establish churches. McAden encountered this firsthand in 1755, during the conflict of the French and Indian War:

Here it was I received the most melancholy news of the entire defeat of our army by the French at Ohio, the General killed, numbers of the inferior officers, and the whole artillery taken. This, together with the frequent account of fresh murders being daily committed upon the frontiers, struck terror to every heart. A cold shuddering possessed every breast, and paleness covered almost every face. In short, the whole inhabitants were put into an universal confusion. Scarcely any man durst sleep in his own house—but all met in companies with their wives and children, and set about building little fortifications, to defend themselves form such barbarians and inhuman enemies, whom they concluded would be let loose upon them at pleasure.[27]

---

[24] Hooker, *Carolina Backcountry on the Eve of the Revolution*, 41, 38, 56.
[25] Townsend, *South Carolina Baptists*, 150.
[26] Foote, *Sketches of North Carolina*, 171.
[27] Foote, *Sketches of North Carolina*, 163.

In 1759 the Presbyterian missionary William Richardson settled at the Waxhaw Church in South Carolina, where he reported, "Almost every night we expect to be awakened with an Indian halloo." Richardson's life was mysteriously cut short when he was found in his room with marks of strangulation on his neck and bruises on his chest. The cause of his death was never settled, but Richardson long after remained a chilling testimony to the violence of the Southern frontier.[28] As one recent study of the Presbyterian Archibald Simpson has emphasized, instilling serious religion on the Carolina frontiers was "an ordeal."[29] Yet despite its obvious challenges, churches knew that establishing a presence in the backcountry was essential for denomination stability.

The Philadelphia Association began expressing an increasing concern to send ministers to the Southern frontier at the beginning of the 1750s. "Oh, if you had heard the mournful complaints and requests of souls destitute of the means of the courts of God and his ordinances sent to us form remote places, it would cause melting compassions in your hearts, as it did ours," they wrote in their 1750 circular letter.[30] Soon the Association was including regular appeals to its churches to release their pastors for itinerate mission work in these regions. "We had affectionate and pressing requests from many places for ministerial help. Our souls are concerned for those who are like to perish for lack of vision; therefore, we entreat you to be fervent and frequent at the throne of grace, that the Lord would send forth many faithful laborers into his vineyard. We earnestly recommend as necessary, that you might be free to spare your ministers some time to supply those who would otherwise be altogether destitute," they wrote in 1755.[31]

As usual, the Philadelphia Association would inspire Hart's own actions in the South. At their 1752 annual meeting, the Philadelphia Association commissioned Benjamin Miller and John Thomas to reform a General Baptist church in Virginia that was reeling from the moral failure of its pastor, the infamous Henry Loveall. It seemed an opportune moment to reclaim the church to the Philadelphia Association's Particular Baptist position. The missionaries also planned to administer the ordinances to another frontier church that Thomas had established on an earlier trip. With these

---

[28] Kidd, *Great Awakening*, 255; Hooker, *Carolina Backcountry on the Eve of the Revolution*, 14, 132–34.
[29] See Moore, *Archibald Simpson's Unpeaceable Kingdom*, xi–xxvii.
[30] Gillette, *Minutes*, 64.
[31] Gillette, *Minutes*, 72.

"A REGULAR CONFEDERATION" 117

plans laid, Miller and Thomas departed, bringing with them a young layman of French Huguenot descent named John Gano. Born in New York in 1727 to a Presbyterian father and a Baptist mother, Gano had experienced the new birth at the peak of the Great Awakening. Afterward he found himself torn over the issue of baptism. Ironically it was the Presbyterian revivalist Gilbert Tennent who nudged him toward his mother's Baptist faith. "Dear young man, if the devil cannot destroy your soul, he will endeavor to destroy your comfort and usefulness; and therefore do not always be doubting in this matter. If you cannot think as I do, think for yourself," Tennent advised. Gano was immersed and joined the Baptist Church at Hopewell, New Jersey. He struck out on the Southern missionary tour with Miller and Thomas, expecting to assist in the background. But to Gano's surprise, Miller and Thomas repeatedly asked Gano to preach. Though hesitant at first, Gano finally spoke up, and performed brilliantly throughout the tour. But he had technically preached without a "regular call," a serious offense among Particular Baptists. The Hopewell church demanded an explanation for his "irregular preaching" when he came home. When Gano insisted, "My own conscience acquitted me" and that he would do the same if placed in the same position again, the church asked him to "exercise his gifts" before them. He did, and they quickly confirmed his call, licensing him to preach on April 14, 1753. He soon began preaching to a group of Baptists in Morristown, New Jersey.[32]

The next year, the Philadelphia Association sent Gano back to the frontier, hoping he could duplicate his earlier success. After being ordained at Hopewell on May 29, 1754, Gano headed south. In North Carolina he made contact with a number of General Baptists "of free will principles." When they denied Gano an audience, he appeared unannounced at a special meeting. Striding to the front, he declared to the shocked house, "I have desired a visit from you which, as a brother and stranger, I had a right to expect; but as ye have refused, I give up my claim, and am come to pay you a visit." He then mounted the pulpit and read from Acts 19:15, "Jesus I know, and Paul I know, but who are ye?" From there Gano's oratory and penetrating interviews persuaded the whole lot to submit to his Particular Baptist position; each church he contacted would go on to join the Philadelphia Association. Gano applied a rigorous standard of examination; he found the conversion testimonies of some of his interviewees to be wanting, and told them so. One General

[32] Wolever, *John Gano*, 25–27, 40–49.

118    OLIVER HART AND THE RISE OF BAPTIST AMERICA

Baptist man agreed to let Gano question him but expressed confidence to his peers beforehand that he should "return triumphant." Gano, however, was not impressed. After hearing the man's personal account, he responded blandly, "I profess, brother, this will not do: this man has yet the needful to seek." When the man's neighbors inquired about the meeting, he said, "The Lord have mercy upon you; for this northern minister put a *mene tekel* upon me!"[33] When all was said and done, Gano congratulated himself on serving a group of misguided frontier Baptists, though outsiders viewed it as an ugly example of the Philadelphia Association's heavy-handed proselytizing.[34]

Pressing further south, Gano preached for John Stephens at Ashley Ferry, South Carolina. Gano's passionate delivery delighted the largely African American congregation. When the slaves formed two lines outside the meetinghouse to thank Gano, Stephens remarked, "You make a very good Negro preacher." Afterward Gano privately remarked in his diary, "This humbled me before God, and I then thought, I would for the future, take more pains with souls, and especially with negroes."[35] It was a notable illustration of how African Americans and white evangelical preachers in the South impacted one other's religious practices in a reciprocal process that lasted throughout the eighteenth century.[36] Gano finally made it down to Charleston, where Hart too opened his pulpit to him, the same occasion on which Gano preached before George Whitefield. Gano returned home to New Jersey in the fall of 1755, marrying Sarah Stites and resuming his ministry at Morristown.

Throughout his career, Hart would serve the South's Baptists less by his own creative genius and more by his ability to adopt tested ministry concepts from other places. In the fall of 1755 he called the Charleston Association to follow the Philadelphia Association and "take into consideration the destitute condition of many places in the interior settlements of this and the neighboring provinces." He recommended following the same program of cooperative funding, collecting "contributions for the support

---

[33] *Mene tekel* is a reference to the Old Testament story of the Babylonian king Belshazzar in Daniel 5. While at a feast, Belshazzar saw a hand writing on a wall, "Mene, mene, tekel, upsharin," which the Hebrew prophet Daniel interpreted to mean that Belshazzar had been "weighed in the balance, and found wanting."

[34] The Philadelphia Association had just ruled in 1752 that persons rejecting the Calvinistic tenets of election and predestination should not be admitted to church membership. See Gillette, *Minutes*, 68. For Gano's interactions with the General Baptists, see Mulder, *Controversial Spirit*, 38–44, and Nettles, *The Baptists*, 109–11.

[35] Wolever, *John Gano*, 47–49, 58.

[36] See Frey and Wood, *Come Shouting to Zion*, xii.

"A REGULAR CONFEDERATION" 119

of a missionary to itinerate in those parts." The Association approved and commissioned Hart to secure a missionary. When the funds came in, Hart boarded the sloop *Fancy* on January 19, 1756, and sailed for Philadelphia. He spent the next nine months back in his home territory, preaching, visiting family, and strengthening ties with the Philadelphia Association. He also met with Gano, urging him to return to the South with him. As usual, Hart was persuasive. He had befriended Gano on the evangelist's earlier Southern tour, probably hosting Gano in his own home. Time and time again throughout his life, Hart's ability to make and keep friends (the two remained close for the rest of Hart's life) proved critical in advancing the Baptist interest. At its 1756 meeting the Charleston Association charged Gano "to visit the Yadkin first and afterwards to bestow his labours wherever Providence should appear to direct."[37]

Gano, whose preaching talents observers often compared to Whitefield's, seemed to find success wherever he traveled. His 1757 campaign led to many conversions, as well as the establishment of a Baptist church in the Jersey Settlement of North Carolina. The young itinerant even inspired one dazzled listener, Samuel Newman, to pen a heroic verse in his honor:

> Go, go, sweet youth, go spread thy master's theme
> For well thou'st learnt his attributes and name.
> Go, in his strength, no cold will thee annoy,
> Go, make the hills and valleys echo joy.
> Proclaim the Savior, this all thy theme,
> Jesus, the Lord, and his blest Gospel's scheme.
> Go sound the trump, for well thou can'st it blow,
> Jesus, the Lord, and his blest merits show.
> Lift up his ensign, show his purple gore,
> That from his side, for sinners, out did pour:
> O! let them, waving in the wind, appear,
> Shew them their sins, the cruel sword or spear
> That pierced his side to make this crimson dye,
> Perhaps they'll tremble, and their sins destroy;
> And own the Lord and his compassions sweet,
> And fall before him, victims at his feet.[38]

---

[37] Wood Furman, *History of the Charleston Association of Baptist Churches in the State of South-Carolina* (Charleston, SC: J. Hoff, 1811), 10; Hart, *Original Diary*, 3.

[38] Wolever, *John Gano*, 118–19.

Gano returned to Morristown after his appointment but received so many pleas to come back to North Carolina that he finally relented, leaving his beleaguered Morristown Church for the third time. He pastored the Jersey Settlement church for three years, leading them to join the Charleston Association. He would not return north until 1760, when the French and Indian War drove him from the frontier.

Hart's initiative to employ a missionary at the Charleston Association meeting in 1755 signaled an important transition for the South's Particular Baptists. Rather than depending on the Philadelphia Association to keep their churches afloat, they were now ready to join the northern Baptists in actively evangelizing America's frontier regions. From this point forward, Baptists in the South would develop a reputation as an aggressively missionary people. In the early nineteenth century a significant number of so-called antimissions Baptists would oppose the concept of denominational fundraising for missions piloted there by Hart, fragmenting large portions of the Baptist South for some years.[39] But ultimately Hart's model would win out. Gano's appointment made him the first in a long line of Baptist missionaries supported by the cooperative funding of his denomination, a line that extends to the present day.

Hart's Charleston Association Baptists were soon joined on the frontier by a host of other competing denominations, including Presbyterians like McAden and Richardson, Anglicans like Woodmason, and later the Methodists and Separate Baptists. The presence of so many different denominations competing for followers could sometimes create confusion among the people and resentment among the clergy. By 1755 McAden was already complaining of a Presbyterian congregation on the North Carolina frontier that had been divided by the influence of a Baptist preacher, likely the Philadelphia Association's Benjamin Miller. "Many adhere to the Baptists that were before wavering, and several that professed themselves to be Presbyterians; so that very few at present join heartily for our ministers, and will in a little time, if God prevent not, be too weak either to call or supplicate for a faithful minister," McAden lamented. "O may the good Lord, who can bring order out of confusion, and all things that are not as though they were, visit this people!"[40] In the mid-1750s the denominational rivalries on the Southern frontier were just warming up.[41]

---

[39] For the story of the antimissions Baptists, see Joshua Guthman, *Strangers Below: Primitive Baptists and American Culture* (Chapel Hill: University of North Carolina Press, 2015), esp. 21–86.

[40] Foote, *Sketches of North Carolina*, 167.

[41] Mulder tells this story well throughout *A Controversial Spirit*.

As the Charleston Association continued to actively evangelize its neighbors over the following decades, the small Baptist denomination increased in number and complexity. The maturation of Hart's Southern Baptist institution is revealed most clearly in the Charleston Association's published minutes and circular letters from the 1770s. A glance at the document from the 1774 annual meeting demonstrates how far Hart's denominational vision had progressed since 1751.[42]

The circular letter, as Hart had proposed, allowed the Charleston Association to share with its churches the news and decisions made at the annual meeting, as well as to stoke the enthusiasm of the Baptist people. "Our souls have been comforted at hearing of the glorious conquests of divine Grace in various places in this province and Georgia," the 1774 letter commented, mimicking the style of the Philadelphia Association's circular letters. Like their northern Baptist brethren, Hart and the Charleston Association leaders used the circular letter to urge Baptists to pray and work for revival. Typically they pitched these requests against the bleak backdrop of the current, lukewarm spirituality in the churches: "But, alas! Much deadness prevails in other places. —Brethren, lift up your hearts to God for success on the word preached, and that God would raise up many faithful Ministers of the Gospel; look out among your young men for such as have promising abilities, and encourage them to improve their talents for the service of the sanctuary." The circular letter also admonished its churches to observe other standard issues of Baptist piety, cling to orthodox teaching, maintain unity in their churches, and "inculcate instruction and promote by example the fear of God in your families."

Like the Philadelphia Association, the Charleston Association attached to their circular letter the minutes of their annual meeting, providing Baptists with a basic outline of what had taken place. It began with opening business: eight total messengers were present from three churches; five churches sent neither messenger nor letter; a moderator (Evan Pugh) and a clerk (the Charleston Baptist layman David Williams) were chosen; and a new congregation at New Savannah, Georgia, was received into the association. Next, John Gano, present as a visiting messenger from the Philadelphia Association, was recognized. Gano stood to read a letter recommending a new measure to strengthen all the Baptists in the colonies. The Philadelphia

---

[42] The following quotations are taken from Charleston Association, *Minutes of the Charlestown Association, February 7, 1774* (Charleston, SC, 1774).

122    OLIVER HART AND THE RISE OF BAPTIST AMERICA

Association proposed "sending out a yearly travelling Minister; who also serves as their messenger, to the several Baptist Associations in America." The Charleston Association officially registered that in this "laudable design we heartily concur," and Hart was appointed to write a letter back to the Philadelphia Association. By 1774 Baptists were developing a growing sense of their denomination across the colonies and consistently expressed a desire to maintain contact with one another. The Charleston Association would also appoint Evan Pugh at this meeting to send letters on their behalf to "cultivate union and a friendly correspondence, amongst all Baptist Associations," which would "promote Christian fellowship, and reciprocally strengthen each others hands, in the cause which, under our Redeemer, we are all engaged in."[43] Nor did this desire for an expanded Baptist community stop with other Regular Baptist churches. The minutes also recorded the presence of two Separate Baptist visitors at the meeting, Timothy Dargan of the Congaree Church and Richard Furman of the High Hills Church, "their company and advice being desired." On the eve of the Revolution, the diverse Baptist groups along the eastern seaboard were closer than ever to coming together.

Signs of a growing associational authority among individual churches are also evident from the 1774 Charleston Association minutes. In the judgment of the messengers, the account of Linch's Creek Church was "very confused" and therefore unacceptable. It was agreed that the Rev. Evan Pugh would act as an official representative of the Association to clear the matter up. He was to "visit them, enquire into their state, and report their case at our next meeting." Pugh was further voted on to be the Charleston Association's messenger to the Association at the High Hills of Santee.

According to Hart's early hopes, the Baptist Association would drive the founding of educational institutions. At this 1774 meeting a plan was presented to fund the establishment of Rhode Island College, with Hart and David Williams appointed to forward all monies collected to the college treasurer. A committee was then appointed to urge the other Baptist associations of America to follow the same fundraising plan. By 1774 Hart's Association had also adopted formal documents to regulate the beliefs and behavior within the institution. The *Charleston Confession*, a lightly edited

---

[43] The Baptist sense of community also extended beyond the colonies. The Philadelphia Association had issued a similar call in 1761, requesting Morgan Edwards and Peter Peterson Vanhorn to "revive and maintain an annual correspondence with the board of Baptist ministers at London, or elsewhere" (Gillette, *Minutes*, 83).

version of the *Philadelphia Confession*, would stake out the doctrinal boundaries; the *Summary of Church Discipline* served as their manual for church order. At the 1774 meeting Hart was charged to determine the number of subscribers for printed copies and called to "put the work to the press" by the first of July. Money was tight, so he was "to print only the number that may be subscribed for."

Finally, the Association formalized plans for the next year's meeting: the first Sunday in February. Hart was appointed to preach the annual sermon, a duty he would fulfill many times over the course of his ministry. The annual sermon to the Association was a kind of rallying cry for Baptists, emphasizing a contended point of doctrine or stirring the churches to some particular united action. Pelot would serve as the alternate "in case of failure." While a meeting of eight messengers from three churches (plus three guests) does not seem overwhelmingly impressive, it signaled that the plans for intuitionalism Hart had set in motion in 1751 had progressed significantly; there was now a fully functioning Baptist denomination in the South.

Founding the Charleston Association endures as Oliver Hart's salient contribution to American history. In an era of religious institution-building across America, Hart was the visionary who saw in the four struggling Particular Baptist churches of South Carolina in 1749 the potential for an organized, energetic Baptist denomination that could duplicate in the South the Philadelphia Association's success in the North: establishing orthodoxy, training ministers, supporting frontier missions, and advancing revival. The birth and growth of Christian institutions like the Charleston Association between 1680 and 1760 constituted a critical step in what Patricia Bonomi has called the "stabilization" of religion in American life, and what Jon Butler has called "the Christianizing of the American people."[44] In a telling comment about the strength of America's Dissenting denominations, the Massachusetts Anglican minister Henry Caner complained in the late 1760s, "We are a Rope of Sand; there is no union, no authority among us; we cannot even summon a Convention for a united Counsell and advance, while the Dissenting ministers have their Monthly, Quarterly, and Annual Associations, Conventions, &c., to advise, assist, and support each other."[45] The proliferation of vigorous, collective denominational institutions like

[44] Bonomi, *Under the Cope of Heaven*, 221. Here she identifies the seventeenth century as the era of "transplantation," the eighteenth century as the era of "stabilization," and holds off the period of "modernization," or a move toward secularism in American life, until the nineteenth century.

[45] Butler, *Awash in a Sea of Faith*, 197.

124　OLIVER HART AND THE RISE OF BAPTIST AMERICA

the Charleston Association was one major reason why America struck early nineteenth-century visitors like Alexis de Tocqueville and Michel Chevalier as an extraordinarily religious place.[46]

The founding of the Charleston Association also stands as an important reminder that the interdenominational cooperation of the Great Awakening did not dilute the various evangelical groups' commitment to their distinctives, nor did it quench their desire for denomination-building. Baptists, Anglicans, Presbyterians, and Methodists might strategically work together in activities specifically focused on producing conversions, but these occasions were brief and fleeting. Rather, as Philip Mulder argues, each of these groups subsequently "particularized and denominationalized" the Great Awakening for their own purposes. By the end of the eighteenth century these groups would engage in fierce competition for the American population with a "controversial spirit."[47] Oliver Hart has been called for good reason "less a precisionist Baptist than a revivalist and moral reformer," but his ambition to create a thriving Baptist denomination in the South and beyond should not be undersold.[48] Hart lacked the edgy personality and strident tone of later generations of separatist Baptists, and he never lost his appreciation for non-Baptist evangelicals. But he was as passionate about advancing the Baptist interest in America as Francis Asbury was about his Methodists.

Founding the Charleston Association in 1751 represented another important move toward the creation of a national, American Baptist denomination. It signaled that Baptists in the South had stabilized, as those in the middle colonies had earlier in the eighteenth century. They now could turn their attention to developing organizations that would allow them to support missionaries, found colleges and seminaries, and undertake large benevolent enterprises. Regional Baptist associations would continue to proliferate through the rest of the eighteenth century. These would in turn enable Baptists to form a chain of communication from Georgia to Maine, giving them the sense that they were part of something much larger than their own local churches or regional associations, eventually leading to the creation of a single denomination that spanned the nation and rivaled that of any of their Protestant neighbors. But these events still lay in the distant future from Charleston in 1751.

[46] Bonomi, *Under the Cope of Heaven*, 217–22.
[47] Mulder, *A Controversial Spirit*, 12.
[48] Kidd, *Great Awakening*, 257.

# 6

# "Every day brings fresh wonders!"

## The 1754 Charleston Revival

Four years into his Charleston ministry, Oliver Hart had substantial cause for satisfaction. In a short span of time he had stabilized the foundering Charleston Baptist Church and successfully organized the South's first Baptist association. Yet the morning of Monday, August 5, 1754, found Hart in a gloomy frame. "I do this morning feel myself Opprest under a sense of my Barrenness," he complained to his diary. He was busy enough with the church, but he feared that he was simply going through the motions: "Alas, what do I do for God? I am indeed employed in his Vineyard, but I feel to little purpose; I feel the Want of the Life and Power of religion in my Own Heart; this Causes such a Languor, and faintness in all my duties to God."[1]

Hart's complaint was characteristic of the piety of the Great Awakening: formal religious activity meant nothing if it was not connected to a passionate, personal relationship with God; this alone constituted "true religion" and "the one thing needful."[2] As Hart put it elsewhere, "It is internal, spiritual experimental religion only, that will be of any avail—the religion of the heart—to this the Lord looks—this he requires—'My son, give me thine heart [Proverbs 23:26].'" Throughout the 1740s Hart had listened to revivalists like Gilbert Tennent reserve their most blistering attacks for mere "formalists," who were denounced as "old secure Professors" carrying on a "dead dry Round of Duties" like the Pharisees of Jesus's day.[3] In many ways, it was the centrality of the felt experience of the indwelling Holy Spirit that separated revivalist Protestants from those who stood on the outside of the movement.[4]

---

[1] Hart, August 5, 1754, Hart MSS, JBDML.

[2] See Hindmarsh, *The Spirit of Early Evangelicalism*, 1–6.

[3] See Gilbert Tennent, *The Righteousness of the Scribes and Pharisees Considered* (Boston, MA: 1741). For a recent discussion of the effect such preaching had on established churches in New England, see Winiarski, *Darkness Falls on the Land of Light*, esp. 367–525.

[4] For the centrality of the personal experience of the Holy Sprit in George Whitefield, see Kidd, *George Whitefield*, 35–36, and Hindmarsh, *The Spirit of Early Evangelicalism*, 33–43.

*Oliver Hart and the Rise of Baptist America*. Eric C. Smith, Oxford University Press (2020). © Oxford University Press.
DOI: 10.1093/oso/9780197506325.001.0001

126 OLIVER HART AND THE RISE OF BAPTIST AMERICA

As Hart saw it, nothing exposed his own decayed spirituality more clearly than his daily calendar. Aspiring to fill each moment of his allotted time on earth with constructive activity, he groaned over what a "poor manager of my time" he had lately been. The model Christian, he believed, awoke early to meet with God in private devotion before stepping out of doors to serve God in the world. Sleeping in was an embarrassing indulgence of the flesh, and Hart's recent failures to rise before dawn weighed heavily on his conscience: "Alas! I am frequently upon my Bed, when I Ought to be upon my knees. To my Shame, sometimes the Sun appears in the Horizon; and begins his Daily Course; before I have paid my tribute of Praise to God; and perhaps while I am Indulging myself in Inactive Slumbers upon my Bed." A truly devoted believer subordinated bodily care for spiritual matters, even if that meant missing sleep or skipping meals. "Oh Wretched Stupidity!" Hart cried. "Oh that for time to come I may be more active for God."[5] Examples of these kinds of complaints are legion among early evangelicals. Joseph Fish (1705–1781), a Congregational minister in Stonington, Connecticut, lamented in 1741 his "wretched Aversion to Duty, To examination To prayer and Everything that is spiritually Good." He despised "This flat Calm! This Cursed Case and Insensibility of my Soul!" and condemned himself as a "*poor, sleepy, Dead, Lifeless* Creature, Fit for nothing but to be Turned Into Hell, and Quickened by its Flames."[6] For eighteenth-century Protestants emerging from the Puritan spiritual tradition, the private diary was the closest counterpart to a Roman Catholic confessional booth at their disposal. This morning Hart used it to unload his overwhelming sense of spiritual failure.

Yet the evangelical diary also served as an altar of covenant renewal, the place where pious vows were made to be more and to do more for God's glory. Thus in the same paragraph, he transitioned from despair to determination. "I would Resolve to be a better manager of my Time than I have hitherto been," he declared. He then proceeded to unfold his new plan for focused and fruitful service, from the moment he crawled out of bed until he collapsed there again that night. With God's help, Hart proposed to

---

[5] Hart, August 5, 1754, Hart MSS, JBDML.

[6] William S. Simmons and Cheryl L. Simmons, eds., *Old Light on Separate Ways: The Narragansett Diary of Joseph Fish, 1765–1776* (Hanover, NH: University Press of New England, 1982), 6–8; see also Winiarski, *Darkness Falls on the Land of Light*, 200–202.

"EVERY DAY BRINGS FRESH WONDERS!" 127

Rise Earlier in the Mornings; to be sooner with thee in Secret Devotion; and oh, that I may be more Devout therein! I would be more Engag'd in my Studies; grant, O Lord that I may Improve more thereby! And when I go out, Enable me better to Improve my Visits; that I always may leave a Savour of divine things behind me. When I go to thy House in order to Speak for thee, may I always go fraught full with Divine things and be Enabled faithfully and feelingly to dispense the Word of Life. In a word, I would begin, and End, every Day with thee; Teach me to Study thy Glory in all I do, and will thou also be with me in the Night Watches; teach me to Meditate on thee, upon my bed, and may I Sleep for thee; and Desire no more than Nature Requires, fit me for thy Service. Thus, Teach me to Number my Days that I may Apply my Heart unto Wisdom.[7]

In years to come, his friends pointed to this diary entry as the quintessential text for understanding Oliver Hart's life. (Richard Furman would quote it entirely at Hart's memorial service.) While his proposal of twenty-four-hour consecration to God may have been naively ambitious, it was sincere. Hart's private spiritual struggles in the fall of 1754 would figure significantly in the development of American Baptists and more broadly the expansion of evangelical Christianity in the colonial South. These "virtuous resolutions and pious breathings of soul" launched him and the Charleston Baptists into an unprecedented season of revival. Within days of this entry Hart would have his chance to learn what it meant to serve God day and night.

\*

Though the First Great Awakening is commonly isolated to the explosive years of 1740–41, the 1750s continued to be a decade of revival for America's Baptists, especially in the South, starting with the Particular Baptists, such as Hart.[8] The South's Particular Baptists have typically been characterized as "quiet, well mannered folk who were not active proselytizers," resisting revivalism until long after the Separate Baptists arrived in the later 1750s.[9]

---

[7] Hart, August 5, 1754, Hart MSS, JBDML.

[8] Jon Butler famously argued that the Great Awakening was an "interpretative fiction" invented by nineteenth-century Christian historians, and the actual event was nothing more than "a short-lived Calvinist revival in New England during the early 1740s." See Jon Butler, "Enthusiasm Described and Decried: The Great Awakening as Interpretative Fiction," *Journal of American History* 69, no. 2 (September 1982): 323–24.

[9] Donald G. Matthews, *Religion in the Old South* (Chicago: University of Chicago Press, 1977), 23. This is the picture of Lumpkin's *Baptist Foundations in the South*, for years the standard work on colonial Baptists in the South. Other influential works that focus on the Baptist scene in Virginia include

128    OLIVER HART AND THE RISE OF BAPTIST AMERICA

This conclusion is largely based on the tendency to focus on Virginia in southern colonial studies, where the Separates found their Particular Baptist counterparts to be few, insular, and suspicious. But in recent years scholars have traveled deeper into the colonial Lower South, where they have found a rich heritage of revivalism among Particular Baptists before the Separates arrived.[10] No figure was more important in this movement than Oliver Hart, and no document more significant for understanding it than his 1754 diary.[11]

*

The earliest sign of revival downpour was like the rising of a cloud no bigger than a man's hand on a clear day. It all began on Saturday, August 10, a Preparation Day for the Charleston Baptists before receiving the Lord's Supper the next morning. Hart had invited John Stephens over from Ashley River to preach to his congregation. As with many denominations that observed communion on an occasional basis, these "sacramental seasons" were treated with serious care. Hart recalled that Stephens "spoke with a good Degree of freedom" about "those provisions made in the Supper of the Lamb" from Revelation 19:9. The Supper of the Lamb was the victory feast of Christ and his people that would mark the consummation of God's Kingdom at the end of history; Stephens noted that the humble meal the Charleston Baptists would share on the morrow foreshadowed that heavenly banquet. The glorious prospect seemed to carry him away. "Lord grant that we may partake thereof when we come to sit down at thy Table!" he exclaimed. His experience the next day did not disappoint, as he noted an unusual awareness of God's presence in worship. "Oh may a sense of the mercy's of God Receiv'd this Day Abide by me! I preach'd twice, and Afterwards Administered the Lord's Supper, the Lord stood by me and encourag'd me in his Work, and particularly in breaking Bread, the Lord broke in with much Sweetness upon my Soul," he wrote in his diary.[12]

The "sweet" sense of the Lord's presence at the Lord's Table was a common experience for the Great Awakening's participants. The promise of holding table fellowship with the risen Christ, as well as the New Testament's call to

Isaac, *The Transformation of Virginia*, and Wesley M. Gewehr, *The Great Awakening in Virginia, 1740–1790* (Durham, NC: Duke University Press, 1930).

[10] For an extended argument on this point, see Smith, *Order and Ardor*.
[11] For an analysis of Hart's diary as part of the era's popular "revival narrative" genre, see Smith, *Order and Ardor*, 52–70.
[12] Hart, diary, August 10–11, 1754, Hart MSS, SCL.

"EVERY DAY BRINGS FRESH WONDERS!" 129

examine oneself spiritually before partaking, made communion an apt vehicle for personal and corporate renewal throughout the revivals.[13] The Presbyterian Samuel Blair reported of a woman in his church that "the Sun of Righteousness at last broke out upon her to the clear Satisfaction and unspeakable Ravishment of her Soul, at a Communion Table," so that it "seem'd to her that she was almost all Spirit, and that the Body was quite laid by; and she was sometimes in Hopes that the Union would actually break, and the Soul get quite away."[14] A Charleston Congregationalist minister named Josiah Smith (1704–1781) felt like he was "eating Bread in the Kingdom of Heaven" when he served communion at George Whitefield's Bethesda Orphanage in 1744.[15] A Lyme, Massachusetts, Congregationalist, Jonathan Parsons (1705–1776), also oversaw an awakening among his young people at the Lord's Table in 1742, on a day he called "our Penticost." Serving three hundred that day, Parsons remarked that "God pour'd out his Spirit in a wonderful Measure," while many moaned and wept over their sins, and others trembled "as tho' they heard the Thunderings and seen the Lightnings from the thick Cloud." Parsons assured his fearful people that the Table proclaimed the "rich Treasures" of God's grace to them in Christ, leading to a worshipful scene of communion. Afterward he said, "I could not but think that the Lord Jesus was come to his Table, and feasting their Souls with his Love."[16]

Hart shared this intimate view of the Lord's Table. It was a place where, as Whitefield had declared at a great Scottish Presbyterian sacramental season, the believer was "one with Christ, and Christ with them." As Christian spiritual writers had for centuries, Hart regularly turned to the romantic imagery of the Song of Songs when preparing for communion, where Solomon's love for his bride typified Christ's love for the believer. Some of his favorite sermon texts for these occasions included "Because of the savour of thy good ointments thy name is as ointment poured forth, therefore do the virgins love thee" (Song of Solomon 1:3); "Draw me, we will run after thee: the king hath brought me into his chambers: we will be glad and rejoice in thee, we will remember thy love more than wine: the upright love thee" (1:4); and "He brought me to the banqueting house, and his banner over me was love"

---

[13] For examples of the Lord's Supper figuring prominently in the Great Awakening, see Kidd, *George Whitefield*, 164–68; Leigh Eric Schmidt, *Holy Fairs: Scotland and the Making of American Revivalism* (Grand Rapids, MI: Eerdmans, 2001), esp. 50–68.

[14] Schmidt, *Holy Fairs*, 115–17.

[15] Kidd, *Great Awakening*, 80.

[16] *Christian History*, July 7, 1744, 2:136–39; see Kidd, *Great Awakening*, 110.

(2:4).[17] Across the South, outsiders would frequently express discomfort with the amorous language that Baptist men and other evangelicals applied to their relationship with God, as yet another sign of revivalist enthusiasm and unmanliness.[18] But the intimacy with God created by the indwelling Spirit was fast becoming a hallmark of evangelical religion in the region. From what Hart could tell, he had not been alone in his heightened enjoyment of God at the Table. "Others also met the Lord at his Table. I believe it was a good Day to many of the Lord's People for which all Praise be unto his Holy Name," he wrote with satisfaction.[19]

After leaving the meetinghouse, Hart gathered "many" of these same people in a private home, where he "expounded" a chapter of the Bible, again with a sense of "great freedom and sweetness." The in-home meetings outside the church's regular gathering times had been an essential measure for promoting revival since Philip Jacob Spener's German Pietist movement in the seventeenth century. Jonathan Edwards had utilized this vehicle in the Northampton revivals of 1734–35, as reported in his widely read *Faithful Narrative of a Surprising Work of the Spirit of God* (1737), and inspired countless ministers to follow his example. The Congregationalist Nicholas Gilman (1708–1748), for instance, followed a pattern among the youth of Exeter, New Hampshire, in 1741, which Hart would use among the Charleston youth in the fall of 1754.[20] Hart was thus working from a well-established template for stoking revival fires. His Monday morning melancholy had vanished after a Sabbath basking in God's presence. "Surely Religion is Good, and a pleasant thing it is to be truly Religious," he sighed happily. His mood, always so closely linked to his perception of the Holy Spirit's activity in his ministry, would remain upbeat for the next three months.[21]

\*

On the following Sunday, Hart voiced for the first time a growing pastoral burden for the youth of the church. The spiritual condition of young people had been a particular concern throughout the Great Awakening, beginning

[17] Oliver Hart, Sermon Register, Hart papers, SCL.

[18] Lindman, *Bodies of Belief*, 65–67; Heyrman, *Southern Cross*, 206–17; Brekus, *Sarah Osborne's World*, 111–12, 116.

[19] Hart, August 11, 1754, Hart MSS, JBDML.

[20] See Winiarski, *Darkness Falls on the Land of Light*, 161–64. For more on the use of Pietistic small groups among the early evangelicals, see John Walsh, "Religious Societies: Methodist and Evangelical 1738–1800," in *Voluntary Religion*, edited by W. J. Sheils and Dianna Wood, Studies in Church History (New York: Oxford University Press, 1986), 279–302.

[21] Hart, August 7, 10, 11, 1754, Hart MSS, JBDML.

with Edwards's *Faithful Narrative*.[22] By refusing to sprinkle the infants of its members for baptism, Baptist churches highlighted the necessity of each child's personal response to God in repentance and faith, but few of the Charleston Baptist youth had made this crucial step. Hart prepared his Sunday afternoon sermon with the Charleston teenagers in mind, selecting a hard-hitting text from Ecclesiastes: "Remember now thy Creator in the days of thy youth, while the evil days come not, nor the years draw nigh, when thou shalt say, I have no pleasure in them" (Ecclesiastes 12:1). Hart's blunt message seemed to land. He commented afterward, "The Lord gave me great freedom blessed be his Name. Found my heart much drawn out in the Afternoon after the Conversion of Young People. Lord take thine own Work, into thine Own Hands." Again Hart supplemented the church's regular services with a smaller gathering that night, this time in his own home. As he expounded Psalm 84 to his wife, children, and slaves, he noted that "several friends" were also present. These extra religious meetings were about to become a regular feature of Hart's nightly schedule.[23]

As Hart closed his diary entry for the day, his language took on a new ebullience: "Afterwards went to Rest: my Soul being much Refresh'd. Glory to God!" Though he did not say so explicitly, he could sense that God was now stirring in a special way.[24] It is not difficult to hear in his diaries echoes of the tone and vocabulary of Whitefield's *Journals*. Aside from Hart's Baptist mentors, no single individual seems to have made a more profound impact on him than the itinerant, whom Hart seems to mimic, whether consciously or unconsciously, throughout his 1754 diaries. This was not unique to Hart, of course. Whitefield's autobiography, journals, and printed sermons were among the colonies most widely read literature in the mid-1700s, prompting untold numbers of Protestant ministers to adopt not only his preaching style, itinerating methods, and introspective piety, but even the very style of his language.[25]

*

[22] For the evangelical fascination with "precocious displays of piety exhibited by the young," see Heyrman, *Southern Cross*, 77–86.

[23] Hart, August 18, 1754, Hart MSS, JBDML. Here again the similarities of Hart's revival measures and those of the Congregationalist Nicholas Gilman in Exeter, New Hampshire, are striking. See Winiarski, *Darkness Falls on the Land of Light*, 161–63.

[24] Hart, August 18, 1754, Hart MSS, JBDML.

[25] Winiarski, *Darkness Falls on the Land of Light*, 198–203.

# 132 OLIVER HART AND THE RISE OF BAPTIST AMERICA

The next morning, Monday, August 19, Hart drew away for quiet reflection. He had never struggled to come up with sermon material before, but the growing demand for impromptu addresses left him gasping to keep pace. He needed a deeper reservoir of spiritual wisdom from which to draw, which meant he simply had to spend more time studying the Bible. This led him to make a new resolution:

> Having been Convinc'd for a Considerable time past, of the Necessity of a Larger, & better acquaintance with; and a more copious knowledge of, the Word of God, I came to a Resolution this Morning, with the Permission, and Assistance of God, to Read ten Chapters every Day, (at least for a time, or till I see an inconveniency arising from it) allowing for times to Travel, and unforeseen events. According to this Resolution I began the New Testament this Morning purposing first to read over that; and then to begin with the Old Testament, and may the Lord grant that I may Read to Advantage.

This new proposal stands in contrast to the emotional pledge he had made two weeks earlier. The reasonable and practical qualifications he added to his Bible-reading commitment suggest he no longer saw himself as scrambling out of a spiritual crisis, but as managing a surprising work of God. He would receive ample opportunity to share the fruit of his new study plan that very week.[26]

The next night, "several Young people" showed up at Hart's house to hear him expound from the Bible. Their unrelenting interest in spiritual things prompted him to admit, for the first time, "I believe that some of them are under some Awakening." It was a thrilling discovery for Hart, who sometimes labored for months at a time without successfully rousing an unconverted listener. Still, an awakening was only a beginning. An "awakened" individual was now alert to his or her separation from God, but these impressions were subject to wear off at any moment. They must be urged to "close with Christ" immediately; Hart knew he must seize the opportunity before him. He prayed, "Oh! May the Lord Carry on his Work in their Hearts; may Conviction End in Conversion, and may none of those Awakened turn back again."[27]

---

[26] Oliver Hart, diary, August 19, 1754, Hart MSS, JBDML.

[27] Oliver Hart, diary, August 20, 1754, Hart MSS, JBDML. For the stages of conversion for eighteenth-century Baptists and evangelicals, see Lindman, *Bodies of Belief*, 52–70, and Goen, *Revivalism and Separatism*, 12–17. A more thorough analysis is found in Cohen, *God's Caress*.

"EVERY DAY BRINGS FRESH WONDERS!"    133

Hart increased his special-called meetings. In addition to his stated Wednesday afternoon lecture, he held private gatherings for inquirers the next three nights. As he saw it, the more he exposed the young people to the gospel, the greater opportunity the Spirit had to work. After Friday's meeting he expressed both fatigue and exhilaration in his diary: "I find when God gives me a Heart to Work for him, he also finds me Work to do: I have for some-time Past felt a love for Expounding, and have had frequent Opportunities so to do. This Evening several People came to my House with a Desire to receive some Spiritual Instruction; which gave me an Opportunity of Spiritualizing blind Bartimaeus; case, I hope to some Advantage." The story of Christ giving physical sight to a blind beggar provided a ready-made analogy for the spiritual conversion Hart's listeners needed. Again Whitefield's influence is apparent; the itinerant loved to draw his listeners into Bible stories to help them encounter Christ and had published a sermon on "Blind Bartimaeus" in 1740.[28] Yet Hart was also beginning to feel the weight of guiding these seeking souls aright. "The Priests Lips are to Retain knowledge, and unto them (the Means) are the people to seek for Wisdom. Lord give me the Wisdom which is from above! That I may teach my people thy fear," he prayed. Despite his pastoral trepidation, the crowds at the meetings were growing. "Blessed be God!" Hart exclaimed. "I have more Reason to believe that some of our Young people are Concerned for their Souls, and it may be that the Revival may prove to be more Extensive than first Expected. Lord grant that many may be Awakened to a sense of their Misery, and Enabled to fly to the Rock of Ages for Refuge."[29]

*

On Monday, August 26, Hart learned of the awakening's first convert. Her name was Margaret Mageay, whom he described as "a Young Woman who hath liv'd in my House almost two years." Apparently Margaret was Hart's slave, someone he considered a member of his household. She would have been included in all of the Hart family prayers and worship gatherings, where Hart observed that she had "been for a long season under some Considerable Concern of Soul." The conversion process had apparently been both emotionally and physically draining for Margaret, but after a protracted struggle,

---

[28] Sermon available in George Whitefield, *The Sermons of George Whitefield*, edited by Lee Gattis (Wheaton, IL: Crossway, 2012), 1:453–66. On Whitefield's sermons from gospel narratives, see Kidd, *George Whitefield*, 155.

[29] Hart, August 23, 1754, Hart MSS, JBDML.

## 134 OLIVER HART AND THE RISE OF BAPTIST AMERICA

she had now "got Comfort." She was not alone. A "Mrs. Stillman" also informed Hart that her son, Samuel, had "also got comfort." Hart resolved to follow up with both young people that day. For now, the mere news of conversion contributed to the building excitement of the revival. In fact the use of information networks, whether word of mouth or print media, played a crucial role throughout the Great Awakening, creating a sense of heightened expectation that God was about to do "here" what he had done "there." As Jonathan Edwards himself remarked, "There is no one thing that I know of, that God has made such a means of promoting his work amongst us, as the news of others' conversion."[30] On receiving news of Margaret and Samuel, Hart rejoiced, "Blessed be God for this Work now going on. Oh, that these may be the first fruits of a far greater Harvest!"[31]

. When Hart interviewed Margaret that night, he found her "able to give a Clear Account how the Lord Manifested himself to her Last Night." Critical to her story was the experience of having a Scripture verse impressed on her mind. She recalled having the words of Jeremiah 31:3, "I have Loved Thee with an Everlasting Love," "set home with so much Light, and Evidence, that she could not avoid taking Comfort from them." She had heard this verse read aloud from the Bible before, but when it arose spontaneously to her memory, the promise seemed to carry more force, as though God's Spirit was personally speaking to her in that moment. This reliance on Bible verses darting into the mind was by now a commonplace in colonial revivals. Jonathan Edwards had observed this phenomenon repeatedly in the Northampton revival of 1734–35. "There is often in the mind some particular text of Scripture, holding forth some evangelical ground of consolation; sometimes in a multitude of texts, gracious invitations and promises flooding in one after another, filling the soul more and more with comfort and satisfaction," Edwards wrote.[32] Whitefield too held up such experiences in his *Journals*, and numberless evangelicals had since taken comfort from hearing God personally speak to them. But by 1754 "impulsive Bible verses" had become one of the most divisive issues in the revivals. Antirevivalist critics viewed testimonies like Margaret's as nothing but feverish enthusiasm, a classic example of radical mysticism. The Congregationalist Josiah Cotton (1680–1756) considered it "the quintessence of Quakerism."[33] Biblical impulses were viewed as

[30] Edwards, *Faithful Narrative*, 176. On this theme, see Lambert, *Inventing the "Great Awakening,"* 143–79, and Noll, *The Rise of Evangelicalism*, 115–19.
[31] Hart, August 26, 1754, Hart MSS, JBDML.
[32] Edwards, *Faithful Narrative*, 172.
[33] Winiarski, *Darkness Falls on the Land of Light*, 233–44.

"EVERY DAY BRINGS FRESH WONDERS!"   135

dangerous because they replaced the authority of the preached Word of God with something like "new revelations," encouraging men and women to act on subjective impressions rather than on reason submitted to God's revelation. They gave recipients an inflated sense of self, as though they were "special favourites of God." Individuals who believed they were acting on God's personal directive could also commit foolish or even immoral acts, such as the notorious "marrying exercise" or what one shocked observer described as "all manner of baudy talk as can be thought of they will cuss and sweir and every thing that is bad."[34] Yet despite these dangers, the antirevivalist Charles Chauncy sneered that one "had as good reason with the wind" as to try to reason with those caught up in the thrill of hearing directly from God.[35]

It is interesting to note that Hart, committed to the Particular Baptist reverence for biblical preaching and the unique authority of the Bible, did not discourage Margaret's experience. By 1754 revivalists who had initially celebrated Bible impulses had backed away from their earlier endorsements. In the hands of radicals like Hugh Bryan and the New England itinerant James Davenport (1716–1757), following Bible impulses had created precisely the kind of chaos that antirevivalists had warned against. Both Edwards and Whitefield had by this point retreated to a more moderate position on the topic, with Edwards publishing three works in the 1740s checking the unbridled enthusiasm he had expressed in *A Faithful Narrative*.[36] Hart would have known all this; he had just been with Whitefield in Charleston earlier that year. The Philadelphia Association would take the same stance against Bible impulses in 1761, declaring, "The Holy Scriptures we profess to be our full, sufficient, and only rule of faith and obedience, and caution all to beware of every impulse, revelation, or any other imagination whatever, inconsistent with, or contrary to, the holy Scriptures, under the pretence of being guided by the Spirit."[37] Yet as Hart noted how "Serene and Comfortable" Margaret now was, and "in a Humble and Holy frame of Soul," it seems the initial excitement of confronting revival overwhelmed his reservations about

[34] Heyrman, *Southern Cross*, 183; for examples of the "marrying exercise" among early Methodists, see Shipp, *History of Methodism in South Carolina*, 275–76.

[35] Charles Chauncy, *Enthusiasm described and caution'd against* (Boston, 1742), 5.

[36] Edwards's three works are *The Distinguishing Marks of a Work of the Spirit of God* (1741), *Some Thoughts concerning the Present Revival of Religion in New England* (1742), and *Treatise concerning the Religious Affections* (1746), all found in Jonathan Edwards, *The Great Awakening*, edited by C. C. Goen, vol. 4 of *The Works of Jonathan Edwards* (New Haven, CT: Yale University Press, 2009). On Whitefield's moderating phase, see Kidd, *Whitefield*, 204–24.

[37] Gillette, *Minutes*, 82.

the dangers of radicalism. He was playing with fire, and not for the last time that night.

While Hart conferenced with Margaret, five more young women entered the room, also "under some Awakenings." Hart responded in a manner altogether unexpected. Rather than take control of the counseling process, he turned to Margaret. At this critical moment he believed the fresh conversion testimony of his young female slave could prove more effective than his own counsel. He asked Margaret "if she could not now tell what God had done for her." She did not hesitate to comply. "Oh yes sir said she, I could now speak for God if the world was to hear; for I now have felt his Love and know that he hath Loved me with an Everlasting Love; Oh! What a night had I last night! What a sweet night!"[38]

The immediate, emphatic assurance Margaret expressed represented another characteristic of Great Awakening piety. As David Bebbington has famously pointed out, earlier generations of Puritan piety had emphasized that assurance was "rare, late, and the fruit of struggle in the experience of believers." Yet the early modern evangelicals believed assurance "to be general, normally given at conversion, and the result of simple acceptance of God's gift."[39] The source of this newfound confidence came, ironically, from the new currents of thought in the Enlightenment, which many evangelicals would have identified with secular humanism rather than with true religion. But Enlightenment thinkers were elevating the role of personal sense experience in arriving at knowledge as never before, seen in John Locke's assertion "All our knowledge is founded [on] *Experience.*" One could be confident about a reality that one had personally "sensed" or "felt."[40] Early evangelicals preached the possibility of an immediate, present salvation, captured in John Wesley's famous sermon *Salvation by Faith* (1739) or Edwards's *A Divine and Supernatural Light Immediately Imparted to the Soul by the Spirit of God* (1734). The message of an immediate, assured, personal salvation struck many listeners as a new and thrilling possibility. Experiential language abounds in evangelical testimonies of the period, and it shows up here in Margaret's words: because she had "felt" Christ's love, she "knew" that she was now born again, and this therefore emboldened her to "speak" with

[38] Hart, diary, August 26, 1754, Hart MSS, JBDML.

[39] Bebbington, *Evangelicalism in Modern Britain*, 43–47. Bruce Hindmarsh has recently provided a helpful discussion on both the novelty and precedent of this evangelical emphasis in *The Spirit of Early Evangelicalism*, 62–68.

[40] For a detailed discussion of the Enlightenment's impact on the evangelical doctrine of assurance, see Brekus, *Sarah Osborne's World*, 95–104.

confidence about her possession of salvation as a slave to a group of white women, though this possession was but a few hours old.

Margaret turned to one of the young women and continued her exhortation in the warmest of terms: "Oh Miss Betsy! Said she, Jesus Christ is Sweet, he is precious, had I known his Sweetness, said she, I would not have liv'd so long without him." Turning to another girl, Margaret cried, "Oh, Oh! Miss Nancy, Christ is Sweet! And since he hath had Mercy on such a vile Wretched Sinner as me, I am sure none need ever to Despair, Oh! Come to Christ! Come to Christ!'" Again Hart's approval of these proceedings is striking, especially when one considers how the Philadelphia Association Baptists had attempted to rein in the black woman at Abel Morgan's meeting and had regulated female Baptist speech later in the 1740s. But as Hart looked on, all he could think about was how the young women were "much Affected" by Margaret's speech and "Could no Longer Contain but Crying out, got up and went out of the house to Vent their grief."[41] The incident bears eloquent testimony to the egalitarian tendency of revival: a white, male, slave-owning, ordained minister deferring to his young, female slave as a spokesperson for the new birth. Admittedly, Margaret's exhortations were directed at other females, in the privacy of Hart's home, and under his supervision. It must also be considered that, as a participant in a coercive relationship, Margaret's testimony was complicated by her relationship to Hart as her master. Nevertheless Margaret discovered that night that evangelical religion gave her a voice in her community she had never before imagined, if only for a moment.

*

Meanwhile, Hart learned that Samuel Stillman's (1737–1807) mother had spoken prematurely about her son's conversion. The young man "seem'd to have some Comfort Yesterday Morning; but lost it in the Evening." Samuel had in fact been struggling for years to attain assurance of salvation. On this occasion, as he later recalled, his "mind was again solemnly impressed with a sense of [his] awful condition as a sinner." This conviction grew stronger and stronger. "My condition alarmed me," Samuel later wrote. "I saw myself without Christ and without hope. I found that I deserved the wrath to come, and that God would be just to send me to hell. I was now frequently on my knees, pleading for mercy. As a beggar I went, having nothing but guilt,

---

[41] Hart, diary, August 26, 1754, Hart MSS, JBDML.

138   OLIVER HART AND THE RISE OF BAPTIST AMERICA

and no plea but mercy."[42] In evangelical parlance, Samuel was experiencing the "terrors of the Law." Sinners like Samuel naturally saw themselves as already righteous before God; "it took a kind of violence to shatter this illusion," Hindmarsh writes, and for preachers like Hart, "the Law was their hammer." Only a thorough exposure to the perfect standard of God's holy Law could break the sinner's spirit of self-reliance and drive him to despair of ever saving himself.[43] On this occasion Hart swung true. The peace that had eluded Samuel on Monday was found on Wednesday afternoon; Hart preached from Matthew 1:21, "He shall save his people from their sins," and Samuel discovered assurance of his salvation. He shared afterward with Hart how he "now obtain'd a clear Sence of his Interest in Christ"; "he had now got Christ and felt the sweetness of his Love." Again the mystical language of experience and intimacy with Christ was prominent in conversion testimony from the Baptist young people. As Stillman reflected on how nearly he had skipped Hart's sermon, he was filled with awe. Hart recalled, "I had like to a missed, said he, going to meeting this afternoon, but I would not have mist for all the world." Unable to contain himself, Stillman turned to a neighbor to testify. "Oh said he, if you had but been there!"[44]

The stories of Margaret and Samuel demonstrate the wide range of individuals touched by the evangelical revival. If only briefly, the experience of the new birth had leveled the differences between an enslaved black female and a privileged white man. The ensuing years would demonstrate just how fleeting the experience had been. Stillman would enter ministry and develop into one of Hart's most celebrated protégés, as the pastor of the First Baptist Church in Boston. Margaret, presumably, would continue to work in Hart's house as a slave.

*

News of Margaret's and Samuel's conversions seemed to open the floodgates of revival within the church, with fresh stories of salvation experiences pouring in rapidly. "Every Day brings Fresh Wonders!" Hart marveled on August 29. "Learn'd this Evening that two persons, Viz: KB and Miss Betsey (^ has comfort since the Society last night)— KB met with Jesus last night,

[42] Samuel Stillman, *Select Sermons on Doctrinal and Practical Subjects* (Boston: Manning & Loring, 1808), vi.
[43] Lindman, *Bodies of Belief*, 57–58. For the preaching of the Law and the formation of the evangelical conscience, see Hindmarsh, *Spirit of Early Evangelicalism*, 180–203.
[44] Hart, August 27, 1754, Hart MSS, JBDML.

"EVERY DAY BRINGS FRESH WONDERS!"    139

and Miss Betsey this morning." As it had throughout the transatlantic revival, the sharing of personal conversion testimonies became a central feature of the Charleston awakening. Hart partially grounded the authenticity of the young people's experience in the fact they had their "mouth fill'd with Praises," as when KB declared, "Jesus Christ is Sweet." Hart now believed that six of the young people had been "brought clear." Later that day he learned of another, a twelve-year-old girl who claimed "she never could say that Jesus Christ Lov'd her till Yesterday: and she told me herself she hop'd Christ Lov'd her." If the key sign of awakening was a sudden realization of God's wrath, the defining mark of conversion was an overwhelming sense of Christ's redeeming love.[45]

As conversions multiplied, the Charleston awakening took a more noticeably emotional turn. The nightly meetings, at first marked by attentive solemnity, were now commonly interrupted by people "crying out" and being "melted down into tears." This was the case not only with young women, like those Margaret had counseled. A group of young men arrived at Hart's house one night "Deeply Concerned to Discourse with me about their Souls' Affairs." What Hart recalled most vividly was their overwhelming sense of personal sinfulness:

> Some Complained, and Cry'd out under a Sence of the Desperate Wickedness & Corruption of their own Hearts: of which they had such a Deep sense, that they seemed to Study to find out such words to express themselves Concerning it, as might set it forth in the strongest Terms.— Some were Crying out under a sense of sin; never were such a Company of great Sinners met together in the world, if they themselves might be Judges; but the most of them were Crying out for Jesus Christ; Oh give me Christ! Give me Christ! Oh if I had but Christ!

Desperate for relief, the young men turned to those who had already "come through" in conversion to "help them to Christ." Before long they could express themselves only by inarticulate moans. To outsiders, the soul-exercises evangelicals underwent during conviction created a spectacle that sometimes amused them and often unsettled them. It was especially disturbing to see white men displaying such emotional excesses in public; some opponents accused Baptists and other evangelicals of "feminizing" men. Others wondered

---

[45] Hart, August 29, 1754, Hart MSS, JBDML.

140  OLIVER HART AND THE RISE OF BAPTIST AMERICA

if ministers like Hart aimed to "first make mad those whom they intended to save."[46]

But Hart made no effort to stifle the boys' wailing. Instead he prayed, "Oh! the Groans and Sighs of these poor creatures; which coming from the Heart, penetrated Heaven's Gates, and I doubt not, Entred into the Ears of the Lord God of Sabbaoth: Lord hear their Cries! And give them a sence of their Interest in thy Love; for thy Son's sake Amen!" Like the Bible impulses, these demonstrative emotional responses had become a flashpoint during the Great Awakening, with many detractors eyeing them as so much attention-seeking delusion. But far from discouraging his young congregants, Hart marked their expressiveness as signs of God's Spirit at work. "Oh may these happy Days Long Continue; may this Work be much more Extensive! And may many have reason to Bless God for these Evening Meetings!" he exclaimed. "Many seem now to be under Soul Concern. there are some appearances of new ones Touch'd almost Every Evening." It seemed beyond question now: Hart was in the middle of a full-scale revival.[47]

*

Hart reveled in the heightened religious excitement at the moment, but later reflection on the excessive emotions and physicality of the Charleston youth also made him nervous. To be sure, there had been far more bizarre manifestations since Whitefield's revivals had begun than anything the Charleston youth had yet exhibited, from visions and dreams to encounters with Satan. And while Hart had vigorously promoted the awakening, he had stopped far short of the most drastic measures available to him: painting lurid pictures of hell, declaring specific individuals to be hell-bound, claiming apostolic powers of prophecy. Yet many conservatives would consider Hart to have already crossed a threshold into radicalism; by August 29 he was beginning to voice concerns of his own. "God Grant that not one of these your Creatures may be Deceived; if one Soul of them should Miscarry, it would be bad; but if it should all prove a Delusion, the Lord pity us! for it would be an Awful Case Indeed." It was as if Hart were consciously pulling himself back to a more moderate perspective, celebrating the freedom of God's Spirit in times of revival, while exercising caution against demonic counterfeits. Yes, Hart admitted, the Charleston awakening could all be a delusion. "But

[46] Heyrman, *Southern Cross*, 35–36; Lindman, *Bodies of Belief*, 64–66; Juster, *Disorderly Women*, 46–74.
[47] Hart, diary, August 26, 1754, Hart MSS, JBDML.

"EVERY DAY BRINGS FRESH WONDERS!" 141

I cannot preswade myself as Yet to think so, but if it should I hope the Lord will prevent its progress; but if it is his Work as I hope and believe it is, Lord Carry it on and Increase it for Thy Name's sake; & for Jesus' sake Amen & Amen." Of all his concerns, Hart seemed most worried about the sinister effects that leading a revival could have on his own soul. Perhaps he could feel himself being swept away in the excitement of it all. "And may the Good Lord keep me truly humble under such Honours Conferr'd upon me," he wrote. "I am afraid of Spiritual Pride." Even the blessing of revival carried the temptation of the deadly sin of self-reliance.[48]

The next day Hart still could not shake his misgivings: he feared that the devil was afoot among the Charleston Baptists. "Felt myself much opprest last night and this morning, under a fear that there may be too much of delusion in this Work going on. If this should be the Case, that Satan Should have a Hand in it, it would be Dreadful," he wrote. While Satan did not command the "nearly obsessive notice" in Hart's lived spirituality as he may have for some early evangelicals, Hart certainly believed in a literal supernatural devil who relentlessly opposed God's work, even through the appearance of revival.[49] His fears drove him to seek the guidance of one Mr. Moody, an older Christian whom Hart called "a good Old Disciple of Jesus Christ." This was the same title Whitefield had used for William Tennent in his *Journals*, indicating that Moody was Hart's elder, a seasoned Christian and observer of religious experience. After Hart gave Moody the details of what had transpired within the church, he advised Hart "not to be Discourag'd; but to Wait, and time would Discover how it was; but he thought, he had seen nothing in it but what might be look'd upon with a favourable Aspect, and as proceeding from the Motions of the Spirit of God." Moody took a realistic approach to revival: "When God Works, the Devil will Work too, and you need not wonder if all don't turn out Right." A mixture of dross with the gold was unavoidable and should not discount the value of the overall movement. It was not far from the position Edwards would take in his later writings on the revival and resonated with Hart and his other moderate revivalist cohorts in Charleston. He was relieved when the Reformed minister John J. Zubly joined their conversation and affirmed Moody's advice. Having "Receiv'd some Necessary Cautions, and Directions from this precious Old Disciple of Jesus Ct.," Hart

[48] Hart, August 29, 1754, Hart MSS, JBDML.
[49] Heyrman, *Southern Cross*, 52; Lindman, *Bodies of Belief*, 56–57. In *Southern Cross*, Heyrman argues that later evangelicals toned down their early focus on the devil's activity to become more palatable to Southern culture (28–76).

142    OLIVER HART AND THE RISE OF BAPTIST AMERICA

declared that he left "with [his] Hopes somewhat Strengthened." Still, he would continue to pray, and fret, about the genuine nature of the work to the end.[50]

\*

The revival continued several more weeks. Hart passed his days in visiting and counseling, occasionally stealing away to study or to write a few letters. His nights were spent preaching to crowded houses. At times the unrelenting pace took its toll on his body. "Slept but little last night, by Reason of my Labours Yesterday; which tired me very much," he wrote on September 2. Yet he wore his exhaustion as a badge of honor. The frenetic religious activity of evangelicals, sometimes termed "meeting mania," struck outsiders as yet another sign of feverish enthusiasm. But to Hart, Whitefield's model of burning the candle at both ends in God's service represented the epitome of Christian devotion. Hart quickly followed his complaint of fatigue by asserting, "Blessed be God, I can say, altho' I am at times weary in my Lord's work, yet I am not weary of it: and I hope I never shall. The more I am engag'd in it, the better I like it; the sweeter I find it! Felt but poorly all Day; oh may I remember my Disolution!" The work remained invigorating, and it took only one good night's rest to recharge Hart for another week of long hours. On September 9 he began the day with another Whitefieldian update: "Slept well last night, blessed be God! And found myself thereby much Refreshed; oh, may I be Enabled to lay out myself for God! I think I am willing to spend, and be spent, in his Service."[51]

\*

By late September it was time to prepare the new converts for baptism. For a Baptist, the immersion and admittance to communion of the new believers was the logical culmination of a revival movement aimed at filling the church with born-again men and women. Hart's interviews with each candidate, usually conducted in his home, provided him the opportunity to question each one about his or her personal experience of grace and grasp of basic doctrine. Margaret and Samuel, for instance, "Both gave Indubitable Evidences of a Work of Grace begun, and carrying on in their hearts. But as to their Doctrinal Knowledge, it is somewhat weak." Their lack of theological

[50]  Hart, August 30, 1754, Hart MSS, JBDML.
[51]  Hart, September 2, 9, 1754, Hart MSS, JBDML.

"EVERY DAY BRINGS FRESH WONDERS!" 143

precision did not discredit their conversions, but Hart set up another meeting to instruct them further in the fundamentals.[52] Sometimes the candidates grew shy before Hart's interrogations. When he "examined the young people round" on a Friday evening, he was disappointed that "most of them had their Mouths Shut up, so that I got but little from them." He prayed, "Lord open their mouths and their Lips shall Shew forth thy praise." At other times the baptismal interviews became the occasion for more conversions. As visitors listened to their young friends speaking about their souls on October 1, Hart reported, "at that time it pleased God to manifest his love to Miss S R. She was so full she could not help discovering of it to all present." This young woman would now take her place with the others in the baptismal waters.[53]

The day came on Thursday, October 10. Hart "Went over the River to Mr. Screven's in Company with most of my People." Here he asked the young converts to testify in public what they had shared with him in private: "Examined ten persons, all gave very good satisfaction: and most of them Spoke Surprisingly of what God had done for their Souls." With this done, Hart "Baptized them according to the primitive Mode, in the Name of the Father etc." Afterward, as he considered the long and dangerous road of discipleship that stretched out before them, he was driven again to prayer: "Lord, they have now made a good profession before many Witnesses; Oh, may they always Act Consistent thereto. Remember them under their particular circumstances: many of them are very young, and will be Expos'd to many temptations: most of them are of the female sex: and therefore their Case is perhaps more Dangerous: take them, O Lord; take them into thy peculiar care, and keep them as the Apple of thine Eye."[54] The work had been God's from the beginning, and God would have to carry it forward to the end.

*

The 1754 Charleston Baptist youth revival forms a little-known but important chapter in the ascendancy of Baptists and, more broadly, of evangelical Christianity in the colonial South. It reminds us that the Great Awakening continued to reverberate throughout America long after Whitefield's famous tour in 1739–41, in numerous small, localized revivals, some all the way down into the Lower South. Evangelicalism was not as late a

---

[52] For the typical Baptist process of examination, see Wills, *Democratic Religion*, 18–20.

[53] Hart, September 27, October 1, October 4, 1754, Hart MSS, JBDML. See also Lindman, *Bodies of Belief*, 58–59.

[54] Hart, October 10, 1754, Hart MSS, JBDML.

144    OLIVER HART AND THE RISE OF BAPTIST AMERICA

development in the South as many scholars have assumed; led by Hart, the Particular Baptists of the Charleston Association were among its lead promoters in the early 1750s.[55]

Hart was the most influential Particular Baptist revivalist in the South at this time, but he was not alone. At the Euhaw settlement his friend Francis Pelot was also working for awakening. Able to preach in both English and his native French, Pelot moved easily among immigrant settlers as he communicated his "truly evangelical" message. Not content with "delivering a little dry morality," Pelot "unfolded and applyed the great and glorious doctrines of the Gospel" and was careful to "rightly divide the word of truth and give the Saint and sinner their proper portion." He engaged in regular itinerant work, preaching to Baptists at Edisto and Hilton Head Island. He also worked with Whitefield when the evangelist swung through the Carolina Low Country. When the Euhaw Baptist Church dedicated its new meetinghouse in 1752, Whitefield preached the first sermon.[56]

Further west, Hart and Pelot's fellow Charleston Association minister Philip James of the Welsh Neck Church practiced an even more radical form of revivalism, one that included visions and dreams. In 1752 James had a mystical encounter with God through a dream, an experience he later related to the Baptist historian Morgan Edwards. At the age of fifty-two James suffered the loss of a favorite child. Overcome with grief, he "fell to the ground as if dead" and was carried to bed. Showing no signs of life for nearly an hour, his family gathered at his bedside, weeping and mourning. When James awoke nearly an hour later, he said, "Had you seen what I have seen you would not be in trouble about this dear little one." He informed his family, "The child now enjoys more happiness in one moment than compensates for all the miseries he endured for life and in the pangs of death also." James based his confidence on a tour of heaven he had just received:

My soul quitted my body [and] the resemblance of a man in black made towards me, and (frowning and chiding and wishing to die) took me up towards the sun, which filled me with fear. As I was ascending, a bright figure interposed and my black conductor was pushed off. The bright men

---

[55] Late dates for the rise of evangelicalism in the colonial South include Heyrman, *Southern Cross*, 9; Samuel S. Hill, ed., *Religion in the Southern States: A Historical Study* (Macon, GA: Mercer University Press, 1983); and John B. Boles, *The Great Revival: Beginnings of the Bible Belt* (Lexington: University Press of Kentucky, 1996).

[56] Hart, *Original Diary*, 7–9; Townsend, *South Carolina Baptists*, 39–40.

took me by the hand and said, "we go this way," pointing to the north. As we ascended, I saw a company of angels and my child among them, (clothed in white and in the full stature of a man) sing with them as the company passed by us, whereupon my bright conductor said "I am one of that company and must join them." And he quitted me and I found myself sinking fast till I came to my body.

For the next three months James "minded no worldly thing but was full of heavenly joy, and attentive only to spiritual concerns." He then died, truly, but the story of his visit to the afterlife lived on in his family, who recorded it in detail and signed it as witnesses.[57]

John Stephens too promoted revival on Ashley River during the 1750s, but "spirits" of a different sort eventually drew his attention away from religion. Morgan Edwards reported that an "unhappy fondness for liquor" drove Stephens from Ashley River pastorate. The Ashley River church records state that the church "being Mett Summoned" Stephens on August 22, 1768, and "admonished him for the Sin of Drunkenness." Stephens made "some Confessions" before the church and was allowed "the Use of the Pulpit for some time longer." But for this "Notorious Crime," it was "Unanimously declared" at the January 31, 1769, meeting that Stephens would no longer be their minister. The church would not survive beyond the Revolutionary War.[58] Morgan Edwards, who was known to overindulge himself from time to time, opined, "But has not a dumb spirit, a deaf spirit, an unclean spirit etc. been cast out? And who knows but Jamaica spirit will one day be exorcised out of this country where it makes such dreadful havock?"[59]

Baptists in the Philadelphia Association continued to reap rewards from the Great Awakening throughout the 1750s. In 1755, for example, the Association received five newly constituted churches: two in Pennsylvania, one in Baltimore, Maryland, and two more in Virginia. At this same 1755 meeting, the Association elected "one ministering brother from the Jerseys, and one from Pennsylvania, [to] visit North Carolina: the several churches to contribute to bear their expense." They also sent ministers to Cape May, New Jersey. In 1757 they received another new church in Newton, New Jersey, and sent two ministers to visit the inhabitants of Dutchess County, New York, in

---

[57] Edwards, *Materials towards a History of the Baptists*, 2:127–29.
[58] Kegley and Little, "Records of the Ashley River Baptist Church," 6–7, 14.
[59] Edwards, *Materials towards a History of the Baptists*, 2:126.

146    OLIVER HART AND THE RISE OF BAPTIST AMERICA

view of starting another. The next year the church gathered there would be admitted to the Association. This new decade of Baptist missions seemed to be a direct result of the numerical growth and activist vigor from the Great Awakening revivals. "Revive the things which are ready to die; and among other things revive Christian conversation; which is so profitable for mutual comfort, growth, and encouragement of religion," the Association wrote in the closing circular letter of the decade. "Labor to make your church fellowship every way useful to each other; watch over your own souls, and over one another for good; use the directions given by the Lord, in order to remove the plague of lukewarmness and indifference from you in the things of God, by prayer and holy practice."[60]

*

The most consequential Baptists revivalism of the 1750s, however, was welling up in the North, as the disruptive forces of the Great Awakening released by Whitefield the decade before continued to crumble the once unified Congregational establishment of New England. Radical supporters of the revival there found it intolerable to remain in churches that included apparently unregenerate men and women who opposed Whitefield's brand of religion. They covenanted to form new, revival-centered churches in which they "attempted to institutionalize many of the evangelist's most innovative, Spirit-centered beliefs, practices, and experiences."[61] Hundreds of these so-called Separate congregations formed in New England between 1740 and 1760. But as the Separate Congregationalists pursued the revival's ideal of a pure church, it was almost inevitable that many would conclude with the Baptists to admit only confessing believers into membership, and that sprinkling infants on the basis of their parents' faith only confused the issue. Besides being driven by the logic of a pure church, the Separates wished to be strict Biblicists; when it became clear that no Scriptural examples of infant baptism existed, "infant-sprinkling, which we called baptism, went away like the chaff of the summer threshing-floor," in the words of Separate Baptist Henry Fisk.[62] In some cases, as with the Separates of Sturbridge and Attleborough, Massachusetts, entire congregations "went to the Baptists" beginning in the late 1740s.[63]

[60] Gillette, *Minutes*, 76.
[61] Winiarski, *Darkness Falls on the Land of Light*, 365.
[62] Quoted in Backus, *History of New England*, 2:94.
[63] For the development of the Separate Baptists out of the Separate Congregational movement, see Goen, *Revivalism and Separatism*, 208–95.

# "EVERY DAY BRINGS FRESH WONDERS!" 147

Of all these Separate Baptists, none would prove more significant for the Baptist South than the fiery Shubal Stearns (1706–1771).[64] After experiencing the new birth under Whitefield's preaching, Stearns formed a Separate congregation at Tolland, Connecticut. Though "but a little man" and without much formal education, Stearns was sharp, gritty, and a powerful orator. "His voice was musical and strong," remembered Morgan Edwards, "which he managed in such a manner as, one while to make soft impressions on the heart, and fetch tears from the eyes in a mechanical way; and anon, to shake the very nerves and throw the animal system into tumults and purtutbations." Apart from his inimitable voice, Stearns could also control crowds with his eyes alone. There was "something very penetrating" in them, which some called an "evil eye" and compared to a rattlesnake transfixing his prey; grown men were known to sink to the ground under Stearns's gaze.[65] By 1751 the Stonington Baptist minister Wait Palmer had convinced Stearns of the Baptist position. Palmer organized a Separate Baptist congregation in Tolland and shortly ordained Stearns as the pastor. In 1753 Stearns's sister, Martha, and her husband, Daniel Marshall, followed him into the Separate Baptist fold. Soon thereafter Stearns made the momentous decision to leave New England for the populous Southern frontier, his soul "fired with zeal to carry light into these dark parts."[66] The Stearns and Marshall families met up north of Winchester, Virginia, and, after a brief stay, moved further south to Sandy Creek, North Carolina, in 1755. The radical revivalism of Stearns, Marshall, and the Separate Baptists would set the frontier ablaze in the second half of the eighteenth century, reshaping the American South in the process.

For a century the Baptist tribe to which Hart belonged had been known as Particular Baptists, to distinguish them from the non-Calvinist General Baptists. With the emergence of the Separate Baptists, they would take on the name of Regulars. The differences between Stearns's Separates and Hart's Regulars lay far more in their origins, worship styles, and cultural preferences than in any substantive doctrinal disagreements. Hart was a moderate revivalist who, in the heat of an awakening, flirted with the same radical practices characteristic of the Separates. Separates and Regulars

---

[64] For Stearns, see John Sparks, *The Roots of Appalachian Christianity: The Life and Legacy of Elder Shubal Stearns* (Lexington: University Press of Kentucky, 2005).

[65] Edwards, *Materials towards a History of the Baptists*, 2:93.

[66] Isaac Backus, *Church History of New England, from 1620 to 1804* (Philadelphia, 1844), 229.

148   OLIVER HART AND THE RISE OF BAPTIST AMERICA

would discover repeatedly over the next decade that, while many of their customs and emphases differed, their essential commitment to revivalism was the same, leading the two groups to unify in the South in the late 1770s. After this union, however, it would be Hart's brand of moderate revivalism that would come to define the new Baptist South into the nineteenth century.

# 7

# "Seals of my ministry"
## Training the Next Generation

It was February 26, 1759, at the Charleston Baptist meetinghouse. From the pulpit Oliver Hart looked out on the two young men whose ordination charge he had risen to deliver. The first was Samuel Stillman, converted five years earlier as a teenager in the Charleston Baptist youth revival. Stillman had immediately exhibited promise, organizing special meetings for his peers and leading them in prayer. As early as 1755 Hart eyed Stillman as an "extraordinary youth" and predicted that he would surely "come to be publicly useful to the Church of Jesus Christ."[1] Now Stillman had accepted a pastoral call on James Island, South Carolina. The second ordinand was an impressive young Englishman named Nicholas Bedgegood (1731–1774). Born at Thornbury, Gloucestershire, Bedgegood had been raised an Anglican and came to America to serve at George Whitefield's Bethesda Orphan House in Savannah, Georgia. There, while reading an Isaac Watts treatise defending infant baptism, Bedgegood was persuaded of Baptist principles, and was immersed by Hart in 1757. Now he sat with Stillman, for ordination to the pastoral post at Welsh Neck, South Carolina.[2]

Hart's ordination charge confronted him with his own inadequacy as a pastor. "Conscious of my own weakness and defects," he wondered aloud how he could "impose a charge, in which I have conducted so unworthily myself?" It was his theology of God's grace that emboldened him to continue. "But, I would not depreciate the grace of God, for it is by his grace I am what I am, and I trust that his grace bestowed upon me hath not been altogether in vain," Hart preached. In the room that very night were visible tokens of God's blessing: "No, blessed be God, some here present, (and among them one however of those now set apart to the great Work) are the fruit of my labours,

---

[1] Oliver Hart to John Hart, September 1755, Hart MSS, SCL.
[2] Townsend, *South Carolina Baptists*, 69; Benedict, *General History of the Baptist Denomination*, 2:180.

*Oliver Hart and the Rise of Baptist America.* Eric C. Smith, Oxford University Press (2020). © Oxford University Press.
DOI: 10.1093/oso/9780197506325.001.0001

150    OLIVER HART AND THE RISE OF BAPTIST AMERICA

the seals of my ministry, my joy and crown." For Hart, the supreme validation of his life's work was the individual men and women he led to the new birth; for some of these men, like Stillman, to then join him in "the most important work in the world" was even sweeter. As Hart moved into his second decade in Charleston, calling, training, and sending new Baptist pastors would become one of the most prominent features in his ministry.[3]

*

At the beginning of the 1760s Baptist ministers were still a rare commodity in the South. The Delaware Valley remained the Baptist center of gravity in colonial America; Virginia, the Carolinas, and Georgia, not the Bible Belt of today, were missions territories. Like other Baptist churches in the South, the Charleston congregation had petitioned Particular Baptist brethren in the Northern colonies and Europe to supply them with a competent preacher. New Baptist "works" were springing up across the Lower South through enterprising itinerants like Hart and Francis Pelot, but they subsisted on the occasional ministry of visiting preachers, sometimes going months or longer without hearing a sermon or receiving the ordinances. These individuals would either do without or would eventually defect to other denominations. If Baptists were to keep up with the South's population, which would grow faster than ever at the conclusion of the French and Indian War in 1763, they must begin to produce their own ministers.

From his earliest days in Charleston, Hart purposed to remedy this problem. He had been called through the discernment of his own local congregation in Pennsylvania, then trained by his pastor, Jenkin Jones, whose personal library furnished Hart's textbooks. Hart wanted to provide this kind of guided mentorship for aspiring preachers in South Carolina, but he also envisioned doing this on a larger scale. In 1750 Congregationalists could send their future ministers to Yale or Harvard, Anglicans to William and Mary, and Presbyterians to the College of New Jersey. Of these, only the College of New Jersey, founded as an evangelical-friendly school during the Great Awakening, was a realistic option for most Baptists. But few could afford the cost, and few saw the need. Hart had been raised fifteen miles from William Tennent's rustic Log College, which had trained a generation of Presbyterian revivalists, and the idea of "a school for the prophets" for Baptists preoccupied him from the beginning of his career.

[3] Hart, Sermon on 1 Timothy 4:16, Hart MSS, SCL.

"SEALS OF MY MINISTRY" 151

Hart knew he must start small, and Samuel Stillman's surrender to preach provided the opportunity to begin. In 1755 he launched a formal program of study he called the Baptist Religious Society, with the goal of assisting "pious young men in obtaining education for the public services of the church."[4] Two years later, he got the Charleston Association involved. At their 1757 annual meeting he asked the messengers "whether there could not be some method concluded upon, to furnish, with suitable degree of learning, those among us who appear to have promising gifts for ministry." The churches each pledged to contribute toward the purchase of a theological library for the Society, collecting a total of 133 pounds. (Half that amount came from the Charleston Church.) Hart, Pelot, and John Stephens would serve as trustees, with Hart acting as treasurer for the humble "education fund." Hart's Religious Society is considered "the first religious partnership among Baptists in America in the interest of religious education."[5]

*

Among the earliest students to enroll in the Society was Evan Pugh (1729–1802).[6] Pugh was born into a Quaker family in Matachin, Pennsylvania, in 1729 but relocated to Winchester, Virginia, as a boy, and later learned practical surveying from George Washington. While teaching school in North Carolina in 1754, he came under the influence of Baptist preaching and was converted to the Baptist way. He eventually made the acquaintance of John Gano, who recommended Pugh to the Charleston Association for acceptance in the Religious Society in 1759. Pugh considered the opportunity a signal mercy of God in his life. "The Lord has indeed done wonders for me, unworthy me!" Pugh wrote to a friend in 1762. "What he designs me for, I know not, but I hope for good; he has returned me to Ch'stown. I'm now studying with dear Mr. Hart, and he seems to signify of their trying to settle me in town which would be very agreeable to me, for I like the place and people much."[7] While imparting doctrinal teaching and technical pastoral skills, Hart also established an affectionate bond with his students, many calling him "father Hart." Pugh often wrote of his meetings with Hart's Society, as on January 1, 1762, when they gathered and "discoursed on ye

---

[4] Furman, *Rewards of Grace*, 26; "Rules for the Society for Promoting Christian Knowledge and Practice, entered to at Charleston, 1755," Furman MSS, JBDML.

[5] Baker, Craven, and Blalock, *First Baptist Church*, 161; Owens, *Oliver Hart, 1723–1795*, 13.

[6] The best source for Pugh is Evan Pugh, *The Diaries of Evan Pugh (1762–1801)*, transcribed by Horace Fraser Rudisill (Florence, SC: St. David's Society, 1993).

[7] Evan Pugh to unknown recipient, April 23, 1762, McKesson Collection, HSP.

152   OLIVER HART AND THE RISE OF BAPTIST AMERICA

secret power of prayer from Matt.6.6." Pugh also studied on his own, though like many young seminarians, he sometimes struggled to surmise their practical import. "This day I studdied Latin till night, then by candal light," he wrote on January 5, 1762. "I read B[ishop] Ushers on Divinity. I feel no particular application of ye present of it to me soul yet. Come Lord Jesus over ye mountain of my provacations & let me taste thine Love."[8] It was a pious wish Hart would have approved of, though he continued to send Pugh back to his books. A minister, in the words of the Apostle Paul, must "study to show thyself approved (2 Timothy 2:5)." In future days Pugh mentioned that he had "begon to learn Greek" and that he "read some Logic. about Syllogisms & am pained with ignorance."[9]

Like any attentive father, Hart formed clear and definite plans for his students, as Pugh indicated, intending for each of them to take a southern Baptist church. Pugh did not disappoint. He accepted a call from the Cashaway Church in 1763, with Hart performing his ordination. Like Hart, Pugh was serious and introspective and struggled often with discouragement as he began to preach. After preaching from Amos 3:8, he confessed, "I made a poor Hand of it, was much scared." The next day, as he prepared for his next sermon, Pugh's condition worsened. "I was much cast down oppressed in Soul co'd not find text for some Time," he wrote. "all appeared very dark & discourag'd to me. I went out cast myself down before God I found words, then I went to stud' &c." He had settled on Hosea 13:9. For the next five consecutive days Pugh "studied all Day very hard" and worked at "writ'g ye Sermon," sometimes in "ye Study," and other times "I went to ye pine Barren." Unfortunately, when Sunday came around, Pugh felt that he again "made a poor hand feel much Discouraged."[10] Though the aspiring preacher continued to wrestle with his calling, he found steady encouragement from both Hart and Pelot and stayed with it. Following Hart's model of revivalism, Pugh also launched an itinerant preaching circuit, traveling to and from Philadelphia in the years 1763–64. Hart worried that Pugh would settle with a Northern congregation, but he returned to South Carolina in 1764, where he remained for the rest of his life.[11]

\*

[8] Pugh, *Diaries of Evan Pugh*, 2.
[9] Pugh, *Diaries of Evan Pugh*, 8.
[10] Pugh, *Diaries of Evan Pugh*, 19.
[11] Townsend, *South Carolina Baptists*, 68.

"SEALS OF MY MINISTRY" 153

Hart could not keep every promising preacher in the South, though. Hezekiah Smith (1737–1805) was born in Hempstead, Long Island, in 1737 to Anglican parents and converted as a young man through John Gano's preaching in Morristown, New Jersey.[12] Smith then enrolled in a new preparatory school begun by the Philadelphia Association in 1756, Hopewell Academy. The Association had proposed that the churches contribute to founding a "Latin Grammar School for the promotion of learning amongst us," under the care of the Hopewell Baptist pastor Isaac Eaton. Eaton, Hart's childhood friend, had been licensed to preach with Hart by the Southampton Baptist Church back in 1746 and shared Hart's burden for educating Baptist leaders.[13] Particular Baptist leaders in both the North and the South were thinking more about an educated and respectable ministry these days, though they would often find it a hard sell among their Baptist constituents. The Association included in their circular letter a plea for the churches to "contribute their mite" to support the school for three straight years, and the academy lasted only eleven.[14] During its brief history Hopewell trained several distinguished Baptist ministers of the rising generation, but few excelled Smith in sheer ability.

Smith was licensed to preach while at Hopewell Academy and then enrolled at the Presbyterian-founded College of New Jersey (today Princeton University). After graduating in 1762, he undertook an itinerant mission to the Southern colonies. He preached wherever he could get a hearing in South Carolina, usually to a positive reception. In February 1762 he crossed on the Strawberry ferry to meet Hart, with whom he shared so many friends in the Philadelphia Association. Hart offered him his pulpit and a place to stay in his home. Over the next several months, Hart often accompanied Smith to his various appointments, guiding him to his more obscure destinations and sharing the preaching duties at places like James Island, Strawberry, and Edisto Island. After nearly a year of itinerating Smith recorded having traveled "4235 Miles and preached 173 Sermons." The crying need for Baptist pastors amazed Smith as he traversed South Carolina, prompting him to recruit other ministers to the region. In a letter to his Hopewell Academy friend Samuel Jones, Smith wrote of thousands on the Pee Dee River without

[12] For Smith, see John David Broome, *The Life, Ministry, and Journals of Hezekiah Smith* (Springfield, MO: Particular Baptist Press, 2004).
[13] Oliver Hart is sometimes erroneously cited as having attended Hopewell Academy under Eaton (i.e., Davies, *Transatlantic Brethren*, 96).
[14] Gillette, *Minutes*, 75–78.

154 OLIVER HART AND THE RISE OF BAPTIST AMERICA

a minister "to break with them the Bread of Life—O, my dear Brother! I hope you will be so moved with Pity and with a probability of a useful Journey, that you will take a Tour this way before you settle." In the mid-eighteenth century the South represented Baptists' most fertile mission field.[15]

Hart urged Smith to settle in South Carolina long term. He had in mind the Cashaway Church in Mount Pleasant, 140 miles north of Charleston, an off-shoot of the Welsh Neck Baptists. Smith went along with the idea for a while, even submitting a handwritten confession of his faith to a committee of Hart, Stephens, and Nicholas Bedgegood, and receiving ordination on September 20, 1763. (Hart again delivered the charge.) But ultimately Smith would not commit to the Cashaway Baptists. Hart did not hide his displeasure over Smith's indecision in a 1763 letter to Samuel Jones (1735–1814). The middle colonies already had a wealth of Baptist preachers, Hart complained, "but Pee Dee is destitute, where Providence seems to open a wide door for Mr. Smith, who refuses, after the warmest solicitations to enter in." Already worked up over Smith, Hart also bristled at Jones's report of Pugh's successful tour though the Northeast. "I am glad Mr. Pugh is so well respected in your parts, but cannot say I am free to his settling there," Hart sniffed. Sure enough, Smith abruptly departed the South for New Jersey in January 1764, leaving the Cashaway Baptists "in a Flood of Tears." Hart mourned over the hole Smith left behind, noting that there were now "two churches entirely destitute on that River, and the People are vastly numerous."[16] Smith ultimately planted a Baptist church in Haverhill, Massachusetts. Like the South, New England was still an underserved area for Baptists, dominated by the established Congregational church. But with Smith's arrival (he would remain in Haverhill for forty years) and the steady rise of strong Separate Baptist congregations, New England Baptist life would begin to thrive in the 1760s. Though Smith had gotten away, Hart never gave up on drawing Baptist preachers to the South.

*

While Hart attempted to coax Smith toward Cashaway, one of Smith's former Hopewell Academy classmates reached out to Hart by mail. Samuel Jones's family had immigrated to Pennsylvania from Wales in 1737, when he was two years old. Jones grew up in the Welsh-speaking Tulpehocken Baptist Church

---

[15] Hezekiah Smith to Samuel Jones, February 23, 1763, McKesson MSS, HSP.
[16] Oliver Hart to Samuel Jones, December 1, 1763, Gratz MSS, HSP; Broome, *Hezekiah Smith*, 234–39; Oliver Hart to Samuel Jones, February 7, 1764, McKesson MSS, HSP.

"SEALS OF MY MINISTRY" 155

in Berks County, Pennsylvania, but was converted and baptized during his student days at Hopewell Academy. After graduating from the College of Philadelphia in 1762, Jones was licensed to preach by the Philadelphia Baptist Church. He soon received a pastoral invitation, delivered by Hart's brother Joseph, a deacon at the Southampton Baptist Church. Jones assumed responsibility for the Baptist churches at both Southampton and Pennepek, making his home halfway between the two, preaching alternate Sundays during the winter months and preaching at both when the weather was good. Since he and Hart already shared so many relational ties, it was natural for the burgeoning pastor to solicit a correspondence with him. Jones's note delighted Hart, who expressed his pleasure at receiving a second letter from Jones before he had responded to the first. "This is an indication that you will be a good correspondent, one who will not stand upon the compliment of a letter, to engage you to write," Hart noted. He assured Jones that in the future he intended to be as attentive in return: "I design, if health permit, that you never shall have cause to complain of backwardness on my part." Before closing, Hart added a patriarchal blessing on the younger man: "May God make you a polished shaft in his Quiver! May your bowe abide in Strength, and your Hands be made string by the mighty God of Jacob! May you be made wise to win Souls; and may you have many to be your joy and crown!" Hart was only about ten years older than Jones, but he embraced the role of a spiritual patriarch to this rising generation of Baptist preachers.[17]

Hart would receive many opportunities to provide Jones with guidance. A year after Jones commenced his ministry in Pennsylvania, he entered a season of spiritual doubt. At his ordination the year before, he had affirmed that the *Philadelphia Confession* was the only "human system he approved." Now, under the strain of serving two churches, adjusting to his first year of marriage, and taking on denominational responsibilities from the Philadelphia Association, he privately questioned some of the doctrines he preached as lacking "certainty, and clear evidence."[18] He shared his anxieties in a candid letter to Hart, who responded in November 1764. Hart underscored the difference between uncertainty and mystery. "Now that there are mysteries in religion I freely grant: but what Truth, or doctrines are

[17] Oliver Hart to Samuel Jones, December 1, 1763, McKesson MSS, HSP. For Jones, see Davies, *Transatlantic Brethren.*

[18] Some of Jones's doubts likely stemmed from the education he received at Philadelphia College, which had jettisoned a medieval curriculum altogether in favor of Enlightenment thought. See Davies, *Transatlantic Brethren*, 92.

156    OLIVER HART AND THE RISE OF BAPTIST AMERICA

handed down to us in the Word of God, as matters of faith, without 'certainty or clear evidence,' I know not," Hart wrote. "True, there are many truths which do not admit of a mathematical demonstration, and with regard to their modus are far beyond the utmost stretch of human reason. Such are the Doctrine of the Trinity, the Union of the two natures on the Person of the Messiah, etc. But therein, are these doctrines, without 'certainty or clear evidence?' I think not." The Enlightenment's emphasis on certainty through empirical experience had influenced Hart in a number of subtle ways, as we have seen. But as he discussed suprarational doctrines like the Trinity, he rejected the Enlightenment's demand for empirical certainty. Human reason was a good gift from God, Hart believed, but it had its limits. There were some truths God never intended his children to prove by the scientific method; they were simply to be received humbly, as articles of faith from God's self-revelation in the Bible. Hart imbibed many tendencies of Enlightenment epistemology and the modern age along the way, but theologically he was a firm supernaturalist and Biblicist who thought within the "Great Tradition" of the church catholic.[19]

Hart encouraged Jones to join him in the submissive posture of faith. "You believe the Scriptures to be the infallible Word of God," Hart reasoned, "and if so, whatsoever is revealed therein, comes handed down to us, with the 'greatest certainty, and upon the clearest evidence.' To suppose the contrary, would be to reflect upon the wisdom, and goodness of the great Author of holy Religion, and which is an impiety I will not suppose you capable of." It seems Jones was also having difficulty accepting the doctrine of "the Covenant of Grace." The traditional Calvinistic understanding of salvation, which exalted God's sovereignty and derided man's natural ability, was growing increasingly unfashionable in the Age of Reason. Hart was happy to defend these truths, but running out of time and space, he simply affirmed, "This covenant is supported by the clearest (even Scriptural) evidence."[20] Hart would at times question his own personal experience of grace, but never doubted the veracity of the Bible or the Calvinistic Baptist system he believed it taught. If Jones had hoped for a conversation partner to encourage him to explore

---

[19] Oliver Hart to Samuel Jones, November 1, 1764, McKesson MSS, HSP. Brekus's *Sarah Osborn's World* is especially helpful on this theme of Enlightenment and early evangelicalism, as is Hindmarsh's *Spirit of Early Evangelicalism*. Another fascinating study regarding the spread of Enlightenment ideas among the "literate but not learned" in colonial America is Sara S. Gronim, *Everyday Nature: Knowledge of the Natural World in Colonial New York* (New Brunswick, NJ: Rutgers University Press, 2009).

[20] Oliver Hart to Samuel Jones, November 1, 1764, McKesson MSS, HSP.

his doubts, he was sorely disappointed; if he wanted a friend to reinforce his confidence in Scripture, he had chosen well. Soon after this exchange, Jones's uncertainties were resolved, and he went on to a fruitful career as the leading minister in the Philadelphia Association. Through his instruction in person and by letter, Hart influenced many Baptists in Jones's generation to stand in the "old paths" of the *Second London Baptist Confession*.

*

About this time, Hart entered a correspondence with another Hopewell Academy graduate, James Manning (1738–1791).[21] Manning was born in Elizabethtown, New Jersey, in 1737. After growing up at the Scotch Plains Baptist Church, he enrolled at Hopewell Academy at age eighteen, where he was converted and received baptism. While at school he formed a close friendship with Samuel Jones and Hezekiah Smith. After graduation he wrote to Jones that he hoped their friendship would "not only last during our stay on earth" but would be a "shadow of that everlasting friendship which shall subsist between kindred souls, through all the future periods of Existence."[22] Manning would partner with Jones, Smith, and other Hopewell classmates to promote the Baptist interest for the rest of his life. At twenty he matriculated to the College of New Jersey to study under its president, the Presbyterian revivalist Samuel Davies (1723–1761). The earliest surviving letter from Manning to Hart is from this period, in which Manning shared the news of Davies's tragic death.

Davies had been the leading figure of the evangelical awakening in Virginia from 1748 to 1759 and was regarded as one of America's finest preachers, even impacting the oratory of Patrick Henry, who heard him as a boy. Davies accepted the presidency at the College of New Jersey in 1759 but died less than two years into his administration, at age thirty-seven. In his reply to Manning, Hart penned an emotional tribute to Davies and to the College:

> And thou, Nassau Hall, lately so flourishing, so promising, under the auspicious management of so worthy a President—what might we not have expected from thee! But alas! How is the mighty fallen in thee! How doth the large and beautiful house appear as a widow in sable weeds! And thy sons,

---

[21] For Manning, see William H. Brackney, "James Manning (1738–1791)," in vol. 3 of *A Noble Company: Biographical Essays on Notable Particular-Regular Baptists in America*, edited by Terry Wolever (Springfield, MO: Particular Baptist Press, 2013), 511–38.

[22] James Manning to Samuel Jones, May 17, 1760, McKesson, HSP.

158    OLIVER HART AND THE RISE OF BAPTIST AMERICA

lately so gay and pleasant, as well as promising and contented—how do they retire into their apartments, and there with bitter sighs, heavy groans, and broken accents, languish out, My Father, my Father!—the chariot of Israel, and the horsemen thereof! But I can write no more.[23]

Though a Baptist minister situated in Charleston, South Carolina, Hart also saw himself as part of an interdenominational, international Christian revival movement; his words of biblical lament over Davies's death indicate how closely he identified with broader evangelicalism and its leaders.

In 1762, Manning graduated from the College, married Margaret Stites (sister of Gano's wife, Sarah Stites), and was ordained for ministry by the Scotch Plains Baptist Church. Hart immediately acted to lure Manning southward. "I congratulate you on your having entered into a new state of life, and hope you will enjoy all the comforts which the married state can afford," Hart wrote, easing into the conversation. "I welcome you into the vineyard of the Lord as one of his laborers. You are now an ambassador for the King of kings. I doubt not but that a sense of the importance of the work lies with weight upon your mind. Well, he who is the Lord our righteousness is also the Lord our strength." These pleasantries aside, Hart made his pitch. He urged Manning, "Come over and assist me in breaking the bread of life to the dear people of my charge." He circled back to the subject again before closing, this time beckoning Manning's new wife to his side: "I have only to say, I hope God will send you upon an embassy to this place, where you will be welcomed to my heart, to my house, and to my people, and where you will have a hopeful prospect of doing much good. Remember me in kind love to your other self. Tell her I wish her joy in her new state, and hope for the pleasure of saluting her in Charleston, where many whose ambition will be to make her happy will rejoice to see her." Despite Hart's best efforts, however, Manning remained in the North. But the two men would work together one day to advance Baptist education through the founding of Rhode Island College.[24]

*

If Hart's young friends initially worried about his willingness to correspond, they quickly learned that he loved almost nothing more than sending and receiving letters. While Hart reserved his diaries for serious, spiritual

[23] Oliver Hart to James Manning, April 27, 1761, Manning MSS, JHL.
[24] Oliver Hart to James Manning, April 27, 1761, Manning MSS, JHL.

# "SEALS OF MY MINISTRY" 159

reflection, his letters often reveal a lighter and more jovial side. In discussing with Samuel Jones the birth of Evan Pugh's second child, Hart quipped that Pugh, whose ministry seemed to lumber along without many visible results, was at least "successful in his generation work if not in that of regeneration."[25]

"Let me hear from you often," he urged Jones in 1764, and he meant it.[26] Hart's epistolary friends often found him, in keeping with his disciplined nature, far more prompt in returning their letters than they were his. When they grew lax in response, he did not hesitate to call them on it. To Samuel Jones he wrote in 1765, "It is long, very long since I received a letter from you. Pray, my good friend, why this silence?" Jones's recent marriage provided no legitimate excuse for Hart. "Sure you have not suffered a Wife to lay an Embargo on your Pen. Are you married? Well, I wish you joy in the matrimonial state. But don't let the fair object attract your whole soul—engross all your time, and cause you to forget a distant friend."[27] In a similar vein, he teased Manning for his delinquency: "Altho' you are already in my Debt, I am about to give you fresh Credit; hoping thereby to induce you to an immediate Discharge of the Whole you owe."

I have Sometimes thought that the Habit, or Disposition of People, is somewhat similar to the Climate in which they live: if so, no Wonder if you Gentlemen, who live so contiguous to the frozen Zone, have cold Hearts. It should seem as if their Hands are cramped with the cold too, and rendered incapable of Holding a Pen. Otherwise, why is it that I hear from them so seldom? Perhaps you are all better employ'd. Convince me of that, and you will atone for every past Neglect. Well, my dear friend, how is it with you?[28]

Promoting piety through friendships, particularly through the medium of friendly letter-writing, was an important feature of the eighteenth-century transatlantic revival. Even when his communication partners disappointed him, Hart's evangelical piety enabled him to turn the subject to the gospel. As he expressed his forgiveness for their neglect of letters, he added, "It is our

---

[25] Oliver Hart to Samuel Jones, June 30, 1769, McKesson MSS, HSP. Excerpts like this reveal that his twentieth-century biographer Loulie Latimer Owens based her assertion that Hart was "completely humorless" on a reading of Hart's diaries alone, without consulting his letters. "Not in one word of his diaries is there the slightest evidence that he ever smiled, much less laughed," she wrote. See Owens, *Oliver Hart, 1723–1795*, 27.

[26] Oliver Hart to Samuel Jones, November 1, 1764, July 15, 1765, McKesson MSS, HSP.

[27] Oliver Hart to Samuel Jones, July 15, 1765, McKesson MSS, HSP.

[28] Oliver Hart to James Manning, December 23, 1767, Manning MSS, JHL.

160    OLIVER HART AND THE RISE OF BAPTIST AMERICA

mercy that we have a long suffering Jesus, who bears with our neglects and imperfections. He is not strict to mark iniquity; otherwise, no flesh could stand before him."[29] But Hart would soon have occasion to apply that forgiveness to a young minister friend on a far more serious occasion than this.

\*

In 1763, Samuel Jones turned the tables on Hart by recruiting his mentor to return to the "better climate" of his native Pennsylvania. As expected, Hart graciously declined: "This does not appear Duty as yet. If I can do any thing, I am persuaded my Service is most wanted in this Place." Among the reasons for remaining at Charleston, Hart cited the anticipated arrival of a new associate minister: "My dear People have procured an Assistant not to dismiss, but to help, and ease me. Mr. Bedgegood is to be my fellow helper."[30] After thirteen years of laborious service, the Charleston congregation had rewarded Hart with a helper; his warm relationship with Bedgegood, whom he had ordained with Stillman in 1759, must have contributed to his excitement over the new arrangement. But what first appeared an ideal partnership turned out to be one of the most painful trials through which Hart would ever pass.

In retrospect, Bedgegood was an unwise choice as Hart's assistant. He was overqualified for the job and destined to be discontented. To begin with, he possessed the formal schooling that Hart never obtained for himself. His obituary identified him as "a classical scholar," having been educated at Tethrington grammar school in England, afterward studying law at Bristol. Furthermore Bedgegood was "an accomplished speaker." His polished sermons to the Charleston congregation convinced some of the wealthier members that he was better suited than Hart for senior leadership. A plan was soon formed to remove Hart from his position and replace him with Bedgegood, and Bedgegood apparently participated in the conspiracy. The ensuing fallout grieved Hart deeply. He was, of course, stung by the betrayal that he suffered from his people. Worse still, his opposition to the plan was predictably spun as resulting from his own petty jealousy of Bedgegood. The church split apart in an ugly dispute. Bedgegood and his supporters ultimately left the church, but they left behind extensive damage.[31]

---

[29] Oliver Hart to James Manning, December 23, 1767, Manning MSS, JHL. On the theme of evangelical friendships and letter-writing, see especially D. Bruce Hindmarsh, *John Newton and the English Evangelical Tradition* (Grand Rapids, MI: Eerdmans, 1996), 241–43.

[30] Oliver Hart to Samuel Jones, December 1, 1763, McKesson MSS, HSP.

[31] Townsend, *South Carolina Baptists*, 69.

## "SEALS OF MY MINISTRY" 161

Estranged from many of his own church members, Hart poured out his troubles to Jones. "Mr. Bedgegood has left us, so that the whole service has devolved on me again," he complained in July, 1765. "As yet I preach twice on each Lord's Day, but whether my strength will be equal to this, through the two following hot months, God only knows." But the increased workload was not the real trouble. "Our Church is now in an unhappy state—much divided, and confused," he wrote. Obviously depressed, Hart wondered if his current plight were not God's discipline. "We are, I am persuaded, guilty before God, in bringing Mr. Bedgegood from a numerous, well-affected people, where he was greatly useful, to serve us, who were not in so much need of help. Hence God has frown'd upon us ever since; so that from step to step, our case has been growing worse and worse, until it is almost become desperate." Hart had violated his own policy of connecting unserviced churches with ministers; now he was paying for it. He felt so defeated, he pondered leaving Charleston altogether. "I am almost ready to conclude that my work here is done, but in that case I know not whither I shall go. Your prayers for me, and for the unhappy people of my charge, are earnestly desired," he confessed. While interested in Jones's prayers, he also sought human intervention in his difficulties. He added in a postscript to Jones, "Do you know of any place where you think I should be useful if God should direct my way to the North?"[32]

The next month he continued in the same vein with James Manning, noting that Bedgegood had aggravated the trouble since departing from the church. "Poor man—he has been vastly imprudent in many things; insomuch that his character is ruined; and I fear his usefulness destroyed. At present he continues in, and about Charles Town, as a thorn in my side, and answers no better purpose." Again he fished for leads on an open pulpit: "Have had many thoughts about Boston, in case I should remove hence. Have lately had a call from the Welsh Neck on Pee Dee. I expect a little time will determine whether I am to continue here or not; but if I must remove, am altogether at a loss where I shall go." Hart was open to anything. He was prone to frequent discouragement in ministry, but at no other point did he openly consider walking away from Charleston and the Baptist South. Throughout this difficult stretch it was the young men he had previously comforted who became his chief comforters.[33]

---

[32] Oliver Hart to Samuel Jones, July 15, 1765, McKesson MSS, HSP.
[33] Oliver Hart to James Manning, August 30, 1765, Manning MSS, JHL.

162    OLIVER HART AND THE RISE OF BAPTIST AMERICA

Despite the pain of his betrayal, Hart remained at his post in Charleston. In the midst of this trial, Samuel Jones had been offered the pulpit of the Boston First Baptist Church, which had finally moved on from the prickly antirevivalist Jeremiah Condy. Jones suggested that Hart take over for him the pastoral charge at both Pennepek and Southampton, the two churches of Hart's childhood, allowing Jones to go to Boston. Hart responded in 1766, "Nothing could be more agreeable to me (if I were to consult my inclination) than to finish my days in my native land. But in this, as in all other respects, I must have an eye to duty primarily." He explained his change of perspective: "Some time ago I really thought my work was nearly at an end here; and perhaps this may be the case yet, but however that may be, things at present wear a different face from what they did. God, I trust, has blest my poor labours to some poor souls, which supports me under many tryals, and indicates that I ought to continue where I am."[34] Visible evidence of fruitfulness in preaching, especially conversions, tended to make all his other problems appear smaller.

Hart's story ended more happily than did Bedgegood's. Bedgegood returned to the Welsh Neck Baptist Church in 1767 but achieved less in this second stint. His successor Elhanan Winchester (1751–1797) caustically recorded in the church book in 1774, "He was never very successful, especially in the latter part of his life; none being baptized after his return." But Bedgegood's personal difficulties in this period cast a darker shadow on his ministry than this. He married a local woman about this time, but their happiness was disrupted when it was reported that he already had a wife in England. Bedgegood had married a Mary Weston years before, but he claimed that she had refused to accompany him to America and that he had since received a report that she had died. In fact she was alive and well, and the Charleston Association summoned him to appear before their body in 1771 "to answer a charge of the sin of polygamy." Likely Bedgegood's behavior toward Hart did not dispose the Association to much sympathy. When Bedgegood refused to appear, the Association disowned him as a minister of the gospel. His Welsh Neck congregation accepted his story and retained him as pastor, but he died under a cloud three years later, in 1774.[35]

As with all of his trials, Hart attempted to view the Bedgegood controversy through the lens of Providence, which he believed lovingly directed

---

[34] Oliver Hart to Samuel Jones, March 7, 1766, McKesson MSS, HSP.
[35] Townsend, *South Carolina Baptists*, 23.

"SEALS OF MY MINISTRY" 163

his life for God's glory and for his own good. This was the counsel he gave by letter around this time to a young woman in Georgia named Hannah Polhill. Weaving into his note a variety of Scripture references, Hart told her:

> The goodness and mercy of God appears conspicuous in many instances, but especially in the gift of his dear Son, for rebellious sinners. And what were we, my dear friend, that we should be made partakers of such great grace? In Christ we have a rich, an immensely rich portion. If Christ is ours, we have all we can wish; an inheritance which waxeth not old, and can never fade away. Clothed in his righteousness, and washed in his blood, we shall appear before God without spot or wrinkle or any such thing. This may reconcile us to all the little trials which fall to our lot in the present life, especially seeing even these, are working together for our good.[36]

As always for Hart, it was the gospel message, "the gift of God's dear Son," that put all of his "little trials" into perspective, even betrayal from one of the very seals of his ministry.

*

A year after the Bedgegood debacle, joy returned to Hart in the form of a twenty-year-old English immigrant named Edmund Botsford (1745–1819). Hart first saw Botsford lingering uncertainly at the gate of the Charleston Baptist meetinghouse one Sunday morning. Hart could not have known the intense inner conflict that the young man was experiencing as church members streamed past him to their seats. Born in Woodburn, Bedfordshire, England, and orphaned by age seven, Botsford had bounced among boardinghouses, the military, and a variety of odd jobs before sailing for the New World to seek adventure with a friend. Now, a year after his arrival in the city, he was alone and directionless. Contemplating his past produced a deep sense of guilt. As a child in a godly woman's boardinghouse, he had been exposed to the Bible and Puritan devotional books like John Bunyan's *Pilgrim's Progress* and *The Holy War*. Just months before, on the voyage to Charleston, he had read Bunyan's *Come and Welcome to Jesus Christ* and considered himself "a converted man" and "the best person on board the ship." But he now realized "Never was a poor creature more deceived." Botsford began attending churches in Charleston, hoping to hear "a gospel sermon"

---

[36] Oliver Hart to Hannah Polhill, May 1764, Hart MSS, SCL.

164 OLIVER HART AND THE RISE OF BAPTIST AMERICA

and find peace for his frightened soul. He was disappointed on both counts. A fellow boarder recognized that he was under spiritual conviction, having squandered away the experience himself. "There is but one minister in this place, who can be of service to you," the young man said, "but he, I am told, is a Baptist; all the rest of the ministers deserve not the name. I would advise you to go hear him." Botsford's hopes rose, believing, "If I could hear the gospel, there would be a possibility of my being saved." This conversation had led him to the threshold of Hart's Baptist meetinghouse.[37]

Botsford talked himself out of going inside that morning—he was already a good man and did not need evangelical conversion, he decided—and instead retreated to the old fortifications at the Charleston Harbor. But as he strolled by the water, conviction fell like a bolt from the sky, and terror filled him. "I had heard of the gospel, and had rejected it; I considered myself a monster, a reprobate; my distress was so great that I cried out, 'I am damned, justly damned!'" he recalled. As his eyes fell on a cannon in the harbor, he wished that he could be "blown to hell" and "be done with his misery." At length he returned to the boardinghouse, passing the next week in gnawing distress.

The following Sunday he resolved to go back to the Baptist church. But as he approached the gate, he almost walked away again. This time, however, Botsford identified his misgivings as "the temptation of Satan." He then "hastened into the house, and seated [him]self in a convenient place." Moments later Hart appeared in the pulpit. Botsford "did not like his dress," presumably objecting to Hart's signature black gown and bands. Still, Botsford could not deny that "there was something in his countenance which pleased me." Hart's earnest, opening prayer intrigued Botsford further. After congregational singing, "the venerable man of God took his text from Acts 13:26, 'Men and brethren, children of the stick of Abraham, and whosoever among you feareth God; to you is the word of this salvation sent.'" Hart's sermon, focused on the basic gospel message, spoke directly to Botsford's troubled soul. "To describe these exercises of my mind under this sermon would be impossible. However, upon the whole, I concluded it was possible that there might be salvation for me, even for me," Botsford remembered. All previous misgivings about the Baptist preacher had now vanished. "I then determined that, in the future, I would attend worship in this place. I do not remember that, when

---

[37] Charles D. Mallary, *The Memoirs of Elder Edmund Botsford* (Springfield, MO: Particular Baptist Press, 2004), 27–28.

able to go, I ever once omitted attending, whilst I lived in Charleston. Indeed, I would not have omitted one sermon for all the riches in the world. Before this, I wished to return to England; but now I was perfectly satisfied to remain, if I lived on bread and water only." It was the beginning of Botsford's evangelical conversion.

On November 1, his twenty-first birthday, Botsford experienced

a day of light, a day of joy and peace. That day I had clearer views than formerly, of sin, holiness, God and Christ, and different views from all I had ever before experienced. I think I was enabled to devote my whole self to God as a reconciled God. I think I then so believed in Christ, as to trust in him, and commit my all into his hands. At that time, and from that time, I considered myself as not my own, but his, *his*, and not the world's, but *his*, and no longer Satan's, *his* for time and *his* for eternity.

His first move was to contact Hart, his spiritual guide throughout the process. "At length I wrote to him, and soon after called upon him, and related to him my experience. On the 13th of March I was baptized, and joined the Baptist Church in Charleston."[38]

Two years later Botsford revealed to Hart that he had been resisting God's call to preach. Hart shared this at the church's next meeting and set a date for Botsford to preach before them "that they might judge of his ministerial gifts." After Botsford's sermon, the church "encouraged him to go forward in the great work," and he began studying with Hart and a church member named David Williams. Botsford kept an extensive diary over the next few years, mostly sermon notes with his own spiritual commentary. Most of the sermons were Hart's, preached at the Charleston Baptist Church. But Botsford also attended the preaching of Hezekiah Smith, who had come south on assignment for Rhode Island College, and Edmund Matthews, a fellow trainee under Hart. Botsford also went to hear the aging George Whitefield, still drawing tremendous crowds in Charleston in 1769 and 1770. At one meeting Botsford noted, "Mr. Whitefield was lifted in at the window, there not being room for him to come in at the door." Botsford maintained that he liked Whitefield's sermon, but "lay aside oratory and Mr. Whitefield's discourse will not do to compare with Mr. Hart's."[39]

---

[38] Mallary, *Edmund Botsford*, 28–34.
[39] Mallary, *Edmund Botsford*, 35–38; Botsford, Diary 1769–1770, JBDML.

# 166   OLIVER HART AND THE RISE OF BAPTIST AMERICA

Hart was by all accounts a fine preacher, but he was no Whitefield; Botsford's remark indicates deep affection for his mentor. Hart's pupils did not simply take down lecture notes in a classroom but shared in every part of his life. They worshipped with him in the Charleston meetinghouse, slept and took meals in his home, accompanied him on itinerant journeys, watched him navigate the highs and lows of daily ministry, unburdened their hearts to him by letter and in person. It is also worth noting that the young men watched Hart interact with his slaves, and this too had a profound impact. Like Hart, Evan Pugh would keep multiple slaves throughout his adult life, and Hart and the Charleston Baptists were directly instrumental in changing Botsford's mind about slavery.

*

Botsford would later claim that when he arrived in Charleston from England, he "had never heard much respecting the negroes, or had seen more than four or five," and "had every prejudice I could have against slavery." Over time, though, slavery no longer appeared to him "in the same light." Apart from Hart's example, Botsford's tutor, the prominent First Baptist layman David Williams, owned two plantations and seventy slaves. "It is true," Botsford admitted, "the slaves have no hope of freedom, and it is also true, they have no proper idea of the nature of freedom. Many in their own country were slaves, and many who were not, were miserable. Several with whom I have conversed, have really preferred their present state in this country to their own country, though in that they were free."[40] Botsford further justified his position by the care he gave his slaves. "Providence has cast my lot where slavery is introduced and practiced. . . . Servants I want; it is lawful for me to have them; but hired ones I cannot obtain, and therefore I have purchased some: I use them as servants; I feed them; clothe them, instruct them, etc."[41] Indeed Botsford insisted that it was better to be "a slave to a good Master than a foot soldier in the British Service for life." Perhaps these were the same arguments he had heard from Hart. After Hart's death, Botsford would complete his evolution by joining fellow Hart protégé Richard Furman in arguing for slavery as a "positive good" for society, in opposition to those "who had not travelled [and] have very wrong Ideas of the situation & of our Negroes."[42]

---

[40] Benedict, *General History of the Baptist Denomination*, 2:110. Talbert and Farish treat Botsford's stance on slavery at length in *The Antipedo Baptists of Georgetown County*, 57–67.

[41] Benedict, *General History of the Baptist Denomination*, 2:110.

[42] Edmund Botsford to John M. Roberts, March 30, 1812, Edmund Botsford Papers, South Carolina Baptist Historical Collection.

Whether by direct precept or merely by observation, Botsford learned from Hart that when in the South, it was in the best interest of Baptist ministers to do as the white Southerners did. Indeed, over time, white Baptist leaders like Hart, Botsford, and Furman discovered creative ways to "sanctify slavery," emphasizing the fatherly role of slave owners and their obligation to instruct slaves in the gospel. This strategy would elevate white Baptists to the status of cultural insiders in Southern society after the turn of the nineteenth century, allowing them to "cross the threshold 'from alienation to influence.'"[43]

For better or worse, Hart's holistic training yielded a new generation of evangelical Baptist ministers for the South. It also produced a host of rich, lifelong friendships. For the rest of Hart's days, the orphaned Botsford called him "my father," and Hart called Botsford "my son." Through Hart's diligent efforts to train younger men for ministry, the Baptist interest in the region took on a different face in the 1760s than it had upon his arrival in 1749. Perhaps more than any other measure, Hart viewed these preachers as the sign that God had placed his seal on his ministry.

*

Hart influenced his young friends toward his own ideal of moderate revivalism, paternalistic slaveholding, and denominational respectability. In terms of numeric growth, organization, education, and refinement (at least among the Regular Baptists), Baptists in the South and beyond were slowly coming to look more like the mainstream American denominations. When Smith, Jones, and Manning wrote to Hart, they had already received more formal education than he ever had; they would one day hold master's and doctorate of divinity degrees. In fact Smith would chastise a critic in 1773 for failing to acknowledge his learning. "In your sermon you did not even call me Rev'd or Mr., tho' I have a Master's degree," he blustered.[44] Learning was as important to these young men as Spirit-filled preaching and worship. Like Hart, they would follow a pattern of moderate revivalism in order to advance the Baptist denomination into the future.

One of the clearest examples of Baptists' growing respectability at the beginning of the 1760s is Hart's protégé Samuel Stillman. Stillman went

[43] Wills, *Democratic Religion*, 51, quoting Nathan O. Hatch, *The Democratization of American Christianity* (New Haven, CT: Yale University Press, 1989), 193; Kidd and Hankins, *Baptists in America*, 98–99.

[44] Hezekiah Smith to Mr. Walker, March 3, 1773, in Backus Papers (ANTS), cited in McLoughlin, *New England Dissent*, 2:743.

168   OLIVER HART AND THE RISE OF BAPTIST AMERICA

to Philadelphia in 1759, where he married and earned a degree from Philadelphia College. He then returned to James Island in South Carolina in 1761, but breathing problems forced him back north. After briefly pastoring two small churches in New Jersey, he was called to be the assistant minister at Boston's Second Baptist Church. This was the congregation that had separated from First Baptist Boston when the pastor Jeremiah Condy had opposed Whitefield's revivalism and Calvinism. By 1765 First Baptist had been dwindling for two decades, and Condy had left the ministry to become a book seller. Weary of watching Second Baptist flourish while they diminished under Condy, members of First Baptist were ready to go in a different direction. After Samuel Jones declined their invitation, they turned to Stillman, who accepted in January 1765. He would remain there for forty years.

Stillman's youth in cosmopolitan Charleston had prepared him well for Boston's refined society. He was "scrupulously neat in his dress" and wore a wig, gown and bands in all public appearances.[45] He was described as "polite" in his address, "combining dignity with condescending kindness, so as to maintain rank with the most eminent though affable with the meanest." The words "dignity" and "decorum" appear in virtually every remembrance of Stillman. His serious, eloquent sermons drew admiration across the city from Baptists and non-Baptists alike, and at various points in his ministry he looked out and saw John Adams, Henry Knox, and John Hancock in the pews. Indeed Stillman came to guard the respectability of the Boston Baptist pulpit jealously, as the black Baptist preacher Thomas Paul (1773–1831) discovered after the turn of the nineteenth century. When Paul offered to address the First Baptist Church, Stillman informed him that "it was Boston, and they did not mix colors." Paul received the same brushoff from Stillman's friend Thomas Baldwin (1753–1825) of the Second Baptist Church, who admitted, "We are too proud to have him preach, and as long as there are other white men to preach, I do not think it best for him to preach here." The deep-seated sense of racial superiority represented by Stillman and Baldwin

---

[45] One contemporary describes Stillman this way: "In his person, Dr. Stillman was slender, and very small of size, agile in movement and erect in bearing, in address polite, combining dignity with condescending kindness, so as to maintain rank with the most eminent though affable with the meanest, and scrupulously neat in his dress; wearing, as in his painted and engraved portrait, a wig, as was in his day common, and a gown, with bands." William B. Sprague, *Annals of the American Baptist Pulpit* (New York: Robert Carter & Brothers, 1860), 79.

"SEALS OF MY MINISTRY" 169

prompted Paul to found an African Baptist Church and an extensive itinerant ministry to black Americans, an important trend in Baptist life during the era.[46]

Stillman published many of his sermons, prompting Harvard to award him an honorary master's degree, and Rhode Island College a doctor of divinity degree in 1788. He also joined a host of community organizations for benevolence, including the Humane Society of Massachusetts, the Massachusetts Charitable Fire Society, Boston Dispensary, and Boston Female Asylum. He also maintained a visible presence at important public occasions, and in 1788 was elected a member of the Massachusetts Ratifying Convention for the federal Constitution. As one contemporary observed, "Whatever might be the character of the circle into which he was thrown, his behavior was always characterized by the utmost discretion and dignity; and, though he could enter, with even keen relish, into the enjoyments of social life, he never for a moment forgot the decorum that belongs to the character of the Christian, and the vocation of the Christian minister."[47] No Boston Baptist could have dreamed of enjoying such a privileged status fifty years earlier.

Not all appreciated Stillman's respectability, of course. The eccentric Elias Smith (1769–1846) complained that Stillman and fellow refined Boston Baptist Thomas Baldwin pressured Smith to dress "more becomingly."[48] They also insisted on stately decorum at Smith's installation service at the Woburn, Massachusetts, church:

Our popery was performed in the Congregational meeting-house, and it was a high day within. We made something of a splendid appearance as it respected the ignorant. We had two doctors of divinity, one or two A.M.'s, and we all wore bands. When we came out of the council chamber and walked in procession to the meeting-house, we looked as much like the cardinals coming out of the conclave after electing the pope, as our practice was like them. Dr. [Hezekiah] Smith said to me after installation: "I advise you to wear a band on the Lord's days." This was a piece of foppery I always

[46] John Dowling, "Rev. Thomas Paul and the Colored Baptist Churches," *Baptist Memorial and Monthly Record* 8 (1849): 295–99; Elias Smith, *Five Letters, with Remarks* (Boston: J. Ball, 1804), 18; Kidd and Hankins, *Baptists in America*, 106.

[47] Sprague, *Annals of the American Baptist Pulpit*, 79. Another contemporary remarked, "There was, indeed, in Dr. Stillman, a happy union of the gentleman, the scholar, and the devoted Christian Minister, calculated to obtain and secure, in any well-principled community, both esteem and love." Sprague, *Annals of the American Baptist Pulpit*, 77.

[48] For Baldwin as a representative of Baptist respectability after the turn of the nineteenth century, see McLoughlin, *New England Dissent*, 2:1114–17.

170    OLIVER HART AND THE RISE OF BAPTIST AMERICA

hated, and when I walked over with it on I then thought I acted with it as a pig does when he is first yoked, and almost struck it with my knees for fear I should hit it. I should not have worn it that day but that Dr. Stillman, who was as fond of foppery as a little girl is of fine baby rags, brought one and put it one me."[49]

But even the most sophisticated Baptist sometimes found himself subjected to public indignities. The Congregationalist William Betley recalled one Sunday when Stillman, whom he described as "a small, frail man," gallantly "carried a corpulent woman into the water" for baptism, according to custom. Unfortunately Stillman "was thrown down by her and was obliged to receive help from the Bystanders." Stillman then gathered what remained of his soggy decorum and completed the rite.[50]

For all his aristocratic bearing, Stillman remained a passionate revivalist. In his opening prayers each Sunday, he often interceded for the sailors working off the Massachusetts coast, eventually drawing many of them to attend worship at First Baptist, sitting in the balcony. He was generally serious and eloquent in his preaching, but when, like Hart, he took flight with a passionate outburst, the sailors would stand in admiration. When listening to the conversion narratives of baptismal candidates, as Hart had done for him, Stillman was known to beam with delight, remarking, "What a wonderfully strange thing religion is! How happy it makes us!" and "Ah, Heaven is not far off, when we feel right." First Baptist Boston numbered fewer than seventy people when Stillman took over for Condy but experienced revival beginning in 1769, adding eighty members in three years. The increase was so dramatic that the Congregational ministers of Boston published a number of tracts to warn young people against going over to the Baptists. The Revolution scattered the church, and afterward it struggled to regain its old vitality, until another revival occurred in 1785 and fifty members were added in three years. In 1790 another season of renewal swept in more than seventy new members over a period of about two years. During these seasons of awakening, Stillman utilized many of the same revival measures he had learned from Hart, including the special Sunday night inquirers' meetings. He gained such popularity throughout the city that many who did not go to

---

[49] Thomas Armitage, *A History of the Baptists* (New York, 1890), 780–81. For Elias Smith, see Hatch, *The Democratization of American Christianity*, 68–80, 128–35.

[50] William Bentley, *The Diary of William Bentley*, 4 vols. (Salem, MA: Essex Institute, 1904–14), 3:85.

his church requested him to visit them at the hour of their death; his prayers on these occasions were known to move physicians to tears, and sometimes even resulted in immediate healing.[51]

Stillman, in other words, was the model pastor according to the moderate revivalist school of Oliver Hart. From the ministries of Stillman, Manning, and Hezekiah Smith in New England, to Samuel Jones in Pennsylvania, all the way down into the Lower South, where Pugh and Botsford served alongside him in the Charleston Association, Hart's influence was showing up on Baptists from north to south by the middle of the 1760s. It was through this growing web of interconnected personal relationships that Hart began to dream of seeing "all the Baptists on the Continent" come together as a single, formidable force for revival in America.

---

[51] Sprague, *Annals of the American Baptist Pulpit*, 76–79; Backus, *History of New England*, 420; Benedict, *General History of the Baptist Denomination*, 393–94.

# 8

# "Promoting so laudable a Design"

## Baptist Development in the 1760s

In the fall of 1766 the Welsh Neck Church was "in a declining state," and everyone knew it. One member, Brother Abel Wilds, wanted to know why. At a monthly meeting Wilds questioned the gathered church for their opinions. The church clerk recorded the brutally honest conclusion: "Upon consideration, it was the unanimous opinion that it was owing to the general dislike of Mr. Pugh." Evan Pugh, Hart's melancholy student in the Baptist Religious Society, had been preaching at the church for the past two years. Pugh's diaries indicate that he had continued laboring to improve his preaching, faithfully attended Religious Society meetings in Charleston, and on many days he simply recorded "in ye Study." He traveled to remote Low Country settlements, preaching, baptizing, officiating at funerals, and performing dozens of marriages for frontier couples. He seems to have been industrious outside the study as well, keeping bees, tending crops, and going hunting with Hart. But for some reason Pugh was not what the Welsh Neck Baptists were looking for. One church member thus made a formal motion, "that it might be considered, whether it would be most for the glory of God for Mr. Pugh to continue our Minister, or to remove to some other place." Realizing the seriousness of the proposal, the church "thought advisable to consider it with deliberation" and "agreed to give each their opinion, and to desire Mr. Pugh to do the same on next Saturday." The result of the meeting was overwhelmingly clear, as the members "unanimously thought it most conducive to the Honor of God in the welfare of the Church for Mr. Pugh to remove." There was little for Pugh to do at this point. He "acquiesced in their opinion and received a Recommendatory Letter."[1] His own report of the event, on December 13, 1766, was typically straightforward: "Had a Church Meeting

---

[1] *An Abstract of the Records of the Welsh Neck Baptist Church, Society Hill, S.C.*, transcribed by Glenn Pearson, May 2000, http://sciway3.net/proctor/marlboro/church/Welsh_Neck_Baptist2.html.

*Oliver Hart and the Rise of Baptist America.* Eric C. Smith, Oxford University Press (2020). © Oxford University Press.
DOI: 10.1093/oso/9780197506325.001.0001

"PROMOTING SO LAUDABLE A DESIGN" 173

I am Dismiss'd from ye Church in ye Welch Neck." He preached the next morning as usual, and on Monday he packed his things.[2] After six years of studying with Hart, Pugh had received an unforgettable lesson in church government. For Baptists, the baptized members of the local assembly constituted the highest authority in religious life. They could call a minister, or they could dismiss him—for the glory of God.

Oliver Hart may not have been happy about the Welsh Neck Church's dismissal of his friend Pugh, but he certainly affirmed their right to do it. He had the doctrine and polity of Baptist churches on his mind in the mid-1760s, working to establish standards of Baptist theology and church government for the churches of the Charleston Association as the Philadelphia Association had done. In 1767 the Association adopted a pair of official documents: the *Charleston Confession* and the *Summary of Church Discipline*. Together they would impact Baptist life in the South for more than a century. In the same period, Hart led the Charleston Association to look beyond their own region and participate with Baptists in the middle colonies and New England to found the first Baptist college in America. By the end of the 1760s Hart's dream of a thriving Baptist denomination, in the South and beyond, was gaining serious traction.

\*

By adopting the *Charleston Confession*, Hart and his fellow messengers in the Charleston Association acknowledged their place in the theological tradition of Dissenting English Calvinists. With only slight alterations, the *Charleston Confession* simply transferred the *Philadelphia Confession* (1742) to the South. The *Philadelphia Confession* had of course been a lightly edited version of the *Second London Confession* (1689), which those Particular Baptists had deliberately intended to reflect the *Westminster Confession of Faith* (1646). The Charleston Association followed the Philadelphia Association except for the article of "laying on of hands," which they omitted. Many Baptists held a deep emotional attachment to this ritual, and it had divided churches through the years (including the Charleston Baptist Church in the days of Thomas Simmons, leading to the creation of the Ashley River Church). The Charleston Association did not wish to make this practice a test of fellowship.[3] Later in the eighteenth century, the

---

[2] Pugh, *Diaries of Evan Pugh*, 61.
[3] Hart believed the practice to be "a mere formal rite, not founded on Scripture," following the interpretation of the English Particular Baptist John Gill. See Hart, *A Gospel Church Portrayed*,

174    OLIVER HART AND THE RISE OF BAPTIST AMERICA

Charleston Association's commitment to a written confession would prove the single greatest obstacle in their union with Separate Baptists, who violently opposed the notion of any creed being imposed on them from outside the local church. Still, the *Charleston Confession* would endure. Its traditional, evangelical Calvinist doctrines would shape the South's Baptists well to the end of the nineteenth century.[4]

*

In addition to affirming the *Charleston Confession*, the Charleston Association charged Hart and Francis Pelot to compose a manual of church order for the South's Baptists. Such manuals had a long history in Baptist life. In 1697 Benjamin and Elias Keach published a short treatise on church discipline along with a condensed version of the *Second London Confession*, and Benjamin Griffith had written a "Treatise on Church Discipline" for the Philadelphia Association in 1743. But the Charleston Association wanted its own. As Hart and Pelot delicately explained, they did not wish to "depreciate the value" of Griffith's "Treatise," but they found it insufficiently "explicit" in some areas, and also believed it contained some articles they considered "exceptionable." Hart and the Charleston Baptists preferred to follow the direction of "the late learned, pious and judicious Dr. [John] Gill" and distance themselves from some of the peculiar traditions of the Welsh Baptists. The resulting *Summary of Church Discipline* was published along with the *Charleston Confession* in 1774.[5]

Unlike the more hierarchical Anglican, Methodist, and Presbyterian denominations, in Baptist churches every member was concerned with the church's government. Hart and Pelot therefore wrote their *Summary* "in the plainest language," to "remove the ignorance" of even the "poor and unlearned."[6] They began by defining the nature of the church itself. They affirmed the reality of a "catholic or universal church" made of "all members

---

23. Hart's Welsh Baptist peer David Jones protested the publication of the sermon in which Hart voiced his opinion. For a detailed treatment of this doctrine and the controversy it sparked among eighteenth-century Baptists, see Davies, *Transatlantic Brethren*, 151–59.

[4] For the pervasiveness of traditional Calvinist theology in the nineteenth-century Baptist South, see Wills, *Democratic Religion*, 102–15.

[5] Charleston Association, *A Confession of Faith*, 1. For a detailed comparison of the two confessions, see James Leo Garrett, *Baptist Church Discipline: A Historical Introduction to the practices of Baptist Churches, with Particular Attention to the Summary of Church Discipline* (Paris, AR: Baptist Standard Bearer, 2004).

[6] Charleston Association, *A Confession of Faith*, 1.

"PROMOTING SO LAUDABLE A DESIGN" 175

of Christ's body throughout the world, whose names are written in heaven." Regular Baptists did not believe one had to be a Baptist to be saved, as evidenced by both Hart's and Pelot's ecumenical revival activity. But as denominational rivalries intensified in the South toward the turn of the nineteenth century, the belief in a universal church would not always be evident in the way Baptists, Presbyterians, and Methodists spoke about one another.[7] By the 1850s some Baptist leaders in the South would become so hardened in their exclusivism that they formed the controversial but widely embraced Landmark movement, declaring Baptists to have the only true churches. "Baptist churches are the churches of Christ," the Landmark leader James Robinson Graves (1820–1893) would write, and "they *alone* hold, and have alone ever held, and preserved the doctrine of the gospel in all ages."[8] Even those nineteenth-century Southern Baptists who rejected Landmarkism often looked on non-Baptists as heretics who had "departed from the Faith of the Gospel."[9] But by acknowledging the reality of an "invisible church," the *Summary* affirmed the value of other Christian traditions, at least in theory. At the same time, the *Summary* insisted that Christ intended all the members of his "invisible church" to become visible to the world by "unit[ing] in distinct churches" that were "true and orderly," and Baptist churches reflected that order best. This was largely because they defined the church as "a company of saints," not a mixed multitude of regenerate and unregenerate, who obeyed Jesus "in all his institutions," including believer baptism.[10] Affirming the salvation of other Christians while promoting their own, firmly held views of church order would always be a point of tension for Baptists in the South.

Hart's *Summary of Church Discipline* provided detailed instructions for how visible churches should be incorporated. Thinking of the many small Baptist works begun on the Southern frontier, Hart and Pelot underscored that size mattered little in forming a true church. Since Christ had promised, "Where two or three are gathered in my name, there I am in the midst of them" (Matthew 18:20), even a handful of believers could form a "church essential." The goal, however, should always be to grow into an independent and

---

[7] See Mulder, *A Controversial Spirit*, 110–67.

[8] On Landmarkism, see James Robinson Graves, *Old Landmarkism: What Is It?* (Memphis, TN: Baptist Book House, 1880); Patterson, *James Robinson Graves*; and E. Brooks Holifield: *Theology in America: Christian Thought from the Age of the Puritans to the Civil War* (New Haven, CT: Yale University Press, 2003), 277–78.

[9] Wills, *Democratic Religion*, 90–97.

[10] Charleston Association, *A Confession of Faith*, 2–5.

176    OLIVER HART AND THE RISE OF BAPTIST AMERICA

fully functioning "church complete," with their own officers. The *Summary*'s prescribed ceremony for constituting a church highlighted the Baptist ideal of separation from the world. The process, overseen by an ordained minister, involved "a strict inquiry" into the new birth experience of all potential members, their doctrinal soundness, and "the goodness of their lives and conversation." All who passed this inspection would then subscribe to the church's written covenant, as all members "bound and obliged themselves to be the Lord's, to walk in all his commands and ordinances, and in all respects to behave toward each other as brethren, agreeable to the spiritual relation they now enter into."[11] One hundred fifty years after the birth of the English Baptist movement, the idea of forming a separated, covenant community of believers remained at the heart of Baptist theology.

Highlighting their identity as a separated community, some churches in the Charleston Association forbade in their official documents common social practices they considered to be sinful. The Cashaway Baptists specified, "No member of this church shall at any time with out lawful call go to any horse race, shooting match, or public place of Carnal mirth, or diversion whatsoever." If ever members were "lawfully called" to such worldly places, they "shall not stay longer there to do his and their business and when any person shall have a call to any of the aforesaid places" and were expected to "produce to the church their reasons for going and the Church shall judge" the propriety. Maintaining separation from the world impacted Baptists' economic decisions as well as their social practices. The Cashaway Baptists further prohibited members from "work[ing] up or down the river on the Sabbath Day without a lawful reason," as well as hiring out one's boat when not working. Again, if "special necessity" required a departure from this ruling, "the reasons shall be produced to the church and the church shall judge whether lawful or not."[12] Upholding the integrity of a "company of saints" this side of heaven was a difficult business in the Low Country.[13]

*

[11] For church covenants, see Champlin Burrage, *The Church Covenant Idea: Its Origin and Development* (Philadelphia, PA: American Baptist Publication Society, 1904), and Charles W. Deweese, *Baptist Church Covenants* (Nashville, TN: Broadman Press, 1990), 24–59.

[12] *An Abstract of the Records of the Cashaway Baptist Church, Society Hill, S.C.*, transcribed by Glenn Pearson, May 2000, https://www.sciway3.net/proctor/marlboro/church/Cashaway_Baptist.html.

[13] Charleston Association, *A Confession of Faith*, 5.

"PROMOTING SO LAUDABLE A DESIGN" 177

The Charleston Association believed that, once constituted, a local church represented the highest form of spiritual authority on earth. In principle, Baptists rejected the power of any other religious body, believing that each local church possessed "the keys, or power of government, within itself, having Christ for its head, and his law for its rule." This meant that the church had "the power and privilege" of choosing its own officers, receiving and dismissing its own members, and administering the Word and ordinances. This granted tremendous spiritual authority to ordinary church members, one reason why the Baptist way would appeal to the South's increasingly democratic sensibilities.[14] In practice, however, Baptist authority was not shared equally among all covenanted members. When decisions were not unanimous, the *Summary* advised that "a majority of male members may determine, and the minority ought peaceably to submit." Despite their rhetoric of spiritual equality, white male members generally occupied the seat of power in Baptist churches much as they did out in Southern society.

Though Baptist women were excluded from governing decisions, they were given a voice in votes related to "fellowship," that is, the receiving and disciplining of members. As in the Philadelphia Association, Charleston Association women could act as witnesses in cases of discipline and, "when aggrieved, are to make known their case, either in person or by a brother, and must have proper regard paid them."[15] A Welsh Neck Baptist woman named Mrs. Jamison tested this stance in 1759, when she "publicly accused Church of dealing too severely with her in an affair subsisting between she and Mrs. Burton last month meeting and the Church." The church heard her out and decided that because only "a small debate" existed between the two women, "if they could freely forgive each other the charge would be satisfied and they take their places." The Welsh Neck Baptists took Mrs. Jamison's grievances more seriously than most other institutions would in South Carolina at the time, an egalitarianism that disturbed many Southerners. Still, when Mrs. Jamison "refused" to forgive Mrs. Burton, she was suspended "till she give proper satisfaction to the church."[16] Thus, in comparison to the broader

[14] On the Southern Baptist equation of New Testament church government with democracy, see Wills, *Democratic Religion*, 28–31. For the general trend toward democratic ideals in American religion, se Hatch, *Democratization of American Christianity*.

[15] Charleston Association, *A Confession of Faith*, 5–6. For an analysis of how Baptist church membership upheld female personhood in Southern society in some ways and upheld the status quo in others, see Stephanie McCurry, *Masters of Small Worlds: Yeoman Households, Gender Relations, and the Political Culture of the Antebellum South Carolina Low Country* (New York: Oxford University Press, 1995), 130–35. See also Juster, *Disorderly Women*.

[16] *An Abstract of the Records of the Welsh Neck Baptist Church*; Wills, *Democratic Religion*, 66.

Southern society, Baptists practiced a remarkable spiritual egalitarianism in church discipline cases. In fact Baptists tended to publicly accuse white men of crimes to a far greater degree than either women or blacks. At the same time, the types of accusations and the penalties for those crimes that Baptist churches issued tended to differ according to gender and race. Baptists, as Greg Wills has observed, "saw in each group different natures and different duties—differences that affected the moral texture of unrighteous acts."[17] Baptists therefore disciplined women for transgressing their God-ordained social roles, especially for sins with sexual connotations such as adultery, dancing, and general flirtatiousness. They also handed down harsher penalties to women than to men. In antebellum Georgia, for instance, Baptist women brought before the church were almost one and a half times more likely than men to suffer excommunication. This disparity was directly tied to Southern society's view of women. Women were to be the guardians of refinement, purity, and piety in the culture; their crimes were therefore more outrageous than those committed by men, who were expected to be rowdier and more wicked. Baptist churches thus felt the pull of the two competing ideals of spiritual equality in the membership and an unequal social order.[18]

*

The *Summary* detailed the appropriate process for maintaining the membership of the company of saints. All applicants must be admitted by common vote of the church, after first sharing his or her experience of grace, receiving immersion, agreeing to the church covenant, and establishing that he or she possessed a scandal-free reputation. Potential members were further expected to have a fairly comprehensive grasp of basic doctrine:

> They should be persons of some competent knowledge of divine and spiritual things; who have not only knowledge of themselves, and of their lost state by nature, and of the way of salvation by Christ; but have some degree of knowledge of God in his nature, perfections, and works; and of Christ in his person as the Son of God, of his proper deity, of his incarnation, of his offices as prophet, priest, and king; of justification by his righteousness, pardon by his blood, satisfaction by his sacrifice, and of his prevalent

[17] Wills, *Democratic Religion*, 66.
[18] Wills treats this issue at length in *Democratic Religion*, 54–59; see also Kidd and Hankins, *Baptists in America*, 82–83.

"PROMOTING SO LAUDABLE A DESIGN" 179

intercession. And also of the Spirit of God: his person, offices and operations; and of the important truths of the gospel, and doctrines of grace.[19]

This doctrinal recitation may seem a rigorous requirement for membership, but the Charleston Association viewed it as essential to maintain the integrity of each Baptist fellowship, which was theological in nature. "How otherwise should the church be the pillar and ground of truth?" they asked.[20] In some cases Baptists excommunicated individuals who demonstrated a deficient grasp of that truth. In the fall of 1779 Elhannan Winchester led a major revival at the Welsh Neck Baptist Church, with dozens of white and black men and women joining each month. Winchester left the church at the close of that revival for the Philadelphia Baptist Church and afterward was discovered to hold universalist views. Coming behind Winchester at Welsh Neck, Edmund Botsford was shocked at the dismal standards Winchester had applied to new church members during the revival. Many white members, but even more blacks, were excommunicated when "upon examination [they] appeared to be very Ignorant of the nature of true Religion." Only if the church was satisfied with the candidate's life and doctrine would it extend the right hand of fellowship and receive him or her into full communion.[21]

Black men and women joined Charleston Association churches throughout the colonial period. On June 27, 1779, Mingo, Plato, Stephen, Darien, and Leannah all received baptism at Welsh Neck. Blacks entered the church on the same terms as whites, implying a radical spiritual equality that did not escape the slaves' notice.[22] Most Baptist churches shared the view of the Welsh Neck Church in 1785 that "truly pious" black members should "enjoy the privileges of Saints," and allowed black members to participate in votes related to fellowship. In reality, however, the social inequality between whites and blacks did not disappear within the church; blacks were still designated as "servants" of their masters in the church record book. As in the case of female members, Baptists applied a different standard of discipline to blacks than to whites. Baptist churches accused white men of crimes far more frequently than they accused blacks, but this was in part due to the churches' low view of the moral and spiritual capacity of black

[19] Charleston Association, *A Confession of Faith*, 16.
[20] Charleston Association, *A Confession of Faith*, 16–17.
[21] *Abstract of the Records of Welsh Neck Baptist Church*; Winchester's case will be explored more thoroughly in chapter 12.
[22] On this theme, see Sylvia R. Frey, *Water from the Rock: Black Resistance in a Revolutionary Age* (Princeton, NJ: Princeton University Press, 1991); and Genovese, *Roll, Jordan, Roll*.

members. White Baptists viewed black brethren much like children in the household of faith, as those whose passions were not subject to the powers of reason. When Baptists did discipline black members—typically for sinning against their role as obedient slaves through crimes such as theft, running away, lying, or drunkenness—they exercised greater severity in an attempt to "arouse feelings of shame and fear." At the same time, also in keeping with their paternalistic posture, Baptist churches were generally quicker to restore black members to church fellowship.[23] Over time it became difficult for black Baptists to resist the conclusion of the social historian Stephanie McCurry that "even in [an] evangelical community, justice ran in the grooves cut by social power."[24] This unequal treatment in white congregations would ultimately inspire many black Baptists in the South to form separate congregations in the late eighteenth and nineteenth centuries.

*

The remainder of the *Summary* was mostly taken up with a nuanced discussion of the discipline of members who violated the church's covenant. The "rebuke" represented the mildest form of correction. It involved "pointing out the offense, charging it upon the conscience, advising and exhorting [the offender] to repentance, watchfulness, and new obedience, and praying for him that he may be reclaimed." Rebukes were common in Charleston Association churches, where common offenses included drunkenness, indiscreet speech, and failing to attend worship. In 1762 the Welsh Neck Church sent a messenger to David Evans to "admonish him for his late disorderly conduct, having drank to excess & attempted to dance in public company." In 1768 a complaint was lodged at the church meeting against Walton Downes (a repeat offender), "for having told untrue and mischievous stories."[25] In 1781 Welsh Neck rebuked Gideon Parish for "plundering," a crime to which he confessed and "promised to make restitution."[26] Other crimes worthy of rebuke mentioned by the *Summary* include wounding the conscience of a brother "through the use of things indifferent," exposing the infirmities of a brother to others, indulging in anger against a brother without just cause, failing to admonish a brother one knows to be guilty of sin, and neglecting church meetings for business or worship with another congregation.

[23] Wills, *Democratic Religion*, 65–66; see also Kidd and Hankins, *Baptists in America*, 82–83.
[24] McCurry, *Masters of Small Worlds*, 136.
[25] Charleston Association, *A Confession of Faith*, 19–20.
[26] *An Abstract of the Records of Welsh Neck Baptist Church.*

"PROMOTING SO LAUDABLE A DESIGN" 181

When a rebuke seemed insufficient, the next level of church censure was "suspension," in which the guilty party was excluded from church office, the Lord's Table, and voting privileges. Crimes rising to the level of suspension included breaking church peace "by janglings and disputings," withdrawing from the church to avoid discipline, refusing the Lord's Table over an offense with another member, promoting heresy, being "a busy tattler and backbiter," slothful neglect of work and care of one's family, and forming a party against church leadership. While suspension removed the offending member from important aspects of "communion" with the church, it did not affect one's essential "union" with the church; the individual was still considered a brother or sister. Upon repentance he or she was restored to full church privileges.

In 1759 the Welsh Neck Church suspended Samuel Rerdon for "obscene conversation," Jacob D'Surrency for "absenting himself from public worship," and John Booth for "publicly quarreling with his Neighbor and using profane language." Suspensions were sometimes issued over lesser crimes when the individual had failed to heed the church's initial rebuke. In 1760 Richard Ponder was suspended less for "excess drinking and racing" than for "refusing to hear the Admonition's of the church."[27] Members who committed gross public crimes and repented were suspended for a season, that the church might test the sincerity of their repentance.[28] In a striking display of Baptist "democratic religion," the Cashaway Baptists even applied this rule to their minister, Joshua Edwards, who confessed to "being overtaken and intoxicated with liquor." The church forgave Edwards but still revoked his privileges for a time.[29] Sometimes the church judged the penitent's sincerity to be lacking. In 1759 the Welsh Neck Church called Jane Poland in for "absenting herself from public worship; and for selling liquor at a horse race." Poland appeared "and acknowledged before the Church the Crimes laid to her charge." But the church judged that, "no sufficient marks of repentance appearing," she was suspended anyway.[30]

Excommunication was the highest form of discipline a church could enact. This "very important, awful, and tremendous" action was "a judicial act of the church in which, by the authority of Christ, she cuts off and entirely excludes an unworthy member from union and communion with the church, and from all the rights and privileges thereof." Early in the

---

[27] *An Abstract of the Records of Welsh Neck Baptist Church.*
[28] Charleston Association, *A Confession of Faith*, 20–21.
[29] *An Abstract of the Records of Cashaway Baptist Church.*
[30] *An Abstract of the Records of Welsh Neck Baptist Church.*

182 OLIVER HART AND THE RISE OF BAPTIST AMERICA

nineteenth century a Georgia Baptist named Jesse Mercer (1769–1841) would assert, "When a Gospel church is sitting, in Gospel order, for the transaction of disciplinary business, there is not a higher court on earth."[31] Practically, excommunication meant withdrawing fellowship from the disciplined individual, refusing to share meals or everyday conversation. Members opened themselves to this shunning when guilty of "notorious and atrocious crimes," as well as for repeated, stubborn offenses of lesser ones. Hannah Murphy was excommunicated for "having vilified several of ye members of ye Church," "neglect[ing] her place" in worship, and having "despised ye authority of ye Church after having made use of all ye means we could tame her, but in vain."[32]

In 1771 Cashaway excommunicated William Owens, a recurring figure in their records. Within months of Owens accusing Big Benjamin James for "having sold a mare to him, but was not delivered," and a woman named Mrs. Jamison (the same who protested her severe treatment by the church) for "drinking too much," the church acted against Owens. It had started with his "sin of Drunkenness," but this was "agrevated and highten" by a string of other crimes: "breaking ye Sabbath, keeping bad company, breaking solem resolution and Declaration, entered into and made by him against Drinking Spiriteous Liqueor— excepting Church advised him to drink." The broken vow was particularly offensive; when he had made his commitment known, "all ye members strongly advised him to keep his vow sacred," but Owens "broak through all." When the church sent for him to attend their disciplinary meeting, he refused to come and "still continued his bad ways of living." On that basis, Owens was "excluded from being a member of this Church until he returns by repentance."[33] Other crimes calling for speedy excommunication included "all sins against the letter of the ten commandments," sins that called for "severe corporal punishment from human laws, provided those laws are not contrary to the laws of God," and "all such sins as are highly scandalous in nature and expose the church to contempt," as when Betsy Raburn was excommunicated by the Welsh Neck Church for "Adultery" in 1785.[34]

[31] Jesse Mercer, "Reply to H.—No. 1," *Christian Index*, February 11, 1836, 67–68, quoted in Wills, *Democratic Religion*, 29.

[32] *Abstract of the Records of Cashaway Baptist Church.*

[33] *Abstract of the Records of Cashaway Baptist Church.*

[34] *Abstract of the Records of Cashaway Baptist Church.* For a discussion of the inequality of men and women in Baptist churches, particularly in church discipline cases involving sexual crimes, see McCurry, *Masters of Small Worlds*, 179–91.

"PROMOTING SO LAUDABLE A DESIGN" 183

Excommunication was a congregational action. The "solemn business" began with calling the accused member to appear, at either a regular or a special called meeting of the church, for a fair trial and an opportunity to provide a defense. Refusal to appear before the church was deemed "a sign of guilt, a contempt of the authority of the church, and an aggravation of his crime," and the church proceeded with excommunication. The Welsh Neck Church sent for Mary Walsh in 1785 because it was reported that she had "entered herself a Scholar in a dancing School." When she did not appear at the next meeting, she was excommunicated.[35] If the accused did appear, after opening with prayer for direction, the individual's case was to be "impartially examined by the Word of God." If the church found the accused guilty, he or she was not immediately cut off but given opportunity to repent while the church mourned and prayed. If the offender continued obstinate and incorrigible, the church proceeded with excommunication.[36]

*

Eighteenth-century Baptist discipline may grate against twenty-first-century sensibilities, but Hart and the Charleston Association believed it to be vital for church health. They were not alone in this opinion. Early American Methodists were also committed to a well-disciplined membership, though they enacted it at a quarterly conference meeting rather than at the congregational level. "Unless the discipline of the church is enforced, what sincere person would ever join a society, amongst whom they saw all ungodliness connived at?" Methodist bishop Francis Asbury asked.[37] Both Baptists and Methodists agreed: properly administered, discipline upheld God's holiness by removing sin in Christ's church; it protected the rest of the fellowship from sin's spreading influence; ultimately discipline even benefited the offender, who was often led to repentance through this confrontation with the church. Such an event took place at Ashley River in June 1738, when Sister Mary Shepherd "came & humbled her self to the Church & desired forgiveness for her offence vis railing agt. Bro: Chanler & Sister Peacock & desired that her Suspension might be taken off & She Restored to her place." In response, it was "accordingly done. The Church looking on her acknowledgements to be Satisfactory, at ye Same time admonishing her to be more Carefull for ye

---

[35] *Abstract of the Records of Welsh Neck Baptist Church.*

[36] Charleston Association, *A Confession of Faith*, 21–23.

[37] Wigger, *Taking Heaven by Storm*, 100; for early American Methodist disciplinary practice, see 98–103.

184  OLIVER HART AND THE RISE OF BAPTIST AMERICA

future wc. She promised by ye help of God to be."[38] Baptists believed that when moved to "shame and repentance," the sinning individual was to be "received again with all love and tenderness, and to be comforted that they may be not swallowed up with overmuch sorrow."[39] Through discipline, churches enacted the love of Christ the good shepherd, who left the ninety-nine behind to pursue a single wandering sheep.

The *Summary of Church Discipline* demonstrates the gravity with which Hart and the Charleston Association Baptists treated the authority of the local church. Churches were not man-made social organizations but "the households of God," and so their order and government were no small matter. The *Summary* remains one of Hart's most significant, if least remembered, contributions. Its adoption by the Charleston Association, along with the *Charleston Confession*, profoundly shaped the traditional ethos of the Baptist denomination in the South for the next century. The *Summary* saw numerous other publications after its initial run. Baptists printed it in 1783 in Wilmington, North Carolina, and again in 1794 in Richmond, Virginia, along with another round of two thousand copies in Charleston that year. Deep into the nineteenth century, Baptists of the South still looked to the *Summary* for guidance in church matters. It was published along with the *Charleston Confession* in 1813, 1831, and 1850.

*

Beyond the South, Baptists took a major step toward denominational strength, respectability, and unity across the American colonies in the 1760s with the founding of Rhode Island College. For many Baptists, an educated ministry was suspicious, a man-made substitute for the unction of the Holy Spirit and too closely associated with the Establishment Pedobaptist denominations that had despised and persecuted Baptists for so long. The Connecticut Congregationalist Joseph Fish noted this in 1768 when he wrote, "The Baptists in general have been so much abused by those who boast of their *Learning*, that it is not strange if many mere prejudiced against such men."[40] In New England most college-educated Baptist ministers were like the Harvard-trained Jeremiah Condy of First Baptist Boston and John Callendar Jr. of First Baptist Newport: Arminian rationalists who opposed revival and were overly concerned with ingratiating themselves with their

---

[38] Kegley and Little, "Records of the Ashley River Baptist Church," 11.
[39] Charleston Association, *A Confession of Faith*, 26–27.
[40] Recorded in Isaac Backus, *A Fish Caught in his Own Net* (Boston, 1768), 109.

"PROMOTING SO LAUDABLE A DESIGN" 185

refined Congregationalist neighbors and who looked down on typical pietistic Baptists.[41] This anti-education attitude was strongest among the Separate Baptists in New England and the South, though it could be found among all Baptist groups. Ebenezer Kinnersley, now on faculty at Philadelphia College, remarked in 1757 how surprised he was that Baptist parents seemed indifferent toward "higher education."[42] Even the refined South Carolina planter-preacher Francis Pelot expressed concern to Hezekiah Smith in 1771 that colleges could turn prospective Baptist preachers into "learned, graceless wretches."[43]

The most ardent supporters of formal education among Baptists came from the Philadelphia Association, which was thinking a great deal about education in the 1760s. In 1761 the Association began lending out books donated by a wealthy London Baptist merchant, Thomas Hollis (1659–1731), who was also a benefactor of Harvard University. Morgan Edwards mentioned the small minister's library in a letter to the board of London Baptist ministers that year, as well as the "infant seminary of learning" lately set up at Hopewell Academy. Noting that the Association had grown from nine churches in 1734 to twenty-eight in 1761, Edwards underscored the value of education initiatives and invited the London Baptists to make a financial contribution to Hopewell Academy. Also in 1761 the busy Edwards called for orders of Baptist catechisms to be printed and distributed among the churches.[44]

Already mentioned several times in this narrative as a chronicler of eighteenth-century Baptist life, Edwards deserves as much credit as anyone of his time for moving Baptists to denominational refinement. Born in Wales in 1722, he had received through the sponsorship of his church two years of formal study at the Baptist Bristol Academy, where he learned Latin, Greek, and Hebrew, afterward claiming that "the Greek and Hebrew are the two eyes of a minister." After Edwards spent a brief time ministering to Baptists in Cork, Ireland, John Gill recommended him to fill the vacant Philadelphia Baptist Church pulpit in 1761. By 1762 he was already promoting the idea of a Baptist college.[45] Rhode Island seemed the obvious location. Edwards called it "the land of the Baptists," estimating that Baptists made up some 40% of the

---

[41] See McLoughlin, *New England Dissent*, 1:282–88, 491–92.

[42] Kinnersely quoted in Davies, *Transatlantic Brethren*, 95.

[43] Francis Pelot to Hezekiah Smith, January 19, 1771, Backus Papers (ANTS), in McLoughlin, *New England Dissent*, 1:499.

[44] Gillette, *Minutes*, 82–83.

[45] Davies, *Transatlantic Brethren*, 95.

186 OLIVER HART AND THE RISE OF BAPTIST AMERICA

colony's population. The Congregationalist Ezra Stiles (1727–1795) guessed in 1760 that of the twenty-two thousand Baptists in New England, 80% lived in Rhode Island.[46] Edwards and James Manning traveled to Newport in the summer of 1763 to begin generating interest for a college.

From the start, the Baptists wished their school to be interdenominational, with non-Baptists helping with the charter and serving as trustees. Baptists, however, were still expected to "have the lead." How this balance between broad catholicity and Baptist confessionalism would be struck in actual practice would prove to be a matter of some controversy. The trouble started with the initial drafting of the school's charter in 1763. At the suggestion of the Newport Baptists, Edwards and Manning asked Newport's highly regarded Congregationalist minister Stiles to draw it up. Reports conflict as to what happened next. Some suggest Stiles acted in good faith on vague instructions from Edwards and Manning, others that he craftily attempted to steal the Baptists' college from them behind the scenes.[47] Whatever his actual motives, Stiles produced a charter for a school not nearly Baptist enough for the Philadelphia Association's taste. He made twenty-two of the thirty-six trustees Baptists but lodged the most significant power with a committee of twelve, eight of whom were Congregationalists. Stiles's draft pleased the Congregationalists and Episcopalians involved with the school, as well as the more sophisticated New England Baptists who desired a "fraternal union" with their Congregationalist neighbors (including those at Newport who had recommended Stiles).[48] Jeremiah Condy, whom many in this group hoped would be president, apparently "desired the College might be on a broad bottom; and that the direction of it might not be confined to any particular denomination."[49] But when the charter was presented at the August 1763 General Assembly, the Philadelphia Association and their like-minded Baptist brethren in Providence scrambled to revise it for the General Assembly's next meeting.

The new charter (authored by Samuel Jones and a Philadelphia Baptist lawyer, Robert Strettle Jones) resulted in a more demonstrably Baptist

[46] McLoughlin, *New England Dissent*, 1:492.

[47] See McLoughlin, *New England Dissent*, 1:493–94 for the former position; for the latter, see James Manning's sympathetic biographer Reuben Aldridge Guild, *Early History of Brown University, Including the Life, Times, and Correspondence of President Manning* (Providence, RI, 1897), 510–49.

[48] For a profile of these New England Baptists, see McLoughlin, *New England Dissent*, 1:278–300.

[49] The words are from the Congregationalist Andrew Eliot of Boston, describing Condy's position to Thomas Hollis in a 1768 letter, in *Massachusetts Historical Collections* 34 (1858): 431. Eliot, speaking for his Congregationalist brethren, called Condy "a Baptist minister of great candor, learning and ingenuity," who "would have been an honor to that or any other seminary."

school. A certain number of Quakers, Congregationalists, and Episcopalians were still represented on the governing board, religious tests of students were forbidden, and it was assured that "Sectarian differences of opinions shall not make any Part of the Public and Classical Instruction." But the charter also stipulated that the president must always be a Baptist minister and that he lead the compulsory chapel services each week. The Stiles party lamented these changes. "It was at first designed to be on a catholic plan, and all denominations united to promote it," wrote the Congregationalist Andrew Eliot, but with the new charter, many non-Baptists pulled their support.[50] In the long run, though, it is unlikely the college could have won the broad support of Baptists for the kind of school Stiles had proposed.

No one supported Rhode Island College more vocally in the Southern colonies than Oliver Hart. Calling himself a "Friend to Learning" in a letter to Samuel Jones in 1762, he wrote that he would "rejoice if a College can be erected in these Parts," and expressed hope that "all the Baptists on the Continent will unite in promoting so laudable a Design." Hart saw the school as advancing two of his lifelong passions: the education of Baptist ministers and the union of American Baptists into an effective, national denomination. He was further delighted by the appointment of his twenty-five-year-old friend James Manning, rather than Jeremiah Condy, as the school's first president. Manning moved with his family to Warren, Rhode Island, in 1764 and was formally appointed "President of the College, Professor of languages, and other branches of learning, with full power to act in these capacities at Warren, or elsewhere," in 1765. In addition to running the new school and teaching its classes, the tireless Manning gathered a Baptist church in Warren and helped found the New England Warren Association.

Hart was so enthused about the college that he volunteered to go on a fundraising tour across Europe. Hart had "corresponded with Dr. Gill, and several more of our London Ministers, for many years past" and believed he could "influence them to contribute in some Way, or other, to so valuable an Institution." This idea may have been little more than a passing fancy, because by the next year Hart had "laid aside all thoughts of it . . . convinced [he] would do but little for the College."[51] The Philadelphia Association wisely sent the far better-connected Morgan Edwards instead, who collected over nine hundred pounds in a 1767 sweep through the British Isles. Edwards

[50] McLoughlin, *New England Dissent*, 1:498.
[51] Oliver Hart to Samuel Jones, February 7, 1764, McKesson MSS, HSP.

188   OLIVER HART AND THE RISE OF BAPTIST AMERICA

would call his efforts on behalf of the college "the greatest service he has done or hopes to do for the honour of the Baptist interest."[52]

Hart was far more valuable to the college in South Carolina than he would have been in Europe. In 1769 he offered the Charleston Baptist Church to the college as a base for raising funds in the South, and his friend Hezekiah Smith, a trustee, came down to lead the effort. Throughout the winter of 1769 and the spring of 1770, Smith's journals contain numerous references to staying in Hart's home and preaching from his pulpit when Smith was not reaching into Baptist pockets. As he had six years earlier, Hart often accompanied Smith as he traveled into the South Carolina backcountry. After Smith returned home, Hart praised him in a letter to Manning: "No man could have done more, and few would have done so much as he has, to serve the institution. He has met with much opposition, and bore many reflections, but none of these things have discouraged him. I heartily wish the benefactions of this province may greatly promote the welfare of the college." North or South, the Baptists of colonial America formed a vast web of interconnected relationships. It would take all the leading figures of that far-flung community to make the vision of a Baptist college a reality.[53]

After Smith returned to Massachusetts, the trustees asked Hart to carry on his fundraising in the South. Specifically the college commissioned Hart, Pelot, and Gano to "address the Baptist Associations throughout America, and urge their cooperation in these efforts to raise funds for the college." Hart subsequently led the Charleston Association in 1774 to adopt a motion, "recommending to every member to pay sixpence sterling, annually, for three years consecutively, to their Elder, or some suitable person; this money to be paid to the Treasurer of the College."[54] Though not a large sum, this financial pledge as war approached indicated a serious commitment to establishing a school. Both the Philadelphia and Warren associations later adopted the Charleston plan.

\*

Hart was transparently committed to Rhode Island College, but the school provided extra incentive for him to raise funds at its first commencement on September 7, 1769. Four years earlier Manning had opened the school with one student, fourteen-year-old William Rogers (destined to become another

---

[52] Davies, *Transatlantic Brethren*, 111.
[53] Oliver Hart to James Manning, April 17, 1770, Manning MSS, JHL.
[54] Guild, *Early History of Brown University*, 22.

"PROMOTING SO LAUDABLE A DESIGN" 189

one of Hart's young protégés). On this day seven received the Bachelor of Arts degree. It was an emotional day for many who had invested so much to make the school a reality. One newspaper reported, "The scene was tender, the subject felt, and the audience affected." Besides graduating Rogers, Manning also awarded several honorary Master of Arts degrees to Baptist ministers in America and Great Britain, including Oliver Hart. Part of Manning's motive, of course, was to induce the honorees to help with fundraising. In one humorous illustration of this, Francis Pelot wrote a letter asking Hezekiah Smith if the rumor were true that Pelot had been awarded one of these honorary degrees; he asked because Manning had written to ask him about collecting for the college in Georgia.[55] Hart certainly held up his end of this bargain. But William Rogers, who could be cynical about honorary degrees, later insisted that "the improvements of his mind by self-application, close reading, and habitual reflection" qualified Hart to receive such a degree more than most. Hart later encouraged Richard Furman, another self-educated minister, to appreciate the degree for what it was: "It is an honorary title, frequently bestowed on persons who have not had the advantage of a liberal education. I know one, at least, on whom it was bestowed, who was every way more undeserving of it than Mr. Furman."[56]

Commencement ceremonies and honorary degrees provided another signal of growing Baptist sophistication in the 1760s. The Philadelphia Association wished to be rid of "vain and insufficient men" who "set themselves up to be preachers" behind the claim of an "extraordinary call" from God. As moderate revivalists, they did not wish to denigrate the indispensable nature of the Holy Sprit's call to preach (though they would be accused of this), but they did not believe a supernatural calling excused a lack of preparation.[57] No doubt, these Baptists were also concerned to improve their social standing among the other colonial churches. They wanted, in the words of Thomas Hollis, "Baptist youth to be educated for the ministry, and equally regarded with Pedobaptists." Forming a school would go a long way toward elevating Baptists into the American religious mainstream. This was especially important in New England, where gaining social cachet would better position the Baptists to fight for equal religious rights.

[55] Francis Pelot to Hezekiah Smith, October 28, 1771, Backus Papers (ANTS), cited in McLoughlin, *New England Dissent*, 1:500–1.
[56] Guild, *Early History of Brown University*, 80–89; Rogers, *A Sermon*, 25; Oliver Hart to Richard Furman, May 30, 1793, Hart MSS, JBDML.
[57] Gillette, *Minutes*, 121–22.

190 OLIVER HART AND THE RISE OF BAPTIST AMERICA

But not all Baptists hailed these changes with enthusiasm. One minister foresaw in 1770 "a new Succession of Scholar Ministers. . . . It has got so far already as scarcely to do for a common Illiterate Minister to preach in the Baptist meetg at providence." To many rural, Pietistic Baptists especially, college degrees were still a hollow replacement for the enabling power of the Holy Spirit and a pandering to the Pedobaptist elites who had been persecuting Baptists for more than a century. Others resented the push for an educated ministry as yet another attempt by the Philadelphia Association to exercise control over Baptists, weeding out those ministers who failed to meet their educational requirements. Reflecting the moderate revivalism of the Philadelphia Association, Hart believed that no academic degree, honorary or earned, could make up for the absence of God's divine call to preach, but learning certainly made "an excellent handmaiden to grace."[58]

*

Hart's honorary degree did nothing to dampen his revivalist zeal. In November 1769 he left with Evan Pugh for a lengthy itinerant preaching journey into the South Carolina backcountry, up through North Carolina and into Virginia to his brother Silas. They would not return until February 1770. As Hart had put it in *A Summary of Church Discipline*, an ordained minister possessed "authority from Christ to preach the gospel and baptize believers in any part of the world where God, in his providence, may call him. But if he should be called unto and accept the pastoral charge of any particular church, he will be more immediately confined to them and they to him." Hart always embraced a dual allegiance, to the particular church he served and the broader world. Local churches largely accepted this arrangement, but parting from a beloved minister for lengthy periods could be difficult. "Left my family and many of my friends in tears," Hart commented. "I committed my people to the Lord and left them under the care of the Rev. Mr. [Hezekiah] Smith." Spreading revival required sacrifice by all.[59]

Hart's 1769 diary reveals the physical challenges itinerant journeys imposed on the minister.[60] Simply navigating unfamiliar paths was a major source of daily anxiety. "Towards evening we went out of the way we intended," Hart noted, but "in the evening reached what is called Drowning

[58] Guild, *Early History of Brown*, 71–72; Hart, *Christian Temple*, 46.

[59] Hart, diary, November 8, 1769, Hart MSS, SCL.

[60] For a more detailed look at eighteenth-century itinerant ministry, see Wigger, *Taking Heaven by Storm*, 48–79, and Woodmason, *Carolina Backcountry*, passim.

"PROMOTING SO LAUDABLE A DESIGN" 191

Creek, where we received better entertainment than we expected." God's providential guidance through a strange country was one of the major themes of Hart's travel record. One day he and Pugh "set off on our way, but were several times at a loss to know if we mist the way we intended to go." Yet "Providence ordered it for the best for about two o'clock we arrived at one Mr. Mayer's." Some mornings the fog was so thick they had to delay their departure; on other occasions torrential rain showers raised the creeks and rivers to impassable levels. While in Virginia, Hart saw more snow than he did in all his years in Charleston. Lodging was rarely ideal. Hart commented on one of his host families, "These were but poor people but received us into their house and did the best for us they could, but our lodging was on some straw spread before the fire, and our covering our own garments. What with the cold and hard lodging I slept but little this night." He went hunting with his brother one snowy day to put meat on the table, though he reported that they "took nothing." Itinerants also had to factor the health of their animals into their plans. Hart's horse sustained multiple injuries to eyes and legs that delayed their trip. Yet even these setbacks served to promote piety in the traveling preacher, as Hart viewed these and other obstacles on the road as opportunities to trust God. "The Lord knows what is best, may we be resigned to his will," he wrote.[61]

Hart encountered a variety of religious groups on his journey. Charles Woodmason, an Anglican itinerant missionary to the Carolina backcountry in this period, spoke of the people being "eaten up by Itinerant Teachers, Preachers, and Impostors from New England and Pennsylvania—Baptists, Presbyterians, New Lights, Independents, and an hundred other Sects—so that one day you might hear this System of Doctrine—the next day another— next day another, retrograde to both. Thus by the Variety of Taylors who would pretend to know the best fashion in which Christs Coat is to be worn none will put it on."[62] The multidenominational race for the frontier was just beginning to raise conflicts that would carry over into the nineteenth century. The itinerating Methodist bishop Francis Asbury often complained about Baptists meddling with his own prospects. They "endeavor to persuade the people that they have never been baptized; like ghosts they haunt us from place to place. O, the policy of Satan!" Asbury groused. In Delaware in 1779 Asbury again found that Baptists were "fishing in troubled water (they always

---

[61] Hart, diary, November 18, 23, 1769, January 1, 5, 1770, Hart MSS, SCL.
[62] Woodmason, *Carolina Backcountry*, 13.

192    OLIVER HART AND THE RISE OF BAPTIST AMERICA

are preaching water to people,) and striving to get into all the houses where we preach."[63] The Anglican Woodmason also despaired of keeping pace with the busy Baptists. If he announced a place and time of preaching, "three or four of these fellows are constantly at my Heels—They either get there before me, and hold forth—or after I have finish'd, or the next Day, or for days together. Had I an hundred Tongues, or as many Pairs of Legs, I could not *singly* oppose such a Numerous Crew."[64] The conciliatory Hart appears largely to have avoided any open controversy with Pedobaptists, though he never shrank from telling them what he thought. Preaching to a group of Presbyterians in 1780, he "endeavoured to prove that believers are the only proper subjects of baptism, and that dipping is the mode of administration," though he admitted afterward that he was unsure how the people received his arguments.[65]

Mostly Hart stuck to preaching his basic, conversion-focused gospel message. He delivered one message on Luke 13:24 at the home of John Davis, but the congregation was so large he "preached out of doors." After another sermon he commented, "I had some freedom and some were affected. I find the longer I stay the more the people are affected to me and my preaching. May my poor attempts be made a blessing to them." He made no comment on the character of his listeners, but he surely found them different from the crowd he normally addressed in Charleston. Woodmason felt it necessary to warn his listeners, "Bring no dogs with you—they are very troublesome." It also distressed Woodmason to no end that many in his audiences "do practice that unseemly, rude, indecent Custom of Chewing or spitting, which is very ridiculous and absurd in Public, especially in women and in Gods House."[66] Once on his journey, Hart received an invitation to preach "in the English Church." He elected for his text Exodus 32:28, "Who is on the Lord's Side?" "I was favored with a good degree of freedom; some were affected, may the Word make an abiding impression on their hearts," he prayed. Whether in the city or on the frontier, standing before Baptists or Anglicans, Hart rarely wavered from proclaiming his core message of the new birth.[67]

If Hart encountered ill treatment from other denominations on his journey, he never mentioned it. Yet Woodmason reported that the "antipathy

---

[63] John H. Wigger, *American Saint: Francis Asbury and the Methodists* (New York: Oxford University Press, 2009), 115.

[64] Woodmason, *Carolina Backcountry*, 111.

[65] Oliver Hart, diary, August 3, 1780, Hart papers, SCL.

[66] Woodmason, *Carolina Backcountry*, 88–89.

[67] Hart, diary, December 17, 24, 1769, Hart MSS, SCL.

which [Baptists and Presbyterians] bear each other is astonishing," and he claimed that a Presbyterian would rather ten of his children became an Anglican than one a Baptist. The fussy Woodmason, who made himself an easy target, complained of a variety of abuses at the hands of Baptists and other backcountry Dissenters. One "Band of rude fellows" brought "57 dogs" into church (Woodmason counted them), which "they set fighting" during the sermon. (Woodmason dismissed the service.) He claimed to have heard Baptists mocking his very name from the pulpit, saying "that tho' I was an Wood Mason, He queried if I was a *Good* Mason—but as Wood was a perishable Matter, and serv'd for Fewel, so that I should perish Everlastingly and serve for fuel to Hell fire." Preachers of all backgrounds suffered from this kind of rowdy backwoods joking; the Baptists apparently called the pale-complexioned Presbyterian William Richardson "The Pale or White Horse of Death, for his People to ride on to Hell."[68]

\*

The Baptists that Woodmason encountered were almost invariably of the Separate variety. Separate Baptists had multiplied at an astonishing rate since Shubal Stearns and Daniel Marshall landed at Sandy Creek, North Carolina, in 1755. Woodmason considered them to be "the most zealous among the Sects, to propagate their Notions, and form Establishments." By 1765 he could write with confidence, "The Baptists are now the most numerous and formidable Body of People which the Church has to encounter with." Morgan Edwards called the Sandy Creek church in 1772 "the mother of all the Separate Baptists," which after seventeen years "is become mother, grandmother, and great-grandmother to 42 churches, from which sprang 125 ministers." Sandy Creek's converts, Edwards said, "were as the drops of morning dew."[69] Though the Separates affirmed the evangelical Calvinism of the Regulars, they expressed these beliefs with a style reflecting the radical revivalism of 1740s New England Separatism. Undomesticated, they cared little for the written confessions, educated ministry, and traditional liturgical patterns of the Philadelphia Association. The Separates stressed instead the immediate, dynamic activity of the Holy Spirit, expressed through loud, passionate preaching and emotionally unrestrained worship. Edwards claimed that all the Separate ministers copied Stearns "in tones of voice and actions of

---

[68] Woodmason, *Carolina Backcountry*, 80, 111.
[69] Edwards, *Materials towards a History of the Baptists*, 2:91–92.

194   OLIVER HART AND THE RISE OF BAPTIST AMERICA

body, and some few exceed him." Philip Mulkey (1732–1801), a Stearns convert who started the first Separate Baptist Church in South Carolina, supplies one example. Mulkey had a voice that Edwards described as "very sweet," and when paired with his perpetually "smiling aspect," had an uncanny ability to "make soft impressions on the heart and fetch down tears from the eyes in a mechanical way." Edwards believed that David Garrick, the most celebrated English actor of the day, could learn from Mulkey how to "spin that sound and mix it with awe, distress, solicitude, or by other affection."[70]

Direct, emotional preaching like Mulkey's and Stearns's connected with the frontier men and women in a way that the rational and meticulously prepared sermons of a Charles Woodmason could not. "The lower class chuse to Resort to them rather than to hear a Well connected Discourse," Woodmason sniffed.[71] The raw passion and apparently otherworldly power of the Separate Baptists resonated in the hearts of the roughhewn frontier people, recalled the Separate Baptist John Leland: "The work among them was very noisy. The people would cry out, fall down, and for a time lose use of their limbs, which exercise made the bystanders marvel; some thought they were deceitful, others that they were bewitched, and many, being convinced of all, would report that God was with them of a truth."[72] The Regular Baptist Morgan Edwards, for one, was a believer. "As for the outcries, epilepsies and ecstacies attending their ministry they are not peculiar to them." He believed that "a pretnernatural and invisible hand works in the assemblies of the Separate-baptists bearing down the human mind, as was the case in primitive churches. 1 Cor 14:25."[73] The openness of more refined Regular Baptists like Edwards and Hart to accepting the unorthodox Separates would prove key in the eventual union of the two groups.

Vivid testimonies of men and women falling under the power of Separate Baptist preaching, often against their will, quickly multiplied across the South. William Coker boasted that "he would rather go to hell than to heaven if going to the latter required his being a baptist." But when he accidentally came upon Dutton Lane (1732–1801) preaching, Coker fell to the ground, "roaring," "Lord have mercy upon me. What shall I do to be saved?" Coker roared for the next hour before coming through as a "humble and pious baptist." John Pickett the dancing master shut down his dancing school "when he

---

[70] Edwards, *Materials towards a History of the Baptists*, 2:140–41.
[71] Woodmason, *Carolina Backcountry*, 20.
[72] Leland, *Writings*, 105.
[73] Edwards, *Materials towards a History of the Baptists*, 2:96–97

"PROMOTING SO LAUDABLE A DESIGN" 195

found Christ"; he would later spend three months in Fauquier Jail in 1770 for preaching the Separate Baptists' gospel.[74]

Philip Mulkey, the charming preacher of Fairforest Creek, left behind one of the most vivid Separate Baptist conversion experiences of all. One night after fiddling for a group of dancers at a party, Mulkey recalled seeing a "hideous specter," so hellish that he immediately fainted and lay as a dead man for ten minutes in the middle of the party. When he came to, he was badly shaken. He knew the specter he had seen was none other than "the Devil, and that he would have me." He quickly mounted his horse, but was tormented all the way home, believing the trees were bowing to strike him and that the stars "cast a frowning and malignant aspect upon me." Once home, he tried to conceal from his wife what had happened. This became difficult when he stopped eating and sleeping for the next several days "and continued to roar out, 'I am damned! I shall soon be in hell!'" In between his fits of terror, Mulkey grumbled against the God he believed had made him for the flames of hell. As Mulkey tried to reform his life, the Separate Baptist John Newton began visiting, reading to him passages about Christ's atonement for sinners from texts like Isaiah 53. One day, as Newton was leaving, the thought came to Mulkey, "There is Lot going out of Sodom! As soon as he disappears fire will come down and burn me." Mulkey ran after Newton, but when he disappeared from sight, Mulkey threw himself on the ground, believing fire and brimstone was about to fall on him. Instead a Bible verse came to mind: "The spirit of Elijah doth rest on Elisha [2 Kings 2:15]." After puzzling over the meaning, this hopeful application dawned on Mulkey: "Who knows but it may mean, that the spirit of John Newton shall rest on Philip Mulkey?" Latching onto the encouragement of this impulsive verse, Mulkey soon found that "the spirit of God came who I found to be a spirit of liberty, comfort, and adoption."[75]

Mulkey immediately began "preaching up conversion" to his wife, but she did not "understand" him. He then turned to his neighbor, a Mr. Campbell, who was even less receptive. Campbell "swore at me desperately, adding, What kind of project are you now upon with the word of God in your hand?'" Campbell then stripped off his clothes, spit on his hands and clinched his fists, and challenged Mulkey to a fight. The beleaguered new convert sat down and wept instead. "You know my dear neighbor, that I am unable to

[74] Edwards, *Materials towards a History of the Baptists*, 2:46, 64.
[75] Edwards, *Materials towards a History of the Baptists*, 2:141–42.

196　OLIVER HART AND THE RISE OF BAPTIST AMERICA

beat you; but now you may beat me if you will; I shall not hinder you!" With that, Campbell put his shirt back on and sat down next to Mulkey, and they both wept. Mulkey eventually returned home without converting Campbell, but he had had one full day.[76]

This was the religion of the Separates that set the frontier ablaze: visions and dreams, encounters with Satan and demon-possessed trees; immediate revelations of Scripture; instantaneous receptions of the Holy Spirit; power and zeal for service and evangelism; boldness in the face of persecution; unashamed baring of emotions. There were even divine healings: at the Fairforest Church in South Carolina, a feverish Richard Kelly was anointed with oil at a love feast and recovered within the hour. Their worship rituals also struck a deep chord. Many Separates practiced nine rites: baptism, the Lord's Supper, love feast, laying on of hands, washing feet, anointing the sick, right hand of fellowship, kiss of charity, and devoting children.[77]

The physicality of Separate Baptist worship provided one more reason to turn off their more refined observers. Hart's friend John Zubly, a Presbyterian minister in Savannah, noted with a roll of the eyes in 1772 the "crazy behavior" of Daniel Marshall, including the fact that he "insisted on washing of feet & the holy kiss as necessary Practices."[78] But no sneer directed at the Separate Baptists approached the level of disgust mustered by Woodmason:

> There are so many Absurdities committed by them, as wou'd shock one of our *Cherokee* Savages; And was a Sensible Turk or Indian to view some of their Extravagancies it would quickly determine them against Christianity. Had any such been in their Assembly as last Sunday when they communicated, the Honest Heathens would have imagin'd themselves rather amidst a Gang of frantic Lunatics broke out of Bedlam, rather than among a Society of religious Christians, met to celebrate the most sacred and Solemn Ordinance of their Religion. Here, one Fellow mounted on a Bench with Bread, and bawling, *see the Body of Christ*, Another with the Cup running around, and bellowing—*Who cleanses his Soul with the Blood of Christ*, and a thousand other Extravagancies—One on his knees in a Posture of Prayer—Others singing—some howling—These Ranting—Those Crying—Others dancing, Skipping, Laughing and rejoicing. Here two or

---

[76] Edwards, *Materials towards a History of the Baptists*, 2:142.
[77] Edwards, *Materials towards a History of the Baptists*, 2:140, 90.
[78] John J. Zubly, *The Journal of the Reverend John Joachim Zubly A.M., D.D., March 5, 1770 through June 22, 1781*, edited by Lilla Mills Hawes (Savannah: Georgia Historical Society, 1989), 21, 24.

3 Women falling on their Backs, kicking up their Heels, exposing their Nakedness to all Bystanders and others sitting Pensive, in deep Melancholy lost to in Abstraction, like Statues, quite insensible—and when rous'd by the Spectators from their pretended Reveries Transports, and indecent Postures and Actions declaring they knew nought of the Matter. That their Souls had taken flight to Heav'n, and they knew nothing of what they said or did. Spect[at]ors were highly shocked at such vile Abuse of [the] sacred. . . . Their Teacher, so far from condemning, or reproving, them, call'd it, the Work of God, and returned Thanks for actions deserving the Pillory and Whipping Post.[79]

It has sometimes been proposed that Regular Baptists like Hart shared Woodmason's contempt for the Separate Baptists and resented their success in the South.[80] Trekking across the countryside of North Carolina and Virginia, Hart and Pugh encountered numerous Separate Baptists, including John Newton, John Overton, James Muse, Nath Towel, John Prior, John Davis, and Elijah Craig. But when Hart described these meetings, he voiced no trace of the suspicion or jealousy that some Regular Baptists expressed toward the Separates in other parts of the colonies. He and Pugh immediately sensed a deep kinship with these Baptist cousins and celebrated the work they were doing. Hart and Pugh stayed in numerous Separate Baptist homes, sharing warm fellowship with each family. After arriving at the home of Thomas Cates, for example, Hart wrote, "His wife received us kindly. Providence has remarkably directed us to houses where we are welcome, among Baptist friends. Here we spent the evening agreeably in religious conversation, after supper we sang and prayed, and so lay down to rest." Hart and Pugh even performed an ordination for the Separate Baptist John Newton at the Congaree Church, though the Sandy Creek Association afterward censured Newton for this.[81] The natural bond Hart felt with the Separate Baptists can be contrasted with his encounter with a Rev. Jackson, a Pedobaptist minister in Virginia. Jackson spent the night at Silas Hart's home one evening. Afterward Oliver Hart commented, "He seems to be very free in conversation, of good learning, but I could wish he were a little more spiritual."

---

[79] Woodmason, *Carolina Backcountry*, 101–2.

[80] See especially Lumpkin, *Baptist Foundations in the South*, v–vi.

[81] Edwards, *Materials towards a History of the Baptists*, 2:146. Newton's personal connections with Hart no doubt contributed to their camaraderie. Newton was also from Pennsylvania, raised Anglican, but baptized in 1752 at Hart's home church in Southampton by Joshua Potts. He had come to South Carolina in 1765.

198   OLIVER HART AND THE RISE OF BAPTIST AMERICA

Jackson gave Hart further cause for regret at the service he conducted the next Sunday. "He sprinkled two twin children by the names of James and John and said he baptized them," Hart noted wryly.[82]

*

As Hart now entered the 1770s, his own revival ministry had been instrumental in expanding the Baptist denomination in the colonial South and throughout America. The Charleston Association, stabilized by the *Charleston Confession* and *Summary of Church Discipline*, was extending its reach throughout the South. Broader denominational initiatives that Hart had supported, notably Rhode Island College, gave further cause for encouragement, as did the success of the Separate Baptists on the frontiers. In the next decade Hart would work to see all these Baptist groups come together in a single denomination.

[82]  Hart, diary, November 22, December 21, 28, 1769, Haart MSS, SCL.

# 9

# "Comforts and mercies, losses and crosses"

## A Transitional Season

The decade of the 1770s began with the conclusion of one of the most formative relationships of Oliver Hart's life. After preaching an estimated eighteen thousand sermons, crisscrossing the Atlantic Ocean thirteen times, and holding together a transcontinental revival movement for over thirty years, George Whitefield died on September 30, 1770, in Newburyport, Massachusetts. The night before, he had begun weakly crawling up the stairs of his host's home to go to bed, but crowds broke into the house and begged for another sermon. Though nearly dead, Whitefield delivered the gospel, as he had done for forty years. He was buried in a crypt under the pulpit of the Old South Presbyterian Church in Newburyport. Whitefield had been the decisive spiritual influence in the lives of countless men and women in his fifty-six years; not least of these was Oliver Hart. Whitefield was perhaps the primary agent in Hart's conversion in 1740, and Whitefield's revivalism in Charleston helped save the Particular Baptists from extinction a decade before Hart arrived there. From 1750 to 1770 Hart had been one of Whitefield's key supporters whenever the grand itinerant had come through Charleston. In fact Hart's last contact with Whitefield had been a revival collaboration, one of their most significant.[1]

*

On March 4, 1770, Whitefield preached in Charleston for the last time. On this occasion a former slave named John Marrant (1755–1791) wandered up. As many had done over the years, Marrant planned to disrupt Whitefield's meeting. Marrant was a musician, and he intended to blow a French horn in the middle of the sermon. But as Marrant unshouldered his instrument, Whitefield locked eyes with him, pointed his finger, and recited his text: "Prepare to meet thy God, O Israel" (Amos 4:12). Marrant fell to the

---

[1] For Whitefield's death, see Kidd, *George Whitefield*, 249–57.

*Oliver Hart and the Rise of Baptist America*. Eric C. Smith, Oxford University Press (2020). © Oxford University Press.
DOI: 10.1093/oso/9780197506325.001.0001

200 OLIVER HART AND THE RISE OF BAPTIST AMERICA

ground, "speechless and silent." It was a half-hour before he regained consciousness; when he did, Whitefield was still preaching. "Every word I heard from the minister was like a parcel of swords thrust into me," Marrant recalled. "I thought I saw the devil on every side of me. I was constrained in the bitterness of my spirit to halloo out in the midst of the congregation." Marrant was carried to the vestry, where Whitefield visited him after the service. "Jesus Christ has got thee at last," Whitefield told him. Marrant was then transported home and put to bed. Before Whitefield left Charleston, he asked Hart to visit the man.[2]

Marrant recalled that when Hart walked upstairs and entered his room, the minister's presence only increased his distress. Hart tried to take hold of Marrant's hand for prayer, but Marrant escaped to the other side of the bed. In his weakened state, he collapsed from the effort, and Hart moved in. He took Marrant by the hand, raised him to his feet, and addressed him warmly with the gospel. When Hart was ready to pray for Marrant's conversion, he fell on his knees, pulling Marrant down with him. After several minutes of fervid prayer, Hart rose and asked Marrant "how he now did"; Marrant replied that he now felt "much worse." Hart was undeterred. "Come, we will have the old thing over again," he said cheerfully, pulling Marrant down to kneel with him again. After several more minutes of earnest prayer, Hart inquired, "How do you do now?" Marrant cried, "Worse and worse," and asked Hart "if he intended to kill [him]." Hart simply bore down harder. "No, no," he replied, "you are worth a thousand dead men, let us try the old thing over again." For a third time Hart and Marrant fell on their knees to pray. This time something inside Marrant broke. "Near the close of his prayer," he remembered, "the Lord was pleased to set my soul at perfect liberty, and being filled with joy I began to praise the Lord immediately; my sorrows were turned into peace, and joy, and love." Hart asked a final time, "How is it now?," and Marrant answered, "All is well, all happy." Hart visited Marrant every day for the next several days. He exhorted Marrant on their final visit, "Hold fast what thou has already obtained, 'till Jesus Christ come."[3]

The test of Marrant's hold came quickly. His new evangelical religion alienated him from his family over the following weeks, and he was forced to flee to the "wilderness." Thus began an action-packed career as a Calvinistic Methodist evangelist. In the forests of South Carolina and Georgia he

[2] Marrant and Aldridge, *A Narrative of the Lord's Wonderful Dealings with John Marrant*, 11.
[3] Marrant and Aldridge, *A Narrative of the Lord's Wonderful Dealings with John Marrant*, 12–13. Hart's last words are a quotation of Revelation 3:11.

learned to speak the language of the local Indians and preached to members of the Cherokee, Creek, Choctaw, and Chickasaw tribes. He later returned to Charleston, where he reunited with his family and preached to slaves until the war. During the Revolution he fought as a British sailor and cannoneer for six years, before suffering a serious injury in an engagement with a Dutch ship. Marrant went to England in 1785, where he received ordination at the Countess of Huntingdon's Bath Chapel. He then carried the gospel and a vision for a holy African community to black Loyalist refugees in Nova Scotia. He returned to England just before his death in 1791 at the age of thirty-five. His published narrative of his life, one of the earliest and most important black autobiographies, saw some fifteen editions.[4]

With many others, Marrant could identify the turning point of his life as the moment of evangelical conversion, facilitated by the partnership of George Whitefield and Oliver Hart. News of Whitefield's death surely stirred Hart to reflect on his own journey since he first heard the itinerant as a teenager. Most of the older men who had influenced Hart back in the 1740s, men like Whitefield, Jenkin Jones, and Gilbert Tennent, had all died. In their places younger men Hart had helped mentor were rising to positions of leadership: Samuel Stillman at First Baptist Boston, Samuel Jones leading the Philadelphia Association, James Manning overseeing Rhode Island College. At forty-seven Hart perhaps sensed he was moving into a new phase of his life, but the next five years would bring many more changes than he could have imagined.

*

An exciting announcement disrupted Hart's routine on Friday, October 16, 1772. Sarah Hart, at age forty-two, was going into labor with their eighth child. By 5 o'clock she had given birth to a baby girl. Oliver and Sarah decided to name her after her mother, but they may have exchanged worried glances when they saw how fragile Baby Sarah was; she would die just three days later. It was a tragic blow to Oliver, but his mind was on his wife. Childbirth was risky at Sarah's age, and her strength had been completely spent in

---

[4] For Marrant, see Cedrick May, "John Marrant and the Narrative Construction of an Early Black Methodist Evangelist," *African American Review* 38, no. 4 (Winter 2004): 553–70; John Salliant, " 'Wipe Away All Tears from Their Eyes': John Marrant's Theology in the Black Atlantic, 1785–1808," *Journal of Millennial Studies* 1, no. 2 (Winter 1999), http://www.mille.org/publications/winter98/saillant.PDF; and Peter H. Wood, " 'Jesus Christ Has Got Thee at Last': Afro-American Conversion as a Forgotten Chapter in Eighteenth-Century Southern Intellectual History," *Bulletin of the Center for the Study of Southern Culture and Religion* 3, no. 3 (November 1979): 1–7.

202 OLIVER HART AND THE RISE OF BAPTIST AMERICA

the delivery. One day after their baby died, Sarah Brees Hart followed her daughter into another world. Oliver had lost his "dear wife," with whom he had spent over half his life. "We lived together 24 years, 7 months, and 25 days when death separated us," he wrote. Numb with grief, he buried his two Sarahs on the same day.[5]

As with most women of the eighteenth century, we know little about Sarah Hart. If she ever wrote a letter or kept a diary, they have not survived. Nor does she figure prominently in Oliver's personal papers, which focus almost exclusively on personal spiritual matters. Throughout their marriage, Sarah remained in the background, quietly supporting her husband through the vicissitudes of church ministry by bearing and rearing his children and keeping up their house. Some of her female neighbors in Charleston revolted against this sort of arrangement. One anonymous woman complained in the *Charleston Gazette*:

> How wretched is a Woman's Fate,
> No happy Change her Fortune knows,
> Subject to Man in every State.
> How can she then be free from Woes? . . .
> Oh, Cruel Pow'rs! Since you've design'd
> That Man, *vain* Man! Should bear the Sway;
> To a *Slave's* Fetters add a *slavish* Mind,
> That I may cheerfully your Will obey.[6]

Sarah knew of such opinions and likely felt their force on some especially trying days. Yet as an eighteenth-century Baptist woman, she pursued what Janet Moore Lindman has called "a domesticated piety," serving God by prioritizing the roles of wife and mother.[7]

Sarah shared a name with the Old Testament wife of Abraham, whom the Apostle Peter praised for "obeying Abraham, calling him lord." The biblical Sarah modeled the Christian feminine ideal of a "meek and quiet spirit" by unquestioningly following her husband on a Quixotic odyssey of trust in an invisible God. When Peter called Christian women to live as Sarah's

---

[5] Hart, *Original Diary*, 6. Catherine Brekus provides some perspective on eighteenth-century childbirth in *Sarah Osborn's World*, 77–78, 89.

[6] Edgar, *South Carolina*, 170–71.

[7] Lindman, *Bodies of Belief*, 112. For a provocative study of how the piety of New England Baptist women was increasingly moved to the domestic rather than the public realm over the course of the eighteenth century, see Juster, *Disorderly Women*.

## "COMFORTS AND MERCIES, LOSSES AND CROSSES" 203

"daughters" by likewise being "in subjection to their own husbands," Sarah Hart strove to live up to her name.[8] She was just eighteen when she and Oliver wed in 1748, and may have expected to settle down to a calm and predictable life in their hometown of Southampton, Pennsylvania. But that changed in their first year of marriage, when Oliver submitted to the call to preach. More changes followed, rapidly. She gave birth to their first child, Seth, in November 1748. The next year she stood in the Philadelphia harbor holding Baby Seth and pregnant with her second child, watching Oliver's ship disappear from sight, bound for Charleston. They would still be separated when she delivered Eleanor the following May, the first of many times she shared her husband for the sake of expanding the Baptist interest.

Domesticated piety came with plenty of risks and sorrows in the eighteenth century. One month after Eleanor's birth, Sarah loaded up her two small children for a twenty-eight-day boat ride to Charleston. The trip itself was successful, but months into settling into her new home, Seth died, just weeks shy of his second birthday. Sadly, these would not be the last tears Sarah would shed over her babies. Two years later she was pregnant with their third child, when a "great and terrible hurricane happened in Carolina" in September 1752. As Oliver recalled, "My house was washed down and all I had almost totally destroyed." The Harts survived but were left homeless. Two months later Hannah was born; the little hurricane baby died nine months later. Soon Sarah was pregnant again, and in November 1754, on the heels of the Charleston youth revival, she gave birth to her fourth child and second son, named Oliver, who would live. Four years later another baby boy arrived, John. In two more years Joseph, Sarah's sixth child, entered the Hart family, but he would live only one year. In 1762 Mary Baker, the seventh Hart baby, was born. She was the last until Baby Sarah, ten years later. Of her eight children, four preceded Sarah in death.[9]

Sarah may never have crossed paths with her contemporary Eliza Lucas Pinckney, the wealthy Anglican plantation owner just outside of Charleston. Yet death visited the families of both devout Low Country women, and Pinckney's expressions of faith upon the death of her husband represent the same ideal to which a Baptist woman like Sarah would have aspired. "We have, my dear children, mett with the greatest of human Evils," Pinckney wrote,

---

[8] See 1 Peter 3:1–6.
[9] Hart, *Original Diary*, 2–6.

204 OLIVER HART AND THE RISE OF BAPTIST AMERICA

but we must drink the cup it has pleased God to give us, a bitter Cup indeed! But aloted us by Infinite Wisdom, and let us ever remember, terrible and grievous as the stroke is, we have still reason to thank the hand from whence it come . . . and we are indebted to the infinitely wise and good God, and above all for the most comfortable and joyous hope that we shall meet in Glory never never more to be separated![10]

Whether facing displacement from home, hurricanes, or the death of a spouse or a child, a significant aspect of domesticated piety for an eighteenth-century woman was learning to resign oneself to the will of God in distress and loss.

Another element of Sarah's domesticated piety involved simply managing the Hart household from day to day. She oversaw the cooking, cleaning, washing, tending the garden and livestock, and raising the children. She seems to have been efficient enough that Oliver was left free to pursue his ministry and private piety without hindrance. Later, when war separated Oliver from his second wife, Anne, he admitted to being completely hapless in the domestic sphere and scrambled to secure a housekeeper by any means necessary. Presumably Sarah had always taken care of these things during their marriage. As household manager she also oversaw the family's slaves, a fixture in their home throughout the Charleston years. The year before Sarah's death, Oliver had purchased a young African woman and her son. "Dinah and her son Friday were bought april 9, 1771. Dinah was then supposed to be about twenty years of age. Friday was born May 29, 1767. The two cost 365 pounds," Hart recorded. Sarah's relationship with the slaves in her home was, of course, marked by the complexity of paternalism. She would have viewed Dinah and Friday as "members of the family" and serving as their mother figure and spiritual guide. While also disciplining their slaves, white women like Sarah often expressed care by making them clothes, helping at the hour of childbirth, acting as nurse in times of sickness, giving out special treats from the kitchen, and of course attending to their spiritual conditions. In this way, moderate evangelical women, along with their men, helped to sacralize slavery by fulfilling familial duties to their slaves.[11]

---

[10] Pinckney, *The Letterbook*, 95.

[11] Hart, *Original Diary*, 2–6. For other treatments of the white conception of slaves as part of the family, see McCurry, *Masters of Small Worlds*, 130–207; Genovese, *Roll, Jordan, Roll*, esp. 83–84; Elizabeth Fox-Genovese, *Within the Plantation Household: Black and White Women of the Old South* (Chapel Hill: University of North Carolina Press, 1988), 23–24; and Robert Manson Myers, *The Children of Pride: A True Story of Georgia and the Civil War* (New Haven, CT: Yale University Press, 1972).

## "COMFORTS AND MERCIES, LOSSES AND CROSSES" 205

From a family perspective, the final years of Sarah's life must have been gratifying. In March 1770 her daughter Eleanor married Thomas Screven, great-grandson of the Charleston Baptist patriarch William Screven. Before the year was up Eleanor had given birth to a daughter, and Sarah held her first grandchild; Eleanor and Thomas named her Sarah. The next year marked another family milestone, as thirteen-year-old John Hart enrolled at Rhode Island College. It was a proud moment for Sarah to see the first family member attend a formal school, particularly one that Oliver helped establish. At the same time, sending their barely teenage son some nine hundred miles away must have stirred no small anxiety in her heart, for another key element of domesticated piety was providing spiritual guidance to one's children, whether in person or by letter. Eliza Pinckney's persistent epistolary counsel to her own sons reflects the same concerns that Sarah would have had for her college-bound son: "For be assured my dear child, I would not hesitate a moment were it in my choice whether I would have you a learned man with every accomplishment or a good man without any," Pinckney wrote. "But as I hope you will be both, I commit you to the Divine Protection and guidance and recommend you to be careful of what acquaintances you make and what friendships you contract, for much depends on the example and advice of those we are fond off, and deviations from Virtue even small ones are extreamly hard to recover."[12] Whether or not Sarah ever wrote to John like this, his later behavior indicates that she had legitimate cause for worry. Yet she also had new concerns at this stage; as her older children were marrying, having children, and moving away, she learned of her own pregnancy, her eighth child.[13]

Beyond serving her household, hospitality represented another important venue for a Baptist woman's domesticated piety. On itinerant missionary journeys, Oliver depended on this aspect of feminine spirituality for his room and board on the frontier; in Charleston, Baptist women like Samuel Stillman's mother opened their homes for Hart's Sunday evening lectures and special revival meetings for inquirers.[14] As a minister's wife, Sarah would have practiced hospitality for religious purposes more than most Baptist women. Oliver's diary of the 1754 revival reveals how frequently the Hart home served as the site of ministry, with individuals showing up at odd hours

---

[12] Pinckney, *The Letterbook*, 159.
[13] Hart, *Original Diary*, 5–6.
[14] For the important relationship between itinerant ministers and their female hostesses, see Heyrman, *Southern Cross*, 161–64, 169–71.

for counsel and much of the church sometimes joining in the family's household devotionals. Thanks to Oliver's gregarious nature with friends and colleagues, Sarah played hostess to an unceasing parade of ministerial guests throughout her time in Charleston.[15] Novice preachers like David Williams, Evan Pugh, and Edmund Botsford filed into the house to study with Oliver through the years, often staying for months at a time. She also hosted visiting preachers like Philadelphia's Morgan Edwards, who stayed with the Harts in Sarah's final year while collecting materials for his Baptist history. When her house was not overflowing with guests, there were many nights when Sarah had to do without Oliver altogether. He was gone for most of 1755 to retrieve John Gano for the Charleston Association and much of the winter of 1769–70 in his preaching mission with Evan Pugh, for example, with many more trips besides.

Sarah's domesticated piety meant that her primary spiritual identity remained rooted in fulfilling the traditional roles of wife and mother. Yet the rise of modern evangelicalism, along with her Baptist faith, also opened to her new opportunities for individual religious expression.[16] Many historians have noted how the experience of the new birth tended to elevate the spiritual status of women.[17] As evangelical ministers encouraged women to explore and express their deepest thoughts and feelings during the conversion process, they instilled in many of the female faithful "a belief in the importance of their individual salvation, a confidence in their personal worthiness, and a sense of their spiritual and moral authority." As Catherine Brekus has observed, this new development of feminine spiritual empowerment reflects one of the most important tensions in the early evangelical movement. "Evangelicals were theological conservatives who believed that women had been created subordinate to men," Brekus writes, "but they also gave women a new vocabulary of individual experience to justify their authority and leadership."[18] Many evangelical women no doubt felt gratified in being able to command the rapt attention of a minister, carefully documenting the details of conversion experiences; other women were held up as guides for spiritual

[15] For a profile of the evangelical woman Sara Edwards's management of her household, see George Marsden, *Jonathan Edwards: A Life* (New Haven, CT: Yale University Press, 2003), 321–23.

[16] On evangelical conversion enhancing a woman's sense of individuality, see Hindmarsh, *Evangelical Conversion Narrative*, 146–49.

[17] Brekus, *Sarah Osborn's World*, 183–90; Heyrman, *Southern Cross*, 165–66. McCurry challenges this idea, proposing that evangelical conversion simply reinforced the suppression of the female self; see especially McCurry, *Masters of Small Worlds*, 195–97.

[18] Brekus, *Sarah Osborn's World*, 183.

seekers, as was the Harts' servant Margaret Mageay during the 1754 revival. Many converted women, including some Baptists, gave voice to their personal relationship with God through diaries and letters, some of which found their way into print as evangelical devotional material. Oliver and Sarah may have encountered the letter of the English Baptist Anne Dutton (1692–1765) to George Whitefield when it was published in Philadelphia in 1743, for instance.[19] If Sarah ever penned an account of her conversion or kept a spiritual diary, these have been lost to history, though Oliver's second wife, Anne, did both.

Baptist women also expressed their spirituality outside the home by meeting with other women for friendship and fellowship.[20] Church gatherings provided important opportunities for women to connect with one another for purposes both social and spiritual. When Baptist women were forced to miss regular church meetings in order to care for the home, they often felt a tremendous sense of loss.[21] Association meetings, which drew Baptists from many churches across large regions, were also special occasions for women like Sarah. Though she would not have participated in the denominational business or even been registered as messenger from her church, Sarah would have looked forward to the fellowship with Baptist women whom she saw only at these annual events. Some Baptist women also attended special, women-only meetings in homes for spiritual discussion. Sarah would have observed the establishment of women's meetings in Philadelphia at the height of the Great Awakening. In 1741 Whitefield organized a "society of young women" there, who he hoped would "prove to be wise virgins" for Christ. Evangelical women continued to organize such societies for themselves in the following years, including a group of Particular Baptist women in Boston which Hezekiah Smith visited.[22]

Particular Baptists were not as open as the early American Methodists to the public leadership roles of women.[23] Yet, as we have already seen, Baptists made more room for women to express their spirituality than did

---

[19] Anne Dutton, *A Letter from Mrs. Anne Dutton to the Reverend G. Whitefield* (Philadelphia, PA, 1743). For Dutton, see Hindmarsh, *Evangelical Conversion Narrative*, 294–301.

[20] Exemplary from this period in this regard is Esther Edwards Burr, Jonathan Edwards's daughter and the wife of New Jersey College president Aaron Burr. See Carol F. Karlsen and Laurie Crumpacker, eds., *The Journal of Esther Edwards Burr 1754–1757* (New Haven, CT: Yale University Press, 1984).

[21] See McCurry, *Masters of Small Worlds*, 121–23.

[22] Lindman, *Bodies of Belief*, 117–21.

[23] For early American Methodist women's roles as preachers, exhorters, and class leaders, see Wigger, *Taking Heaven by Storm*, 152–57.

many denominations in the eighteenth century. This began with the Baptist membership process, which required Baptist women to make an individual public confession of faith, receive baptism, and agree to the church covenant. The spiritual equality with men signaled in these rituals simultaneously empowered Baptist women and threatened non-Baptist husbands.[24] When the Virginia Anglican William Hickman's wife became a Baptist, he recruited a zealous Episcopalian minister to steer her back. Mrs. Hickman informed the minister that she "was fond to hear him preach, but she could not pin her faith to his sleeve."[25] Perhaps most unconverted husbands reacted to the evangelical religion of their wives with "a combination of masterful indulgence and bemused condescension," but plenty responded with violence. Stories abound, especially in Anglican Virginia, of angry husbands refusing to share a bed with their wives, tearing their wives' clothes off to prevent them from attending church, beating them if they received baptism, and confronting Baptist ministers with guns. In these tense episodes, Baptist churches found themselves forcing women to choose between loyalty to their husbands and to their own individual sense of duty to Christ, one of the most controversial aspects of early Baptist life in the South.[26]

Some of the more radical Baptist clergy may have relished "colluding" with a woman's defiance of her husband for the sake of Christ, but a moderate revivalist like Oliver Hart found the position very uncomfortable. In a letter to Richard Furman, Hart commented on the "cruel manner" in which a young woman named Sally was "deprived of that which her soul longs for" by a husband who would not permit her to "come forward and openly profess the religion of Jesus." He urged Furman to "watch for an opportunity of conversing with her," believing that he would "easily trace the footsteps of the Divine Spirit in her exercise, and discover most ardent breathings of soul after Divine things." He added, "O what a pity that such a soul should be bound by the bigotry and humor of—anyone!"[27] Still, he did not recommend overturning the entire family structure to have the conversation. Yet even when facing an intractable husband, many Southern women chose to join the Baptists, regardless of the consequences in the home.

---

[24] Heyrman clearly outlines the sense of vulnerability experienced by unconverted Southern men when their wives experienced the new birth (*Southern Cross*, 179–81).

[25] Lindman, *Bodies of Belief*, 114.

[26] Heyrman, *Southern Cross*, 166; Matthews, *Religion in the Old South*, 101–9.

[27] Oliver Hart to Richard Furman, August 27, 1793, Hart Papers, JBDML.

## "COMFORTS AND MERCIES, LOSSES AND CROSSES" 209

Baptist church discipline, explored in detail in the previous chapter, also gave women a unique voice in Southern society. Baptist women were held accountable as responsible individuals for their own fidelity to the church covenant, of course, and could be disciplined before the church. But women could also defend themselves, make accusations of their own, provide testimony in discipline trials, and serve on investigative committees.[28] In some cases, church discipline against an erring husband provided a Baptist woman greater recourse for protecting her rights than most anything she could find in society at the time.[29] Baptist churches were willing to intervene in marriage relationships when they involved the sinning of covenant church members, as Bakers Will of Ashley River discovered in December 1738. He came under suspension for "his disorders particularly with respect to his useing unjustifiable Severity towards his wife in Beating of her."[30]

Morgan Edwards was one minister who understood the influence that Baptist women could wield in a church. Opposing the rulings of the Philadelphia and Charleston Associations, which allowed for female voting, Edwards noted, "The vote of a woman is equally decisive of that of man, and the women, who are always the most numerous, have it in their power at any time to decide everything against men."[31] In the early nineteenth century a Georgia Baptist named Jesse Mercer would express the same fear, pointing to the disproportionate number of women in Baptist churches to argue *against* their participating in governmental votes of the church.[32] Clearly the ideal of "democratic religion" that Baptist men strenuously promoted sometimes created difficulties when it came to managing the female members of their church. It is hard to resist Christine Heyrman's wry conclusion that "early Baptist and Methodist preachers knew that they depended on women a great deal, but perhaps wished that they needed them a good deal less."[33]

Yet within their clearly defined boundaries, Baptist women found a variety of ways to wield influence within the church. They made financial contributions to the church and to denominational initiatives, and later in the nineteenth century would express their piety through

---

[28] Wills, *Democratic Religion*, 54.

[29] See McCurry, *Masters of Small Worlds*, 131–35, 191–94.

[30] Kegley and Little, "Records of Ashley River Baptist Church," 11.

[31] Edwards, *Customs of Primitive Churches*, 102.

[32] Wills, *Democratic Religion*, 58. Donald Matthews estimated the ratio of women to men in evangelical churches to be 65:35 (*Religion in the Old South*, 47).

[33] Heyrman, *Southern Cross*, 177.

210 OLIVER HART AND THE RISE OF BAPTIST AMERICA

voluntary societies, especially related to missions.[34] In private conversations and informal settings, Baptist women might provide spiritual guidance to men, sometimes even to their minister. Once when returning from a funeral with a bereaved mother, Oliver Hart recorded the deep impact her testimony of faith had on him. He noted that he was "much pleased with her conversation," for it was evident that "God has done great things for her during her afflictions. They have operated kindly, brought her to the feet of Jesus, weaned her from earthly things and taught her to make the Lord her *all.*" The submissive widow's faith challenged his own. "In short, she delighted me much, and yet made me ashamed when I saw how far short I come of acting the Christian and minister. O Lord, revive thy work in my heart, remove deadness from my soul, teach my tongue to speak thy praise!"[35] Though they would never hold public religious office, women like Sarah Hart and this godly widow constituted the backbone of Baptist churches.

It is regrettable that more details about Oliver and Sarah's marriage, and more of Sarah's own thoughts, have not been preserved. Most of Oliver's writings during his marriage to Sarah were lost in 1780, when the British ransacked his home, and the only surviving lines he wrote about her are the few he dashed off on the event of her death. But the more substantial record of his relationship with his second wife shows that he was attentive and affectionate—even romantic. This relationship will be explored in a later chapter, but it appears to give credence to his friends' memory of him as a "loving and tender husband." On his part, Oliver praised to his younger friends "all the comforts which the married state can afford."[36] Sarah's death in 1772 was surely the cause of great sorrow for him. She stands in a long line of women who played a quiet but vital role of support for the public ministries of their husbands. It is impossible to know from this distance what Sarah thought about her life of domestic piety. Perhaps she felt some of the tension voiced by the nineteenth-century woman Mary Brown, who confessed, "I would rather be a simple unambitious loving wife than to be empress of the world! But can it be so now? Can this wild heart ever be tamed to gentle and familiar duties, to know and desire nothing for itself . . . to become a *living sacrifice*, a meek and uncomplaining sacrifice to another's happiness?"[37] Brown's presentation of marriage is a bit grim, but no doubt

---

[34] For female participation in benevolence and missions societies, see Wills, *Democratic Religion*, 57–58; Guthman, *Strangers Below*, 80–83; Heyrman, *Southern Cross*, 308n44.

[35] Oliver Hart Diary, October 15, 1781, Hart MSS, SCL.

[36] Oliver Hart to James Manning, April 27, 1761, Manning MSS, JHL; Rogers, *A Sermon*, 23.

[37] Quoted in McCurry, *Masters of Small Worlds*, 197.

"COMFORTS AND MERCIES, LOSSES AND CROSSES" 211

articulates the fears of many eighteenth- and nineteenth-century evangelical women. However much Sarah may or may not have experienced such an internal struggle over her domesticated role, she ultimately embraced it. She died as she lived, sacrificially serving her family.

*

As Oliver grieved for Sarah, he was cheered by his "son in the ministry," Edmund Botsford. After two years of study in Hart's Baptist Religious Society, Botsford was licensed to preach in 1771 and soon moved to the Euhaw Church to assist Francis Pelot. There his education continued. After delivering what he thought was an especially commanding sermon, he eagerly asked Pelot if he thought he had the gift to preach. To his disappointment, Pelot replied cryptically that he was not prepared to answer. Botsford soon received another opportunity to preach but was as disgusted with this second effort as he had been pleased by the first. Afterward Pelot invited him for a walk, and Botsford braced himself for a scathing critique. Instead Pelot gently noted, "I could not answer your question the other day, for I thought perhaps Botsford might be one of those preachers who can preach when they please; but now I perceive that Botsford cannot always preach just when Botsford pleases; I am therefore encouraged to hope that he is called of God, and that he may venture forward in the work." For moderate revivalists like Pelot, Hart, and Botsford a preacher's worth was not measured by his rhetorical ability but by his dependence on the Spirit.[38]

About this time, a branch of the Euhaw Church, meeting at Tuckaseeking, forty miles from Savannah, Georgia, sent for Botsford. For the next two years he preached with relentless energy all over the Georgia and South Carolina frontier, seeing many conversions. In March 1773 he paused long enough for Hart and Pelot to ordain him, authorizing him to baptize his new converts. In August he reported riding 650 miles, preaching forty-two sermons, baptizing twenty-one persons, and administering the Lord's Supper twice. "Indeed, I travelled so much this year, that some used to call me the *flying preacher*," he recalled. Many of the individuals touched by Botsford's labors on the frontier came from immigrant families. After one service at Stephen's Creek, South Carolina, he invited any of his listeners desiring baptism to relate their testimony. A Dutch lady called Mrs. Clecker came forward, but deferred the question of her baptism to her husband's permission. Botsford

---

[38] Mallary, *The Memoirs of Elder Edmund Botsford*, 38–39.

immediately called out to Mr. Clecker, asking if he objected. Put on the spot, Clecker stammered, "No, no, Got forpit I shout hinter my vife, she was one good vife." But Botsford learned afterward that the little Dutchman was not at all pleased with either his wife's baptism or Botsford's forwardness with him in a public meeting. When the gathering disbanded, Clecker raged and swore against Botsford, "Vaut, to ax me pefore all de people if he might tip my vife!" Yet witnessing his wife's immersion deeply affected Clecker. Botsford found him afterward in an orchard, in great distress. "O Sir, I shall go to de tivel, and my vife to hefen," he cried. "I am a boor lost sinner; I can't be forgifen; I fear de ground will open and let me down to de hell, for I cursed and swore you vas one goot for noting son of—. Lort have mercy on me!" Within months Clecker too found peace in believing Botsford's gospel, and also requested baptism. As Mr. Clecker followed the spiritual lead of his wife, he provided yet another example of how itinerant evangelical ministry on the frontier challenged traditional family dynamics.[39]

On November 28, 1773, Hart and Pelot traveled to Savannah to constitute the New Savannah Baptist Church, made up of those converted under Botsford's ministry. Hart preached from the solemn text of Hebrews 13:17, "Obey them that have rule over you, and submit yourselves: for they watch for your souls, as they that must give an account, that they may do it with joy, and not with grief: for that is unprofitable for you." Afterward Botsford served the Lord's Supper to his church for the first time. The scene overwhelmed the recently widowed Hart. He had been instrumental in Botsford's conversion, call to ministry, training, and ordination. Now his spiritual "son" was fulfilling Hart's dream for planting Spirit-filled Regular Baptist churches throughout the region. "It was a day of rejoicing," Hart wrote. By investing in young ministers like Botsford, Hart was helping to remake the religious scene of the colonial South and expand the territory of America's Baptists.[40]

*

Meanwhile Hart still had his biological children to care for. His two oldest, Eleanor and Oliver, were on their own, but ten-year-old Mary Baker was still home, and teenage John was at Rhode Island College. Even across the country, John gave Hart the most trouble. In 1786 Botsford would tell Hart, "Whatever *you* may have known, *we* all knew J. to have been the wildest of

---

[39] Mallary, *The Memoirs of Elder Edmund Botsford*, 45–46.
[40] Mallary, *The Memoirs of Elder Edmund Botsford*, 46–47; Hart, *Original Diary*, 6.

"COMFORTS AND MERCIES, LOSSES AND CROSSES" 213

Mr. Hart's children."[41] A prime example came in 1773, when John's misbehavior at school gained the attention of Hart's friend, the college's president James Manning. In an official statement from the school, John Hart is recorded as having been reprimanded "for habitually neglecting [his] studies, being out of College in the evening in town beyond the time specified in the laws and absent from his room in study hours and making disturbance by noise or otherwise, and suffering others to spend their time idly in his room at entertainments or otherwise."[42]

Manning dutifully relayed these developments by mail to Hart, who was mortified. In a shamefaced response, Hart expressed frustration with his son. "I am sorry John has conducted [himself] so as to give you so much trouble, and to forfeit the place he had under the management of Mrs. Manning," Hart apologized. "Had I been apprised of his unworthy conduct sooner, perhaps I should have remanded him back to Carolina; for I am not in such affluent circumstances as to throw away money in the education of one who has no view to his own advantage." Surely feeling the absence of Sarah's support in the home, Hart reached out for any assistance his old friend could provide: "I thank you, however, for all the pains you have taken with him, and that you have made trial of the discipline of the rod. Let me entreat you unweariedly to exert your best endeavors for his advantage. Who knows but God may give him a turn? I should be sorry if he should return a worthless blockhead." Hart also addressed some other subjects in the letter to Manning, sharing the good news of Botsford's ministry success. He likely revealed some loneliness as he inquired about mutual Baptist friends from whom he had not heard. "I should be glad to see an account of your late Commencement in print. Pray, how goes on the great man of Haverhill [Hezekiah Smith]? I have heard nothing from him for a great while past; and I hear almost as little about Mr. Stillman, or our affairs in Boston. How is Mr. Davis's place supplied? Has that church any minister?" But at the close of the letter, he returned to John: "Could you not prevail on John to write to me? I have received but one letter from him for the space of twelve months past, although I have sharply reproved him for his neglect, over and over again." For the first time in his life Hart was learning what it meant to balance his many ministry commitments with the task of guiding his children as a single parent. If he

[41] Mallary, *The Memoirs of Elder Edmund Botsford*, 48–49, emphasis in original.
[42] James Manning, "Public admonition of a number of students," Manning MSS, JHL.

214    OLIVER HART AND THE RISE OF BAPTIST AMERICA

had ever questioned the value of Sarah's domesticated piety before, he surely realized it in this bewildering period.[43]

\*

Hart began the year 1774 by forming a new friendship that would alter the rest of his life, as well as the future of American Baptists. He left Charleston on December 27, 1773, to attend a "Big Meeting" of the Separate Baptists on the South Carolina frontier, at a place called the High Hills of Santee. He preached at several churches during this trip, including the High Hills Baptist Church on New Year's Eve. But the highlight of the trip was a sermon he heard. On January 2, 1774, he listened as eighteen-year-old Richard Furman preached before the Lord's Supper from Colossians 2:6, "As ye have therefore received Christ Jesus the Lord, so walk ye in him." Hart called it afterward "a time of refreshing to the people of God." It was the first of many occasions in which Furman would impress him.[44]

Richard Furman was born in Esopus, New York, in 1755, but his father, Wood Furman, moved the family to a backcountry settlement in South Carolina called High Hills when he was still an infant. This was an untamed land in every sense, a place the Baptist preacher Jeremiah Dargan called "a wild, wild place, a wicked, wicked neighborhood." Dargan believed that he preached there "to no purpose except provoking them to outrage." The Furman family moved to other places in South Carolina throughout Richard's youth, but by 1770 they were back at High Hills. At this time the Separate Baptist Joseph Reese was leading a revival in the region. Born in 1736 at Duck Creek in Kent County, Pennsylvania, Reese had been raised Anglican. He moved to the Congaree in 1745, where he was converted under the dynamic preaching of the Separate Baptist Philip Mulkey and baptized in 1760. Reese soon followed Mulkey into the ministry, and like his mentor developed a reputation for his uncanny command over hearers' emotions while preaching. Morgan Edwards commented, "His voice and countenance affect like an enchantment." Reese was known to transform entire crowds with his messages: men who had defiantly kept their hats on removed them and wept; hecklers planning to launch pine knots at him dropped their missiles in shame; one man wielding a hickory club came threatening to "wear it on the bawling dog's back," but ended the meeting begging for salvation.[45] As

[43] Oliver Hart to James Manning, November 27, 1773, Manning MSS, JHL.
[44] Hart, *Original Diary*, 6.
[45] Edwards, *Materials towards a History of the Baptists*, 2:145–46.

## "COMFORTS AND MERCIES, LOSSES AND CROSSES" 215

expected, Charles Woodmason bitterly criticized the almost cult-like allegiance Reese seemed to enjoy among his Separate Baptist folk, especially the ladies. "What Man amongst all the Beaus and fine Gentlemen of the Land has such Influence over the Women as *Joseph Reez?* It was but a few Sundays past, That to make display of their Veneration for Him, and shew the Power He had over them, that He made them strip in the Public Meeting House, quite to their Shifts, and made them all walk home barefooted an bare legged," Woodmason scoffed, "And had He only said it, they would have stript off their Smocks, and gone home stark Naked."[46] The nominally Anglican Furman family had never met anything like Reese or the Separate Baptists.

When sixteen-year-old Richard heard the gospel from Reese, he felt a new "sense of guilt and unworthiness" and saw himself "as a sinner willing to accept the free grace of the Gospel." When Reese interviewed Richard for baptism, his thorough, heartfelt answers penetrated his mother's heart, and she too was converted. Reese baptized them both on the same day. Soon afterward Furman began informally preaching, prompting the High Hills church to approach him about "exhorting" at their services. As an exhorter, he would follow the preachers' sermons with pointed questions and personal encouragements for the congregation. Some of Furman's peers mocked him for his earnestness, but crowds began to gather around the boy preacher. He had a warm heart and an uncommonly sharp mind, and his words made a deep impact on many. In 1774, the same year he met Hart, Furman was ordained by Joseph Reese and Evan Pugh as pastor of the High Hills Baptist Church. He was just nineteen years old.[47]

*

Hart's budding friendship with Furman proved pivotal in the union of the Regular and Separate Baptists in the South. Since the Separates had arrived in North Carolina in 1755, every effort at uniting had sputtered. In 1762 Philip Mulkey sent several inquiries about a union to the Charleston Association, prompting them to send Hart and Pugh to a Separate Baptist meeting in North Carolina. Nothing came of their visit. In 1769 the Regular Baptists of the Ketocton Association in Virginia ("armed off" from the Philadelphia Association in 1766) sent a letter to another Separate Baptist

---

[46] Woodmason, *Carolina Backcountry*, 113.

[47] Furman, *Charleston Association*, 72; Townsend, *South Carolina Baptists*, 150; Nettles, *The Baptists*, 125–27.

meeting in North Carolina, drawing attention to their common Baptist and revivalist convictions: "If we are all Christians, all Baptists—all *New Lights*—why are we divided? Must these little appellative names, *Regular* and *Separate*, break the golden bond of charity?" These overtures accomplished little. Reese learned just how dimly the Separates regarded the Regulars in a painful firsthand experience. Despite his flamboyant preaching style, Reese apparently handled the Scriptures to the satisfaction of his more buttoned-down Regular Baptist listeners. Morgan Edwards noted that though he was "no more than an English scholar," he was yet "surprisingly successful and judicious," and Hart and Pugh found Reese commendable enough to oversee his ordination at Congaree Church in 1769. Yet afterward Reese suffered a public reprimand by the Sandy Creek Association.[48] In 1772 the Separates of Congaree Association in South Carolina began corresponding with the Philadelphia Association at Morgan Edwards's request, and sent messengers to the Charleston Association the next year. But negotiations for a merger broke down when the Separates "would be satisfied with nothing short of the Regulars coming fully into their own views."[49]

The persistent division between the Regulars and the Separates stemmed largely from cultural differences, especially their divergent attitudes regarding written confessions of faith. As the Separate Baptist John Leland explained, "The Regulars adhered to a confession of faith, first published in London, 1689, and afterwards adopted by the Baptist Association of Philadelphia, in 1742; but the Separates had none but the Bible." Coming out of New England Congregationalism, the Separate Baptists believed extrabiblical confessions were intended to control and to persecute other Christians who disagreed with them. They worried that such "creeds" displaced the Bible and would "usurp a tyrannical power over the conscience." Thus when the Regulars proposed to unite with the Separates around the *Second London Confession*, the Separates "expressed fears, that the confession of faith might in time bind them too much, as there were some objectionable parts." For their part, the Regular Baptists had found written confessions vital for summarizing biblical truth, guarding Scripture from heretical interpretation, and providing the essential doctrinal standard of unity for their fellowships since the end of the seventeenth century.[50]

---

[48] Edwards, *Materials towards a History of the Baptists*, 2:146.
[49] Furman, *Charleston Association*, 33; Semple, *A History of the Rise and Progress*, 68, emphasis in original.
[50] Leland, *Writings*, 105; Semple, *A History of the Rise and Progress*, 67.

"COMFORTS AND MERCIES, LOSSES AND CROSSES" 217

The worship styles of the two movements also differed drastically. In his *Customs of Primitive Churches*, Morgan Edwards outlined the orderly liturgical pattern Regular Baptists typically followed: "a short prayer suitably prefaced; reading a portion of Scripture; a longer prayer; singing; preaching; a third prayer; singing a second time; administering the Lord's Supper; collecting for the necessities of the saints; a benediction." The frontier meetings of the Separate Baptists were altogether different. Under the Spirit's immediate influence, the Separates "jerked" with muscular contortions, "barked" and yelped like dogs, "rolled on the ground in agonized dread of hell-fire and eternal damnation," and "leaped into the air with ecstatic shouts at the glory of their newfound salvation." In the heat of revival, Separate Baptists cast aside traditional concerns about ordained leadership, encouraging men and women alike to speak openly in their gatherings when so led. To the Separates, Regular Baptists were far too "solemn and rational"; they longed for spontaneous, physical, visceral experiences of God's presence.[51]

Patterns of speech and style of dress also represented matters of disagreement between the Baptist groups. Richard Furman's son Wood identified among "the peculiarities of the Separates" a certain "preciseness in dress and language, somewhat similar to the Quakers." Separate Baptists believed that maintaining a strict dress code served as an important expression of Christian holiness in the midst of a worldly society. Separate Baptist men "cut off" their hair and repudiated "superfluous forms and modes of dressing . . . [such as] cock't hats." The austere appearance of the Separates made them the object of ridicule among the Anglican gentlemen of Virginia. It also caused them to stand out from the more refined Regular Baptists, who did not share their convictions about dress. The Separates considered the Regulars to have compromised with the world, "not sufficiently particular in small matters, such as dress, etc." The Regulars maintained that the Separates' scruples over clothing were extrabiblical requirements and unnecessarily restrictive.[52] It was a classic case of moderate and radical revivalists struggling to understand one another.

For all these differences, however, the essential beliefs of the Regular and Separate Baptists were not far apart. Both operated from a basic theological

[51] Leland, *Writings*, 105; Semple, *A History of the Rise and Progress*, 320; William Taylor Thom, *The Struggle for Religious Freedom in Virginia: The Baptists* (Baltimore, MD, 1900), 493.
[52] Isaac, *Transformation of Virginia*, 162; for a Separate Baptist defense of "serious living," see Thomas, *Virginian Baptist*, 59–60; Semple, *A History of the Rise and Progress*, 67; Furman, *History of the Charleston Association*, 33.

## 218 OLIVER HART AND THE RISE OF BAPTIST AMERICA

framework of evangelical Calvinism, and both had been heavily influenced by the eighteenth-century revivals.[53] This became clear to the Regulars and Separates whenever they actually spent time with one another. When John Gano visited a Separate Baptist meeting in 1759, for example, the Separates at first eyed him with suspicion. But Gano's passionate revival preaching quickly won them over. Gano reported of the Separates to the Philadelphia Association, "Doubtless the power of God was among them; that although they were rather immethodical, they certainly had the root of the matter at heart."[54] A 1787 statement published by a general committee of Separate and Regular Baptists in Virginia further underscores their basic doctrinal agreement; it asserted, "The doctrine of salvation by Christ and free, unmerited grace alone ought to be believed by every Christian and maintained by every ministers of the gospel. Upon these terms we are united; and desire hereafter that the names *Regular* and *Separate* be buried in oblivion."[55] The Separate Baptist preacher John Taylor (1752–1835), initiator of the revival in Kentucky in the 1780s, stated that he could unite in fellowship with Regular Baptists because he "found no difference as to doctrinal opinions."[56] In 1772 Edmund Botsford encountered the Separate Baptist patriarch Daniel Marshall on Kiokee Creek, Georgia. "Well sir," Marshall asked Botsford, "are you come to preach for us?" "Yes sir, by your leave," Botsford replied, "but I confess I am at a loss for a text." "Well, well, look to the Lord for one," advised the old man. Botsford preached from Psalm 66:16, "Come and hear, all ye that fear God, and I will declare what he hath done for my soul," speaking about the experience of the new birth. Afterward Marshall took Botsford by the hand and said, "I can call thee brother, and give thee the right handoff fellowship, for some how I never heard *convarsion* better explained in my life; but I would not have thee think thou preaches as well as Jo Reese and Philip Mulkey. However, I hope you will go home with me." Despite their different histories and styles, both Regulars and Separates embraced a revivalist Calvinism.[57]

---

[53] The Separate Baptists have often been misidentified as Arminian in their theology because of their rejection of the *Second London Confession* and their passionate evangelistic appeals. Though many Separates shunned controversies regarding God's eternal decrees as overly precise, they were not classical Arminian.

[54] Semple, *A History of the Rise and Progress*, 101.

[55] Semple, *A History of the Rise and Progress*, 101, 67.

[56] John Taylor, *Baptists on the American Frontier: A History of Ten Baptist Churches*, edited by Chester Raymond Young (Macon, GA: Mercer University Press, 1995), 141.

[57] Mallary, *The Memoirs of Elder Edmund Botsford*, 41–43.

"COMFORTS AND MERCIES, LOSSES AND CROSSES"    219

As the story of Botsford and Marshall indicates, personal friendships often accomplished more than formal actions in unifying the two Baptist groups. It should come as little surprise that Hart led the way in all such bridge-building efforts. From the Separates' first arrival in the South, Hart seemed eager to include them in his Baptist denomination, making several journeys to frontier Separate Baptist congregations in the 1760s and 1770s. He celebrated the "happy revival of religion in the interior parts of this province, among the Separate Baptists." He mentioned two visits to the Separates, once with Pugh to ordain John Newton and Joseph Reese, and later to witness ten new believers receive baptism. One of the converts, a little girl, impressed Hart by giving "an amazing account of the Lord's work on her heart." He remembered both visits with the Separates were "much to [his] satisfaction."[58] In April 1775 he would return to the High Hills of Santee to assist Richard Furman in ordaining the Separate Baptist Joseph Cook (1750–1790). Two years later Hart helped Cook ordain another Separate Baptist, Lewis Richardson, at the Charleston Baptist meetinghouse.[59] In a 1775 tour of the Carolina backcountry, Hart lodged with Philip Mulkey of Fairforest Church, even submitting, at Mulkey's insistence, to the Separate Baptist rite of foot washing. "This evening before we lay down to rest, Brother Mulkey requested that he might wash my feet," Hart recalled. "With some reluctance I consented. After declaring that I did not believe it to be an ordinance of Christ, he then, being girded with a towel, and having water in a basin with great humility and affection, proceeded to wash my feet, talking religiously and affectionately all the time." Hart's broadmindedness and intentional friendships would go a long way in promoting the Baptist interest in the colonial South.[60]

*

On April 5, 1774, Hart married Anne Marie Sealy Grimball (1741–1813), a thirty-four-year-old Charleston belle, seventeen years his junior. Anne's first husband, Charles Grimball, had died in 1770, leaving her with two small children. Hart had for two years watched as Anne "demeaned herself with so much prudence, circumspection, and integrity as to gain the esteem and applause of all her acquaintances. In short, as a maid, a wife, and a widow, she

---

[58] Oliver Hart to Samuel Jones, June 30, 1769, McKesson MSS, HSP.

[59] Hart, *Original Diary*, 6–13.

[60] J. Glenwood Clayton and Loulie Latimer Owens, eds., "Oliver Hart's Diary of the Journey to the Backcountry," *Journal of the South Carolina Baptist Historical Society* 1 (November 1975): 22. See Thomas R. McKibbens, "Over Troubled Waters: Baptist Preachers Who Were Bridge Builders," *Baptist History and Heritage* 40, no. 2 (Fall 1984): 42–52.

## 220 OLIVER HART AND THE RISE OF BAPTIST AMERICA

has sustained an unsullied character, and been a pattern and ornament to her sex." Anne was a member of Hart's church, though she had remained unconverted long into her first marriage. She described herself as "thoughtless and gay" in Charleston society, though through Hart's preaching at the Baptist church, she eventually came through in conversion. "After many struggles with my frail and corrupted nature," she wrote, "many conflicts with a hard head of unbelief, our condescending Lord made me willing to follow him into the watery grave. I was baptized by Mr. Hart, May 5, 1770 (in my 29th year). Thus the Lord in his abundant mercy led me on from step to step as I could bear with afflictions—with comforts and mercies—with crosses and losses—until I was made willing to trust him, alone, for the whole of my salvation." A shared experience of evangelical conversion and Baptist immersion bound Oliver and Anne together.[61] He doted on Anne, or "Nancy," as he called her. One year after their wedding he wrote, "I esteem that as one of my happiest days that put such a prize into my bosom. All this I could seal with my blood." For the rest of his days, this remained the typical way in which he spoke about her.[62]

*

Yet the joy of his new marriage was mingled with grief for Hart in the fall of 1774. He had asked his friend Pelot to officiate the ceremony in April, having performed the same favor for Pelot in 1761. But in November 1774 Pelot suddenly died. Hart was shocked. Just the month before, he had preached in Pelot's pulpit with his friend in attendance. Hart believed that "a greater loss the Baptist interest could not have sustained by the death of any one man in the Province"; on a personal level, Hart had "lost the best friend and counselor I ever was blest with in the world." For more than twenty-four years the two Baptist pioneers had enjoyed "the most intimate friendship." As Hart reflected on his friend's most admirable traits, he remembered his "vivacity of temper, a great flow of spirit, which being regulated by a principle of grace rendered him [an] . . . agreeable companion. His conversation was not only pleasing but profitable, as he had a fine turn of introducing religion and spiritualizing most occasions in life." Together the two men had worked through many problems on behalf of the South's Baptists. "He knew how to solve doubts and clear up difficult cases of conscience," Hart wrote.

---

[61] Anne Hart, *Narrative of Anne Maria Sealy Grimball Hart, born 1741, South Carolina*, HSP. For a more detailed analysis of Anne's conversion, see Smith, *Order and Ardor*, 35–36.

[62] Hart, *Original Diary*, 6–7.

"COMFORTS AND MERCIES, LOSSES AND CROSSES" 221

"To say no more, he was the sincere, open, constant, and hearty friend, could keep a secret, and in short, few men were ever better qualified for friendship than he."[63]

Hart paid his friend a final service by preaching his funeral sermon at the Euhaw Church Pelot had so long served. Hart selected for his text John 14:19, "Because I live, ye shall live also." He was keeping a promise he had made to his friend. Three years earlier, Pelot had asked Hart to "perform this last kind office of respect to him" and had chosen the passage on that occasion. Hart delivered an emotional message to a full house. "Most were in tears and gave visible marks of the regards they bore to the memory of their late dear minister," Hart remembered. As in every trial, Hart sought the hidden purposes of a wise and good God even in this sorrowful event. "May God sanctify the affliction and repair the loss to all concerned," he prayed. His portrait of Pelot provides a glimpse into the virtues of friendship that he admired and aspired to himself. American Baptist leaders in the eighteenth century often expressed this sort of deep kinship with one another; it was out of this web of close-knit personal relationships that the Baptist denomination grew.[64]

\*

The early 1770s were, in Anne Hart's words, a period of equal parts "comforts and mercies" as well as "losses and crosses" for Hart. He had said goodbye to George Whitefield and buried his first wife, his baby daughter, and his best friend. He had married off his oldest daughter and sent his youngest son to college. Now he was married again. In the field of ministry, the young men he had nurtured and trained were making their own way as revival leaders, and the prospects of union between the Regular and Separate Baptists seemed more promising than ever. But as Hart passed through a season of dramatic personal transition, change was in the air throughout Charleston. In the fall of 1774 South Carolina sent five delegates to Philadelphia for the First Continental Congress. War was on its way, and Oliver Hart soon would find his life turned upside down.

---

[63] Hart, *Original Diary*, 7–8.
[64] Hart, *Original Diary*, 8. For the friendship networks of eighteenth-century Baptist men, see Lindman, *Bodies of Belief*, 164–73, and Davies, *Transatlantic Brethren*. To compare these dynamics to those among early American Methodist itinerants, see Wigger, *Taking Heaven by Storm*, 62–71.

# 10

# "The rising glory of this continent"

## The American Revolution

On August 14, 1765, Samuel Stillman, twenty-eight years old and about ten years removed from his conversion in Oliver Hart's Charleston youth revival, was the new pastor of Boston's First Baptist Church. Nothing could have prepared him for the scene playing out before him. Protesters filled Boston's streets, hanging an effigy of the British stamp agent Andrew Oliver (1706–1774), then cutting off its head and lighting it on fire on Fort Hill. After setting the effigy ablaze, the crowd returned to vandalize the house of the real Andrew Oliver, who had already fled and would promptly resign his post.

Stillman's Boston neighbors were protesting the hated Stamp Act. Passed by the British Parliament against the American colonies in 1765, the Stamp Act required colonists to purchase many commonly used printed materials on paper produced in London, which carried an embossed revenue stamp. The Stamp Act was part of a larger effort by Parliament to recoup their massive debts from the French and Indian War of 1754–63. Parliament's Sugar Act of 1764, which imposed tax on a variety of consumer goods, from sugar to cloth, had elicited growls from many American leaders, who protested that only a people's elected representatives had the power to tax. Yet because the Sugar Act directly affected only merchants and politicians, colonial resistance was limited. When Parliament followed the Sugar Act with the further-reaching Stamp Act in 1765, however, an entire continent exploded with outrage. Hart too witnessed violent protests, by the citizens Charleston, emboldened by the "laudable example" of the Northern colonies. When the "obnoxious" stamp paper arrived in Charleston Harbor on October 18, 1765, an association of rebels gathered near the docks with the intention of destroying the cargo. Lieutenant Governor William Bull ordered the stamp paper placed under protection at Fort Johnson. The next day protestors carried an effigy of their local stamp collector through the streets in a coffin,

*Oliver Hart and the Rise of Baptist America.* Eric C. Smith, Oxford University Press (2020). © Oxford University Press.
DOI: 10.1093/oso/9780197506325.001.0001

"THE RISING GLORY OF THIS CONTINENT" 223

before burning it that night to wild applause. They then vandalized the stamp distributors' homes and threatened them with violence.[1]

Astonished by this vehemence, Parliament repealed the Stamp Act in 1766. The colonials were elated. In Boston, Stillman celebrated the repeal in a sermon to the First Baptist Church, praising his neighbors for being so "tenacious of rights and liberties." He viewed the repeal as proof that King George III was a "most gracious sovereign" and "father of his people." With this recent misunderstanding cleared up, Stillman declared that he and his fellow colonists were "inviolably attached to his Majesty's most sacred person."[2] But the exhilaration was short lived. In 1767 Parliament passed the Townshend Acts, imposing duties on glass, lead, paints, paper, and tea imported into the colonies. The colonists submitted a series of protests against these acts as autocratic abuse of power, but their cries went unheard, and the relationship continued to deteriorate. When Boston's citizens threw a large shipment of British tea into Boston Harbor in December 1773, Britain responded with the "Intolerable Acts," or Coercive Acts, against the colony of Massachusetts in 1774. After this, delegates from the thirteen colonies assembled in Philadelphia as the First Continental Congress in the fall of 1774 and petitioned the Crown to ease its repressive measures. Yet the colonists again found no relief from the king. On May 8, 1775, Hart received the news that the king's troops had "commenced hostilities" by opening fire on American militia at Lexington and Concord on April 19, 1775.[3] War had come; he knew it would soon visit Charleston.

*

Most colonial Baptists ultimately supported American independence, but in the years leading up to the Battle of Lexington and Concord in 1775, this position was anything but certain.[4] Baptists in New England were especially ambivalent early on, and some remained so throughout the conflict.[5] After

---

[1] Keith Krawczynski, *William Henry Drayton: South Carolina Revolutionary Patriot* (Baton Rouge: Louisiana State University Press, 2001), 28–29.

[2] Samuel Stillman, *Good News from a Far Country*, (Boston, 1766), 7, 31–34; Kidd, *God of Liberty*, 12.

[3] Hart, *Original Diary*, 9.

[4] Kidd surveys well the range of evangelical responses to the Revolution in *The Great Awakening*, 288–307, highlighting the dangers of viewing early evangelicals as a monolith.

[5] McLoughlin notes how Baptists in rural New England never wholeheartedly supported the war, even to the end. In 1780 Connecticut's Woodstock Church wrote to the Warren Association, "We feel but little heart to hold the sword against a British invader while our country men are endeavoring to deprive us of liberty of conscience." See McLoughlin, *New England Dissent*, 1:572, n6. There were also a few conscientious objectors among Baptists during the war, including Peleg Burroughs of Tiverton, who in 1778 refused to read from his pulpit an address from Congress "to rouse the People up to War"

all, the civic leaders crying for their inalienable rights represented a group that had been depriving Baptists of religious freedom since the days of Roger Williams. Throughout the 1760s and early 1770s, New England Baptists were still being taxed for the placement and support of Congregational ministers. They were fined and jailed when they did not present certificates stating that they belonged to an acceptable Dissenting church (and were sometimes still punished when they did), had their property seized, and were generally looked upon as second-class nuisances. New England Baptists had traditionally found the king of England more sympathetic to their plight than the leadership in New England. Ebenezer Smith, minister of the Baptist Church in Ashfield, Massachusetts, where city officials seized hundreds of acres in 1770, spoke for many when he scorned the Sons of Liberty as those who desired "liberty from oppression that they might have liberty to oppress."[6] Thus New England Baptists were likely to view the fight with George III as the Congregationalists' War, while *their* fight was for religious freedom at home. In 1773 Isaac Backus, the Revolutionary era's most articulate spokesman for freedom of conscience, published his famous *Appeal to the Public for Religious Liberty*. It was not until a much later date that many New England Baptist leaders came to believe that political independence could in fact clear a path for obtaining religious liberty.[7]

In 1774, at the First Continental Congress in Philadelphia, Baptist leaders from the Warren and Philadelphia associations, along with some Quakers and other Dissenters, met with a delegation from Massachusetts that included John and Sam Adams. Led by Isaac Backus, the Baptists urged the disestablishment of Congregationalism, citing numerous recent cases of state-sponsored persecution. The meeting went poorly; John Adams later said that he was "greatly surprised and somewhat indignant" to be called before this "self-created tribunal" of motley Dissenters. Samuel Adams sneered at the Baptists as "enthusiasts who made a merit of suffering persecution." John Adams flatly told Backus, "We might expect a change in the solar system, as to expect they would give up their establishment."[8] Such

---

and instead "laboured hard" to convince his people "how wrong it is for a Disciple of Christ to engage in outward War" (1:582).

[6] Quoted in Preserved Smith, "Chronicles of a New England Family," *New England Quarterly* 9 (September 1936): 424.

[7] Kidd and Hankins, *Baptists in America*, 49. For a more detailed account of the development of New England Baptist thought regarding independence, see McLoughlin, *New England Dissent*, 1:569–87.

[8] See McLoughlin, *New England Dissent*, 1:556–61.

"THE RISING GLORY OF THIS CONTINENT" 225

dismissiveness from Patriot leaders obviously did not endear their cause to the Baptists, who continued to stand aloof from them. In turn, New England Congregationalists deeply resented their Baptist neighbors for their tepid support, often painting them as Tories and traitors. From Newport, Rhode Island, Ezra Stiles seethed against the Baptists, who he believed were being played against the patriots by the Crown. "They will leave the general Defence of American Liberty to the Congregationalists to the Northward and Episcopalians to the Southward," he grumbled.[9]

\*

In the middle colonies, Philadelphia Association leaders sympathized with the plight of their New England brethren but attempted to maintain neutrality in the early 1770s. In 1770 the Philadelphia Association heard a report of the Ashfield case in Massachusetts from Hezekiah Smith. They then moved that, as their brethren in New England were "sorely oppressed this year again, and no redress obtained, though diligently sought for; their case is to go home soon, to be laid at the feet of our gracious sovereign." They took up a collection to finance Smith's journey home to Haverhill.[10] William Rogers of Philadelphia's First Baptist Church, though later to become a Continental Army chaplain, reprimanded Backus by letter in March 1775 for addressing the First Continental Congress. Rogers believed the Congress to be "a Body of Men from whom we may expect no Relief." The Philadelphia Baptist Robert Strettle Jones also urged Backus not to squander the option of appealing to Great Britain for religious rights, writing, "This channel we ought ever to keep open."[11] Morgan Edwards, perhaps the Philadelphia Association's most prominent minister, was an open Loyalist whose son fought in the king's army throughout the war. Edwards was almost certainly the author of an anonymous, pro-Anglican and pro-English article printed in the Pennsylvania *Chronicle* on November 26, 1770, which declared:

Truly it is the Interest of the Baptists that the Chh of Engld. should multiply in Massachusetts & Connecticut, so far as to form a Balance of Ecclesiastical power there, as in other colonies. And as for Bishops they are welcome there: their coming thither is an Object worthy of Petitions: we

[9] Ezra Stiles, *The Literary Diary of Ezra Stiles*, 3 vols, edited by F. B. Dexter (New York, 1901), 1:473.
[10] Gillette, *Minutes*, 114.
[11] McLoughlin, *New England Dissent*, 1:565; Hovey, *A Memoir of the Life and Times of Isaac Backus*, 223–24.

226   OLIVER HART AND THE RISE OF BAPTIST AMERICA

cannot be Worse off; we may be better; they are Gentlemen at least & have some Generosity for vanquished Enemies. But the New-Englnd People (of a certain Denomination) are supercilious in Power, and Mean in Conquest. I will venture to say, that all the Bishops in Old England have not done the Baptists there so much despite for eighty years past, as the Presbyterians have done this year to the Baptists of New England.[12]

The article predictably evoked a strong reaction in New England. Ezra Stiles raged against Edwards as a man of "inveterate Malice against the Congregationalists" and a "Tool of the Ministry." Though forced to sign a recantation of his Toryism on August 7, 1775, Edwards would never regain the position of prominence he held among American Baptists before the war.[13] Most Baptists in the middle colonies and New England were not outspoken Loyalists like Edwards, but by 1775 they had developed a reputation of unreliability in wartime. Stiles complained in November 1774, "Tho some few Baptists and Quakers are hearty with us, yet too many are so much otherwise that was all America of their Temper and Coolness in the Cause the Parlt. Would easily carry their Points and triumph over American Liberty."[14]

*

Virginia Baptists faced a similar predicament as their brethren in New England. Under Anglican establishment, they had endured the most intense physical persecution of any colonial Baptists, especially from the late 1760s to the beginning of the war. Separate and Regular Baptist preachers alike risked physical attack whenever they stood to preach. Morgan Edwards reported that John Waller was gagged with a horsewhip by the parish minister, then dragged to the local sheriff, who "immediately received him and whipped him in so violent manner (without the ceremony of a trial) that poor Waller was presently in a gore of blood, and will carry the scars to his grave."[15] Virginia Anglicans knocked Baptists down, "dragged [them] about by the hair of [the] head," fired guns at them, rushed them with drawn swords, hunted them down with dogs, and all but drowned them in cruel parodies of immersion. Virginians disrupted Baptist meetings by swearing and catcalls, launching stones, apples, and other projectiles, riding horses

---

[12] McLoughlin, *New England Dissent*, 1:577.
[13] See Guild, *Early History of Brown University*, 13.
[14] Stiles, *The Literary Diary of Ezra Stiles*, 1:492.
[15] Edwards, *Materials towards a History of the Baptists*, 2:55.

"THE RISING GLORY OF THIS CONTINENT" 227

through the congregation, and flinging hornets' nests and poisonous snakes at the worshippers. Between 1768 and 1778 fifty dissenters were jailed for preaching without a license in Virginia, most of them Baptists. When incarcerated, Virginia Baptists continued to endure mistreatment, especially when they attempted to use their persecution as a platform for their message. Jailed Baptist preachers were nearly suffocated by the burning of pepper pods and brimstone outside their cells; others had their faces urinated on; one claimed explosives were set off beneath his cell; some were moved to solitary confinement to prevent access to open windows.[16] Even when not experiencing overt abuse, one Piedmont planter summed up the Baptist experience in Virginia when he noted that they "weare held in contempt by most of the people."[17]

On the eve of the Revolution, it was thus entirely reasonable to expect Virginia Baptists to support the Crown, which had historically protected Virginia's dissenters, rather than the local leaders who had persecuted them.[18] Yet as armed conflict loomed closer, Virginia's leaders grew increasingly aware of their dependence on the military service of their despised but sizable Dissenting population. Recognizing a golden opportunity, Baptists and other Dissenters in Virginia entered into a lengthy period of negotiation with the Virginia legislature that would last from 1768 to 1786, in which they demanded, first, greater toleration from the state, and later full religious freedom.[19] This coalition of Dissenters began petitioning the House of Burgesses for reform in 1770. In 1775 the Virginia Baptist convention announced their intention to support the Patriot cause, even fighting in the Continental Army. They acknowledged that while they were "distinguished from the Body of our Countrymen by appelatives and sentiments of a religious nature," they nevertheless considered themselves "members of the same community in respect of matters of a civil nature," and endorsed the "military resistance against Great Britain in her unjust invasion, tyrannical

---

[16] For the Virginia Baptist experience, see John A. Ragosta, *Wellspring of Liberty: How Virginia's Religious Dissenters Helped Win the American Revolution and Secured Religious Liberty* (New York: Oxford University Press, 2010), 28–36; Isaac, *Transformation of Virginia*, 161–205; Semple, *A History of the Rise and Progress of the Baptists in Virginia*; Edwards, *Materials towards a History of the Baptists*, vol. 2; James Ireland, *The Life of Rev. James Ireland* (Winchester, VA, 1819); and Thomas, *The Virginian Baptist*.

[17] Chester Raymond Young, ed., *Westward into Kentucky: The Narrative of Daniel Trabue* (Lexington: University Press of Kentucky, 2004), 128.

[18] For British protection of Dissenter interest in Virginia, see Ragosta, *Wellspring of Liberty*, 40–42; Foote, *Sketches of Virginia*, 103, 157–60, 165; and Isaac, *Transformation of Virginia*, 151–52.

[19] Ragosta recounts this negotiation process in *Wellspring of Liberty*, 43–70.

228   OLIVER HART AND THE RISE OF BAPTIST AMERICA

oppression, and repeated hostilities."[20] As the war progressed and Virginia grew more desperate for the Dissenters' help, the Baptists would shrewdly negotiate for more and more religious freedom.

*

In South Carolina, Hart and the Charleston Association Baptists appear to have backed the Revolution from the beginning. Having never faced religious persecution, Hart and his Regular Baptist friends in the Lower South had existed on friendly terms with churches of other denominations and with Charleston's cultural elites for decades. They thus had fewer reservations about supporting local Patriot leadership than did Baptists in other areas. While Hart certainly intended to leverage the Revolutionary moment to obtain full religious freedom for Dissenters in South Carolina and beyond, his support of American Independence never seemed to be in doubt.

Out on the Carolina frontier, Baptist support for the war varied. Some Separate Baptists, including Joseph Reese and Richard Furman, endorsed the Patriot cause from an early date. Yet many Separates, far removed from the daily clamor for independence Charleston had known for the past decade, were loyal to the king and averse to helping the aristocrats of Charleston. Baptist James Miles of Cross Roads Meeting House near the Haw River in North Carolina vociferously rejected the American position. "Show him a great man with a half moon in his hat with liberty written upon it and his hat full of feathers," he said, "and he would show you a devil, and that poor men were bowing and scraping to them, and [the Patriots] leading them to hell as soon as they had come from the Congress." He insisted that Patriots "were blow'd up as big as a blather and that he did not value the Congress nor the Committee [of Correspondence] no more than as [a] parcel of raccoon dogs, for he got his [commands] from the King and the field officers got their [commands] from hell or the devil."[21] Miles was more outspoken than most, but many backcountry inhabitants, including a number of Separate Baptists, shared his sentiments.

South Carolina officials were well aware of this. In the wake of Lexington and Concord, the colony's Provincial Congress assembled in June 1775 to make serious preparations for war. They called for 1,500 troops, created a

---

[20] See "Journal of Convention, August 16, 1775," in Charles F. James, ed., *Documentary History of the Struggle for Religious Liberty in Virginia* (Lynchburg, VA: J. P. Bell, 1900), 52.

[21] Marjorleine Kars, *Breaking Loose Together: The Regulator Rebellion in Pre-Revolutionary North Carolina* (Chapel Hill: University of North Carolina Press, 2002), 213–14.

"council of safety" vested with vast executive powers, and composed an oath of allegiance to the American colonies called "the Association." As they scrambled to gain commitments to the Association, they knew their biggest challenge lay in the backcountry. British officials were already working hard to stoke the embers of anti-Whig feelings among South Carolina's interior settlers. In June the South Carolina Committee of Intelligence learned of a plan by North Carolina's governor Josiah Martin to raise an insurrection among pro-British backcountry men. If the South Carolina Council of Safety did not quickly suppress backcountry Loyalism, they faced the real and terrifying prospect of fighting a war on two fronts. The Committee of Intelligence sent letters into the colony's interior to raise support for their cause in the spring and summer of 1775, but a greater effort was needed. Col. William Thomson (1721–1796), a Whig regimental commander, suggested that if some men "of the most noted Character" traveled to the backcountry to clarify the "unhappy disputes" in a "proper Light," the Council of Safety stood a chance of persuading key backcountry leaders of signing the Association. The Council of Safety thus appointed a team of three men "to make progress into the Back Country, to explain the causes of the present disputes between Great Britain and the American colonies." At the time, it seemed as if South Carolina's desperate hopes hung on the success or failure of this backcountry commission.[22]

The Council of Safety's chairman, Henry Laurens (1724–1792), appointed William Henry Drayton (1742–1779), a wealthy planter, lawyer, and statesman of Charleston, as leader of the Commission.[23] The vain and passionate Drayton, now thirty-three years old, was an aggressive Patriot and a future president of the South Carolina Provincial Congress. The second team member was thirty-one-year-old William Tennent III (1740–1777), pastor of the Congregational church in Charleston and grandson of William Tennent, founder of the Log College and a preacher Hart had heard as a teenager. A riveting orator, Tennent held master's degrees from both New Jersey College and Harvard. He also established the reputation of being a "Firebrand Parson" for his outspoken political views, thanks largely to an impassioned patriotic sermon he published in 1774, *An Address, Occasioned by the Late Invasion of Liberties of the American Colonists by the British Parliament.* Laurens called

---

[22] Krawczynski, *William Henry Drayton*, 159–60; Thomson to Laurens, 22 July 1775, in Alexander Samuel Salley, *The History of Orange County, South Caroline* (Orangeburg, SC: R. L. Berry, 1898), 160; *Baptist Courier*, March 9, 1793, quoted in Owens, *Oliver Hart, 1723–1795*, 16.

[23] For Drayton, see Krawczynski, *William Henry Drayton*.

230    OLIVER HART AND THE RISE OF BAPTIST AMERICA

on Hart to fill the third spot. Apart from his evangelical kinship to Tennent, Hart stood out drastically from the other two men. The self-taught Baptist minister moved in different circles from his companions, and at fifty-two he was about two decades older than both. But Hart, it was reasoned, could communicate with the large segment of backcountry Baptists. The letter he received, signed by Laurens, assured him, "Your compliance will be esteemed by the Council of Safety as an instance of your zeal in public service, when the aid of every freeman and lover of constitutional liberty is loudly called for."[24] As other state governments would do throughout the war, South Carolina intended to use the so-called black regiment of American clergy to their fullest advantage in this conflict.[25]

Hart eagerly accepted the charge. His cousin John Hart (1713–1779) would sign his name to the Declaration of Independence on behalf of New Jersey. His brother Joseph (1715–1788) would serve as an officer in the Continental Army of Pennsylvania. His son John, home from Rhode Island College, enlisted under South Carolina's war hero Gen. William Moultrie (1730–1805). Oliver Hart was too old to fight, but he could preach the message of liberty to ordinary Baptist folk. He wrote in his diary, "On Monday, July 3, 1775, I set off for the frontiers of the province, being appointed by the Council of Safety to accompany the Honorable William Henry Drayton and the Rev. Wm. Tennent to try to reconcile a number of the inhabitants, who are disaffected to the government." It would be a costly mission. As Hart rode away, his new wife, Nancy, was pregnant with their first child. Silas Hart would be born August 30, while his father was still gone. Tragically the boy would die less than a month later, when Hart was again missing, this time at the bedside of his deathly ill daughter, Nelly. "I was absent at the birth and death of the child, a heavy trial to my dear Nancy," Hart would write regretfully. Like other colonists who enlisted in the cause of liberty, Hart's patriotic service came at a steep price.[26]

*

Though Hart would rendezvous with Drayton and Tennent at various points on the journey, each member of the Commission followed a different route,

---

[24] Krawczynski, *William Henry Drayton*, 160–62; Owens, *Oliver Hart, 1723–1795*, 16. Colonial leaders asked other clergy to perform similar recruiting tasks during this period; see Bonomi, *Under the Cope of Heaven*, 211.

[25] For other "patriot evangelicals" who went on similar recruiting missions during the Revolution, see Kidd, *Great Awakening*, 293–94.

[26] Hart, *Original Diary*, 9.

"THE RISING GLORY OF THIS CONTINENT" 231

seeking out their respective target audiences. Hart rode first to the familiar Congaree Baptist Church, where his friend Joseph Reese served as pastor. There, on August 2, Hart preached from John 8:36: "If the Son therefore shall make you free, ye shall be free indeed." It was a well-loved passage for all evangelicals, extolling the spiritual freedom Jesus gives his followers. But Hart deftly shifted to the theme of political liberty, addressing his listeners with "the subject of the times." It was the first time on record that Hart departed from his typical pattern of preaching the plain meaning of the text, but his politicizing of Scripture would become common in the years ahead. Many Dissenting preachers all over America were infusing biblical passages with political meaning at this time: the great "tyrant" oppressing Christians these days was more often George III than Satan, and the "liberty" all men should desire was not freedom from sin but "the individual rights secured to all people by the Enlightenment."[27] Hart's congregation heartily approved his message. Afterward Hart prevailed on Reese to join him on the rest of his journey. As the two men traveled together, they talked with anyone who would listen about "the state of the times." At one stop Hart delivered another creative twist on a classic evangelical text, Galatians 5:1: "Stand fast therefore in the liberty wherewith Christ hath made us free, and be not entangled again with the yoke of bondage." Harry Stout has pointed out that while biblical references to "liberty" and "freedom" are relatively rare, "patriot ministers seized on every instance of the term and extracted from it a double meaning which, they believed, was intended especially for them."[28] Of these treasured "liberty texts," none was more popular than Galatians 5:1. Hart "took occasion to speak on the state of national affairs," while the people "heard with attention." He learned afterward that "one opposer was convinced, and sharply reproved one who quarreled with the sermon." Hart was quickly learning how effective the language of Zion could be in the service of politics.[29]

The most pleasant event in the journey came on August 21, at William Wofford's home on the Tyger River. There, Drayton, Tennent, and Hart hosted a picnic for the locals, where "a beef was barbecued, on which we dined." The free food attracted a large crowd, and after the meal the team followed the basic program of an evangelical revival meeting. Reese, a good singer,

---

[27] John Fea, *The Way of Improvement Leads Home*, 151–52. Mark Noll also addresses how Christian language was used as a "Republican Disinfectant" in *America's God*, 82–85.

[28] Stout, *The New England Soul*, 298–99. See also Daniel Dreisbach, *Reading the Bible with the Founding Fathers* (New York: Oxford University Press, 2017), esp. 189–99.

[29] J. Glenwood Clayton, and Loulie Latimer Owens, eds., "Oliver Hart's Diary of the Journey to the Backcountry," *Journal of the South Carolina Baptist Historical Society* 1 (November 1975), 19–20.

loosened the audience up with a song. Drayton, the passionate and persuasive orator, then spoke for over an hour on the recent developments between the colonies and the Crown. Hart recorded that the people listened attentively, and at the end of the meeting more than seventy men came forward to sign the Association Agreement. In fact the people were "so active and spirited" that they insisted on forming a provincial regiment on the spot.[30] A song, a sermon, and an invitation: this was nothing less than a revival meeting for the sake of political freedom. It was a prime example of how evangelical rhetoric and practice were influencing the American Revolutionary generation. Whether the speaker held to evangelical convictions (like Hart and Tennent) or not (like Drayton), American orators used patterns of evangelical communication to great effect throughout the war.[31] This was also the team's most successful engagement of their commission.

Not every stop was so encouraging. On August 10 Hart and Reese arrived at the home of Separate Baptist Phillip Mulkey at Fairforest Creek. Mulkey had built a very popular ministry in the backcountry with his homespun charisma. In the late 1760s Charles Woodmason had marveled at Mulkey's influence with the people: "Would any Mortal three Years past have dreamed or imagin'd that such a Person as the infamous Mulchey, who came here lately in Rags, hungry, and bare foot can now, at his beck, or Nod, or Motion of his finger lead out four hundred Men into the Wilderness in a Moment At his speaking the Word—Without asking any Questions, or making the least Enquiry for what or for why."[32] The "infamous" Mulkey was indeed serving under a moral cloud by 1775, which Hart detailed in a letter to James Manning in 1767. Hart praised Mulkey for leading the most dynamic revival in Baptist life, but added that he had "sadly fallen, having become the father of a spurious child by a widow woman, a member of his own church. On account of which religion has suffered much, especially in those parts, and among those people."[33] Morgan Edwards added in 1772, "A thorn was put into [Mulkey's] flesh about 4 years ago which will . . . teach his votaries that he is but a man."[34] Mulkey maintained a significant following despite

[30] Clayton and Owens, "Journey to the Back-Country," 23.

[31] See Harry S. Stout, "Religion, Communications, and the Ideological Origins of the American Revolution," *William & Mary Quarterly* 3rd ser., 34, no. 4 (October 1977): 524–25; and Isaac, *Transformation of Virginia*, 265–67. Jon Butler, who wishes to emphasize the secular character of the Revolution, downplays the impact of evangelical rhetoric and ideas in "Enthusiasm Described and Decried," 320–21.

[32] Woodmason, *Carolina Backcountry*, 112.

[33] Oliver Hart to James Manning, December 23, 1767, Manning MSS, JHL.

[34] Edwards, *Materials towards a History of the Baptists*, 2:141.

"THE RISING GLORY OF THIS CONTINENT" 233

his checkered past, though his repeated sins of the flesh eventually caught up with him. The Charleston Association would ultimately dis-fellowship him in 1790, warning its members of his "enormous crimes; such as adultery, perfidy and falsehood, which have been attended with very aggravating circumstances, often repeated and continued in for years; and part of the time, united with his highest pretensions of zeal and piety."[35] But on this night in 1775, the saddle-weary Hart and Reese, in no position to be fastidious, knocked on Mulkey's door anyway. He welcomed them inside.

To Hart's dismay, Mulkey revealed that he was a staunch Loyalist. Along with all his neighbors, he had come under the sway of a prominent Tory leader named Col. Thomas Fletchall (1725–1789). Fletchall was a big operator in the area in every way: he ran a gristmill and a sizable plantation, and weighed over three hundred pounds. "I find that Col. Fletchall has all those people at his beck, and reigns amongst them like a little king," Hart remarked. Fletchall had even composed a Counter-Association, in which he called his neighbors to pledge loyalty to the Crown. Hart scoffed at the pledge as "a jejune incoherent piece," but admitted that it "serves to delude the people." As Hart engaged Mulkey's neighbors in conversation, he saw that they too were "so on the side of the ministry, that no argument on the contrary side seemed to have any weight with them." The next day Hart addressed a few dozen men when a crowd of angry Loyalists interrupted, shouting that they "wished 1,000 Bostonians might be kill'd in battle," and one "wish'd there was not a grain of salt in any of the coast towns on the continent." Hart wrote that night, "On the whole, they appear to be irritated in the extreme."[36] This conflict struck him considerably. Fearing British interception, he began writing his diary in code.

He had good reason to be nervous; Loyalist resentment ran deep against the Patriots in many portions of the backcountry. At one gathering, Colonel Fletchall and his "Gang of Leaders" met the commissioners "double Armed" with pistols, swords, and rifles, their scowling features indicating "dark Designs." A few altercations between the hot-headed Drayton and Tory leaders nearly touched off a civil war. Adding to these anxieties, the group chose an unseasonably rainy August to travel across the frontier, and the muddy roads and swollen creeks made progress difficult. Hart reports crossing "several deep creeks," and rivers that were "very high and

[35] Townsend, *South Carolina Baptists*, 125.
[36] Clayton and Owens, "Journey to the Back-Country," 20–21.

234    OLIVER HART AND THE RISE OF BAPTIST AMERICA

ran rapidly." On August 23 he determined that he had done all he could and headed back to Charleston. He would arrive home with great relief on September 6.[37]

The fact that Tennent and Drayton would continue their travels for another few weeks raises the obvious question of why Hart broke off early. Drayton's biographer Keith Krawczynski, who takes a rather dim view of Hart's contribution to the Commission, suggests that Drayton and Tennent may have "lost confidence in the Baptist minister." After all, Hart had been "browbeaten" and "ridiculed" by the opposition at many stops; he finally trudged home "disappointed and jaded." Krawczynski wonders if Hart was a good choice for the mission in the first place, citing not only his advanced age but his lack of Drayton's self-confidence and Tennent's personal charisma. The truth is, Hart probably was a bit out of place on this mission. It seems the constant threat of violence bothered him more than he expected, and his lifelong tendency to grow discouraged by rejection was not ideally suited for this rugged work. In the end, Hart was simply a Baptist preacher trying to do his part in the war effort.[38]

Whatever Hart's personal impact may have been, the backcountry mission was hailed as a great success back in Charleston. After covering over three hundred miles in a month's time, speaking an average of once a day, and holding hundreds of personal conversations about "the state of the times" with backcountry neighbors, Hart and his party garnered numerous pledges of loyalty to the South Carolina Council of Safety, raised enough volunteer companies to increase the Patriot forces by over six hundred, and gathered invaluable information about the state of the backcountry for the Council of Safety. In addition, Drayton negotiated an important peace treaty with the residents of Ninety-Six, South Carolina. The Provincial Congress formally thanked the commissioners on November 29, 1775. The Baptist historian Loulie Owens calls Hart's participation in the commission "the most significant contribution to the American Revolution by any individual South Carolina Baptist."[39]

*

[37] Krawczynski, *William Henry Drayton*, 179; Loulie Latimer Owens, "Oliver Hart and the American Revolution," *Journal of the South Carolina Baptist Historical Society* 1 (November 1975): 5–12; Clayton and Owens, "Journey to the Back-Country," 26.

[38] Krawczynski, *William Henry Drayton*, 162, 188.

[39] Owens, "Oliver Hart and the American Revolution," 2; Krawczynski, *William Henry Drayton*, 192–94.

The issue that ultimately won the majority of America's Baptists over to the Patriot cause was the prospect of obtaining full religious freedom under the constitution of a new republic. Since the fourth century, traditional Christian wisdom had held that because religion was essential to a virtuous and stable society, the state must sponsor a given church and require its citizens to attend it and support it financially. While not all American Baptists suffered for their beliefs at the time of the Revolution, all abhorred the concept of state-established religion. Hart, who was never oppressed for his Baptist beliefs, nevertheless called the union of church and state "the sole cause of all those horrid persecutions which have so much disgraced Christianity and set the world on fire."[40] Even in colonies that enjoyed a relatively high degree of religious freedom, like South Carolina, Baptists felt a deep kinship with their suffering brethren in other colonies. At their February 6, 1775, meeting, the Charleston Association "agreed to recommend to our Churches, to contribute to the Relief of our Brethren, suffering under Ecclesiastical Oppressions, in the *Massachusetts Bay*. And that the Money raised be sent to the Rev. Oliver Hart, to be by him remitted to Rev. Isaac Backus, for that Purpose."[41] On other occasions they expressed solidarity with fellow Baptists by letter and through corporate prayer. At their 1778 meeting the Charleston Association read a letter from the Warren Association, "by which it appears that the Baptists in some parts of New England are still laboring under religious oppressions; which they justly deem doubly gauling at such a period as this, when they are equally engaged, with their fellow-citizens, in procuring and defending the civil rights of America."[42] Whatever their geographical location, Baptists across the American colonies viewed it as their duty to seize the moment of Revolution to obtain the freedom to worship according to one's own conscience, what Hart called "a capital blessing" and "the natural and inalienable right of all men."[43] Revolutionary-era Baptists truly saw themselves as fighting a war on two fronts.

South Carolina was a beacon of religious freedom compared to Virginia or Massachusetts, but it still collected taxes from all property holders for the Church of England and also required religious qualifications to participate in the political process. In lobbying for religious freedom, Baptists

[40] Oliver Hart, *America's Remembrancer, with Respect to her Blessedness and Duty* (Philadelphia, PA: Dobson, 1791), 15.

[41] Charleston Association, *Minutes of the Charleston Association, February 6, 1775.*

[42] Charleston Association, *Minutes of the Charleston Association, February 2, 1778* (Charleston, SC, 1778).

[43] Hart, *America's Remembrancer*, 15.

found it effective to unite with other Dissenting denominations.[44] In South Carolina the most impassioned and effective spokesman for soul freedom was Hart's friend William Tennent III. When, in 1776, South Carolina's state constitution gave preferential treatment to the Anglican Church, Tennent led the Dissenters movement in petitioning the state congress for full disestablishment. He decried the "odious discrimination" against the new state's Dissenters and noted the inconsistency of calling them to fight for political liberty while denying them religious liberty. By now there were in fact far more Dissenting congregations in South Carolina than Anglican—why must all be forced to fund the Church of England? "Equality or nothing! Ought to be our motto. In short, every plan of establishment must operate as a plan of injustice or oppression," Tennent thundered. He exhorted the assembly to "yield to the mighty current of American glory and freedom," by granting equal rights to all citizens, regardless of religious conviction. Hart cheered his friend on.[45]

In 1777, as Tennent was moving his aged mother home with him from New York, he reached the High Hills of Santee and contracted a fatal nervous disorder. Richard Furman rushed to Tennent's bedside and later reported to Tennent's wife, "I was with him in his last moments—his life went gently from him—almost without a struggle or groan. He told me in almost the last words he spoke, that his mind was calm and easy, and he was willing to be gone."[46] South Carolina's most articulate defender of religious liberty was dead at the age of thirty-seven. In a poignant tribute to the bond that held evangelical Dissenters together during the war years, Hart preached a memorial sermon for his fallen friend at the First Baptist Church, based on 2 Samuel 3:38, "Know ye not that there is a great man fallen this day in Israel?" He took the occasion to declare the principles he and Tennent shared so deeply: "I am clear in my opinion, that the peace, welfare and happiness of this state, depends much upon our having our religious, as well as our civil liberty constitutionally fixed."

> All who have just notions of freedom, and have embarked in the glorious cause, will certainly expect this. It is so just and equitable, that the meanest citizen may demand it, as his right. It is our inalienable property, as much so as limb or life; and we cannot dispose of it, without being guilty of great

[44] For the story of the Dissenters' coalition in Virginia, see Ragosta, *Wellspring of Liberty*.
[45] See Kidd, *God of Liberty*, 180.
[46] Rogers, *Richard Furman*, 38.

injustice to ourselves, and impiety toward God. We hope therefore, that our representatives will do justice to their constituents, by fixing religious liberty on the broadest bottom, and the most permanent foundation.[47]

\*

While religious liberty united Baptists with their Dissenting neighbors, it also drew them closer to one another. Baptists across America had grown increasingly aware of one another in the decade leading up to the war, and many, like Hart, wished them to unite as a single denomination. This desire is evident at the 1774 Charleston Association meeting. There they received letters from "three Sister Associations," the Warren, Philadelphia, and Fairforest. They then sent letters in return, as well as to the Ketocton Association in Virginia, and elected messengers to attend the meetings of each association on their behalf. They also received a proposal from Mulkey, in attendance as a guest from Fairforest, for "uniting the several Association in this Province into one." The Charleston Association was "well pleased" by the idea, believing that this union would "tend to the Interest of the Churches in general," and "resolved to promote it." The Association voted down a proposal to change the time of their annual meeting, because in the present arrangement, a single Baptist messenger "from the Northward" could "attend all the BAPTIST ASSOCIATIONS on the Continent, except that at *Ketocton*."[48] Clearly, the aspiration to link all the Baptists on the continent was growing, but their far-flung geographical locations, as well as the cultural differences among the Regulars and Separates, continued to hinder this.

The common cause of religious liberty was perhaps most responsible for finally effecting the desired union. In September 1775 Isaac Backus and a committee from the Warren Association in New England proposed a national congress composed of delegates from "all the Baptist societies on this Continent," modeled after the Revolutionary actions of the Patriots. The goal of the meeting would be to frame a course of action for creating a united front for religious liberty in the new nation. When this congress failed to materialize, it was suggested that another "continental association" should meet in Virginia the following year, but by 1776 the times had become too difficult to meet.[49] Hart no doubt regretted the failure of these plans on the national

[47] Hart, *Character of a Truly Great Man*, 29–30.

[48] Charleston Association, *Minutes of the Charleston Association, February 7, 1774* (Charleston, SC, 1774).

[49] McLoughlin, *New England Dissent*, 1:567–68.

level, but he continued to use religious liberty as a lever for Baptist union in the South. In 1777 he wrote to Furman, "We now have a hopeful prospect that we shall obtain religious liberty, in its full extent, in this state; it cannot fail if the Dissenters will be careful to attend the next Session of Assembly." Furman had by now developed his own voice as an ardent patriot among the Separate Baptists. In 1775 the twenty-year-old pastor had written a letter condemning Parliament for trampling on Americans' rights and calling on his fellow backcountry men to resist. South Carolina's Col. Richard Richardson of the High Hills had copied Furman's letter and distributed it in the backcountry in the winter of 1775, just before quelling a Loyalist rebellion at Ninety-Six.[50] Hart now urged Furman to bring his Separate Baptists into union with both the broader Dissenters' coalition as well as with the Regular Baptists in the Charleston Association. "I am the more for this junction, because I fear that some of the Baptists on the frontiers will be deemed unfriendly to government," Hart wrote. "Therefore let all of us who are in support of our happy constitution unite together in one band; we shall thereby appear the more respectable in the eyes of government." Hart knew some might accuse him of abandoning piety for political machinations, but he was untroubled by this. "Let not these thoughts be rejected as human policy. While in the world, we must be concerned with it, and I am sure the religion of Jesus forbids us not our making ourselves as comfortable in it as possible."[51]

Hart proved persuasive. At the October 1778 meeting of the Charleston Association, Furman led his large High Hills church, along with one of its daughter churches, Lynch's Creek, into the Association. It was a historic milestone in Regular-Separate Baptist relations. "We cannot but rejoice at the happy prospect of a greater union among the churches in this state than ever there has been," reported the Charleston Association circular letter. "We believe the time is coming, when brotherly love shall abound among all the saints, and people of God, when divisions shall cease and be no more, and the gospel shall have free course, run and be glorified." Sure enough, the South Carolina Constitution of 1778 disestablished the Anglican Church: any Protestant would be allowed to hold office, and all Protestant churches could legally incorporate. The jubilant tone of the Charleston Association's circular letter later that year reflects the Baptist sense of triumph: "We esteem it as a singular blessing of Providence, that our civil and religious privileges are

---

[50] Rogers, *Richard Furman*, 28–30; Kidd, *God of Liberty*, 85.
[51] Oliver Hart to Richard Furman, February 12, 1777, Hart MSS, JBDML.

# "THE RISING GLORY OF THIS CONTINENT"  239

established on the broadest bottom, and most permanent foundation." The cause of religious liberty was drawing Baptists together all over America; it was also a primary reason for the confidence of Hart and other Baptists that, even in the darkest hours of the war, God was indeed on their side.[52]

*

In fact there were times when Hart's perception of God's hand on America moved him to worship. In one remarkable passage from a 1778 letter to his brother Joseph, Hart cast off all restraint in speaking of America's future in terms typically reserved by evangelicals for the final consummation of the kingdom of God:

> During the whole of this struggle, the Providence of God hath appeared evidently in our favor, and it would be impious to doubt of a happy issue. After the virtue of America hath combatted a few more difficulties, all will be well. With joy I often look forward and contemplate the rising glories of this continent; its inhabitants nourished by the most free, generous, and perfect form of government ever modeled; and cherished by the best of rulers, chosen by ourselves, whose interest and inclination will conspire to make the ruled happy. When peace, like the swelling tide, shall flow over the mountains and cover the whole land. When Religion, freed from its shackles—learning and virtue, encouraged and promoted, shall spread far and wide. Wisdom and knowledge shall increase, and every peasant be qualified for a Senator. Every man shall sit down under his own vine, and under his own fig tree; and the trade, favour, and protection of America will be courted by all nations under Heaven. This is the prize for which we are contending, and this is the legacy which we mean to bequeath to our posterity; in the enjoyment of which our children's children to the last stages of time, will rise up and call us blessed. But I am lost in the boundless prospect; may Heaven be propitious to our hopes.[53]

Hart was coming to believe that America was specially blessed by God, a notion that would gain adherence among many Baptists as the war progressed,

[52] Charleston Association, *Minutes of the Charleston Association, October 19, 1778* (Charleston, SC, 1778).

[53] Oliver Hart to Joseph Hart, July 5, 1778, Hart MSS, SCL. Harry Stout discusses how Patriot orators applied the language of millennial texts to the American Revolution in *New England Soul*, 306–9.

240     OLIVER HART AND THE RISE OF BAPTIST AMERICA

as they at long last gained religious freedoms many of them had previously only dreamed about.[54] This belief in American Exceptionalism, already evident in Hart's 1778 letter to his brother Joseph, would gain increasing prominence in his thoughts and in his preaching all the way to the end of his life.

Some scholars have noted this growing tendency among American evangelicals to wed God and country as another clear sign of the influence of Enlightenment epistemology. As Americans grew more confident in their ability to know things once considered hidden in God's mysterious counsels, they applied their new powers of insight to the destiny of America. It seemed so self-evident that the Almighty was guiding the American enterprise, bound up as it was with freedom and virtue, that to suggest otherwise would be nothing less than "impious." As the historian John Fea described Hart's contemporary Philip Vickers Fithian, "The Calvinist belief that human sin clouded one's capacity to discern God's providence was exchanged for a modern certainty that the Revolution was divinely inspired."[55] Whether a Presbyterian like Fithian or a Baptist like Hart, many Revolutionary evangelicals did not hesitate to identify the cause of Jesus Christ with the cause of America, participating in the emergence of an American civil religion that remains familiar among American evangelicals to this day.

*

While political events often consumed his thoughts, Hart struggled to remember that his primary concerns belonged to the kingdom of another world. For Baptists, wartime presented both unique challenges and opportunities for promoting conversion, holy living, and the building up of local churches. However convinced many Baptists may have been of the righteousness of the America cause, war was an awful thing that suggested disciplinary judgment from God's hand. Accordingly, at its February 1775 meeting the Charleston Association urged its churches to observe three days of fasting and prayer in the coming year. Their leaders wished for Baptists "to humble ourselves before Almighty God for our sins, to supplicate his mercies, and to deprecate the judgments which we have justly deserved; and which from the present alarming circumstances of affairs, appear to be hanging over us."[56]

---

[54] See Kidd and Hankins, *Baptists in America*, 56–58; Fea, *Was America Founded as a Christian Nation?*, 3–17.
[55] Fea, *The Way of Improvement Leads Home*, 214; see also the argument of Noll in *America's God*.
[56] Charleston Association, *Minutes, February 6, 1775*.

For those who had ears to hear, the drums of war were a wake-up call to get right with God.

As Hart surveyed Charleston's spiritual landscape, he was especially concerned by his community's ongoing attachment to frivolous amusements in the face of God's judgment. The city's almost frenetic devotion to the worldly pastimes of dancing, theatergoing, and horse racing had long been a concern of the evangelical community, and Hart had frequently preached against it. In 1778, in response to "many earnest solicitations," he published *Dancing Exploded: A Sermon, Shewing The Unlawfulness, Sinfulness, and bad Consequences of Balls, Assemblies, and Dances in general.* The sermon was an old fashioned jeremiad, a rhetorical genre perfected by New England's Puritans. In the jeremiad, the minister seized upon some public calamity as evidence of God's chastening a community that had grown spiritually and morally lax.[57] Like the Old Testament prophet Jeremiah, the preacher would then urgently call the people to repentance, extending hope that the Almighty would again restore his former favor if they would heed the warning. Hart followed this time-tested strategy in *Dancing Exploded.* "The judgments of God are now spread over our land, and the inhabitants ought to learn righteousness," he thundered, citing "the clangor of arms—the garments rolled in blood—the sufferings of our brethren in the northern states, and of others in a state of captivity." As one nineteenth-century reader remarked, the sermon "blazed with the pure old Puritan fire."[58] Hart knew that his pronouncements would not aid his popularity, but like any faithful prophet, he was willing to stand alone. "By some I may be pitied for my folly, by others, despised and ridiculed," he acknowledged. "[But] if I had not been willing to endure the scoff of the world, I should never have made an open profession of the religion of Jesus, much less should I have become a preacher of his much-despised gospel."[59] When it came to worldly pleasures, moderate evangelical Baptists never minded vocally opposing their society.

For thirty-two passionately argued pages in *Dancing Exploded,* Hart took dead aim at Charleston's dancing culture, citing its tendency toward sexual misconduct, its waste of time and money, and its general failure to glorify God and benefit the soul. He concluded his sermon with a series of probing questions: "For what was I made? Do I answer the end of my being? Is God

[57] Stout, *New England Soul,* 62–63, 75–76, 95.
[58] Moses Coit Tyler, *The Literary History of the American Revolution, 1763–1783* (New York, 1897), 296.
[59] Hart, *Dancing Exploded,* 5–6.

242 OLIVER HART AND THE RISE OF BAPTIST AMERICA

glorified in all my actions? Is living in pleasure to live like a Christian? Must I not shortly die, and give an account of my actions to God? Have I any time to spare from transacting business for eternity?" "If this advice were universally regarded," he insisted, "we should hear no more of balls, assemblies, and dances; instead of which, our temple gates would be crowded, and the general cry would be, 'Lord, what shall I do to be saved?'" Like all good Baptist preachers, Hart found a way to get to the issue of conversion, even from the dance floor. Though it may not have changed many opinions in Charleston society, *Dancing Exploded* remains a particularly vivid example of how many American evangelical preachers attempted to promote piety during the Revolutionary War through preaching.[60]

A number of Hart's Baptist friends also promoted wartime piety by serving as chaplains to the Continental Armies, including Hezekiah Smith, Samuel Stillman, and John Gano. Hart was no longer physically up for such strenuous work, but he still sought to minister to the Patriot troops however he could. One opportunity came on July 22, 1777, when a young soldier called Malcolm was sentenced to die for deserting the American army, along with two companions. Hart, dressed in his gown and bands, went to the military barracks to visit the three men, where he "conversed and prayed with them" for some time. Afterward he walked with them to the scaffold. He "conversed with them all the way," speaking to Malcolm over the noise of fife and drums. Despite his best efforts, Hart "discovered but little signs of penitence in either of them." Still, he accompanied the three soldiers to the place of execution, where he prayed with them again, and said farewell. When one of Malcolm's commanding officers addressed him a final time, the young soldier called for Hart. Though Hart suspected that "all he wanted was to protract time," he prayed with him once more, and then watched in sorrow as Malcolm, blindfolded, kneeled before the firing squad and was shot. The other two soldiers had been led to believe they would be executed with Malcolm. Instead they received a fierce reprimand from their commanding officer and were told that if they would continue serving in the war, they would be pardoned. For all parties involved in the war, these were desperate days indeed.[61]

\*

[60] Hart, *Dancing Exploded*, 30–32. For the use of jeremiads by ministers throughout the war, see Bonomi, *Under the Cope of Heaven*, 212–13, and Butler, *Awash in a Sea of Faith*, 208–9.
[61] Hart, *Original Diary*, 11.

As Hart's diaries and correspondence in 1778 and 1779 reveal, the war had shattered the peaceful lives he and his family had so long enjoyed. A friend, James Murray, was killed "by the bursting of a great gun" on Edisto Island. With horror, Hart recalled that Murray survived the accident for a few minutes "but was insensible and never spoke." The memory of the ghastly scene prompted him to comment, "Thus uncertain is life. O may I always hold myself in readiness for death." These were indeed serious times. Hart was particularly disturbed by reports of the conduct of the British soldiers toward prisoners and civilians. "The policy of Britain, in the present controversy, would disgrace the most barbarous nation; and the conduct of the British Army in America, will remain in indelible characters of blood to future generations," he fumed to his brother Joseph. "Their cause is unjust, and their measures diabolical. For my part, I cannot trace the ravages of their army without horror and indignation." Red Coats aside, one never knew what the South Carolina Loyalists were plotting. After his harrowing experience in the backcountry, Hart declared without hesitation, "Tories are some of the basest creatures under the heavens." He suspected their handiwork behind every misfortune in Charleston. When a fire broke out at three in the morning and consumed several houses, Hart bitterly remarked, "There is the greatest reason to believe this was done by the hands of some vile Tory." He shivered at rumors of British Loyalists arming the local Creek Indians and stirring them up to slaughter Charleston's citizens.[62]

The war also intensified the city's ever-present fear of a slave uprising. Like the rest of his white neighbors, Hart dreaded the prospect of a slave majority seizing an opportunity to join forces with the British. One night his worst fears seemed to have been confirmed. On March 4, 1779, at 10 o'clock, the clanging bells of St. Michael's awakened sleeping Charleston. When several men rushed to investigate the steeple, they found "a negro man, pretending to be fast asleep, and apparently drunk." When they roused the man, he claimed "he knew nothing about ringing the bells." Hart worried that this was not an isolated prank but "a signal for the perpetration of some diabolical plot. It may be for burning the town, or perhaps something worse. Thro' mercy, no harm came of it." Never had the tension in Charleston been higher.[63]

Still, family life went on. Hart's son John, like many young South Carolinians, was straining for action on the battlefield. Hart worried about

---

[62] Oliver Hart to Joseph Hart, March 24, September 10, 1778, Hart MSS, SCL.
[63] Hart, *Original Diary*, 10–13.

244    OLIVER HART AND THE RISE OF BAPTIST AMERICA

his reckless boy. "John is still in the army, and seems to long for an opportunity of proving his valour," he told his brother Joseph. "Indeed I doubt not his courage, but wish he may have equal conduct, and not be too rash."[64] John would receive his chance for heroism at dawn on October 9, 1779. The united French and American forces under the command of Count d'Estaing (1729–1794) attempted to storm the British lines just below Charleston at Savannah, Georgia. They were repulsed by the British defense and many were killed, including Count Casimir Pulaski (1745–1779). John had the command of a company in that battle. As Hart recorded it in his diary, John had been "in the thickest danger, with bullets falling all around him like hail, but God in mercy spared his life."[65] It seemed that John always landed on his feet, though he contributed to his father's graying head in the process.

The Hart family received a brief interlude of joy on November 19, 1778, when Hart had the honor of officiating the wedding of his oldest son, Oliver, who would go on to practice medicine in Charleston. The young man took "Miss Sarah Brockinton" as his bride. Hart commented that she was "a poor girl, but sustains a virtuous character which is preferable to riches. May God bless them, and make them blessing to each other." The war was impoverishing everyone, it seemed. Prices on daily goods had skyrocketed, stretching family resources to the extreme. "We now feel the effects of war in the purchase of every article of life. Upon an average we pay eight hundred percent advance upon marketing liquor and dry goods; which make it hard upon the poorer sort, who have no resources," Hart wrote. And yet his family never went hungry. On two separate occasions in the first month of 1779, Hart reported two visitors calling at his house, bearing generous cash gifts of three hundred dollars and seventy dollars. "Thus God supplies my necessities. May I be thankful and my kind benefactors rewarded," Hart wrote.[66]

*

As the British troops drew closer to Charleston, Hart's friends feared that his conspicuous patriotic service made him a target of military repercussions. The British would in fact arrest sixty-five known civilian Patriots upon capturing Charleston in 1780, imprisoning them for a time at St. Augustine, Florida. These prisoners were later paroled, but then were deported with

[64] Oliver Hart to Joseph Hart, January 14, 1779, SCL.
[65] Hart, *Original Diary*, 13.
[66] Hart, *Original Diary*, 13–14.

their families from the state.[67] It does appear Hart was a marked man. In 1781 his wife Nancy reported reading an article in a British political magazine that condemned his backcountry mission, casting it as incitement of Indian rebellion. Along with Tennent, Hart was described as one of "two rebel clergy" who went on "the pious mission to the Cherokee Nation to endeavor to draw over those people to the interest of America, to bribe them to take the superintendent, if they failed to do this, way lay him and assassinate him."[68] Accordingly, when the British initially threatened Charleston in October 1775, Hart moved his family and their possessions by schooner to Euhaw, where they stayed with the widow of Francis Pelot. In the process Hart contracted a fever that kept him from preaching for more than a month. It was August 3 of the following year before the Harts felt safe enough to return to Charleston.[69]

In February 1780 Sir Henry Clinton (1730–1795) again brought the British Army against Charleston. Doctors advised Hart, suffering from another fever, "to leave town for a change of air, especially as the enemy had landed and it was supposed Charleston would soon be attacked." His health had deteriorated significantly over the past year. Just months before, he appeared to have suffered a stroke. He awoke to a sudden "paralytic complaint" in his right shoulder, which quickly spread down his arm and to his hand. He had been unable to write or preach for some time, and even after the initial severity wore off, there remained a "fixed numbness" on his right side that he feared he might "carry with [him] to the grave." He had written around this time, "As to myself, I am in but a poor state of health, and have been so about two months past, and God only knows whether ever I shall be a hearty man again. I visibly feel the effect of age, which reminds me of my Disolution; may grace prepare me for my great Change." In this weakened condition Hart and Nancy vacated the city for the house of his son-in-law, Thomas Screven, in St. Thomas Parish. There Hart convalesced for two months, where he received reports of Clinton's impending arrival. Hart shared in the anxiety of all Charleston citizens during these tense days. He wrote, "Often did I petition God with prayers and tears that poor Charles Town might be spared, and not suffered to fall into the enemy's hands. Never could I give it up until I heard of its surrender."[70]

---

[67] Edgar, *South Carolina*, 237–38.
[68] Anne Hart to Oliver Hart, July 19, 1781, Hart MSS, SCL.
[69] Hart, *Original Diary*, 9.
[70] Hart, *Original Diary*, 13.

246　OLIVER HART AND THE RISE OF BAPTIST AMERICA

News of the city's fall reached Hart on May 21, 1780. He acted quickly: "To escape being made prisoner, I left my family, and travelled northward." He made his way north to Georgetown, where he found lodging with old friends. But his rest was cut short by the news that "1,500 of the enemy were on the march for this place." He immediately hurried out of town. By May 22 he had arrived at the home of Evan Pugh, now serving as pastor of the Pee Dee Baptist Church. By the end of the next week another former student had joined Hart, "my dear son in the gospel, Rev. Edmund Botsford." Botsford too had been forced to leave his congregation when the British troops landed at Savannah. A group from Pee Dee was already preparing to leave for North Carolina and invited Hart and Botsford to join them. Hart was "distressed at the thought of leaving my dear Mrs. Hart and family in the hands of the enemy, but it was out of my power to help them. Committing them into the hands of a merciful God therefore, I proceeded on my journey." From June 2 to 26 Hart, Botsford, and their party traveled "by slow marches" until they reached the house of Hart's brother Silas in Augusta County, Virginia.[71]

*

Ever looking for an opportunity to be "useful," Hart and Botsford began preaching for a Presbyterian congregation at Stone River. They generally confined their messages to topics congenial to their common evangelical convictions. One night, however, a member of the Presbyterian church, Capt. John Stephenson, visited Hart for a discussion about their distinctions. Stephenson informed Hart that he had become "convinced of the invalidity of infant sprinkling and the validity of believer's baptism, to which he desired to submit." Hart examined Stephenson, who satisfied Hart with his "gracious experience and knowledge of gospel doctrines." A few weeks later Hart gathered "a large congregation" for a service "under the shade of trees, near the banks of N. River." He preached to the Presbyterian crowd for half an hour from Mark 16:16, "He that believeth and is baptized shall be saved." As he explained the Scripture's meaning, he "endeavoured to prove that believers are the only proper subjects of baptism, and that dipping is the mode of administration." This was radical talk for his Pedobaptist listeners, and he confessed, "How the people felt I don't know." Still, they all "behaved decently, and heard with much attention." After the sermon Hart stepped down into the river. There, "in the face of the whole congregation, I baptized Capt. John Stephenson, a

---

[71] Hart, diary, May 21, 1780, Hart MSS, SCL; Hart, *Original Diary*, 13.

"THE RISING GLORY OF THIS CONTINENT" 247

man of good character, and member of the Presbyterian Church." The ritual held the audience spellbound. According to Hart, Stephenson was "the first person ever baptized in these parts or in this river, hope numbers may follow the example, though a new and strange thing to almost all who saw it. Never did I see people behave with more decorum." Afterward Hart added, "I hope he will not disgrace the Baptists by embracing their principles." Hart could speak the ecumenical language of evangelicalism as well as anyone and was happy to do so in order to promote revival. But when the opportunity arose, he never shrank from promoting the Baptist way.[72]

By August 31 Hart and Botsford had learned of Gen. Charles Cornwallis's (1738–1805) humiliating defeat of Maj. Gen. Horatio Gates's (1727–1806) troops at the battle of Camden on August 16. This news cut off all hope of returning to Charleston. The companions decided to press further north for the home of Hart's brother Joseph in Pennsylvania. Their route took them through beautiful country, crossing the Picket Mountains at Massanutten Gap and the Blue Ridge Mountains through what Hart called "Thoms Gap." They arrived in Orange County, Virginia, on September 21, where they stayed at the home of John Leland, the most significant Separate Baptist minister in Virginia of the late eighteenth century, a major revival leader and outspoken advocate for religious liberty. Leland was recovering from "a severe fit of sickness" when the two arrived, but still managed to introduce his guests to several important Separate Baptist leaders, including John Waller, William Dawson, and David Thomas. Each had paid a steep price for conducting Baptist ministry in Anglican-established Virginia. For more than a week Hart and Botsford shared many meals and preaching platforms with the Separate Baptists as they rode throughout the region and "were very happy together." If there lingered any suspicions between these Regular and Separate Baptist ministers before this visit, their shared experience in the war as well as in ministry was quickly dissolving them.[73]

After riding some seven hundred miles together, Hart parted with Botsford in Prince William Parrish and continued by himself for Joseph Hart's house in Pennsylvania. He passed through Frederick Town, Baltimore, and London Tract, preaching at every stop, reuniting with old friends and making new ones. Along the way he received bad news from home. His house had been lost, and the Charleston Baptist Meetinghouse had been taken over for the

---

[72] Oliver Hart, diary, July 14, August 3, 1780, SCL.
[73] Hart, *Original Diary*, 14.

248   OLIVER HART AND THE RISE OF BAPTIST AMERICA

storage of salt beef.[74] British troops frequently seized the opportunity to deface Dissenting meetinghouses, viewing them as hotbeds of Revolutionary sentiment. Finally, on October 10, 1780, he arrived in Philadelphia. He was immediately welcomed into the home of an erudite young Baptist named William Rogers. He had been the first student at Rhode Island College and now served as a military chaplain and professor of belles lettres at the University of Pennsylvania. After nearly six months of travel, Hart had reached his destination. From the beginning of his exhausting journey to its completion, he was sustained by the kindness of his network of diverse Baptist friends. He would need them in the days to come.

[74] Hart, *Original Diary*, 13.

# 11

## "Directed in the path of duty"

### Staying the Course

Hart made it to Philadelphia just in time for the annual meeting of the Philadelphia Association in October 1780. He had been in South Carolina for thirty years, but through his extensive communication network, he had maintained many close friendships with northern Baptists. The Association immediately admitted Hart as a messenger, and then unanimously asked him to preach. Hart impressed the young minister William Rogers that night as "a great and good preacher" and "an animating Christian."[1] For Hart, this address to his Northern peers must have been pregnant with meaning: three decades earlier, this Association had commissioned him as a raw licentiate to begin a pioneering work in the South. Now he stood before them a respected and accomplished leader, exiled from his church and family in Charleston. Many new faces had replaced the leaders of that earlier generation. No longer concerned with merely gaining stability in the New World, these Baptists were now expanding throughout colonial America and establishing institutions to rival those of any other denomination. So much had changed for Hart and for Baptists since 1749.[2]

*

Yet many things remained the same. The Hopewell Baptist Church in New Jersey immediately asked Hart to fill their vacant pulpit in November. He agreed. Reflecting on God's strange Providence in his life, he wrote, "Tomorrow, Deo volente, I am once more to be employ'd in the great work of dispensing the Word of Life to the Inhabitants of my native land. O for the assisting aids of the Spirit of God. Thou, O Lord knowest that without Thee I can do nothing, wilt thou be my help, for Christ's sake, Amen."[3] The

---

[1] William Rogers to Isaac Backus, October 26, 1780, Backus MSS, Andover Newton Theological Seminary.

[2] Gillette, *Minutes*, 169–70.

[3] Oliver Hart, diary, November 12, Hart MSS, SCL.

*Oliver Hart and the Rise of Baptist America.* Eric C. Smith, Oxford University Press (2020). © Oxford University Press.
DOI: 10.1093/oso/9780197506325.001.0001

250  OLIVER HART AND THE RISE OF BAPTIST AMERICA

Hopewell congregation totaled 216 members—recorded as 122 females, 87 males, and 7 "Negroes"—more than double the size of the next largest church in the Philadelphia Association.[4] The Hopewell Baptists had been seeking a minister since the untimely death of Isaac Eaton in 1772, the scholarly pastor who had served them for more than twenty-six years. The congregants revered Eaton, even burying his remains under the church and erecting his tombstone in front of the pulpit. The inscription read, in part, "In him with grace and eminence did shine, the man, the Christian, scholar, and divine." Eaton's immediate successor, Benjamin Coles, had found him to be a difficult act to follow. During his years as their minister, from 1774 to 1779, Coles oversaw more than one hundred conversions, leading to Hopewell's rise as the Philadelphia Association's largest church. Yet because Coles was uneducated and relied more on emotion in his delivery than had Eaton, the church opposed him so strongly that leadership eventually advised Coles to resign.[5] It was a revealing testimony to the diversity of tastes and preferences that existed in Baptist life. In Oliver Hart, the Hopewell Baptists saw a man in the same mold as Eaton: the two men had in fact been childhood friends, were licensed to preach in the same service back in 1747, and were both committed to an educated ministry. On December 7 a committee from the church extended Hart a call "to act as their minister as long as it might be agreeable to them and me," assuring him that they would "use their endeavours to render me as happy as they could in life."[6]

The call to Hopewell further intrigued Hart because of his extensive family ties to the church and community. The property on which the Hopewell meetinghouse stood had been donated by his cousin, John Hart, in 1747. John was a local celebrity. Born in Hopewell in 1713, he became a successful farmer and mill operator in the region, and by the 1770s was the largest landowner in Hopewell, with over six hundred acres to his name. His original stone house and barn still stand on Hart Avenue in Hopewell today. Known as "Honest John," he had an excellent reputation, remembered by Founder Benjamin Rush as "a plain, honest, well meaning Jersey farmer, with but little education, but with good sense and virtue enough to pursue the true interests of his country." During the 1760s the people of New Jersey elected John to a number of important civic positions, including the Colonial Assembly (1761–71), the committee to elect and appoint delegates to the First Continental Congress

---

[4] Gillette, *Minutes*, 179.
[5] Maring, *Baptists in New Jersey*, 76.
[6] Oliver Hart, diary, December 7, 1780, Hart MSS, SCL.

(1774), the New Jersey Committee of Correspondence and Committee of Safety (1776), and the New Jersey Provincial Congress (1776). John was designated to sign the new "bill credit notes" issued by the state of New Jersey, and signed over twenty-five thousand notes by hand. In 1776 he was elected as one of five delegates to the Second Continental Congress, where he became the thirteenth delegate to sign the Declaration of Independence. In December of that year the British and Hessians invaded the Hopewell area. In spite of his imminent danger, John refused to leave the side of his dying wife. After her death, he narrowly escaped the British invaders and lived as a fugitive in the New Jersey woods for a year. He returned home to substantial damage to his home and property after the American victories at Trenton and Princeton. In June 1778, while serving as speaker of the Assembly, he invited Washington's troops to camp on his farm. Twelve thousand men stayed by the creek that flowed through the farm until June 24, four days before fighting and winning the Battle of Monmouth. Soon thereafter John died of kidney stones at the age of sixty-six, a little more than a year before Oliver returned to the area, on May 11, 1779.[7]

Oliver Hart was more than open to supplying the Hopewell pulpit, but his concern for Baptist church order prevented him from immediately accepting. It bothered him that the entire church had not been present at the decision to call him. He politely requested that due notice be given of a special church meeting. If, at that meeting, the church unanimously ruled to extend the invitation, he would accept. Accordingly, the church gathered on December 16, and Hart received his unanimous vote. After reserving "the liberty of making occasional excursions, to which I think Providence called," Hart agreed to come. There remained only the matter of determining the housing package for their homeless minister. The committee asked if he would prefer to live in the church-owned parsonage or to secure his own quarters. Here, Hart apparently played coy. "I hinted that were it not for the trouble it might put the church to, I should chuse the parsonage, but if that could not be come as easily, I would shift as well as I could," he said. After a brief private conference, the church unanimously agreed to fix up the parsonage for Hart, or to invite him to live in any of their houses. With these terms settled, Hart turned to prayer in his diary: "O Lord, I beseech thee to direct me by thy providence and grace, how to act; and as I am now to have the charge of a numerous

---

[7] For John Hart, see Maring, *Baptists in New Jersey*, 73.

## 252  OLIVER HART AND THE RISE OF BAPTIST AMERICA

people, heretofore divided, grant me wisdom, and every needed grace that I may be made a blessing to them. Amen." He was a pastor again.[8]

*

As thankful as Hart was to secure a new living and return to his roots, the separation from his family prevented him from enjoying the new call fully. "I should be happy enough, were it not for the doleful thoughts arising in my mind respecting my poor dear wife, children, and connections, now in the hands of the enemy," he recorded on November 11. "O may God pity them and supply their wants."[9] He struggled to begin a new life without Nancy and the children. Moping around Philadelphia one afternoon, purchasing "sundry necessary articles," he found the wartime prices "dear, beyond all reason."[10] He moved into the parsonage on December 25, 1780 (these Regular Baptists did not observe Christmas Day), the first place he could call home since fleeing Charleston in the spring. Yet Nancy's absence hovered over the day like a dark cloud. "Felt somewhat happy at once more having a home of my own, if it may be proper to call it my home without having my dear Nancy in it," he wrote. Many members of the church showed up with housewarming gifts. In the coming months, the people of Hopewell would continue to do all they could to make their new, distinguished minister comfortable; Hart acknowledged that they treated him "with the greatest kindness and respect."[11] In several diary entries he mentions church members mending his fences, plowing his fields, cutting his wood, inviting him over for meals and visits, and otherwise attending to his needs. As with all his temporal blessings, Hart traced Hopewell's kindness back to God's providential care. "Thus the Lord puts it into the hearts of his people to provide for my subsistence," he wrote in March 1781. "Bless his name."[12]

The church's help notwithstanding, Hart had no intention of keeping house himself. After decades of relying on a wife and a staff of slaves, it was unthinkable for the fifty-seven-year-old to start cooking and cleaning now. Hart's first order of business after moving into the parsonage was therefore to send for his niece, Nelly Thomas, who lived with his brother Joseph in nearby Warminster, Pennsylvania. As Hart saw it, Nelly would not only provide

---

[8] Oliver Hart, diary, December 16, 1780, Hart MSS, SCL.
[9] Oliver Hart, diary, November 11, 1780, Hart MSS, SCL.
[10] Oliver Hart, diary, December 23, 1780, Hart MSS, SCL.
[11] Oliver Hart, diary, December 25, 1780, Hart MSS, SCL.
[12] Oliver Hart, diary, March 1781, Hart MSS, SCL.

"DIRECTED IN THE PATH OF DUTY" 253

domestic services; she was a family member "in whom I can confide," and as his niece, she could live in his house "without censure from a censorious world." Hart wrote to Joseph on December 23 requesting his permission for her to come. The truth is, his letter left them little choice: "Should she refuse, it will be to me a shocking disappointment. I cannot see that her coming can be any detriment to Nelly or anybody else." Who would not want to wait on him?, the letter suggested. He informed Joseph that he was so confident that Nelly would come, he was already sending Deacon Barton Stout and his wife, Rachel, with an empty wagon to Nelly's home in Pennsylvania to get her. In closing, he slipped in one more appeal for good measure: "If after all the attempt should fail of success, I should hardly know how to hold up my head, or look my friends in the face; therefore must beg you to use your influence in my favor."[13] Hart had marshaled his greatest powers of loving manipulation, but after the Stouts left on December 26, he still worried over the result. "I trust Providence will favor me in sending her," he wrote, "for I know not how to manage without her." He certainly intended to trust God to take care of him, but he was also known to help the Almighty with his own maneuvering from time to time. To his immense relief, the Stouts pulled up to his house on December 29 with Nelly. It was for Hart "a pleasing circumstance, for which I desired to be thankful."[14]

Still, Nancy consumed his thoughts. On January 1, 1781, Hart followed the Puritan Pietistic tradition of gathering the church and marking New Year's Day. Together they reflected on God's work in their lives over the past year, considered their spiritual gains and losses during that time, and resolved to live more earnestly for Christ in the year ahead. Hart selected a classic Puritan text for the purpose, Romans 13:11, "And that, knowing the time, that now it is high time to awake out of sleep: for now is our salvation nearer than when we believed." But after the service all he could think of was Nancy. "O that this year may be by me devoted unto God," he recorded in his diary. "The last has been a trying, and, as to anything I have done, a very unprofitable one. How glad should I be now to hear from my Nancy, and to know that she fares as well as her fugitive husband."[15] On January 27 an otherwise comfortable evening by the fireside was likewise spoiled by Nancy's absence. "When shall she come that will remove these sore calamities? Lord I would patiently wait thy

---

[13] Oliver Hart to Joseph Hart, December 23, 1780, Hart MSS, SCL.
[14] Oliver Hart, diary, December 23, 26, 29, 1780, Hart MSS, SCL.
[15] Oliver Hart, diary, January 1, 1781, Hart MSS, SCL.

254 OLIVER HART AND THE RISE OF BAPTIST AMERICA

pleasure," he prayed.[16] A few weeks later, on February 18, Hart again sought to trust his difficult lot to God. Reflecting on the twelve-month anniversary of his departure from Charleston, he wrote, "The viscisitudes I have since passed through are not to be expressed; grievous enough they have been, yet God has been good beyond description. O may I be humble and thankful. May I never be suffered to repine. And may I be directed for time to come in the path of duty. Amen." Focusing on duty kept Hart moving forward, at least for the time being.[17]

*

At the beginning of 1781, American morale had sunk to an abysmal level, as the war seemed to drag on interminably. General Washington wrote to John Laurens around this time, "The people are discontented, but it is with the feeble and oppressive mode of conducting the war, not with the war itself."[18] Hart observed the disgust of America's troops firsthand, in the mutiny of the Pennsylvania Line on the first week of the year. The 2,400 soldiers of the Pennsylvania Line were encamped at Jockey Hollow, New Jersey, about forty miles north of Hopewell. Their living conditions were horrendous. Many had served for three years without receiving any pay beyond their initial twenty-dollar bounty. On New Year's Day the soldiers armed themselves and deserted camp to carry their grievances to Congress. When others tried to stop them, they fired shots, killing one of their own officers. The mutineers promised not to defect to the British, but insisted on a hearing with Congress and set up camp at Princeton. When the Hopewell militia was called out to confront the defectors, Hart met them at the Baptist meetinghouse to preach to them.[19] "What the consequence of this defection will be is hard to say, but I dread it," he wrote.[20] Lurid reports of British atrocities compounded his dread. On February 15 he read an article in the *New Jersey Gazette* reporting that Congress had approved enforcing the Law of Retaliation, treating British prisoners as the American prisoners had been treated. "This law cannot but be just, and yet it seems to be severe and cruel," Hart mused, "for it is certain

[16] Oliver Hart, diary, January 27, 1781, Hart MSS, SCL.

[17] Oliver Hart, diary, February 18, 1781, Hart MSS, SCL.

[18] Library of Congress, "The American Revolution, 1763–1783," George Washington to John Laurens, January 15, 1781, http://www.loc.gov/teachers/classroommaterials/presentation-sandactivities/presentations/timeline/amrev/homefrnt/gwtojl.html.

[19] On the Pennsylvania Line Mutiny, see E. Wayne Carp, *To Starve the Army at Pleasure: Continental Army Administration and Political Culture, 1775–1783* (Chapel Hill: University of North Carolina Press, 1990), 179–203.

[20] Oliver Hart, diary, January 3, 1781, Hart MSS, SCL.

"DIRECTED IN THE PATH OF DUTY"    255

that Americans, in general who have been taken prisoners by the English have been treated with the most cruel barbarity. O for an end to this unnatural war!" His hopes rose when he learned of Brig. Gen. Daniel Morgan's decisive victory over Col. Banastre Tarleton back home at the Battle of Cowpens in Cherokee County, South Carolina. It would prove a turning point in the Southern campaign. "I trust the Almighty will continue to own our righteous cause, spirit up our troops, and subdue the enemy, until the independence of America is fully established. Amen," Hart prayed.[21]

The war hindered correspondence, but Hart still managed to exchange several letters with Nancy, who filled her six surviving letters with explanations as to why she had not yet joined him in Hopewell. She complained of her broken physical condition in a February 23 letter, professing, "I am now very weak, scarce able to walk out—live almost in my chamber."[22] At many points she spoke as though they would never see one another again. On May 14 she further indicated that she intended to stay in Charleston by announcing that she had opened a school in her home. Apparently she had taught school before and would "endeavor once more in this poor but not ungenteel way to get my living." She urged Hart to picture her "with my little tribe around me, endeavouring to lay the foundation for some abler hand to raise the superstructure of education upon."[23] Launching a home school seemed inconsistent with her earlier testimony that she could not even get out of bed. But she seemed willing to say and do almost anything if it would keep her in Charleston.

Meanwhile Hart continued to confess his lonely misery to his diary. On some nights, when his friends from the church had gone home and Nelly was out socializing, he found the solitude unbearable. He mooned on April 24, "I am now all alone, my niece Nelly being absent, no one to converse with, to amuse me. My thoughts, therefore much employed about my better half. O could I but have her with me I should have some of the best company, how sweetly would the hours then glide away. Often have I hung upon her lips and been charmed by her sweet conversation."[24] When he learned that the *Flagg* was arriving in Philadelphia from Charleston in June, he excitedly rode the forty miles there, expecting to meet Nancy on board. Instead he found only some Charleston friends bearing her letter from May, along with

[21] Oliver Hart, diary, February 15, 1781, Hart MSS, SCL.
[22] Anne Hart to Oliver Hart, February 23, 1781, Hart MSS, SCL.
[23] Anne Hart to Oliver Hart, May 14, 1781, Hart MSS, SCL.
[24] Oliver Hart, diary, April 24, 1781, Hart MSS, SCL.

256 OLIVER HART AND THE RISE OF BAPTIST AMERICA

a care package for him of socks, four handkerchiefs, and a hymn book. Hart expressed his bitter disappointment to Nancy in a June 12 letter. While he carefully avoided overtly accusing her of not caring for him, he came very close. "Perhaps some evil demon whispers in the ear, 'Was her affection equal to yours, she would break through every obstacle, and fly to your arms to render you happy,'" he suggested. He was getting desperate, and he wanted her to know it.[25]

Hart tried everything to woo Nancy to Hopewell in this letter. Here she would not need to operate a school because his new living was sufficient to keep them both comfortable. And since Nancy was loath to leave her son and female slave, he assured her that they too would be welcome. He also painted an idyllic scene of his life at Hopewell:

> I am settled on a pretty little farm; capable with proper management, of producing many good things. One thing only is lacking; you only can supply that. With ease I can fancy I see you, as heretofore, with your little chicks around you, but this affords me no pleasure; much rather would I actually see you, on my farm, busying yourself with your poultry, traversing the fields, admiring the flocks and herds, or within, managing the dairy.

Fearing that visions of domestic labor might not be sufficient to uproot Nancy from the comfort of Charleston, Hart shifted his approach to shameless sweet-talk:

> I am free to stake the whole of my reputation, with the best connoisseurs, on the prudence I manifested in the choice of a wife. Doth this savor of pride? Pardon it, my Love, you are the Object; and none other can like this, excite the passion of laudable pride in my breast. The moment I had the happiness of calling you my own, I thought myself one of the happiest of men, and truly you have rendered me so, to the utmost of my wishes. With regard to conjugal felicity, few have enjoyed a greater share of it than we have been favored with, until the fatal period which obtruded this painful separation.

Ultimately, though, Hart knew that the decision must be hers. Reflecting on the spiritual purpose of his sorrows, he wondered aloud if God were not disciplining him for elevating Nancy too high in his affections: "I told my

---

[25] Oliver Hart to Anne Hart, June 12, 1781, Hart MSS, SCL.

"DIRECTED IN THE PATH OF DUTY" 257

dear, that I lov'd her too much—I have indeed placed her in the room of him who justly claims my supreme affection. I am now chastised for it, as it is fit I should. God will have no rivals." The letter, Hart's only surviving epistle to a spouse, provides a rare window into his marital relationship. As he was discovering, he was utterly dependent on his wife.[26]

Nancy responded to Hart's letter on July 19. She expressed her blushing gratitude for his "courtly letter," but also reacted defensively to his veiled questioning of her love. She professed that the same demon he mentioned also oppressed her with doubts about his affection. After all, how could he have left her in Charleston, "penniless, friendless," and "to crown it all," now "liable to banishment, to transportation, for actions not her own."[27] It is unknown if Hart's public patriotism actually placed Nancy in any danger. But four days later she offered a new excuse for staying home, her fear of sea travel: "What a poor thing am I, timorous and fearful, want to go, yet rather stay, and thus lingering, lose the time." With a melodramatic flourish, she added, "And what if I get a watery grave? Will you blame yourself at the innocent cause? No, no my dear must not do this."[28] Whatever might be said about the traditional roles of women in Baptist homes, Nancy in her own way clearly wielded a great deal of power in this relationship.

*

On Saturday, September 1, Hart watched as General Washington led his American troops, along with the French soldiers under Count de Rochambeau (1725–1807), move southward through Trenton and Princeton. Washington was responding to recent intelligence from French admiral Count de Grasse (1722–1788), reporting that his twenty-nine-ship fleet with three thousand soldiers was moving toward the Chesapeake Bay, where British general Lord Cornwallis was encamped at the Yorktown peninsula. Hart took the opportunity to visit with John Gano, who was serving as Washington's chaplain.[29] Baptist legend has long held that Gano actually immersed Washington during the war at the general's request. According to one account, Washington approached Gano and said, "I have been investigating the Scripture, and I believe immersion to be the baptism taught in the Word of God, and I demand it at your hands. I do not wish any parade

---

[26] Oliver Hart to Anne Hart, June 12, 1781, Hart MSS, SCL.
[27] Anne Hart to Oliver Hart, July 19, 1781, Hart MSS, SCL.
[28] Anne Hart to Oliver Hart, July 24, 1781, Hart MSS, SCL.
[29] Oliver Hart, diary, September 2, 1781, Hart MSS, SCL.

258   OLIVER HART AND THE RISE OF BAPTIST AMERICA

made or the army called out, but simply a quiet demonstration of the ordinance." Gano is then said to have baptized Washington in the Hudson River before forty-two witnesses. Baptists have long cherished this story, for obvious reasons.[30] But the account can in no way be substantiated. For example, Gano would certainly have shared this triumph with Hart at this meeting. Yet Hart, who went out of his way to praise Washington, never mentions the incident in his numerous later references to the Patriot leader, casting further doubt on the beloved American Baptist fable. Nevertheless Gano's willingness to serve the Continental troops as a chaplain, along with other prominent Baptist leaders like Hezekiah Smith, Samuel Stillman, and William Rogers, helped solidify Baptists' identification with the burgeoning American nation.[31]

The next day Nancy finally arrived in Philadelphia. It had been some eighteen months since she and Oliver had seen one another. "Blessed be the name of the Lord for this renewed token of his kindness," Hart wrote in his diary. After two weeks he was still aglow with the joy of his reunion: "I would be thankful that I have a home, and blessed be God, I now have the happiness of my dear Nancy with me, a blessing I have long wished and prayed for. God has heard and answered my prayers in restoring to me the joy of my heart. O that she may have her health perfectly restored, may we live together as heirs of the grace of life, and enjoy the same conjugal felicity as heretofore." Three years later, when Oliver was sixty-one, Nancy gave him a final son: William Rogers Hart.[32]

*

On October 24, 1781, Hart received more good news. He was in Philadelphia for the annual meeting of the Philadelphia Association when he heard the Liberty Bell toll. Washington's troops had combined with the French fleet to corner Cornwallis at Yorktown. The Americans laid siege to the British Army until Cornwallis surrendered more than eight thousand troops on October 19. Hart wrote, "This day arrived, from General Washington, the account of the surrender of Lord Cornwallis and the whole army under his command to General Washington on the 19th inst. A glorious event! . . . The Philadelphians manifested their joy by illuminations, bonfires, fireworks,

---

[30] See John K. Nelson, *A Blessed Company: Parishes, Parsons, and Parishioners in Anglican Virginia, 1690–1776* (Chapel Hill: University of North Carolina Press, 2003), 225.

[31] Kidd and Hankins, *Baptists in America*, 40, 56–57.

[32] Oliver Hart, diary, September 2, 1781, Hart MSS, SCL.

etc., but unhappily the mob committed sundry depredations, breaking the Quakers' (Tories) windows, etc."[33] Hart, who had little love for Tories, could not bring himself to cast a stone in their direction on this night. The occasion was far too happy to be spoiled with malice, even toward Loyalists. Small battles would continue until the signing of the Treaty of Paris in 1783, but after Yorktown, Hart knew that the long war would soon be over.

For Hart, the Revolution had been a monumentally disruptive event in his life. It had drawn him into important roles of public service, had dislodged him from Charleston and the South where he had labored for thirty years, and had convinced him of God's hand of blessing on the American enterprise. For Baptists as a whole, the war would prove to be just as significant. The conflict had increased American Baptists' awareness of one another across regional lines and had served to unify them, particularly for the cause of religious liberty. While many Baptists had begun the 1770s ambivalent in their support of the Revolution, the end of the war found most enthusiastic about a special work God had purposed to do in the new republic, and the role that they would play in it, no longer as a minor out-group but as a mainstream denomination. Furthermore, the democratic forces released by the Revolution would work overwhelmingly in the Baptists' favor in the years following the war. Baptists, who had always opposed hierarchical church government, emphasized the primacy of the individual conscience, and empowered ordinary men and women by stressing the priesthood of all believers, now found themselves in a society tailor-made for their populist religious message. As a result, Baptist membership would multiply tenfold in the three decades after the war's conclusion.[34]

\*

With the war and his separation from Nancy behind him, Hart set out to establish a routine of ministry at Hopewell. He adopted the same patterns he had followed in Charleston, beginning with a commitment to conversionist preaching. For instance, on December 17, 1780, he reported preaching to "a pretty good congregation" from one of his favorite texts, Psalm 110:3, "Thy people shall be made willing in the day of thy power." The verse was a classic resource among early evangelical preachers for explaining the new birth as a gift of divine grace from Jesus Christ. The Psalm envisioned God's

---

[33] Oliver Hart, diary, October 24, 1781, Hart MSS, SCL.
[34] Hatch, *Democratization of American Christianity*, 3; Noll, *America's God*, 149.

260 OLIVER HART AND THE RISE OF BAPTIST AMERICA

enemies presenting themselves as loyal subjects to King Jesus, through the heart-change wrought by God's Spirit. In the years 1773–94, Hart preached from this text more than any other, over a dozen times.[35] On this day he was pleased to find that "the hearers were exceeding attentive, and I had good freedom, hope the Word was blest to some."[36] His diaries find him regularly at prayer for his people and carrying on his former practice of preaching to small groups in private homes to stimulate revival. On Monday, March 12, 1781, he spoke extemporaneously to "a good number of people" from John 21:17, "Simon, son of Jonas, lovest thou me?" He remarked, "I trust the Lord enabled me to be faithful, although an unstudied and perhaps an unconnected discourse."[37]

Hart married Hopewell's young people and buried their dead. He constantly rode to members' homes for prayer and spiritual conversation and visited their sick. Some of these visits occasioned concern; after leaving the home of Mary Ann Little, for example, he remarked, "Very ill, very ignorant, and poorly prepared for death." Other visits prompted worship, as at the deathbed of the Widow Baldwin: "For some time during her illness she labored under great distress of soul but some days before her death she was brought out into gospel liberty and died rejoicing."[38]

Despite his energetic efforts, Hart made little progress with the church. No matter how vigorously he preached up the new birth, he found the response of his listeners to be lacking. Passages like this one are common in his diary: "Lord's Day, February 10: a fine day and a pretty good congregation. The Lord enabled me to preach with freedom from Matt 11:28. Come unto me. My soul longed earnestly to see sinners coming unto Jesus weary and heavy-laden with sin. But alas, conversion work is a strange work in this place."[39] Hart struggled just to get them to come to church. Many of his scheduled preparation days before the Lord's Supper, honored as special occasions for worship and personal reflection in Charleston, were poorly attended. Even the weather seemed against him. On more than one snowy Sunday morning, he arrived at the meetinghouse prepared to preach, only to find that none of his two hundred church members had chosen to brave the cold. He glumly reported, "As no congregation attended, returned home

[35] Oliver Hart, Sermon Record, Hart MSS, SCL.
[36] Oliver Hart, diary, December 17, 1780, Hart MSS, SCL.
[37] Oliver Hart, diary, March 12, 1781, Hart MSS, SCL.
[38] Oliver Hart, diary, October 15, 18, 1781; February 18, 23, 1782, Hart MSS, SCL.
[39] Oliver Hart, diary, February 10, 1782, Hart MSS, SCL.

without preaching." Like many pastors who oversaw revival during the early years of the Great Awakening, Hart found the adjustment to obscure and ordinary ministry with fair-weather members a painful one.[40]

*

Hopewell's apathy was especially disappointing to Hart as he considered that the years 1776–83 were marked by significant revival advance among several American evangelical groups, especially Baptists. In the South the Separate Baptists continued to multiply at an astonishing rate. The itinerant evangelist John Leland, for example, baptized 130 individuals in Virginia by himself from November 1779 to July 1780.[41] The black Baptist minister George Liele extended the Baptist reach into the Caribbean in 1782 when he fled Savannah, Georgia, from the British. He landed in Kingston, Jamaica, where, along with "four brethren from America," he planted that city's first Baptist church. By 1791 the Kingston church had 225 members in full communion and 350 adherents.[42]

Baptists in Nova Scotia and New England experienced the most dramatic awakenings of all, participating in what would later become known as the "New Light Stir."[43] Isaac Backus judged that these revivals "spread the most extensively and powerfully through New England, than any revival had done for forty years"; an estimated two thousand New Englanders received immersion in 1780 alone.[44] One small church touched by the awakening, the Third Baptist Church of Middleborough, Massachusetts, received fifty-four newly converted members through baptism between May and July 1780. Their pastor, Asa Hunt, said of one of their more intense meetings that "the Divine power was like pentecoste."[45] As on the first Pentecost, the New Light Stir came complete with its own signs and wonders. The most famous took place on May 19, 1780, when a dramatic darkness enveloped the entire region so completely that candles had to be lit in the middle of the day. Many observers explained away the incident as smog, an eclipse, or some other meteorological aberration. Others viewed the phenomenon as a divine signal that "the day of judgment was come," in Backus's words. Multitudes responded

---

[40] Oliver Hart, diary, February 10, 1781, Hart MSS, SCL.
[41] Leland, *Writings*, 21.
[42] Frey and Wood, *Come Shouting to Zion*, 131–32.
[43] Baptists in Nova Scotia experienced substantial gains through revival during this season of awakenings, led by the radical revivalist Henry Alline. See Kidd, *Great Awakening*, 309–12.
[44] Backus, *History of New England*, 2:264–65.
[45] Backus, *History of New England*, 2:272n1.

to the so-called Day of Darkness by fervently seeking God, and the Baptists were perhaps the greatest beneficiaries. In 1781 the New Hampshire Baptist medical doctor–turned-pastor Samuel Shepard baptized seventy-eight souls on a single itinerant journey and witnessed the formation of eight Baptist meetings in New Hampshire. Shepard reported to Backus, "Some hundreds of souls are hopefully converted in the counties of Rockingham, Strafford, and Grafton, in New Hampshire, within a year past."[46] The number of New England Baptist churches alone increased from fifty-three to eighty-nine between 1778 and 1782. Hart devoured these reports; the only thing he enjoyed more than hearing about Baptist revival was experiencing revival at his own church.

Yet the New Light Stir in New England and other revivals in the early 1780s passed the Hopewell Baptists by. "I long to see some fruit of my labour in Hopewell," Hart wrote in July 1781, "But alas, we are all too carnal and worldly minded. The things of the world engross our attention too much."[47] One of the nagging issues in the congregation appears to have been the existence of old divisions between members. Hart alluded to this on April 8, 1781, when he prayed to be "an instrument of uniting, and building them up in the most holy faith."[48] When William Rogers looked back on Hart's time at Hopewell, he indicated that dealing with church disunity consumed a significant portion of Hart's time and energy. He said in an address to the church after Hart's death, "No more will you behold him, presiding in your assemblies, or stepping forth as a healer of your breaches. You certainly will never forget his uniform prudential deportment, and his anxiety for the prevalence of unanimity among you!"[49] Perhaps the bickering in the church had to do with the handful of large families that composed the church's membership, or the flood of new people who had suddenly entered the church during Benjamin Coles's tenure. Still, Hart trusted that God intended to sanctify him through his spiritual and ministerial struggles. "Had much less freedom than common," he confessed after a flat Sunday morning sermon in 1781. "However, the Lord does all things well. It is fit I should be left sometimes to teach me where my great strength lies." In his estimation, humble dependence on Jesus was the pinnacle of evangelical piety. Whatever God chose to

---

[46] Backus, *History of New England*, 2:280.
[47] Oliver Hart, diary, July 15, 1781, Hart MSS, SCL.
[48] Oliver Hart, diary, April 8, 1781, Hart MSS, SCL.
[49] Rogers, *A Sermon*, 35.

use in order to cultivate the reliance of faith in his self-reliant children should be embraced—even the mortification of failing to lead a revival.

\*

Meanwhile, the Philadelphia Association scratched Hart's itch for action. As the 1780s began, the Association's quest to expand and solidify Baptist church order in the young nation continued with great energy. Hart joined the Association in fielding a variety of questions from perplexed churches in these years, from whether or not Jesus was a proper object of prayer,[50] to the perennial question regarding the propriety of foot-washing among Baptists (an issue addressed three times, in the years 1771, 1773, and 1792), to whether or not a Baptist meeting not yet formally constituted as a church could receive the Lord's Supper.[51] The Association also promoted Baptist order by mediating church disputes. They still notified Baptists of excommunicated individuals masquerading as preachers, like the former Stamford pastor Robert Morris, relieved of his duties for "gross immoralities" in 1781.[52] The Association encouraged its churches to learn their own history by purchasing copies of Backus's *A History of New England, with Particular Reference to the People called Baptists*, in 1785.[53] But nothing exercised the Philadelphia Association Baptists in the early 1780s like contending with the growing threat of heterodox religious sects springing up in the wake of the American Revolution.

The greatest concern came from the Universalists, who denied the doctrine of the eternal punishment of the unconverted. American Universalism is typically traced back to John Murray (1741–1815), an Englishman converted by George Whitefield, who imbibed Universalist ideas from James Reilly of London. (Universalism was sometimes known as "Reillyism" at this time.) Murray came to America in 1770, preaching often in Separate and Separate Baptist congregations in New England. In 1779 he organized the

---

[50] Gillette, *Minutes*, 200. The Association answered unequivocally that it was right to pray directly to Jesus, citing several New Testament examples and expressing some horror that the issue would ever be called into question (fearing it sprung from a deistic tendency to deny the divinity of Christ). Yet the matter was not settled, but instead touched off a strange controversy that dragged on for about three years, led by the rather prickly David Jones, at this time an itinerant preacher and member of Great Valley Baptist Church. See Gillette, *Minutes*, 217–18. Hart may have been involved as well, against Jones. Jones and Hart would tilt at one another again over the issue of laying on of hands.

[51] Gillette, *Minutes*, 206. The Association found this question important enough to delay their response until the following year.

[52] Gillette, *Minutes*, 173.

[53] Gillette, *Minutes*, 206.

264    OLIVER HART AND THE RISE OF BAPTIST AMERICA

first Universalist church in America, in Gloucester, Massachusetts, and also published Reilly's *Union, or a Treatise on the Consanguinity between Christ and his Church.*[54] It is likely that Murray made contact in the 1770s with the most influential propagator of Universalist ideas among colonial Baptists, Elhanan Winchester (1751–1797).

A native of Brookline, Massachusetts, Winchester began his career as an itinerant evangelist, preaching widely across his home colony from 1773 to 1774 and enjoying great success. In 1774 he ended up at the Baptist church in Welsh Neck, South Carolina, of the Charleston Association. Over the next five years he emerged as perhaps the most dynamic revivalist in American Baptist life. In 1776 he baptized forty new members into the church, attracting attention from Baptists on both sides of the Atlantic. English Baptists Caleb Evans (1737–1791) and John Rippon (1751–1836) published news of Winchester's revival in the circular letter of the Western Association in England.[55] In the fall of 1779 Winchester baptized a staggering 240 new members at Welsh Neck, including enough African slaves to form a separate black church.[56] Hart was overjoyed by this news, writing to Backus in 1779, "At Pee Dee there has been a glorious display of ye Power, and goodness of God, in the Conversion of hundreds." Hart considered Winchester "a valuable man" and "greatly useful" to "the Baptist interest."[57] That winter Winchester toured New England, preaching at Congregational and Baptist churches alike. There, from December 1779 to May 1780, he baptized another 109 converts. "His success is wonderful," Backus exclaimed.[58] As Winchester's rising star reached its peak in the fall of 1780, he was offered the most prestigious of American Baptist pulpits, the First Baptist Church of Philadelphia. The church convinced the twenty-nine-year-old evangelist to accept the post on a six-month trial.[59]

Unbeknownst to them, however, Winchester already considered himself "half a convert" to Universalism. By now he had come to appreciate the Universalist writings of the German Baptist George Klein-Nicolai, who had published an English edition of *The Everlasting Gospel* under the pseudonym

---

[54] McLoughlin, *New England Dissent*, 2:717–18.

[55] Davies, *Transatlantic Brethren*, 161.

[56] Townsend, *South Carolina Baptists*, 296.

[57] Oliver Hart to Isaac Backus, February 16, 1777.

[58] Kidd, *Great Awakening*, 316. See also McLoughlin, *Diary of Isaac Backus*, 2:1034, 1045, 1049, 1058; and Hatch, *Democratization of American Christianity*, 41–42.

[59] Elhannan Winchester, *The Universal Restoration, Exhibited in Four Dialogues between a Minister and his Friend* (Worcester, MA, 1803), xv.

Paul Siegvolck.[60] Once in Philadelphia, Winchester encountered several more Universalist influences, including George Stonehouse's *The Restitution of All Things*, Andrew Ramsay's *The Philosophical Principles of Natural and Revealed Religion*, along with the pious example of several German Baptist Universalists he met in Germantown.[61] Winchester continued to preach conversionist messages in the revival style at First Baptist Philadelphia, again with great results. But in the spring of 1781, as his six-month trial drew to a close, he came out openly for Universalism. For evangelical Baptists, of course, denying the necessity of the new birth to gain heaven was the ultimate heresy. Winchester's teaching touched off an explosive controversy in the church.

The Philadelphia Association immediately stepped in, appointing Hart to a committee of five ministers to investigate the situation. Hart traveled to Philadelphia and met with the church in the first week of April 1781.[62] His committee confirmed that Winchester had transgressed the bounds of orthodoxy, and the offender soon left. The committee advised the Philadelphia Association to "beware" and "not admit him, or any who advocate 'universal salvation' to the office of public teaching, or suffer any who avow the same to continue in their communion." In a report to the Warren Association in Rhode Island, Hart voiced deep concern over the discovery of Universalism in the heart of Baptist life: "The minds of but too many are poisoned with the heresy, and the Philadelphia Church is reduced to a deplorable situation." Winchester and his Universalist party would even attempt to seize the church property through the court system, though they ultimately failed. "God knows where these things will end," Hart sighed. "We have thought it our duty, however, to bear an open testimony against this damnable doctrine. Churches, in every capacity, ought to be pillars of truth."[63] The Winchester saga would not be the last time Hart and the Philadelphia Association would confront Universalism in the post-Revolutionary years.

*

---

[60] Winchester would pen the preface to a new American edition of *The Everlasting Gospel* in 1794.

[61] Nathan A. Finn, "The Making of a Baptist Universalist: The Curious Case of Elhanan Winchester," paper presented to the Baptist Studies Group at the Evangelical Theological Society, San Francisco, 2011, 9–10.

[62] Oliver Hart to Isaac Backus, February 16, 1777; Gratz MSS, HSP.

[63] Gillette, *Minutes,* 174; Oliver Hart to Warren Baptist Association, April 22, 1781, Backus MSS, ANTS.

Meanwhile their New England brethren contended with a host of other new religious groups cropping up in the 1780s, many of which contained radical elements. In the early 1770s a New Hampshire tailor named Benjamin Randall (1749–1808) underwent an evangelical conversion after learning of the death of George Whitefield.[64] Randall had heard Whitefield in one of the evangelist's final public appearances, and though Randall had scorned his message at the time, news of Whitefield's death sobered him. "Whitefield is now in heaven, while I am in the road to hell," he lamented.[65] After his conversion Randall separated from his antirevivalist Congregational church in 1775, and in 1776 received immersion in a Baptist church and began to preach. His evolution, however, was not complete. Along with many Americans at the turn of the nineteenth century, Randall began to question the Calvinist doctrines of predestination that had thus far been a mainstay in American evangelicalism. As he puzzled over these issues, he retreated to the solitude of a cornfield, where he poured out his concerns to God. There he received a vision. He was first stripped of all pride before the majesty of God, and then covered by a white robe so that "I looked down all over me, and I appeared as white as snow." Randall recalled, "A Bible was then presented before the eyes of my mind, and I heard a still small voice, saying look therein." From his vision Randall gathered that the Scriptures "ran in perfect connection with the universal love of God to men—the universal atonement in the work of redemption, by Jesus Christ, who tasted death for every man."[66] His mystical encounter in the corn marked the birth of the Free Will Baptist movement. He found a ready audience for his anti-Calvinist message in rural New England, opening fourteen new congregations in Maine and New Hampshire within a year of his vision. By 1830 the Free Will Baptists in American could boast 450 churches.[67]

American Baptists would encounter even more radical sects during the Revolutionary era, and few were as colorful as the Shakers. Birthed in Manchester, England, as a kind of evangelical spin-off of Quakerism, the Shakers looked to "Mother" Ann Lee (1736–1784) as their leader.[68] Lee had

[64] For Randall, see Caldwell, *Theologies of the American Revivalists*, 150–54; Scott Bryant, *The Awakening of the Freewill Baptists: Benjamin Randall and the Founding of an American Religious Tradition* (Macon, GA: Mercer University Press, 2001), 65–138; and John Buzzell, *The Life of Elder Benjamin Randall Principally Taken from Documents Written by Himself* (Limerick, ME, 1827).

[65] Buzzell, *Life of Elder Benjamin Randall*, 18.

[66] Buzzell, *Life of Elder Benjamin Randall*, 88–89.

[67] I. D. Stewart, *The History of the Freewill Baptists* (Dover, NH, 1862), 1:450.

[68] For Ann Lee, see Brekus, *Strangers and Pilgrims*, 97–113.

"DIRECTED IN THE PATH OF DUTY" 267

left her blacksmith husband to pursue public ministry after losing four children in infancy. She claimed to be Christ's successor on earth and insisted that sexual intercourse was the cause of evil and original sin. Persecution in England drove her and her followers to America in 1774, and by 1775 the Shakers had settled into a celibate commune at Niskayuna, New York, nine miles outside of Albany. Even the demonstrative worship of the Separate Baptists could not compare to what took place in Shaker meetings, which featured speaking in tongues, prophesying, singing and dancing, and violent bodily shaking. Shakers became known for promoting pacifism, faith healing, and preparing the way for Christ's second coming through their communal lifestyle.

Many Baptists resonated with the Shakers' message, among them the Connecticut Baptist Joseph Meacham (1742–1796). Disillusioned with the Baptists and every other "standing order," Meacham struck out for New York to proclaim "the full work of salvation." There he stumbled upon the Shakers and became "convinced that these strange people professed the spirit, kingdom, & work which he had so earnestly prayed, & sought, & of which he had prophesied," and that "Mother Ann was the Bride, *the lambs wife.*"[69] Meacham became a key leader among early Shakers, who spread out from Niskayuna and attracted many other Baptists from 1780 to 1785, especially in New England. It became common for church records in these days to report that a handful of members "went off to the Shakers," among them numerous Baptist elders. In Pittsfield, Massachusetts, an entire Baptist congregation converted to Shaker ways.[70] Backus compared the Shakers to "papists" in their devotion to Mother Ann Lee. "Their doings are unnatural and violent," he added, and they "propagate their scheme with a strange power, signs, and lying wonders." Backus, James Manning, and other Baptist leaders missed no opportunity to pass on salacious Shaker stories, including those involving the naked dancing of men and women "to imitate the primitive state of perfection," or the "carnal fruits" that "inadvertently resulted from their chaste embraces."[71] Shaker influence would cool by the late 1780s, though they would experience revitalization in the frontier camp meetings after 1800. For

---

[69] Kidd, *Great Awakening*, 318–19. See also Theodore Johnson, ed., "Biographical Account of the Life, Character, & Ministry of Father Joseph Meacham . . . by Calvin Green, 1827," *Shaker Quarterly* 10 (1970): 23–27; and Stephen Stein, *The Shaker Experience in America* (New Haven, CT: Yale University Press, 1992).

[70] McLoughlin, *New England Dissent*, 2:715–17.

[71] Backus, *History of New England*, 2:297–98; Guild, *Early History of Brown University*, 364.

268 OLIVER HART AND THE RISE OF BAPTIST AMERICA

a brief window of time, however, they seemed to pose a significant threat to American Baptists.

Other innovative groups multiplied during the era, as the young republic moved toward what Jon Butler has called "the Antebellum Hothouse" of religious diversity that marked pre–Civil War America.[72] It was a strange new world for American Baptists, who throughout the colonial period had largely been viewed as a radical fringe sect. Now, in the increasingly pluralistic environment of post-Revolutionary America, Baptists looked like a tame and respectable denomination, fending off a new generation of innovative movements. Some, like the Free Will Baptists or the New Divinity movement (examined in the next chapter), were to Hart regrettable departures from the old paths of traditional Calvinism, though not beyond the pale of the Christian faith. Other movements, like Universalism, and to a lesser degree the Shakers, represented far more serious errors. For Hart, defending against all perversions of biblical truth was simply part of an ancient spiritual battle. "This is one of the games at which Satan hath play'd in every age of the Christian Church," he wrote to Backus. "More especially in times of revival, the Enemy will sow such tares among the wheat."[73] Baptists now found that they were the conservative voices in the tumultuous religious landscape of early America.

Hart took every opportunity to hold the line for Baptist orthodoxy, and found one in 1782, when the Association elected him as its moderator. His duties included expounding an article of the *Philadelphia Confession* for the annual circular letter, for which he was assigned chapter 8, "On Christ the Mediator." The ten-page letter he produced represents the most thorough doctrinal exposition from his hand. In the face of many theological innovations, Hart upheld the traditional, covenantal understanding of the redemptive work of Jesus Christ. He explicitly affirmed the doctrines of original sin, the Trinity, eternal election, the indissoluble union between the divine and human natures of Christ, justification by faith alone in Christ alone, particular redemption, and the perseverance of the saints. The Baptist historian Tom Nettles has noted that Hart quotes verbatim from the *Baptist Catechism* at least seven times in this essay. The exposition lends credence to William Rogers's later assessment of Hart, that "the sum and substance of all his discourses were founded on the great atonement, yet he studied variety,

---

[72] See Butler, *Awash in a Sea of Faith*, 225–56.
[73] Oliver Hart to Isaac Backus, July 25, 1781, Backus MSS, ANTS.

"DIRECTED IN THE PATH OF DUTY" 269

for he never lost sight of the Bible-system in any of its parts."[74] Hart closed his letter by saying, "Thus, dear brethren, have we endeavored to treat of Christ the Mediator, and we trust that his fullness and suitableness have, in some measure, been made to appear. That you may live to, for, and upon him, and at last live and reign with him, is the prayer of yours in the faith and fellowship in the gospel." Though the winds of doctrine were shifting in Baptist life in the 1780s, Hart had lashed himself to the mast of the traditional Calvinism of the *Philadelphia Confession* and the doctrines that had upheld his personal faith for more than thirty years.[75]

*

In 1783, the year Hart turned sixty, the Philadelphia Association asked him to deliver the opening sermon at its annual meeting. His message revealed how desperately he still thirsted for revival. He aimed his sermon at rousing an apathetic church to the "flaming love, burning zeal and assiduity in religion" that had characterized Baptists during the Great Awakening. Using the Old Testament description of building the Jewish temple as a metaphor for spiritually building up the church, Hart exhorted his listeners, "The gospel means of revival are still in our hands. Let us then rouse from our lethargy: gird on our strength, and work vigorously in repairing the Christian Temple, which through sloth and negligence is too much gone to decay." For Hart, the answer to the church's woes was vigorous, Spirit-empowered action. Just as all the Jews in Haggai's day helped build the Temple, "even so should Christians of all ranks and characters, labor in building up the church of Jesus Christ. Every one has a work to do; none should be idle." Calling the Association's messengers to "persevering constancy" in their service, he drew on military imagery. His metaphor of the devoted soldier would have carried special force in the wake of the Revolution:

> The Lord will have no three months, nor three years men employed in his service. All these artificers should enlist for life, and constantly persevere in the work till disabled by death. Some who have engaged in this service, have grown weary of it, and given up. Others, on account of some difficulties, have slunk away, like cowards, and deserted the cause. Many, upon finding that building the Christian temple might interfere with their ease,

---

[74] Rogers, *A Sermon*, 24.
[75] Gillette, *Minutes*, 182–91; Nettles, *The Baptists*, 459n68.

270    OLIVER HART AND THE RISE OF BAPTIST AMERICA

health, interest, or reputation, have given over, and left the work to other hands. Blessed be God, all are not of this stamp. Christ hath still some faithful servants left, who adhere firmly to the work assigned them. Should we say unto such, as Jesus said unto the twelve, "Will ye also go away?" each one would answer, "God forbid! Lord, to whom should we go. I love my Master—I love his work. Let him bore mine ear through with an awl, for I will serve him forever."[76]

The Association approved Hart's message with gusto, immediately ruling, "The subject of the introductory sermon being very important, and treated much to our satisfaction, Brother Hart is requested to prepare the same for immediate publication."[77] Hart had opened his sixth decade with a decisive statement: he, and the Baptists for whom he spoke, had no intention of retreating from advancing revival in America. But would he finish his career in Hopewell, New Jersey, or return to Charleston? This was the question that confronted Hart as he moved to the middle of years of the 1780s.

[76] Hart, *Humble Attempt*, 4, 7, 38–39.
[77] Gillette, *Minutes*, 193.

# 12

## "The Baptist Interest"

### A Respectable Denomination in a New Nation

The war halted life at the Charleston Baptist Church for over two years, its meetinghouse requisitioned and its minister in exile. But as matters returned to normal in the spring of 1783, the church's trustees invited Oliver Hart to resume his pastoral charge. It was a natural request, but it launched an awkward, four-year saga, filled with tension and miscommunication. Their proposal attracted Hart from several angles. Hopewell's people were kind but spiritually apathetic, and Hart yearned to know revival again. He lamented that he had been "so unprofitable in the Lord's work": "If God has made use of me at all in this Place, it has been principally in healing the unhappy breach which had taken place in the Church. For this I would be grateful, but I long to see sinners enquiring the Way to Zion." Further, the South was the site of his life's work and home to his and Nancy's closest friends and family.[1]

Yet Hart initially decided against a return. Among the reasons he listed in his June reply were "the providential direction he had received to Hopewell— the strength of mutual attachments—the pleasing prospects of the church he then served—his own better health—his opinion that a younger and more active man was necessary for them—and his comparative want of success during the latter part of his residence in Charleston."[2] Each of these legitimate factors no doubt contributed to his decision. He also left unmentioned another factor: the Charleston church could not provide him with the stable living he enjoyed at Hopewell. Hart told his brother in 1785 that Hopewell paid him "200 Dollars per annum, besides the Benefits of the Parsonage, which they are to assist me in working; and the Farm will be rendered more than profitable by an Addition of about 37 Acres, which the Church and Congregation have lately purchased. With these advantages, I hope, my

---

[1] Manly, *Mercy and Judgment*, 47; Oliver Hart to Richard Furman, October 9, 1784, Hart MSS, JBDML.

[2] Manly, *Mercy and Judgment*, 47.

*Oliver Hart and the Rise of Baptist America*. Eric C. Smith, Oxford University Press (2020). © Oxford University Press.
DOI: 10.1093/oso/9780197506325.001.0001

272    OLIVER HART AND THE RISE OF BAPTIST AMERICA

Living here will be tolerably easy, altho' not grand." The postwar Charleston Baptists could offer no such security. Hart penned a gracious rejection letter, suggesting that the trustees engage a series of short-term supply preachers until they could adequately support a full-time pastor. But he also included a statement that would contribute to a long season of confusion on both ends of the correspondence: though he was turning down their offer, he admitted he was still "not clear in [his] duty."[3]

The church took Hart's advice. After a year of entertaining supply preachers, the Charleston trustees asked their favorite to take permanent charge of the church. On March 8, 1784, they extended a call to Richard Furman, the talented, twenty-nine-year-old Separate Baptist minister from the backcountry. The prospect of following Hart, whom he revered, in this prominent pulpit must have appealed to Furman in many respects. But he too declined. God still had work for him, Furman believed, at the High Hills Church, which was experiencing revival at the time. He also suspected that Hart did in fact want to return to Charleston.

On Furman's advice, the trustees renewed their invitation to Hart. Hart admitted that this second call threw him into "a distressing perplexity," but he again turned them down. He insisted that they go back after Furman, calling him "a prize of inestimable worth." Hart promised the trustees that if Furman refused, he would either return to Charleston or send someone better. Above all, though, he advised them to pray, for if Furman "comes in answer to prayer, he will come with a blessing."[4] Hart had laid out a decisive plan for the committee. But he again short-circuited the process by mentioning he was still "not clear" as to where his duty lay. He told Furman the same in an October 9, 1784 letter:

> Hitherto I have been detailed in this place, and whether I shall ever return to Charleston or not is a matter yet undetermined. I have my health so well here am so well settled, and the situation of this church is such, that I scarce know how to leave the Place. Yet wish my old charge to be supplied. I understand they have had an eye upon you. I have wrote to them to give you a call, which hope you will accept, if you can see your way clear, as I know not of anyone that I should choose in preference, to fill up that Place. I hope God will direct you in this great Affair, for his own Glory, and the good of

[3] Oliver Hart to Joseph Hart, April 18, 1785, Hart MSS, SCL.
[4] Manly, *Mercy and Judgment*, 49; Rogers, *Richard Furman*, 52.

his Church. The struggles I have had in my own mind, to know Duty, perhaps have not often been experienced. I now leave it with Him whose I am, [whom] I desire to serve and who can guide all my Ways.

Hart repeatedly rejected the Charleston call in one breath, and then expressed his uncertainty in the next. Furman was convinced that Hart wanted to return, and would, if he received a better financial offer. Whether or not Hart was fishing for a raise, his failure to make a clean break with the committee created much consternation in Charleston, strained his relationship with Furman, and extended the negotiations far longer than they should have gone.[5]

Hoping to clear the air once and for all, Furman wrote Hart a long and deferential letter on January 26, 1785. He expressed his "real sorrow" that Hart was not returning to South Carolina and gently criticized the Charleston trustees for failing to make Hart a more suitable proposal. Furman also voiced his fear that talk of his own acceptance of the Charleston pastorate may have hindered Hart from accepting the call. He therefore gave Hart "a full account" of his dealings with the trustees, beginning with his initial advice "not to make the least mention of obtaining another minister until they had the fullest answer from you." Furman's message was as clear as Hart's had been ambiguous: if Hart had the least interest in returning home, Furman wanted no part of Charleston.[6]

Ultimately it was the frustrated Charleston trustees who brought closure to the discussion. Hart told his brother Joseph in 1785, "It is now probable that I shall fix here, for my former Charge in Charleston have wrote me, as their opinion, that it is my Duty to continue in Hopewell, and beg me to send them a suitable Minister."[7] But even with Hart out of the running, Furman lingered at High Hills for two more years. He was loath to leave his beloved backcountry congregation and perhaps a bit intimidated to take on the refined city church. He did not finally relent until November 1787. The handoff had been clumsy, but the leadership of the Charleston Baptist Church was now fully transferred to Furman. It was a momentous occasion for many reasons, not least because a Separate Baptist minister now led the flagship church of the Regular Baptist South. With the long-desired union between

[5] Oliver Hart to Richard Furman, October 9, 1784, Hart MSS, JBDML.
[6] Richard Furman to Oliver Hart, January 26, 1785, Furman MSS, JBDML.
[7] Oliver Hart to Joseph Hart, April 18, 1785, Hart MSS, SCL.

274   OLIVER HART AND THE RISE OF BAPTIST AMERICA

the two Baptist groups finally solidified, a new era in American Baptist life had begun.[8]

*

Meanwhile, Edmund Bostford's revival exploits in the Lower South continued to impress. On March 30, 1785, he wrote Hart of "a pretty good work begun" in Charleston. During an eight-week visit, Botsford preached forty-one public sermons and visited many individuals in their homes to discuss conversion. The response, especially among the slaves, had been tremendous. "I have hardly enjoyed an hour to myself since I have been in town," Botsford wrote. "Numbers of blacks come to see me, and some whites; and many I must go and see. I doubt not that if there was a minister settled here, there would soon be a flourishing Church. Who would have thought that your poor son Botsford would have been owned as an instrument to bring souls to the Charleston Church?" Through their interactions in Charleston and across the South, African and Anglo-Americans were having an important reciprocal effect on one another's religious practices, contributing to the revival culture of that region for years to come.[9] The scene Botsford painted must have transported Hart back to the awakenings he had participated in thirty years before: "Crowds attend public meetings, which are held three times on Lord's days, and on Wednesday evenings; every other evening we have meetings at private house, in which I have introduced praying for those poor distressed souls who ask." Botsford's report demonstrates the persistence of the Great Awakening in the South through the end of the eighteenth century.[10]

The letter made for bittersweet reading for Hart. He rejoiced over the Spirit's activity in Charleston and at the emergence of his young protégés Furman and Botsford as revival leaders. At the same time, the lethargy of his Hopewell congregation depressed him. After decades in the middle of the revival action, Hart now pastored a church in decline. Hopewell had been by far the largest congregation in the Philadelphia Association when he arrived in 1780, registering 212 members. Despite his best efforts, however, he watched that number steadily slide downhill after his arrival. By 1788 Hopewell recorded only 164 members at the annual meeting of the Philadelphia Association.[11] The reasons for this reduction are unclear,

[8] Rogers, *Richard Furman*, 53–59.
[9] See Frey and Wood, *Come Shouting Zion*, xii, 97, 144.
[10] Mallary, *Edmund Botsford*, 63–65.
[11] Gillette, *Minutes*, 263.

though the church would continue its downward trajectory after Hart's death. They would embrace a hyper-Calvinist, anti-missions position in the 1830s, and kept shrinking throughout the nineteenth century. Writing in 1901, Thomas Sharp Griffiths reported, "It is only a question of time, when First Hopewell will be extinct." He further conjectured that "Isaac Eaton, Oliver Hart, the Stouts and Hautons and Blackwells, could they know of the ruin that has come of the work of their lives, would be filled with shame."[12] Shame, perhaps, but not shock. All the way back in 1788 Hart had written, "O, how did my soul long for the conversion of my hearers! But conversion is strange work in Hopewell."[13]

*

Two more painful events in 1788 reinforced Hart's sense of personal decline. At the end of May he traveled to First Baptist Church in New York City to fill the pulpit for his old friend John Gano, who had recently left the church to preach in Kentucky. Hart set off with excitement, enjoying visits with preacher friends at Southampton and Scotch Plains on the way. But when he arrived in New York, the church asked him to preside over a special meeting to examine baptismal candidates. Only one woman presented herself, and the interview went poorly. Hart "was not satisfied with her experience" and rejected her request for baptism.[14] It was a dismal note on which to begin a preaching tour, and, unfortunately, it foreshadowed more disappointments to come.

Though Hart preached from all his favorite texts in the coming weeks, he looked back on virtually every sermon with disgust. He "felt exceedingly bound up" and "straitened" each time he spoke. He found his soul "shut up," "not set at liberty." He believed he lacked the power of the Holy Spirit. "O how I did long for a divine communication" he moaned after another abysmal performance. "O that the Lord would condescend to add a blessing." He fared no better in the other duties he carried out in Gano's place. A woman he visited on her deathbed he found to be "extremely ignorant" of basic Christian truth. A priest had just left after sprinkling her with holy water, "by which she seemed to think her sins were done away. Horrid stupidity!" Hart muttered. He toured the city, viewing the markets, buildings, forts, docks, and shipyard,

---

[12] Thomas Sharp Griffiths, *A History of Baptists in New Jersey* (Hightstown, NJ, 1904), 71.

[13] Oliver Hart, diary, June 22, 1788, Hart MSS, SCL.

[14] Oliver Hart, diary, May 30, 1788, Hart MSS, SCL.

276 OLIVER HART AND THE RISE OF BAPTIST AMERICA

but his inability to preach with power covered the entire trip with a dark cloud. After his last, unsatisfactory sermon, he gloomily wrote, "The Lord knows what is best for me, may I be humbled before Him. I have indeed been pretty much mortified in this excursion, were I to judge of usefulness by my own feelings should conclude nothing has been done for God or the souls of men." Perhaps God designed even this embarrassing chapter in his life for good.[15]

The stinging memory of his New York excursion could have been erased by another trip Hart scheduled in the fall of 1788. For the first time in eight years he would travel south, to attend the annual meeting of the Charleston Association. It promised to be a sweet homecoming and a refreshing reminder of happier days. Hart left on September 2 in high spirits. Two days later, though, he came down with a cold. At age sixty-six, he no longer rallied from such physical setbacks as in his earlier itinerant days. Worse still, the home in which he lodged that night did not hold family prayers the next morning. Hart had counted on this time of devotion, having omitted rising early enough for private prayer in his own chamber. As he set off that morning, the predicament reminded him of a story about a minister who failed to commit his trip to God and then met repeated obstacles as a result. The old tale was more reflective of common superstition than the gospel of grace he had been preaching for forty years, but it still haunted him as the miles passed. "I thought of this again and again, and could hardly help anticipating disaster," he confessed. Sure enough, the crosspiece of Hart's sulky broke on a rough road that afternoon, forcing him to turn aside in Downingtown, Pennsylvania. Hart and his guide resumed their journey the next day, but he reported, "The roads were so bad, I almost wish I was at Hopewell."[16]

By the time they reached the house of Hart's brother Silas in Winchester, Virginia, the trip had fallen apart. Hart's cold was worse, the roads looked awful, and his guide's horse had come up lame. Hart had no choice but to turn back for home. He was devastated. In one of the most poignant entries in his extensive diaries, he wrote:

But no one knows how much these things have affected my spirits, they rob me of my natural rest, I feel a perturbation of mind which I cannot describe,

---

[15] Oliver Hart, diary, May 27–June 10, 1788, Hart MSS, SCL.
[16] Oliver Hart, diary, September 4, 1788, Hart MSS, SCL.

and what is worse, Satan and unbelief rob me of my spiritual comforts (if ever I knew anything of religion, which I am tempted to doubt) so that my burthen is great. These indeed are precious words—Cast thy Burthens upon the Lord, and He will sustain thee. I see many gracious promises and declarations, and have been attempting to plead the blood and righteousness of Christ, and to lay hold on the skirts of his Robe, but the Arm of faith seems to be withered. I try to say, Lord, I believe, help thou mine unbelief—O Lord give me faith.

> From this vile heart purge thou the dross;
> Cleanse this polluted den;
> Cherish my soul, fill it with grace;
> Sweet Jesus, say Amen. [17]

Hart's faith had withstood many tests, but growing old was proving to be the stiffest yet.

The journey home only extended the trial. The bright spot came when Hart fulfilled a long-held desire to meet the famed Separate Baptist preacher James Ireland (1745–1806) in Buck Marsh, Virginia.[18] Ireland was one of the Virginia Baptists who had preached to crowds from his jail cell during the years of religious persecution before the war, and had endured, among other things, an attempt to blow up his cell with a keg of gunpowder. Meeting Ireland and preaching in his pulpit one night was a highlight of Hart's otherwise unhappy journey. His joy was afterward dampened on a ferryboat ride, however, when he slipped and fell into the river. He rode the rest of the day soaking wet.[19] "This to me has been the most trying and fatiguing journey that ever I took; both to body and mind," he sighed after his return.[20]

The failed trips to New York and Charleston in 1788, the falloff of Hopewell Baptist Church, and his own diminishing health all underscored a painful reality for Hart: he was no longer leading the charge in the American Baptist revival. About this time, he confided to Furman, "My thread must be near run out, and consequently my work near done, yet I feel anxious desires that the small remnant of my days may be devoted to the service of God and terminated in his Honor." The center of gravity for Baptist America was beginning to shift from North to South, due in no small part to Hart's

---

[17] Oliver Hart, diary, September 24, 1788, Hart MSS, SCL.
[18] Oliver Hart, diary, October 5, 1788, Hart MSS, SCL.
[19] Oliver Hart, diary, October 10, 1788, Hart MSS, SCL.
[20] Oliver Hart, diary, October 19, 1788, Hart MSS, SCL.

278    OLIVER HART AND THE RISE OF BAPTIST AMERICA

own labors in Charleston between 1750 and 1780. The younger men he had mentored—Furman, Botsford, Samuel Stillman, Samuel Jones—had moved to the front lines; Hart was drifting to the rear. He had assumed many roles among American Baptists since 1749 and now was settling into that of elder statesman.[21]

*

The Americans finalized their independence from Great Britain with the Treaty of Paris in 1783. But now the task of nation-building had begun, and the American leaders faced the massive duty of determining a new form of government. Since 1781 the states had operated under the Articles of Confederation, a relatively loose agreement upholding the sovereignty of each individual state. The war years had convinced many leaders that a stronger, centralized federal government was essential for preserving the states' hard-won liberty. These individuals, counting among their number George Washington, James Madison (1751–1836) of Virginia, and Alexander Hamilton (1755–1804) of New York, came to be known as Federalists. Other Americans feared that investing power over thirteen diverse and far-flung colonies in a small, elite class of rulers simply invited a reprisal of British tyranny. These devotees of decentralized government, led by Patrick Henry (1736–1799), became known as Anti-Federalists. In the summer of 1787, fifty-five delegates from twelve of the colonies convened in Philadelphia, ostensibly to revise the Articles of Confederation. But when the Constitutional Convention adjourned three months later, its members had framed an entirely new form of government, expressed in a 4,200-word document known as the Constitution of the United States. Henry had suspected some such Federalist maneuver and had famously remained home during the Constitutional Convention because he purportedly "smelt a rat." Over the next year the Federalists, led by Hamilton and Madison, labored to educate the public about the new government and persuade the states to ratify the Constitution over the protests of their Anti-Federalist opponents.[22]

---

[21] Oliver Hart to Richard Furman, June 15, 1791, Hart MSS, JBDML.

[22] Many excellent works treating the constitutional era exist, including Gordon S. Wood, *The Creation of the American Republic, 1776–1787* (Chapel Hill: University of North Carolina Press, 1998); Woody Holton, *Unruly Americans and the Origins of the Constitution* (New York: Hill and Wang, 2008); Richard Beeman, *Plain, Honest Men: The Making of the American Constitution* (New York: Random House, 2009); and Pauline Maier, *Ratification: The People Debate the Constitution, 1787–1788* (New York: Simon and Schuster, 2010). For the Constitution and the desire to establish virtue in the new republic, see Kidd, *God of Liberty*, 209–27.

"THE BAPTIST INTEREST" 279

Many Baptists were skeptical. Virginia Baptists were the most sensitive to the danger of religious oppression and had fought hard throughout the 1770s and 1780s to obtain full religious liberty in Virginia. It concerned them to find nothing in the proposed Constitution explicitly securing these rights of conscience. Madison, who had long been Virginia Baptists' greatest political ally in these matters, had found such a Bill of Rights unnecessary since the Constitution did not explicitly grant the government power to infringe in these arenas. But Virginia Baptists were not interested in assuming that their freedoms would be upheld; this now formidable voting bloc stood prepared to oppose ratification. This realization sent Madison scrambling to persuade Virginia Baptist leaders like John Leland to support ratification on the promise of a forthcoming Bill of Rights.[23] Many New England Baptists shared the Virginians' dubious perspective. Isaac Backus, pleased that the new Constitution refused to impose any religious test or oath on officeholders, supported ratification. Still, he estimated that two-thirds of the other twenty Baptist delegates at the Massachusetts state ratifying convention remained strongly Anti-Federalist.[24]

Baptists in the middle colonies generally viewed the Constitution more favorably. They had not shared the persecution experiences of their brethren from Virginia and New England and had witnessed at close range the inefficiency of the Articles of Confederation throughout the war. Philadelphia Association leaders therefore declared the recent Constitutional Convention to be "the kind interposition of Divine Providence" in their 1787 circular letter and endorsed ratification. They bemoaned the "national dishonor, injustice, anarchy, confusion and bloodshed, which have already resulted from the weakness and inefficiency of the present form" of government, and feared this to be "but the beginning of sorrows, unless the people lay of hold on this favorable opportunity offered to establish an efficient government."[25] Hart counted himself among this group of Baptist constitutional supporters. He read the *Federalist Papers* with glowing approval and cheerfully recorded in his diary each of the state's votes to ratify. On June 21, 1788, New Hampshire became the ninth state to ratify. The new government would begin on March 4,

---

[23] See Mark S. Scarberry, "John Leland and James Madison: Religious Influence on the Ratification of the Constitution and on the Proposal of the Bill of Rights," *Penn State Law Review* 113, no. 3 (April 2009), https://ssrn.com/abstract=1262520; and L. H. Butterfield, "Elder John Leland, Jeffersonian Itinerant," *American Antiquarian Society Proceedings* 62 (1952): 155–242.

[24] Kidd and Hankins, *Baptists in America*, 73.

[25] Gillette, *Minutes*, 230.

280   OLIVER HART AND THE RISE OF BAPTIST AMERICA

1789, with George Washington elected as America's first president on April 30.

President Washington proclaimed November 26, 1789, "a day of public thanksgiving and prayer to be observed by acknowledging with grateful hearts the many signal favors of Almighty God especially by affording them an opportunity peaceably to establish a form of government for their safety and happiness."[26] Hart was only too happy to support "our beloved Commander-in-Chief." Over the past decade Hart had become adept at using the pulpit to promote the independence and rising glory of America. On a government-called Thanksgiving day on Wednesday morning, December 30, 1778, he had preached from 1 Samuel 7:12, "Hitherto the Lord hath helped us." On more than one fast day he had preached from 2 Chronicles 7:14, "If my people, which are called by my name, shall humble themselves, and pray, and seek my face, and turn from their wicked ways; then I will hear from heaven, and will forgive their sin, and will heal their land."[27] These carefully chosen texts, invariably drawn from Old Testament passages about theocratic Israel, expressed important assumptions that many early American preachers made about the identity of the new republic. In the Old Testament, Israel was a nation in special covenant with God, who had pledged to bless them as well as to discipline them, according to their response to his divinely given law. The Puritan leaders in Massachusetts Bay had been applying this covenantal language to their own colony in New England since its founding, a move that powerfully shaped the people's sense of identity as God's new chosen people. Now, in the Revolutionary era, Protestant clergy throughout the republic, including Baptists like Hart who had always been on the wrong side of theocratic New England, were applying these assumptions to America as a whole. As William McLoughlin has demonstrated, this was a key move for eighteenth-century Baptists, as they transitioned from colonial outlaws to a mainstream American denomination.[28] The tendency to view America as a "Christian nation" in covenantal relationship with God persists among

---

[26] George Washington, "Thanksgiving Proclamation," October 3, 1789, George Washington Papers, Library of Congress, https://www.loc.gov/resource/mgw8a.124/?q=1789+Thanksgiving&sp =132&st=text.

[27] Other fast day texts Hart used are Esther 4:3, preached on July 4, 1775, "And in every province, whithersoever the king's commandment and his decree came, there was great mourning among the Jews, and fasting and weeping, and wailing; and many lay in sackcloth and ashes"; and Nehemiah 9:2, preached on March 6, 1777, "And the seed of Israel separated themselves from all strangers, and stood and confessed their sins, and the iniquities of their fathers." See Oliver Hart, Record of Sermons, Hart MSS, SCL.

[28] McLoughlin, New England Dissent, 1:ix–xxi, 2:741–42, 751–53, 1107–27.

American Baptists and other evangelicals to the present day, with biblical texts like 2 Chronicles 7:14 remaining in heavy use to encourage national repentance, moral rectitude, and social action.[29]

On Washington's 1789 Thanksgiving day, Hart delivered to the Hopewell Baptist Church a carefully prepared address later published as *America's Remembrancer, with Respect to her Blessedness and Duty*. It provides a classic, Providentialist interpretation of American exceptionalism. Hart chose Numbers 23:23 as his text, "Surely there is no inchantment against Jacob, neither is there any divination against Israel: according to this time it shall be said of Jacob, and of Israel, What hath God wrought!" The statement originally referred to God's unique protection of Old Testament Israel against all her enemies' curses and attacks. Hart happily applied the prophecy to America: "The several nations of the world, beholding the mighty Revolution, and the many great and wonderful events which have taken place, are struck with astonishment, and constrained to a supernatural power, even the operations of Deity, asking, 'What great, unexpected things hath God wrought for America?'"[30]

Hart began his sermon by tracing God's favor on the American enterprise all the way back to the divine appointment of Christopher Columbus; God had used the explorer's "bold and enterprising genius" to "discover to the enlightened nations this vast continent." Hart also honored the memory of Plymouth's Separatist Pilgrims, "a hardy, determined, pious people," whose desire for religious freedom compelled them "to combat every difficulty, rather than wound their consciences or dishonor God." He carefully noted that earlier attempts to settle the continent by "men of the world, actuated wholly by selfish motives," had failed. But the Pilgrims were different; they were largely "stimulated by religion" and thus enjoyed God's preservation against obstacles of "hunger, cold, and the savage natives of the land." Hart remained consistent in his interpretation when he reached the Revolution. He left no doubt that Americans "claimed the patronage and agency of the Divine Being" throughout the war. Most recently, the formation of the First Continental Congress represented further evidence of God's work. Thinking of the wrangling over the Constitution just past, Hart recalled that "however much divided with regard to locality, religion, personal interests, tempers and prejudices, they all united as one man," and "who, but the Being who governs

---

[29] For more on this tendency and its effects, see Fea, *Was America Founded as a Christian Nation?*, 3–76.

[30] Hart, *America's Remembrancer*, 4–5.

282 OLIVER HART AND THE RISE OF BAPTIST AMERICA

the heart, could effect this?" In this last statement he was now inching closer to applying the language evangelicals used to describe the divine inspiration of the Bible to describe what took place in Philadelphia. By the end of the sermon, it would become clear that one of Hart's major rhetorical goals was to defend the new Constitution as a divinely blessed document worthy of American support.[31]

As Hart turned his attention to postwar America, he confessed that he would "do violence to [his] own feelings" not to praise God for George Washington, "a name which no additional title or epithet can emblazen or dignify!" He lauded the president as "the boast of his country, the wonder of the world, and the darling of Providence." Clearly Hart had no trouble with the strong executive powers the Constitution had granted Washington. He called the new government "the mature production of the most wise and approved patriots, legally chosen as our representatives, from whom we had everything to expect and nothing to fear." He then made several attempts to soothe any Anti-Federalist anxieties among his listeners. Since the Constitution's framers were citizens of the republic, Hart reasoned, "they could have been under no temptation to form an oppressive Constitution." Coming from a Calvinist who for decades had proclaimed his belief in man's total depravity apart from divine grace, this sweeping statement of trust in the good intentions of men is more than a little surprising. Yet Hart's confidence in the Constitution's authors seemed to know no bounds. To him, the new government was "open, free, and generous, although energetic— calculated to render the citizens of the United States happy, as it secures unto them all their rights and privileges, upon the most permanent basis." He believed that the principle of representative government neutralized any fears of a developing tyranny. After all, "while our rulers are amenable to ourselves, and amenable to us, we must be safe; especially while a Washington presides." Hart did not entertain the unpleasant notion of what life could be like with a lesser man than Washington in that powerful executive office. He was convinced that history would vindicate the Constitution. "Under its benign influence, I trust, religion, agriculture, manufactures, trade and commerce, and the more liberal arts and sciences will all flourish," he predicted. It sounded as if the Constitutional Congress had been the last crucial step before ushering in the millennial reign of Christ.[32]

---

[31] Hart, *America's Remembrancer*, 3–13.

[32] Hart, *America's Remembrancer*, 12–14. From Boston, Hart's protégé Samuel Stillman expressed the same glowing perspective regarding the Constitution, declaring his willingness to ratify "without

"THE BAPTIST INTEREST" 283

Wrapping up his speech, Hart urged his listeners to respond to God's special favor by leading contented, thankful, and humble lives. As Americans, they should submit cheerfully to their new leaders, live together in love, lead active and useful lives, and contribute to the exigencies of both church and state. Above all, of course, they must devote themselves to religion: "Considered as rational creatures, God has done great things for us. But as Americans, what has he not done?"

*America's Remembrancer* represents well the almost unhinged enthusiasm that many Baptists felt at the dawning of the new republic. The Warren Association of New England had declared in 1783, "Nor is it all improbable, that America is reserved in the mind of Jehovah, to be the grand theater on which the divine Redeemer will accomplish glorious things."[33] In a July 4 speech in 1795, Jonathan Maxcy (1768–1820), president of Rhode Island College, proclaimed that the founding of the United States represented nothing less than "the resurrection of liberty, the emancipation of mankind, [and] the regeneration of the world." Maxcy envisioned "the Angel of Liberty descending, dropp[ing] on Washington's brow the wreath of victory, and stamp[ing] on American freedom the seal of omnipotence. . . . We tread a new earth, in which dwelleth righteousness; and view a new heaven."[34] Other evangelicals shared in this euphoria, but Baptists believed they had special cause for celebration. They had lived as religious and cultural outsiders since the days of Roger Williams; many Baptists, particularly those in New England and Virginia, had suffered significant religious persecution in this era. For them, finally obtaining religious freedom represented the answer to generations of prayers; it was the dawn of a new era of hope. In a letter to the Warren Association in 1790, the New England Baptist Richard Montague celebrated America as the place where "now liberty is gained for all of the Sects and denominations of Christians by ye Constitution we live under."[35] Certain that God had chosen America, and especially his Baptist faithful there, for

any amendments at all," believing that "while Americans remain in their enlightened condition, and warmly attached to the cause of liberty they cannot be enslaved." In Jonathan Elliot, *The Debates in the Several State Conventions* . . . (Philadelphia, PA, 1876), 162. Isaac Backus too applied millennial language to the future of the United States under the new government: "Such a door is now opened for the establishment of righteous government and for securing equal liberty as never was before opened to any people on earth" (148–51).

[33] Cited in Kidd and Hankins, *Baptists in America*, 57–58.
[34] Jonathan Maxcy, *An Oration, Delivered in the Baptist Meeting-House in providence* (Providence, RI, 1795), 5–6.
[35] Richard Montague to Warren Association, September 3, 1790, Backus Papers, ANTS.

284 OLIVER HART AND THE RISE OF BAPTIST AMERICA

unique blessing, nothing seemed impossible to Hart and many other Baptists at the beginning of the 1790s. "Shielded by Omnipotence, and replenished by the Divine Munificence, America is safe, and must be happy while the Lord her God continues to work for her," Hart declared.[36]

Hart's story reflects the persistent tendency of American evangelicals to blend gospel ministry with political activism. After a Congress-called Day of Thanksgiving and Prayer in December 1781, Hart delivered another rousing speech identifying America as a new Israel, based on Jeremiah 51:15, "For Israel hath not been forsaken." Afterward he wrote, "Thro' mercy had a pretty good Degree of Freedom, and the People were very attentive. As at my first preaching here I openly declared my religious Principles, I now gave them a specimen of my political ones."[37] Hart dispensed these specimens more freely the older he got. As he became more deeply involved in the Revolution, he often co-opted traditional evangelical language about the new birth and revival for political purposes, conflating the spiritual freedom of Jesus with the political freedom of the American patriots. His habit of applying biblical promises of Christ's millennial glory to the future of America under the new Constitution also suggests that the location of his hope had shifted, at least temporarily, from a heavenly to an earthly kingdom. It is tempting to speculate that as Hart found fewer causes for encouragement in his local church ministry at Hopewell, he increasingly looked for signs of revival in the American political landscape. Yet by dipping into politics he ran the same risk that all politically inclined evangelicals have ever since: of confusing the Christian gospel with the affirmation of a set of government policies or a particular political party.[38]

\*

As much as American politics stirred Hart, the subject that dominated his personal writings in his final decade was what he often called simply "the Baptist interest." The 1787 Philadelphia Association circular letter indicates that Baptists were by now spreading in every direction in the republic. The Association received a letter from Virginia, announcing that there, too, the long-divided Regular and Separate Baptists had finally come together in a Plan of Union. The Philadelphia Association also read a stack of other letters detailing "the progress of the gospel" in Charleston, New England, Kentucky,

---

[36] Hart, *America's Remembrancer*, 14–24.
[37] Oliver Hart, diary, December 1781, Hart MSS, SCL.
[38] Hart, diary, December 7, 1781, Hart MSS, SCL.

and Georgia. At these reports the Association was moved "to rejoice in the prosperity of Zion throughout this continent: and encouraged to believe that the purity of the doctrines and ordinances of the gospel of Christ are prevailing more and more."[39] When Hart had been a teenager in the 1730s, Baptists had only one association in America and were struggling to establish their place in the colonies. In 1788 the Philadelphia Association sent letters to the Warren (New England), Shaftsbury (western Massachusetts), Charleston, Ketocton (Virginia), Stonington (Connecticut), Salisbury (Maryland), and New Hampshire associations, with more churches being planted and associations forming constantly. The Philadelphia Association proudly published a table in its 1790 circular letter, listing thirty total associations, stretching from Massachusetts down to Georgia.[40] These were high times to be a Baptist in America.

The late eighteenth-century Baptist surge was due largely to the meteoric rise of the Separate Baptist movement in the South. At their 1787 meeting, the Philadelphia Association read a letter from the Virginia Separate Baptist John Leland, informing them that about 1,200 people had been baptized and added to their churches in the past two years.[41] Hart rejoiced at the news, gushing in a letter to Furman about "thousands who are flocking to Christ in Virginia": "I saw a letter from there the other day mentioning the numbers in four churches and the whole amounted to about 2,100. The Minister's names were Waller, Leland, Piggot, and Mason. Highly favoured men!" Surveying the explosion of Baptist churches on the frontier, he marveled, "It should seem as if trees had become men and them men Baptists. This is the Lord's doing, and it is marvelous in our eyes. Little did I think when Brother Pugh and I travelled through that Wilderness in so solitary a manner, that so great a change would have taken place in so short a space of time, if ever." The reports provoked Hart to work and pray harder for similar victories in Hopewell: "May you and I, dear brother, become more successful in the Gospel."[42]

Baptists were also moving west in the 1780s. As mentioned earlier, John Gano, among the most celebrated of American Baptist preachers of the eighteenth century, had left his New York City pulpit in 1787 for Kentucky. So many Virginia Baptists moved to Kentucky in this period that the historian Robert

[39] Gillette, *Minutes*, 227–28.
[40] Gillette, *Minutes*, 269.
[41] Gillette, *Minutes*, 227.
[42] Oliver Hart to Richard Furman, September 28, 1789, Hart MSS, JBDML.

286    OLIVER HART AND THE RISE OF BAPTIST AMERICA

Semple called the territory "the vortex of Baptist preachers," questioning "whether half the preachers who have been raised in Virginia have not emigrated to the western country."[43] In 1781 Elijah Craig of Upper Spotsylvania Baptist Church in Virginia relocated his entire congregation to Kentucky, declaring that "the rich and illimitable acres of a western Canaan were offered to them" in the American West. Craig's so-called Traveling Church involved upwards of six hundred people undertaking a six-hundred-mile journey, the largest single migration of Virginians to Kentucky of the day. Craig would go on to found two of Kentucky's earliest Baptist churches, Gilbert's Creek (1781) and South Elkhorn (1783). In 1785 four churches joined to form the Elkhorn Association, adopting the *Philadelphia Confession*. One member of the original Travelling Church, a slave named Peter Durrett, would found First African Baptist Church of Lexington in 1790. From 1788 to 1798 the number of Kentucky Baptist congregations increased from eleven to thirty-two, and 559 to 2,376 members. In the next three years Kentucky Baptists grew to number 4,853.[44]

*

Hart found the Baptist expansion into all these new areas to be exhilarating, but the Baptist South maintained a special place in his affections. In addition to assuming Hart's former pastorate in Charleston, Furman had also inherited his role as leader of the Charleston Association. "Keep up that Institution," Hart urged his younger colleague.[45] This caution proved to be unnecessary, because Furman outstripped even Hart as a denominational visionary and institution-builder. Furman pushed in 1785 for the Charleston Association to incorporate under state law in order to hold and administer funds and property for educational purposes. At the 1786 meeting a covenant was prepared supporting the incorporation, and a committee was appointed to petition the legislature, with Furman serving as chairman. In the coming decades Furman would lead in establishing the South Carolina Baptist Convention, along with a host of educational, benevolent, and missionary activities. Most Baptists in the South welcomed this growing

---

[43] Semple, *Rise and Progress of the Baptists in Virginia*, 226.

[44] Kidd and Hankins, *Baptists in America*, 70–71. For more on the Baptist migration to Kentucky, see George Washington Ranck, *"The Travelling Church": An Account of the Baptist Exodus from Virginia to Kentucky in 1781* (Louisville, KY, 1910); William Warren Sweet, ed., *Religion on the American Frontier: The Baptists, 1783–1830* (New York: Henry Holt, 1931); and Taylor, *Baptists on the American Frontier*.

[45] Oliver Hart to Richard Furman, March 2, 1790, Hart MSS, JBDML.

"THE BAPTIST INTEREST" 287

denominational structure as a mark of progress and sophistication. Others, like Edmund Botsford, expressed concern, fearing that the denomination would soon invade the independence and eclipse the priority of the local churches. Botsford voiced his displeasure to Furman and to Hart, noting that while he loved Furman, he hoped that his plans "would not take place during my day." But Hart encouraged Furman to keep going, and stepped in to calm Botsford's fears. "It gives me much pleasure," Hart wrote Furman, "that your charitable fund receives such liberal supplies. If I once presumed to find fault with your Association, I must now be done, and do freely own, you far exceed us. May you go on and prosper. I am glad my son Botsford is become friendly to your measures."[46] Through Furman, many of Hart's long-held hopes for the Baptist South would come to fruition.

*

Numerical growth and denominational sophistication were two signs that Baptists had moved into the mainstream of American religious life. Another was their increased concern for an educated ministry. "I wish for the interest of the Religion we profess, we may all grow in grace, knowledge, and understanding, that the Baptists may be distinguished by something superior to folly and meanness," Hart wrote to Furman in 1790.[47] His letters from this period are filled with the names of "promising young men" entering Baptist ministry, along with his wishes that they receive proper training. He read with excitement the printed sermons of a young South Carolina Baptist named Henry Holcombe (1762–1837), pastor of the Euhaw Church in South Carolina and later at Savannah, Georgia. Hart praised Holcombe to Furman as "a truly great and good man, possessed of first-rate abilities." Yet Hart lamented that Holcombe and other Baptists like him failed to achieve widespread recognition for want of formal qualifications. "Had he been favored with a liberal education he might have shone among Doctors in Divinity, as it is, he is superior to many of them, and as to solid Divinity, not inferior to any of them. His discourse on the Sovereignty and Unchangeableness of the Deity, in my opinion, exceeds anything I ever read on the subject," Hart wrote.[48] Like many Baptist ministers of his day, Hart seems to have borne certain insecurities about his own lack of education compared to ministers of

---

[46] Oliver Hart to Richard Furman, May 7, 1792, Hart MSS, JBDML.
[47] Oliver Hart to Richard Furman, March 2, 1790, Hart MSS, JBDML.
[48] Oliver Hart to Richard Furman, August 27, 1793, November 26, 1793, Hart MSS, JBDML.

288 OLIVER HART AND THE RISE OF BAPTIST AMERICA

the older denominations. He urged younger Baptists to earn degrees and established ministers to accept honorary titles. When Furman expressed reluctance to accept an honorary master's degree from Rhode Island College, Hart pushed him to reconsider: "I know it cannot make you a greater or better man, but it may possibly render you more respectable and useful; and the Baptist interest, at Charleston, may be no loser thereby."[49] One detects this same desire for respectability at work in the Philadelphia Association's 1791 letter, which whenever possible distinguished its leaders not with the older, Pietistic titles of "brother" or "elder" but as "Doctor Rogers," "Doctor Jones," and "Doctor Manning."[50]

Baptists were now outpacing many of these older churches in sheer growth, but if Baptists were to obtain equal status with them in society, they needed to provide their leaders with theological credentials. Hart used his final address to the Philadelphia Association in 1791 to wave this banner. He described ministers as the "pillars" of the church, which must be "hewn by the axe of the law, smoothed by the plane of the gospel, painted by the gifts and graces of the Spirit, and varnished by human erudition." It was that final step in the process, receiving the "varnish" of theological education, to which so many of his Pietistic brethren objected. Hart often bemoaned the anti-intellectual tendencies of his Baptist brethren. While he agreed that education could not replace a divine calling to preach, he insisted that it was "a qualification of great importance, and ought never to be dispensed with, when it can be obtained." He then gave voice to a long-held dream, the establishment of a Baptist theological seminary: "In ancient times, there were schools of the prophets; and they are not less needed now. May such institutions be encouraged. We can do little or nothing else towards preparing these pillars. It is a pity that we are so reluctant in this. I am sorry to say, that several young ministers, of bright natural parts, and gracious endowments, are groaning for want of this advantage." Hart would not live to see the Baptist seminary of his dreams, but he took every opportunity to sow the seeds that successive generations of Baptists would water and harvest.[51]

*

The years immediately following the Revolution were marked by growth and revival for American Baptists; they were also years of theological innovation.

---

[49] Oliver Hart to Richard Furman, September 26, 1792, Hart MSS, JBDML.
[50] Gillette, *Minutes*, 270.
[51] Hart, *A Gospel Church Portrayed*, 16–17.

For Hart, promoting the Baptist interest meant guarding against all forms of heterodox teaching. The rise of New Divinity theology among Baptists, also called "Hopkinsianism" after Samuel Hopkins (1721–1803), especially concerned him.[52] Hopkins, Joseph Bellamy (1719–1790), and the other New Divinity leaders were New England Congregationalists who sought to extend the theological legacy of Jonathan Edwards into a new generation. Both Hopkins and Bellamy had studied with Edwards and maintained close friendships with him until his death in 1754. They were particularly enamored by Edwards's ideas about the nature of true virtue. The goal of the redeemed, they argued, was a "disinterested benevolence": to love God and others without any thought to one's own selfish benefit, to love as God loves, even at great personal cost. This concept of disinterested benevolence led New Divinity proponents to a number of provocative conclusions: that the sign of a true conversion is not that one loves God for what he does for one, but because one has seen the beauty of God oneself and loves God for who he is apart from anything God does for one. Pressing this point further, Hopkins argued that the truly converted sinner is so overwhelmed with love for God, that he or she is willing to be damned if that is what God wishes.

Another unique feature of the New Divinity was the extrapolations it made on Edwards's anthropology. On the one hand, Hopkins so stressed the absolute sinfulness of humanity that he insisted that everything the sinner does before conversion arises only from self-love and is thus wicked in God's sight. He therefore concluded that sinners should not be encouraged to use the "means of grace" to seek conversion, as generations of ministers had counseled, for this would only deepen their condemnation. At the same time, following Edwards, Hopkins stressed that while sinners lacked the "moral ability" to respond to the gospel, they did not lack any "natural ability" to do so: they *could* believe, if they only *would*. It was only the sinner's own stubborn heart keeping him or her from receiving the gospel. Hopkins concluded that sinners should not be counseled to use the means of grace but to immediately repent and believe. This complex, philosophical reasoning drew jeers from many traditional Calvinists, including the Baptist William Rogers, who dismissed the New Divinity with this doggerel: "You can and you can't;

---

[52] For a recent introduction to the main lines of New Divinity thought, see Caldwell, *Theologies of the American Revivalists*, 75–100. Other helpful resources include Holifield, *Theology in America*, 126–56; Douglas A. Sweeney and Allen C. Guelzo, eds., *The New England Theology: From Jonathan Edwards to Edwards Amasa Park* (Grand Rapids, MI: Baker Academic, 2006); and Oliver D. Crisp and Douglas A. Sweeney, eds., *After Jonathan Edwards: The Courses of the New England Theology* (New York: Oxford University Press, 2012).

290   OLIVER HART AND THE RISE OF BAPTIST AMERICA

You shall and you shan't; You will and you won't; You'll be damned if you do, and damned if you don't."[53] Another critic called the system "a ready way to throw [sinners] into the devil's arms."[54] Yet Hopkins's stress on immediate repentance would exercise tremendous influence over the next one hundred years of American revivalist theology.

The New Divinity attempted to make Edwards's thought more amenable to the Age of Reason; it was a quest for a logically consistent Calvinism. Ultimately this led its proponents to modify a number of central Reformed doctrines, sometimes in shocking ways. While stoutly affirming the reality of original sin, they denied the federal imputation of Adam's sin to the human race, an idea they found both unscriptural and abhorrent to reason. Adam's sin created the conditions by which all men now surely choose a sinful course, but each individual sinned because he so chose. They further altered the traditional Reformed view of Christ's atonement and the justification of sinners. They objected to viewing Christ's death as paying an actual sin-debt on behalf of the elect. Instead they promoted what has become known as the "moral government theory," in which Christ embraced the consequences of sin for all people, thereby allowing God to grant forgiveness to sinners in a manner consistent with his holiness. Their doctrine of justification also rejected the concept of imputation, or sinners receiving the personal right-eousness of Jesus Christ before God upon believing the gospel. Rather, they again emphasized the "principle of personal merit," by equating justifica-tion with the forgiveness of sins and stressing the new birth as leading to righteous, moral lives. These sweeping changes to core Reformed Christian teachings provoked strong reactions. Backus charged Hopkins with having "filled our land with controversy and given the enemy an occasion to re-proach the truth, especially about the sovereignty of grace and the earnest and free calls of the gospel to all sinners, without any good in them."[55] Hart, equally disgusted, quipped that it was "a poor divinity and jargon loose, such that will never build the house."[56]

Despite this criticism, the New Divinity would exert a powerful influence on American theology for more than a century, and many Baptists found in it a strong appeal. A number of New England Baptist elders were dismissed

---

[53] William Rogers to Isaac Backus, December 10, 1792, Backus Papers, ANTS.
[54] Brekus, *Sarah Osborn's World*, 279.
[55] Isaac Backus to Jonathan Maxcy, March 17, 1797, Backus Papers, ANTS.
[56] Oliver Hart to Richard Furman, August 27, 1793, Hart MSS, SCL.

"THE BAPTIST INTEREST" 291

from their churches for promoting its tenets in the 1770s and 1780s.[57] In 1790 the Philadelphia Association felt compelled to warn Baptists, "We apprehend danger, lest by these fine spun theories, and the consequences which are drawn from them by some, the great doctrines of imputation of Adam's sin, and Christ's proper atonement, imputed righteousness, &c., should be totally set aside, or at least, the glory sullied. We therefore advise that great care should be taken to guard against innovations not calculated to edify the body of Christ."[58] Especially after Manning's death in 1791, Hart feared that Rhode Island College had become "headquarters" for New Divinity thought and was turning out dozens of "Hopkinsians" into Baptist pulpits. Manning's successor, Jonathan Maxcy, was the most important promoter of New Divinity thought among Baptists at this time, in 1796 publishing a classic essay on the governmental theory of the atonement.[59] In 1793 Hart learned that the Baptist church at Georgetown, South Carolina, had rejected the candidacy of a Rhode Island College graduate, John Waldo, as pastor over his New Divinity leanings. Hart confessed that he was "glad the Georgetown people have been better taught than to embrace such sentiments or to approve of such preaching." To Hart, the Baptist interest would flourish in the new century only insofar as it held fast to the traditional teachings of the *Second London Confession* that he had so long preached.[60] Yet somewhat ironically, it was to be the Edwardsian concept of "disinterested benevolence," transmitted through the British Baptist Andrew Fuller, that would lay the groundwork for Baptist missionary activity, of which Hart would strongly approve, in the nineteenth century.[61]

*

More pernicious than the New Divinity was the growing Baptist fascination with Universalism, which Hart described as "gaining ground among us" at the beginning of the 1790s. William McLoughlin claims that almost

[57] McLoughlin mentions Noah Alden being dismissed from the Baptist church at Stafford, Connecticut, in 1765 and Samuel Hovey from Chemsford in 1770. See McLoughlin, *New England Dissent*, 2:734–35.

[58] Gillette, *Minutes*, 256.

[59] Holifield, *Theology in America*, 283. Maxcy's essay was entitled "Discourse Designed to Explain the Doctrine of the Atonement"; he later successfully spread New Divinity teaching to the Baptists of the South as the first president of the University of South Carolina.

[60] Oliver Hart to Richard Furman, May 30, 1793, Furman MSS, Furman; Oliver Hart to Richard Furman, August 27, 1793, Hart MSS, SCL; Talbert and Farish, *Antipedo Baptists of Georgetown* 36–37.

[61] See Michael A. G. Haykin, "Great Admirers of the Transatlantic Divinity: Some Chapters in the Story of Baptist Edwardsianism," in Crisp and Sweeney, *After Jonathan Edwards*, 197–207.

every Baptist church in New England lost some members to Universalism during this period, and "many lost ten or twenty."[62] Every year, it seemed, another Baptist minister was being outed as a Universalist. The Philadelphia Association confronted "the wild notion of universal salvation" in its 1790 circular letter, comparing it to "leprosy" and "a plague" in Baptist life.[63] Hart informed Furman of two ministers who had been recently "excluded" by the Philadelphia Association, William Worth and Artist Seagreaves of Pittsgrove, New Jersey. They were soon followed by Nicholas Cox of Kingwood, who "artfully and strenuously" promoted Universalism. Hart lamented, "Schism, disorder and confusion has taken place in that late flourishing church. [Cox's] influence among them is so great that a majority adheres to the man, if not to the sentiments." Hart was pleased that a minority group at Kingwood had risen up and excommunicated Cox. Following the standard Baptist practice of church discipline, the Kingwood congregation announced that they could no longer endorse Cox's salvation and refused to serve him the Lord's Supper. But Cox "paid no regard" to his church exclusion; he continued preaching, and even tried to seize the Kingwood church property through litigation. At this point Hart inserted himself into the conflict: "I have wrote pretty freely to Mr. Cox, with respect to his defection, and advised him, if he would desire to retain the character of an honest man, to do, what he ought to have done before he had kindled the flame among his brethren, resign all claim to institutional authority in Kingwood Church, and to the Temporalities thereof."[64]

Cox's defection seemed a harbinger of more theological tumult for American Baptists. "Where these things will end I know not, but they have a gloomy aspect," Hart wrote. By August 1793 Joseph Stephens of Upper Freehold had also been excommunicated for espousing Universalism. "Indeed he has always been an odd character," said Hart, and "never brought any honor to the interest of religion." Hart believed the American Baptist body could remain healthy only if it were "kept free from this Infection, and from all other heretical Tenets."[65] But the doctrinal perspectives among American Baptists would only continue to fragment in the new century.

\*

[62] McLoughlin, *New England Dissent*, 2:721.
[63] Gillette, *Minutes*, 257.
[64] Oliver Hart to Richard Furman, July 15, 1790, Hart MSS, JBDML.
[65] Oliver Hart to Richard Furman, July 15, 1790; August 27, 1793, Hart MSS, JBDML; Gillette, *Minutes*, 247, 256.

"THE BAPTIST INTEREST" 293

The largest threat to Baptist growth at the turn of the nineteenth century would turn out to be a group of fellow evangelicals, the Methodists. John Wesley had sent his first two Methodist missionaries to America, Joseph Pilmoor and Richard Boardman, back in 1769; Hart had befriended Pilmoor in his visit to Charleston and even invited him to address the Charleston Baptists. American Methodism grew slowly in its first fifteen years, owing to a combination of its unfavorable Arminian and perfectionistic doctrines, as well as its very English episcopal government and Wesley's vocal support of the king of England. By 1789 Isaac Backus complained that Methodist teachers "have taken great pains to draw off people from all other religious communities in our land by compounding works and grace together," yet he believed that "their influence is now in decline."[66] In this assessment Backus proved to be very wrong. American Methodists formally separated from the Church of England in 1784, organizing under the leadership of Bishops Thomas Coke and Francis Asbury. In the subsequent years Methodism's reach into America extended dramatically, thanks largely to its vast itinerant network and its lay leadership outside America's urban centers. Between 1786 and 1788 alone, Methodist membership increased from 18,791 white and 1,890 black members to 30,809 white and 6,545 black members, an 81% increase overall. The Methodists also expanded their number of circuits from fifty-one to seventy-six and the number of traveling preachers from 117 to 165.[67] Clearly Backus had misread the situation; Methodists were emerging as Baptists' single-greatest religious rival in the new American nation.

As with the Separate Baptists, the passionate, plain-spoken revival preaching of the Methodists was well-suited to the developing populist religious ethos of America. Botsford, who had himself led many frontier revivals in the Lower South, grumbled to Backus over the Methodists' backwoods enthusiasm: "They sing, pray, clap hands, fall down. Laugh, haolloo, etc. some times all together, that you would think they were deranged." Botsford added that they also courted persecution and were censorious of all other churches and that "their conversions [were] of a short duration." Backus too expressed his skepticism about the legitimacy of Methodist growth. "Many have doubtless been reformed by their means, and some converted," he admitted, "but they readily receive awakened persons to communion without a profession

---

[66] Isaac Backus to his wife, March 29, 1789, Backus Papers, ANTS, quoted in McLoughlin, *New England Dissent*, 2:725.
[67] See Wigger, *American Saint*, 165.

294    OLIVER HART AND THE RISE OF BAPTIST AMERICA

of regeneration." What especially chafed Baptists was that "if any one who was sprinkled in infancy is not satisfied with it and will join with them, they will go into the water and baptize them."[68] To the Methodists, the practice of immersion-upon-request exhibited a charitable flexibility and their belief that the meaning of the sacrament was more important than the mode. To Baptists, it was crass pragmatism; out-traveling and out-preaching them to gain adherents was one thing, but hijacking their most distinctive ritual was too much. The stage was being set for the intense denominational competition between the two groups that marked the nineteenth century.[69]

*

As Hart observed the growth of denominations like the Methodists, he and other Baptist leaders placed new stress on distinctive Baptist doctrines. At the height of the Great Awakening, Hart had often overlooked issues not pertinent to eternal salvation in order to promote revival with a coalition of non-Baptist evangelicals (including Methodists). By 1790 he still affirmed evangelical catholicity in principle, but his concern to guard the Baptist interest into the next century shifted his focus toward Baptist precisionism. A prime example came when he learned that the Charleston Association had affirmed that Baptist churches should grant members letters of dismissal to join Pedobaptist congregations. In a closely reasoned letter to Furman, Hart objected warmly to the ruling: "It cannot be consistent with *good order* to dismiss our Members to any Church whatever which is so disorderly as to set aside an Ordinance [i.e., baptism], which Christ in his Gospel holds as essentially necessary to Church Communion and Fellowship." For a Baptist church to bless one of its members joining a Pedobaptist congregation communicated "a tacit Acknowledgement that Infant Sprinkling is equally valid with Believers Baptism" and opened the door for Baptists to "slide into the Bosom of Pedobaptist Churches." Hart knew that Pedobaptists would "never" dismiss their members into communion with a Baptist church, because this would legitimize believers' baptism and "would end to bring down their Infant-Sprinkling." He closed by emphatically stating, "There need be no dismissing of members to churches with whom we are not in communion; for we ought to hold communion with all *True Christian Churches*."[70]

---

[68] McLoughlin, *New England Dissent*, 2:726.
[69] On this phenomenon, see Mulder, *A Controversial Spirit*, esp. 110–29.
[70] Oliver Hart to Richard Furman, March 2, 1790, Hart MSS, JBDML.

"THE BAPTIST INTEREST" 295

In taking this hard line, Hart knew that he opened himself to charges of narrow sectarianism. He attempted to defend his position as he continued:

I hope nothing that I have said will be construed into Bigotry, or the want of Christian Regard to Pedobaptists. I think the whole Tenor of my Conduct acquits me from such a Charge. I sincerely declare, that I esteem a number of Pedobaptists as Christians, in Preference to many Baptists, and could freely commune with them at the Lord's Table, if my Master did not forbid by making Baptism an *essential* Prerequisite to Church Membership; and we are to walk by this. With regard to our Pedobaptist Brethren I wish them well and forbid them not, though they walk not with us.[71]

To a Methodist like Francis Asbury, Hart's attitude displayed the typical Baptist penchant for mistaking "a controversial spirit for the spirit of religion" and making "dipping" the "*ne plus ultra* of Christian experience."[72] To Hart, correct church practice was simply a matter of obedience to Christ's commands in the Bible. While not essential to salvation, they were nevertheless important. As they had from the beginning, American Baptists in the new century would have to sort out how to balance evangelical catholicity with doctrinal precision.

*

If Hart was growing more entrenched with age regarding Baptist distinctives, he was opening up to new ideas about race and slavery. For much of the eighteenth century there had been nothing unusual about a white Baptist minister owning slaves in any part of the country. Along with Hart, Northern Baptist leaders such as Hezekiah Smith, Samuel Stillman, James Manning, and Ephraim Bound of Boston each owned at least one slave at some point.[73] It was not until the 1770s that this position encountered any real challenge from within the Baptist fold. One of the earliest and most striking examples came from the Baptist itinerant Elhanan Winchester, who had not yet begun stirring controversy over Universalism. In *The Reigning Abominations: Especially the Slave Trade, Considered as Causes of Lamentation* (1774), Winchester spoke openly of "the impropriety of the slave trade," denouncing slavery as

[71] Oliver Hart to Richard Furman, March 2, 1790, Hart MSS, JBDML, emphasis in original.
[72] Quoted in Mulder, *Controversial Spirit*, 118–19.
[73] See McLoughlin, *New England Dissent*, 2:766.

employing "every vice that degrades human nature."[74] These were inflammatory words, especially for a Baptist preacher in South Carolina. Perhaps Winchester's unpopular convictions about slavery provided further motivation for his relocating to Philadelphia in 1780.

Antislavery sentiment gained traction among Baptists in the North in the 1780s, thanks in part to the reforming efforts of the Quakers, as well as to the application of the "disinterested benevolence" doctrine by New Divinity spokesman Samuel Hopkins.[75] Prominent Baptist ministers began to identify with the antislavery cause, publicly petitioned to end the slave trade, and joined abolition societies. In 1789 the Quaker Moses Brown formed a society for the abolition of the slave trade in Rhode Island, which Manning (who had sold his slave boy, Cato, twenty years earlier) joined, as did Stillman. Hart's friend William Rogers served as vice president for the Philadelphia-based Pennsylvania Society for Promoting the Gradual Emancipation of Slavery, in 1790.[76] In 1789 the Philadelphia Association commended "the several societies formed in the United States and Europe, for the gradual abolition of slavery of the Africans, and for guarding against their being detained or sent off as slaves, after having obtained their liberty," and encouraged the Baptist people to form their own organizations for the same purpose.[77]

According to Rogers, these antislavery developments among Baptists had a profound effect on Hart. Throughout his thirty years in Charleston, Hart had taken the typical, moderate evangelical position: he had ministered to slaves as spiritual equals and decried cruelty and abuse toward them. But he had not only declined to oppose slavery, he bought and owned slaves himself. This stance had allowed him and other evangelicals to be accepted in Southern culture. Now, it seems, Hart was changing his ideas. "A mind like his was always open to conviction," Rogers remembered. While as late as 1780 Hart still "labored under some prejudices in favor of the slavery of the poor Africans and their descendants," Rogers continued, "his benevolent soul, soaring above every selfish motive, was soon brought to contemplate the whole with horror—and to wish, yea more, fervently to pray for success

---

[74] Elhanan Winchester, *The Reigning Abominations, Especially the Slave Trade; Being the Substance of a Discourse Delivered in Fairfax County, Virginia, December 30, 1774* (London: H. Trapp, 1788), 17–18.

[75] For Samuel Hopkins and the New Divinity's influence on the antislavery movement, see Brekus, *Sara Osborne's World*, 284–88, 209–313, 339.

[76] Nash, *Forging Freedom*, 103–106; Sprague, *American Pulpit*, 6:147; McLoughlin, *New England Dissent*, 2:766–69.

[77] Gillette, *Minutes*, 247.

to attend the endeavours of those individuals or societies who are laudably engaged in promoting the happiness of the great human family!" By the time the Philadelphia Association publicly endorsed abolition in 1789, it would appear that Hart added his own "amen."

Still, Hart found the practical application of his new convictions complicated. As Rogers told it, "Mr. Hart, by his will, has left a young negro man free, after a few years service—who has since been disposed of to a good master for five years.—Mrs. Hart, since the death of her husband, has liberated a Negro Woman, with her youngest child, and disposed of her other two children, each till the age of 25—when they are to be free also." Even after embracing abolition, Hart retained slaves to the end of his life, though he made arrangements for their liberation by the age of twenty-five. Like many evangelicals, Hart apparently believed that such an incremental policy provided slaves the best opportunity to flourish in society as free men and women. Nevertheless the scene of Mrs. Hart's female slave and her baby being separated from the other children remains heartbreaking. It serves as a reminder of the inevitable tragedies accompanying the slave system and the myriad thorny, practical problems evangelicals like Hart faced as they acted on their emerging social conscience about race.[78]

Nor should these stories suggest that Hart and his fellow white Baptists came to recognize black men and women as equals, even after coming to denounce slavery. A story told by a contemporary admirer of Stillman reflects the persistent assumptions of racial superiority among the most forward-thinking of Northern white Baptists. Intending to be complimentary, Stillman's friend remembered him for being "in the best sense, condescending" toward those who "regarded themselves as his inferiors," thinking especially of African Americans. This admirer went on to relate a time when Stillman, out walking with his friends in Boston, met "a coloured man." This man "very politely took off his hat, and bowed to the Doctor, who instantly reciprocated the civility. His friend, unused to such demonstrations, could not help asking why he took off his hat to that black man. 'Why,' replied Dr. Stillman, 'the man made his obeisance to me, and I should be loth to have it said that I had less manners than a negro.'" Reflecting on this scene, Stillman's friend remarked, "There was in his constitution a remarkable blending of moral greatness with all the more gentle and retiring of the

[78] Rogers, *A Sermon*, 24.

# 298 OLIVER HART AND THE RISE OF BAPTIST AMERICA

Christian virtues."[79] As it would be for all Americans, progress in the arena of race relations would be for Baptists a long, slow journey.[80]

*

Though faced with the reality of his own physical decline and his failure to lead the kind of revival at Hopewell he had known in Charleston, the closing years of the 1780s were not all disappointment for Hart. One frigid Saturday morning in January 1789, a Mrs. Patience Blackwell shared with the Hopewell church the account of her recent conversion and "offered herself as a candidate for baptism." The church had gathered to prepare for the Lord's Supper the next morning, and Mrs. Blackwell was eager to be immersed so that she could join the rest of the faithful at the table. Hart and the church immediately repaired to the home of Deacon Nathaniel Stout, through whose farm ran Beden Brook, their usual baptismal site. The problem, of course, is that the creek had long since yielded to the bitter temperatures of the New Jersey winter, resulting in an imposing layer of ice. Undaunted, Hart recorded in his diary quite matter-of-factly that the church simply "cut away the ice (which was of considerable thickness)." The sixty-six-year-old pastor then led Mrs. Blackwell down into the slushy, bone-chilling waters. There, "according to the ancient practice," Hart "baptized her in the Name of the sacred Trinity. We then came up out of the water, and neither of us received any damage, altho' there was snow on the ground as well as ice in the brook," he wrote.[81]

For forty years Hart had demonstrated this same, rugged determination in promoting the ancient ways of the Baptist interest in America. In spite of countless dangers and setbacks during those years, they, like Patience Blackwell, had somehow emerged not only unharmed but apparently bearing the blessing of God. As he now entered the final decade of the eighteenth century, though his own physical decline and absence of revival at Hopewell discouraged him, the rising glory of both the American republic and the Baptist people gave him cause for hope. He had long envisioned a day when the various regional associations of Baptists now scattered across the country would be joined in a single, thriving denomination. This prospect now seemed more attainable than ever.

---

[79] Sprague, *Annals of the American Baptist Pulpit*, 77.
[80] Kidd and Hankins treat this theme extensively throughout their recent monograph *Baptists in America*.
[81] Oliver Hart, diary, January 24, 1789, Hart MSS, SCL.

# 13

# "All the Baptists on the Continent"

## A Dream Briefly Realized

Oliver Hart and Richard Furman, along with Shubal Stearns the South's most important Baptist leaders between the years 1750 and 1825, carried on a regular correspondence during the first half of the 1790s. The tensions between the two men regarding the pastoral succession at the Charleston Baptist Church were now far behind them. The letters they exchanged were easy and affectionate, ranging over a wide field of subjects. Politics remained a major interest for both men, and they mused about the trajectory of the French Revolution and commiserated about the ongoing presence of British Loyalists in American public life. They kept one another apprised of the younger men who were filling Baptist pulpits in their respective areas, and sent along printed copies of recommended sermons and associational minutes. Hart, showing his age, never failed to update Furman on his aches and pains, nor to inquire about the latest local gossip around Charleston. Always they inquired about one another's families. Theirs was a leisurely, familiar correspondence characteristic of eighteenth-century evangelicalism.

But their most frequent topic of discussion was the need for revival among the Baptist people. Virtually all of Hart's letters included a report in this regard. He utilized a dazzling range of metaphors to describe the same old reality of spiritual lethargy: "Vital piety and practical godliness among professors in these parts, seem to be almost cashier'd. We have had no late additions to our Church."[1] "Would to God that I could close my letter by communicating some such good tidings respecting these parts, but we seem to be at a stand."[2] "Our religious concerns are not so promising as I could wish; altho' three were baptized and added at our last communion."[3] "As to the state of religion in these parts, it is nearly a dead calm. I am sorry to say

---

[1] Oliver Hart to Richard Furman, June 15, 1791, Hart MSS, SCL.
[2] Oliver Hart to Richard Furman, May 7, 1792, Hart MSS, SCL.
[3] Oliver Hart to Richard Furman, September 26, 1792, Hart MSS, SCL.

*Oliver Hart and the Rise of Baptist America.* Eric C. Smith, Oxford University Press (2020). © Oxford University Press.
DOI: 10.1093/oso/9780197506325.001.0001

there is not the least appearance of a revival in our church."[4] "I have to lament of too much leanness of soul, and too little success in the Lord's work. Indeed I know not of any visible revival in any of these northern states."[5] "After all, the state of religion remains in status quo."[6] "As to the State of Religion in these states, it is at a low ebb, very much so in Hopewell."[7] In Charleston, Furman's estimation was no different; the condition of the churches from his view was "truly melancholy."[8] The imagery changed with each letter, but the story remained the same: Baptists needed revival.

Hart's assessment of Baptist decline was not unique in the 1790s. The previous decade had seen bursts of religious fervor in various regional pockets, such as New England's New Light Stir and the Great Revival in Virginia in the late 1780s. But now, throughout America, Baptist leaders were expressing similar anxieties about the spiritual state of the new nation. As the Charleston Association summed up the situation in 1793, "That religion is in a low and languishing state throughout the continent, admitting a few exceptions, and that it is greatly so with us, is evident, from the best testimony and our own observation."[9] Insidious, heterodox notions seemed to menace the Baptists on every side, whether the Universalism of Elhanan Winchester, the Deism of Thomas Paine, or the out-and-out infidelity associated with the French Revolution.[10] The Goshen Baptist Convention of Virginia declared it to be "a dark time with the church, and many false teachers are gone out into the world."[11] Just as concerning as overt false teaching was the general carelessness and secularism that seemed to blanket the American people. Especially in the South, ministers of every denomination complained in these days of empty church houses and the general "falling off" of religious commitment. The newly opened western territories, where thousands had flooded to grab land in the 1780s, were now notorious for irreligion and immorality. Edmund Botsford was so discouraged by his own congregation's dismal spirituality in Georgetown, South Carolina, that he commented to Furman in the

[4] Oliver Hart to Richard Furman, May 30, 1793, Hart MSS, SCL.
[5] Oliver Hart to Richard Furman, June 20, 1793, Hart MSS, SCL.
[6] Oliver Hart to Richard Furman, November 26, 1793, Hart MSS, SCL.
[7] Oliver Hart to Richard Furman, April 10, 1794, Hart MSS, SCL.
[8] Richard Furman to Sarah Furman Haynsworth, August 23, 1792, Richard Furman papers, JBDML.
[9] Charleston Association, "Minutes, 1790–1804," p. 6, microfilm, Southern Baptist Historical Library and Archives, Nashville, Tennessee.
[10] John B. Boles details these perceived threats to evangelicals in the 1790s in *The Great Revival*, 12–24.
[11] Goshen Baptist Association Minutes, 1795, "Circular Letter," p. 7, microfilm, Southern Baptist Historical Library and Archives, Nashville, Tennessee.

"ALL THE BAPTISTS ON THE CONTINENT" 301

spring of 1796, "I was in hopes some time ago it was midnight with us, but I now begin to fear I was mistaken.... In cold winter nights, it often seem[s] a long time from midnight to morning."[12]

*

Gloomy as these prospects were, veteran revivalists like Hart knew better than to despair. Since Old Testament times, God had worked among his people in a familiar, cyclical pattern of decay and renewal, degeneration and revitalization. In this light, even seasons of the most pronounced religious decline could be viewed as invitations from the Lord to abandon all religious self-reliance and depend on him alone for fresh outpourings of the Spirit. It was a hopeful perspective that kept Hart and his colleagues always living in expectancy for the next great move of God. As Mark Noll has written, it was this widespread longing for revival, even more than the experience of revival itself, that caused evangelicalism to take root in America.[13] And while the sending of revival remained God's prerogative, his people certainly could and should ask, seek, and knock at Heaven's door. Accordingly, Baptists and evangelicals all over America responded to the nation's spiritual crisis by declaring fasts and praying for revival throughout the 1790s. "O pray for us that we may have days of refreshing from the presence of the Lord," Hart exhorted Furman, that "the Spirit of the Lord may breathe on these dry Bones, that they may live."[14] Hart's letters from this period voice the hopes and fears of an evangelical movement that produced a steady stream of revivals in America from the 1730s until deep into the nineteenth century.[15]

While waiting out the long, dreary winter, Hart remained always alert for the first budding of spring. When he thought he glimpsed a sign on Sunday morning in 1791, he excitedly shared his story with Furman. Hart preached "very comfortably to a large congregation" that day, from Colossians 3:1. It was a classic text for admonishing Christians to spiritual-mindedness, well-suited to the times: "If ye then be risen with Christ, seek those things which are above, where Christ sitteth on the right hand of God." Afterward the congregation "repaired to the water" for a baptismal service, joined by "some hundreds of spectators." As always, Hart said a few things "respecting the

[12] Edmund Botsford to Richard Furman, May 3, 1796, South Carolina Baptist Historical Collection, Furman University, Greenville.
[13] Noll, *Rise of Evangelicalism*, 137.
[14] Oliver Hart to Richard Furman, June 15, 1791, Hart MSS, SCL.
[15] On the continuity between the First and Second Great Awakenings, see Kidd, *The Great Awakening*, 321–24.

302 OLIVER HART AND THE RISE OF BAPTIST AMERICA

Nature and Design, the Subject and Mode of the Ordinance"; then he waded out into the river and baptized five people. The crowd generally "behaved with the greatest decorum," Hart reported, and some were noticeably affected by what they witnessed. One man, "who had never seen the ordinance administered . . . could say nothing against it." Another woman, "to whom it was also quite new, said it was the prettyest sight she had ever seen in her life." Hart wondered aloud to Furman if this could be a portent of a greater awakening to come: "Query, whether such behaviour and such approbation, or the most insolent opposition and ridicule, is most likely to be followed with success? I know which is more pleasant. Will you pray, my brother, O pray earnestly that these may be the first fruits of a great harvest. Who knows but God will hear you for us."[16]

This hopeful seeking of revival had defined Hart's ministry for nearly five decades. It would continue to mark America's Baptists into the final years of the eighteenth century, when, along with other evangelical denominations, they would experience a fresh religious awakening that would reshape the entire nation's religious landscape.[17] In New England, New Divinity Congregationalists like Timothy Dwight (1752–1817) of Yale College, Edward Dorr Griffin (1770–1837), Asahel Nettleton (1783–1844), and Lyman Beecher (1775–1863) presided over an Edwardsian awakening that resulted in not only numerous conversions but an unprecedented burst of evangelical activism. The western frontier saw a more emotional, unruly brand of revivalism break out at an outdoor communion service in Logan County, Kentucky, in July 1800. "The people fell before the word, like corn before a storm of wind," remarked one amazed participant.[18] From there, the Great Revival washed over the rest of the South, all the way back to the Carolinas, where Furman witnessed mass conversions at outdoor meetings held in the "Kentucky Stile." Furman initially expressed reservations about the demonstrations among those of a more "enthusiastick disposition," but he readily admitted that there was also "strong evidence of supernatural

---

[16] Oliver Hart to Richard Furman, August 26, 1791, Hart MSS, SCL.

[17] For an overview of the Second Great Awakening, see Caldwell, *Theologies of the American Revivalists*, 102–6; Daniel Walker Howe, *What God Hath Wrought: The Transformation of America, 1815–1848* (New York: Oxford University Press, 2009), 164–202; Barry Hankins, *The Second Great Awakening and the Transcendentalists* (Westport, CT: Greenwood Press, 2004); and Sydney E. Ahlstrom, *A Religious History of the American People*, 2nd ed. (New Haven, CT: Yale University Press, 2004), 415–71.

[18] Boles, *The Great Revival*, 57.

"ALL THE BAPTISTS ON THE CONTINENT" 303

power and gracious influence" among many.[19] There had not been such a widespread, interdenominational revival of this intensity since the days of George Whitefield.[20]

But Oliver Hart, who had so earnestly prayed for such a day for so long, would not live to see it.

*

Puritan realist that he was, Hart began telling his friends by the middle of 1795 that he was "a dying man." In truth, he had been preparing for death most of his adult life. Even in his early thirties a bout of sickness or fatigue would prompt him to pray, "Lord, may I be ready for my dissolution." But now, in the final week of December 1795, the restless activist was confined to his bed, fighting for every breath. Attending Hart was the son born to him in the autumn of his life, eleven-year-old William Rogers Hart. Oliver had named his last child after one of his younger friends, the Baptist minister and educator William Rogers, who had been instrumental in changing Hart's mind about slavery. As the boy waited on his father, he silently reminded Hart of so many of the things he had invested his life in: the promotion of the Baptist interest in colonial America, the training and education of ministers, the cultivation of evangelical friendships, the pilgrimage of the Christian life. William took in every detail of his father's final days, and afterward shared his observations with his namesake.

Many visitors passed in and out of Hart's room in that last week of the year. They came to sit at the venerable preacher's bedside and to recall to him his hope in Christ, as Hart himself had done for others so many times in fifty years of pastoral work. Hart needed this; his pain was so acute that his body was sometimes racked with convulsions. The struggle for each breath grew so intense that on more than one occasion he burst a blood vessel and spat up substantial quantities of blood. He tried not to complain, but every so often he would wearily raise his hands and murmur, "Poor, mortal man." When one of his visitors responded by offering Hart the promise of resurrection from the Apostle Paul, "This mortal flesh shall put on immortality," Hart answered, "Yes! Yes!" He had often preached about walking by faith rather than by sight; now faith was all he had. As his outer nature was wasting away,

---

[19] Boles, *Great Revival*, 77; Benedict, *General History*, 2:167–71; McCurry, *Masters of Small Worlds*, 148–50.

[20] Kidd and Hankins survey Baptist participation in the Great Revival in *Baptists in America*, 76–97.

304    OLIVER HART AND THE RISE OF BAPTIST AMERICA

he believed that his inner nature was being renewed, day by day, straining ahead to the consummation of the miracle that had been inaugurated by the new birth at the height of the Great Awakening.[21]

On other occasions it was Hart who ministered to his visitors. The Baptist preacher William Van Horne came to see him and asked if his friend felt comfortable in his bed. Visibly suffering, Hart nevertheless testified to a deeper comfort in his final hours, gasping out, "God is an all sufficient Savior!" Later, when his pain became more intense, another visitor suggested, "How happy for Mr. Hart that he has but one work to do." Yet even in the throes of death, the mention of "doing a work" while preparing to stand before God instantly engaged Hart's evangelical reflexes. For over half a century he had declared that sinners were not saved by their own works of obedience but by grace-wrought faith in the finished work of Jesus Christ. Hart immediately replied by quoting Romans 10:4, "Christ is the end of the law for righteousness to everyone that believeth!" He had spilled much ink and many tears over his open diary through the years, inspecting his heart for evidence of godliness. But the time for self-examination was past. As he prepared to step out into eternity, Oliver Hart was fixing his eyes on Jesus.[22]

As Hart's time drew near, he called for the friends and family around him to "help him praise God for what he had done for his soul." His friends and family encircled his bed, rehearsing through prayer, song, and Bible reading the victory of the resurrected Jesus over the grave, a triumph in which they all now shared by virtue of the new birth. Caught up in this atmosphere of worship, one friend knelt at Hart's head and reminded him that he would soon exchange his present company for the glorious assembly of the angels and the saints from all the ages. To this, Hart could only lift a hand and reply, "Enough, enough!" It was more than his frail heart could sustain.

The next day, December 30, Hart rested his head on his pillow, closed his eyes as if he were going to sleep, and died.[23]

*

The Baptist America on which Hart closed his eyes looked dramatically different from the one he had first encountered some seventy-five years earlier. American Baptists in 1700 counted roughly eight hundred members in twenty-four churches. By 1740 those numbers had risen to just three

[21] Rogers, *A Sermon*, 28.
[22] Rogers, *A Sermon*, 28.
[23] Rogers, *A Sermon*, 28–29.

thousand members in sixty churches. The nineteenth-century Baptist observer David Benedict recalled how, in those early years, "the sect as a whole was denounced as the dregs of Christendom." Baptists were "reproached with a wild and fanatical pedigree, or, in other words, as being descendants of the *madmen of Munster*," referring to the revolutionary Anabaptists of sixteenth-century Germany.[24] No doubt many negative opinions about Baptists persisted in 1790, but it was becoming impossible not to take them seriously in American society. Their number had exploded to sixty-seven thousand Baptist members in 979 churches, grouped into forty-two associations.[25] Thanks to the wide-scale embrace of Baptist principles by African Americans, the Baptist movement was also far more diverse at the close of the eighteenth century than at the beginning. The Savannah African Baptist Church, for instance, would grow from 80 to 1,400 members between 1788 and 1812, and would reach 2,800 members by 1832; Augusta's Springfield African Church, begun in 1791, would reach 1,300 members by 1832.[26]

No one was more astonished by this transformation than the Baptists themselves, who often commented on their drastic change of fortunes in these days. In his "Century Sermon" to the Philadelphia Association in 1807, Hart's longtime friend Samuel Jones selected Isaiah 54:2 as his text: "Enlarge the place of thy tent, and let them stretch forth the curtains of thine habitations: spare not, lengthen thy cords, and strengthen thy stakes; for thou shalt break forth on the right hand and on the left." Jones declared with exuberance, "During the last century . . . there has been a fulfillment of the prophecy in the text among us." Baptists by this time were becoming experts at statistical reporting, and Jones calculated that, if one took into account that there are "three hearers in a congregation for every communicant in the church," there must be 735,000 people on any given Sunday sitting under a Baptist ministry, or "one-eighth part of the whole population of the Union."[27] The long-suffering Baptists of New England shared in Jones's exultation. "If we compare the present state of our denomination in this land with the state it was in 50 years since, we shall see great cause of encouragement and

[24] Benedict, *Fifty Years among the Baptists*, 33. For the Anabaptists and the Muenster rebellion, see Norman Cohn, *The Pursuit of the Millennium: Revolutionary Millenarians and Mystical Anarchists of the Middle Ages*, rev. ed. (New York: Oxford University Press, 1970), 255–80.

[25] Robert Gardner, *Baptists of Early America: A Statistical Study* (Atlanta: Georgia Baptist Historical Society, 1983), 35.

[26] Michael Sobel, *Trabelin' On: The Slave Journey to an Afro-Baptist Faith* (Westport, CT: Greenwood Press, 1979), 350–55.

[27] Gillette, *Minutes*, 453–59.

306 OLIVER HART AND THE RISE OF BAPTIST AMERICA

thankfulness," wrote the Boston Baptist Association in 1814. "We were then oppressed; we have now full liberty to worship God according to the dictates of our own consciences. We were then few in number; we have now increased to a multitude. The Lord has indeed done great things for us whereof we have reason to be glad."[28] Once a despised sect fighting for survival on the Pennsylvania frontier and meeting secretly in hostile New England, Baptists would enter the nineteenth century in a two-horse race with their fellow religious upstarts, the Methodists, for the soul of the American people.

*

American Baptists' impressive growth in the eighteenth century was due in large measure to the ascendancy of Baptists in the South, where Hart had played such a seminal role. When he arrived in Charleston at the close of the 1740s, the handful of Particular Baptist churches in the Lower South were small, weak, and disconnected. There existed among them no plan for organization, no strategy for missionary outreach into the growing frontiers, no vision for training and educating new ministers. Inspired by his participation in the Great Awakening in Pennsylvania, Hart came to Charleston on a mission to change all that by implementing the denominational model of the Philadelphia Association in the region. Over the next thirty years he succeeded in doing just that.

Hart connected pastorless congregations with ministers through the American Baptist network and organized the South's Particular Baptist churches into the Charleston Association in 1751. Committed to educating young Baptist preachers, he established the Baptist Religious Society, the first cooperative effort for ministerial education by Baptists in America, in 1755. In the same year, he proposed the first cooperative missionary effort among the South's Baptists, raising funds to secure John Gano as an itinerant evangelist on the North Carolina frontier. He personally befriended, corresponded with, and trained numerous younger men who would become Baptist leaders of the next generation, in the South and beyond. He shaped the beliefs and practices of the South's Baptists for more than a century by leading the Charleston Association to adopt the *Charleston Confession* and the *Summary of Church Discipline*, the latter of which he coauthored. This included the growing number of black Baptist churches in the South that practiced the

---

[28] Boston Baptist Association Minutes, 1814, 14, quoted in Mcloughlin, *New England Dissent*, 2:1110.

same rigorous Baptist discipline during the nineteenth century Hart had outlined and that embraced his Calvinism at least until Emancipation.[29] When the radical Separate Baptists arrived in the region, Hart did not hold them at arm's length, but played a decisive role in uniting them with the South's Particular-Regular Baptists, most importantly through his friendship with Richard Furman. Hart had also worked for religious liberty for Baptists and all Dissenters under the new South Carolina Constitution, contributing to the growing acceptance of Baptists in mainstream society. Then there was Hart's revival-oriented pastoral ministry at the Charleston Baptist Church, which established that once unstable congregation as the mother church of Southern Baptists. No one did more to lay the groundwork for the denominational life of the Baptist South in the eighteenth century.

*

After Hart's death, Furman built on Hart's foundation. In his twenty-five years as moderator of the Charleston Association, Furman's relentless lobbying for ministerial education resulted in the formation of a General Committee, which in turn laid the foundation for Baptist schools like Furman University (1826) and Mercer University (1833). Without a doubt, American Baptists were being recognized for their learning as never before; for instance, Jonathan Maxcy would become the first president of the University of South Carolina in 1804, and South Carolina Baptist Basil Manly Sr. would become president of the University of Alabama in 1837.[30] But education was just one arm of Furman's strategy for Baptist expansion. As Baptist associations across South Carolina multiplied, he urged the creation of the Baptist Convention of South Carolina in 1821, further enlarging Baptist efforts in evangelism, education, and benevolence. Beyond the borders of the South, Furman provided leadership in the hour when "all the Baptists on the Continent" finally came together for unified action.

*

In 1810 a young Congregationalist minister named Adoniram Judson (1788–1850), freshly graduated from Andover Theological Seminary, helped

---

[29] See Wills, *Democratic Religion*, 67–83.

[30] Francis Wayland, who became the fourth president of Brown University (formerly Rhode Island College) in 1827, would publish widely praised textbooks on ethics, philosophy, and political science in the 1830s. For Wayland, see Kidd and Hankins, *Baptists in America*, 130–35, and McLoughlin, *New England Dissent*, 2:1274.

create the American Board of Commissioners for Foreign Missions, the first organization in the United States committed to supporting international missionaries. In 1812 Judson and his new wife, Ann (1789–1826), boarded a ship bound for India. On the way over, Judson prepared for his impending encounter with the English Baptist missionaries already in the field by undertaking a thorough study of the New Testament doctrine of baptism. To his surprise, he arrived in Calcutta thoroughly convinced that the infant baptism that he and his denomination practiced was unbiblical. He requested immersion for him and Ann from one of the Baptist missionaries and, along with his colleague Luther Rice (1783–1836), resigned from the American Board of Commissioners. American Baptists suddenly found they could lay claim to a group of international missionaries, but also that they would need support from the Baptist people. Inspired by the Judsons' story, Baptist leaders from all over the nation gathered in Philadelphia in 1814. It was a distinguished gathering; the names of almost every minister on the program were preceded by the title "Dr.," including Hart's friends Furman and Rogers. Though still motivated by revivalism, this august assembly in Philadelphia seemed far removed from an earlier generation of more radical Baptists, who spoke of tours of hell, received revelations through dreams and trances, employed female exhorters, and practiced divine healings. It was a testimony to the staying power of Hart's moderate brand of revivalism.[31]

After much prayer and deliberation, the Baptist leaders resolved to form the General Missionary Convention of the Baptist Denomination of the United States of America, for Foreign Missions, adopting the Judsons as their first sponsored missionaries. Because they agreed to meet every three years, the organization soon became known as the Triennial Convention. They elected Furman as the first president.[32] In his inaugural address, Furman memorialized the momentous step Baptists were now taking by working together for foreign missions. He also cast a vision for a larger denominational work, adding, "Many other and most important advantages may arise to the interests of Christ from our acting as societies and on the more extended scale of a Convention in a delightful union." Baptists across America

[31] For the tendency of denominations to moderate the more "radical" elements of their earlier religious expressions, including the reassertion of traditional gender roles, see Juster, *Disorderly Women*; Brekus, *Strangers and Pilgrims*, 66 and passim; and Noll, *Rise of Evangelicalism*, 263–66.

[32] Gregory A. Wills, "From Congregationalist to Baptist: Judson and Baptism," in *Adoniram Judson: A Bicentennial Appreciation of the Pioneer American Missionary*, edited by Jason G. Duesing (Nashville, TN: B&H Academic, 2012), 153–58; Robert G. Torbet, *A History of the Baptists*, rev. ed. (Valley Forge, PA: Judson Press, 1963), 249–50.

had remained for so long "ignorant of each other to a lamentable degree.... Why prevent us from uniting in one common effort for the glory of the Son of God?" Furman confessed that as he watched so many previously unacquainted Baptists from across the union sharing fellowship at the Triennial Convention, "it was as if the first interviews of heaven had been anticipated." The support of the Judsons and foreign missions was just the first step, Furman announced; in the years that followed, the Triennial Convention intended to expand its work to include home missions, ministerial education, and other benevolent causes.[33]

Expand they did, and quickly. In 1817 the Triennial Convention sent Isaac McCoy (1784–1846) as a missionary to the Indian tribes in Indiana, Illinois, and Michigan. In 1821 representatives of the Triennial Convention established Columbian College (today George Washington University) in Washington, D.C., fulfilling a long-held desire of George Washington to have a national university within the nation's capital.[34] In 1824 the Baptist General Tract Society was founded to publish educational materials, and in 1832 the Convention formed the American Baptist Home Mission Society to oversee domestic missions.[35] Baptists in America could now claim a "national Baptist superstructure," with an influence that reached into the nation's capital and clear to the other side of the globe.[36] Hart, one can only imagine, would have been beside himself with joy.

*

But the union of all the Baptists on the continent would be short lived. As with their Methodist and Presbyterian brethren, the American Baptist denomination ultimately foundered on the rock of slavery.[37] For a small window of time in the early 1790s, it seemed possible that a number of other white Baptists in the South might follow the same antislavery trajectory as Hart had. In his *Virginia Valediction* before departing for Massachusetts in 1790, John Leland spoke pointedly and at length to the issue. "The whole scene of slavery is pregnant with enormous evils," Leland preached. "On the

---

[33] *The Baptist Magazine for 1815*, vol. 7 (London, 1815), 24.

[34] See George Thomas, *The Founders and the Idea of a National University: Constituting the American Mind* (New York: Cambridge University Press, 2015), 2–3.

[35] *Proceedings of the Baptist Convention for Missionary Purposes* (Philadelphia, PA, 1814), 42–43.

[36] Noll, *America's God*, 197.

[37] On the splintering of antebellum American denominations, see C. C. Goen, *Broken Churches, Broken Nation: Denominational Schisms and the Coming of Civil War* (Macon, GA: Mercer University Press, 1985).

master's side, pride, haughtiness, domination, cruelty, deceit and indolence; and on the side of the slave, ignorance, servility, fraud, perfidy and despair." Leland himself had no ready solutions, but he sensed that matters would soon reach a breaking point if action were not taken: "Something must be done! May Heaven point out that something, and may the people be obedient.... If they are not brought out of bondage, in mercy, with the consent of their masters, I think that they will be, by judgment, against their consent."[38] In 1794 the Georgia Baptist Association approved a petition to the legislature calling for a ban on the importation of slaves. And in 1796 the Ketocton (Virginia) Association received a query from Happy Creek Church: "Can the present practice of holding Negros in slavery be supported by Scripture and the true principles of a republican government?" The Association declined to answer, deeming it to be a "proper subject of legislation," a common Baptist position on race issues in these days. But the following year these Virginia Baptists adopted a position against "hereditary slavery" as "a transgression of the Divine Law" and recommended to the state a program of gradual emancipation.[39]

But whatever hopes for change across the Baptist South may have existed at the beginning of the 1790s quickly dissolved with Eli Whitney's invention of the cotton gin in 1793. In 1788 South Carolina had produced 1.5 million pounds of cotton; by 1801, that number had skyrocketed to 20 million pounds. In 1834 it would reach 65 million pounds. A massive slave labor force was now far too integral to the Southern economy to think of dispensing with it. Many white Baptists still lamented slavery as a moral evil, but to challenge the institution seriously would ensure their marginalization as radicals in Southern society. Furman, like most white Baptist Southerners, opted instead to stick with the standard moderate evangelical policy Hart had followed during his Charleston years: sanctifying slavery as essential to the Divine order, beneficial to the benighted African race, and a holy burden for those white masters charged with the physical and spiritual care of black members in their "households." In 1807 Furman stated baldly his belief that it was "the order of providence that a considerable portion of the Human race must necessarily move in a humble sphere and be generally at the disposal of

---

[38] Leland, *Writings*, 94–98.
[39] *Minutes of the Ketocton Baptist Association* (Dumfries, VA, 1796), 4, and *Minutes of the Ketocton Baptist Association* [1797], 4, 6, both cited in Kidd and Hankins, *Baptists in America*, 100.

"ALL THE BAPTISTS ON THE CONTINENT" 311

their fellow men."[40] To oppose the prevailing social order of the South was to oppose the Divine order.

Furman penned the classic exposition of white evangelical paternalism in a letter to South Carolina's governor Thomas Bennett (1781–1865) in 1822. After the free black carpenter Denmark Vesey (d. 1822) was accused of staging a massive slave uprising that same year, Furman felt compelled to publicly defend the institution of slavery on behalf of the South Carolina Baptist Convention. He frankly acknowledged the many evils that had arisen from abolitionist rhetoric, namely to "disturb the domestic peace of the State, to "produce insubordination and rebellion among the slaves" and "to infringe the rights of our citizens." Further, abolitionism served "to deprive slaves of religious privileges, by awakening in the minds of their masters a fear, that acquaintance with the Scriptures, and the enjoyment of these privileges would naturally produce the aforementioned effects." Furman forcefully asserted "that the holding of slaves is justifiable by the doctrine and example contained in Holy writ; and is, therefore consistent with Christian uprightness, both in sentiment and conduct." Certainly, he admitted, there were many regrettable abuses of slavery, for which God would hold masters accountable. Yet the institution itself was part of "that order of things, which the Divine government has established." In this divine order, slaves "become part of the family," their temporal and eternal welfare resting heavily on the shoulders of the master. In God's providence, slavery could be the instrument "for the civilization and conversion of the Africans." Following a bewildering line of logic, Furman even suggested that slavery was "a means of saving life" and that "Africans brought to America were, in general, slaves, by their own consent." He concluded that "a master has a scriptural right to govern his slaves so as to keep them in subjection; to demand and receive from them a reasonable service; and to correct them for the neglect of duty, for their vices and transgressions; but that to impose on them unreasonable, rigorous services, or to inflict on them cruel punishment, he has neither a scriptural nor a moral right."[41]

Furman's message was clear: if the governor of South Carolina was looking for allies in the fight to maintain slavery, he need look no further than the nearest Baptist church. Furman's position, echoed by his successor at First

---

[40] Furman quoted in McCurry, *Masters of Small Worlds*, 212.

[41] Richard Furman, *Exposition of the views of the Baptists relative to the coloured population of the United States in a communication the governor of South Carolina*, in Rogers, *Richard Furman*, 274–86.

# 312 OLIVER HART AND THE RISE OF BAPTIST AMERICA

Baptist Charleston, Basil Manly Sr., and the entire white Baptist South in the decades leading up to the Civil War, ensured that Baptists would remain at the heart of Southern society.[42] Indeed, after 1820 the once-marginal sect had become the established religion of the region. As one twentieth-century author would quip, Baptists in the South constituted "the center of gravity."[43] Yet while their proslavery position helped the South's white Baptists build bridges with their Southern neighbors, it drove a wedge between them and their Northern Baptist brethren.

\*

The Baptist Triennial Convention began to fracture by the early 1830s. When British Baptists, in the wake of Britain's Slavery Abolition Act in 1833, admonished their American brethren to work for swift and total abolition, 180 Northern Baptists responded with a letter of commendation, announcing, "SLAVEHOLDING is now the most heinous sin with which America is chargeable."[44] But the white Baptist South merely dug in its heels. The Charleston Association condemned those "deluded and mischievous fanatics" who dared to "interfere with the domestic institutions of the Southern and Slave-holding States." These South Carolina Baptists regarded the meddling of their Northern counterparts "not only as officious and unfriendly but incendiary and murderous."[45] For many years the Triennial Convention attempted to remain neutral on slavery, leaving the matter to individual consciences, so that the board could continue its work. But by 1844 the sectional tensions had reached a boiling point. Georgia Baptists tested the Convention's neutrality policy by nominating the slaveholder James Reeves as a missionary to the Cherokee Indians; the Home Mission Society voted Reeves down seven to five. In response, Alabama Baptists, led by Basil Manly Sr. (now president of the University of Alabama), submitted an inquiry to the Foreign Mission Board, asking if slaveholders could be appointed as missionaries. The Board's response was blunt: "One thing is

---

[42] For Manly's proslavery position as pastor of First Baptist Charleston, see Fuller, *Chaplain to the Confederacy*, 106–29. On the general theme of white Baptist and evangelical endorsement of slavery, see especially McCurry, *Masters of Small Worlds*, and Heyrman, *Southern Cross*.

[43] See Edward L. Queen II, *In the South Baptist Are the Center of Gravity* (Brooklyn, NY: Carlson, 1991). Many works document this phenomenon, including Rufus Spain, *At Ease in Zion: A Social History of Southern Baptists, 1865–1900* (Tuscaloosa: University of Alabama Press, 2003), and Ammerman, *Baptist Battles*, 18–71.

[44] Andrew T. Foss and Edward Mathews, eds., *Facts for Baptist Churches* (Utica, NY: American Baptist Free Mission Society, 1850), 20.

[45] Foss and Mathews, *Facts for Baptist Churches*, 26; Kidd and Hankins, *Baptists in America*, 125.

"ALL THE BAPTISTS ON THE CONTINENT" 313

certain: we can never be a party to any arrangement which would imply approbation of slavery."[46] That was all Manly and the white Baptist Southerners he represented needed to hear. On May 8, 1845, over three hundred Baptists convened in Augusta, Georgia. By the time they adjourned, the delegates had passed a constitution for the Southern Baptist Convention, consisting of 4,126 churches and 351,951 total members.[47] Unlike Presbyterians and Methodists, America's Baptists would not reunite after the Civil War; never again would all the Baptists on the continent exhibit the visible unity they had in the early decades of the nineteenth century.

*

Hart's dream of a nationwide Baptist denomination did not last, but his legacy continued in the new Southern Baptist Convention. Southern Baptist delegates formed their own Foreign and Domestic Mission Boards at Augusta in 1845, echoing Hart's proposal to fund John Gano's frontier missions back in the 1750s. Hart, the passionate organizer, would be gratified to know that these continue to operate to the present day under different names, along with a host of other Southern Baptist entities. Then, in 1859, a young Furman University professor named James P. Boyce (1827–1888) realized Hart's dearest institutional wish by founding a seminary to train the young Baptist ministers of the South.[48] Boyce, along with fellow founding professor Basil Manly Jr. (1825–1892), had been reared at the Charleston Baptist Church. Among the first books placed in the library of the Southern Baptist Theological Seminary, in Greenville, South Carolina, were those first purchased a century earlier by Oliver Hart, with funds from the Charleston Association's humble Baptist Education Fund. The seminary's theology would be stamped by Hart's traditional, evangelical Calvinism: Manly Jr. would base the school's confessional document, *The Abstract of Principles*, on the *Charleston Confession* that he and Boyce had learned as boys. Faculty at Southern Seminary, located since 1877 in Louisville, Kentucky, are still required to sign this document today.

Beyond the institutions of the early Southern Baptist Convention, Hart's influence remained discernible in a variety of other ways. Southern Baptists

[46] Foss and Mathews, *Facts for Baptist Churches*, 136.

[47] For Manly's role in creating the Southern Baptist Convention, see Fuller, *Chaplain to the Confederacy*, 212–27.

[48] See Gregory A. Wills, *The Southern Baptist Theological Seminary 1859–2009* (New York: Oxford University Press, 2009), 3–52. For Boyce, see Tom J. Nettles, *James Petigru Boyce: A Southern Baptist Statesman* (Philipsburg, NJ: Presbyterian & Reformed, 2009).

remained passionate promoters of revivalism and heartfelt evangelical piety, producing thousands of conversions and swelling church roles throughout the nineteenth century. For many years they continued to practice the careful discipline of Baptist church members as Hart had prescribed in his *Summary of Church Discipline*, though these exclusionary practices would fall out of fashion in the enormous and increasingly pragmatic denomination by the end of the nineteenth century.[49] They would wrestle publicly with how they should relate to other denominations, and, while retaining a stronger separationist streak than Hart had, would ultimately reject the exclusionary Landmark position in a move that would have pleased Hart, the principled ecumenist. Of course, Southern Baptists also exhibited the same conflicted social conscience that dogged Hart's ministry, prophetically denouncing the sins of Southern leisure culture like dancing, gambling, card playing, and novel reading, while keeping in lockstep with Southern culture on the larger matters of race relations.[50] Southern Baptists also moderated the eighteenth-century Separate Baptists' radical stance on the public roles of women. They became a bastion of conservatism in the arena of gender politics even while continuing to extend women opportunities to participate in church life that outpaced many of their Protestant neighbors. This unusual adaptability enabled Southern Baptists to gain a remarkable foothold in Southern culture, attaining status as the so-called Catholic Church of the South and, in time, the world's largest Protestant denomination.

At almost every level, then, for better or for worse, the Southern Baptist Convention, torn asunder from his beloved American Baptist denomination, was covered in Hart's fingerprints. This is in some ways surprising, because as he knew of himself, he did not possess many of those "striking, dazzling qualities" associated with major religious leaders. Hart became Southern Baptists' most important pioneer by his earnest and steady piety, his unparalleled gift for cultivating and keeping fruitful friendships, and his skillful blending of the Philadelphia Association's Baptist denominationalism and the Great Awakening's moderate revivalism in Charleston. Yet as is the case with most pioneers, who clear and plant so that those who follow can build and harvest, Hart's name is forgotten today, attached to none of the multitude of Baptist institutions and buildings his life helped make possible. We cannot know, of course, what Hart might say about how this story developed. It is

---

[49] Wills tells this story in *Democratic Religion*, 116–38.
[50] On this theme, see especially Spain, *At Ease in Zion*.

possible, though, that he would reply with something similar to his remarks from a 1759 ordination sermon:

And however sensible of very great degrees of weakness, and unworthiness, yet I am not altogether without an inward testimony of some degree of faithfulness, sincerity, and engagedness in my Master's work.[51]

[51] Hart, Sermon on 1 Timothy 4:16, Hart MSS, SCL.

# Bibliography

## Archival Material

Backus, Isaac. Papers. Franklin-Trask Library Collection, Andover Newton Theological Seminary at Yale Divinity School, New Haven, Connecticut.

Botsford, Edmund. Papers. James B. Duke Memorial Library, Furman University, Greenville, South Carolina.

Furman, Richard. Papers. James B. Duke Memorial Library, Furman University, Greenville, South Carolina.

Hart, Anne. *Narrative of Anne Marie Sealy Grimball Hart, Born 1741, South Carolina.* Historical Society of Pennsylvania, Philadelphia.

Hart, Oliver. *A Copy of the Original Diary of Rev. Oliver Hart of Charlestown, Pastor of the Baptist Church of Charlestown.* Mimeographed copy. James P. Boyce Centennial Library, Southern Baptist Theological Seminary, Louisville, Kentucky.

Hart, Oliver. Letters. Gratz Collection. Historical Society of Pennsylvania, Philadelphia.

Hart, Oliver. Letters. McKesson Collection. Historical Society of Pennsylvania, Philadelphia.

Hart, Oliver. Papers. James B. Duke Memorial Library, Furman University, Greenville, South Carolina.

Hart, Oliver. Papers. South Caroliniana Library, University of South Carolina, Columbia.

Manning, James. Papers. John Hay Library, Brown University, Providence, Rhode Island.

Pugh, Evan. Letters. Gratz Collection. Historical Society of Pennsylvania, Philadelphia.

## Primary Sources

*An Abstract of the Records of the Cashaway Baptist Church, Society Hill, S.C.* Transcribed by Glenn Pearson, May 2000. https://www.sciway3.net/proctor/marlboro/church/Cashaway_Baptist.html.

*An Abstract of the Records of the Welsh Neck Baptist Church, Society Hill, S.C.* Transcribed by Glenn Pearson, May 2000. http://sciway3.net/proctor/marlboro/church/Welsh_Neck_Baptist2.html.

Backus, Isaac. *A Fish Caught in His Own Net.* Boston, 1768.

Backus, Isaac. *Church History of New England, from 1620 to 1804.* Philadelphia, 1844.

Backus, Isaac. *A History of New England, with particular reference to the Denomination of Christians called Baptists.* Boston: Edward Draper, 1777.

Bentley, William. *The Diary of William Bentley*, 4 vols. Salem, MA: Essex Institute, 1904–1914.

Broome, John David. *The Life, Ministry, and Journals of Hezekiah Smith: Pastor of the First Baptist Church of Haverhill, Massachusetts, 1765 to 1805 and Chaplain in the American Revolution, 1775 to 1780.* Springfield, MO: Particular Baptist Press, 2004.

318 BIBLIOGRAPHY

Chanler, Isaac. *New Converts Exhorted to Cleave to the Lord. A Sermon on Acts XI 23 Preach'd July 30, 1740 at a Wednesday Evening-lecture, in Charlestown, Set Up at the Motion, and the Desire of the Rev. Mr. Whitefield; With a Brief Introduction Relating to the Character of that Excellent Man . . . With Preface by the Reverend Mr. Cooper of Boston, N.E.* Boston: D. Fowle for S. Kneeland and T. Green, 1740.

Charleston Association. *A Confession of Faith, Put Forth by the Elders and Brethren of Many Congregations of Christians (Baptized upon Profession of their Faith) in London and the Country. Adopted by the Baptist Association in Charlestown, South-Carolina. To which is annexed, A Summary of Church Discipline.* Charleston, SC: David Bruce, 1774.

Charleston Association. *Minutes of the Charleston Association, February 7, 1774.* Charleston, SC, 1774.

Charleston Association. *Minutes of the Charleston Association, February 6, 1775.* Charleston, SC, 1775.

Charleston Association. *Minutes of the Charleston Association, February 3, 1777.* Charleston, SC, 1777.

Charleston Association. *Minutes of the Charlestown Association, February 2, 1778.* Charleston, SC, 1778.

Charleston Association. *Minutes of the Charleston Association, October 19, 1778.* Charleston, SC, 1778.

Charleston Association. *A Summary of Church Discipline.* Shewing the qualifications and duties, of the officers and members of a Gospel-church. Charleston, SC, 1794.

Chauncy, Charles. *Enthusiasm described and caution'd against.* Boston, 1742.

Chauncy, Charles. *Seasonable Thoughts on the State of Religion in New-England.* Boston: Rogers and Fowle, 1743.

Dutton, Anne. *A Letter from Mrs. Anne Dutton to the Reverend G. Whitefield.* Philadelphia, PA, 1743.

Edwards, Jonathan. *The Great Awakening.* Edited by C. C. Goen. Vol. 4 of *The Works of Jonathan Edwards.* New Haven, CT: Yale University Press, 2009.

Edwards, Jonathan. *Religious Affections.* Edited by John E. Smith. Vol. 2 of *The Works of Jonathan Edwards.* New Haven, CT: Yale University Press, 1959.

Edwards, Morgan. *The Customs of Primitive Churches, or A Set of Propositions Relative to the Name, Materials, Constitution, Power, Officers, Ordinances, Rites, Business, Worship, Discipline, Government, &c. of a Church; to Which Are Added Their Proofs from Scripture; and Historical Narratives of the Manner in Which Most of Them Have Been Reduced to Practice.* Philadelphia, PA: Andrew Stuart, 1768.

Edwards, Morgan. *Materials towards a History of the Baptists.* 2 vols. Edited by Eve B. Weeks and Mary B. Warren. Danielsville, GA: Heritage Papers, 1984.

Fleetwood, William. *A Sermon Preached before the Society for the Propagation of the Gospel in Foreign Parts, at the Parish Church of St. Mary-le-Bow, on Friday the 16th of February, 1710/11.* London: Joseph Downing, 1711.

Foss, Andrew T., and Edward Mathews, eds. *Facts for Baptist Churches.* Utica, NY, American Baptist Free Mission Society, 1850.

Furman, Richard. *Rewards of Grace Conferred on Christ's Faithful People: A Sermon, Occasioned by the Decease of the Rev. Oliver Hart, A.M.* Charleston, SC: J. McIver, 1796.

Garden, Alexander. *Take heed how ye hear.* Charleston, SC: Peter Timothy, 1741.

Gillette, A. D., ed. *Minutes of the Philadelphia Baptist Association, from A.D. 1707 to A.D. 1807.* Philadelphia, PA: American Baptist Publication Society, 1851.

## BIBLIOGRAPHY 319

Hart, Oliver. *America's Remembrancer, with Respect to her Blessedness and Duty*. Philadelphia, PA: Dobson, 1791.

Hart, Oliver. *The Character of a Truly Great Man Delineated, and His Death Deplored as a Public Loss: A Funeral Sermon, Occasioned by the Death of the Rev. William Tennent, A.M.* Charleston, SC: David Bruce, 1777.

Hart, Oliver. *Dancing Exploded: A Sermon Shewing the Unlawfulness, Sinfulness, and Bad Consequences of Balls, Assemblies, and Dances in General*. Charleston, SC: David Bruce, 1778.

Hart, Oliver. *A Gospel Church Portrayed, and Her Orderly Service Pointed Out—A Sermon, Delivered in the City of Philadelphia at the Opening of the Baptist Association, October 4, 1791*. Trenton, NJ: Isaac Collins, 1791.

Hart, Oliver. *An Humble Attempt to Repair the Christian Temple, Shewing The Business of Officers and Private Members in the Church of Christ, and How Their Work Should Be Performed; with Some Motives to Excite Professors Ardently to Engage in It*. Philadelphia, PA: Aitken, 1785.

Ireland, James. *The Life of Rev. James Ireland*. Winchester, VA, 1819.

Karlsen, Carol F., and Laurie Crumpacker, eds. *The Journal of Esther Edwards Burr 1754–1757*. New Haven, CT: Yale University Press, 1984.

Keith, George. *An Exhortation and caution to Friends Concerning Buying or Keeping of Negroes*. Edited by George Moore. New York, 1693.

Leland, John. *The Writings of the Late Elder John Leland*. Edited by L. F. Greene New York: G. W. Wood, 1845.

Lumpkin, William L. *Baptist Confessions of Faith*. Valley Forge, PA: Judson Press, 1969.

Mallary, Charles D. *The Memoirs of Elder Edmund Botsford*. Springfield, MO: Particular Baptist Press, 2004.

Marrant, John, and William Aldridge. *A Narrative of the Lord's Wonderful Dealings with John Marrant, a Black, now Going to Preach the Gospel in Nova-Scotia, born in New-York, in North America*. London: Gilbert and Plummer, 1785.

Maxcy, Jonathan. *An Oration, Delivered in the Baptist Meeting-House in providence*. Providence, RI, 1795.

McCoy, Isaac. *History of Baptist Indian Missions*. New York, 1840.

Muhlenberg, Henry. *The Journals of Henry Melchior Muhlenberg*. Translated by Theodore G. Tappert and John W. Dobberstein. 3 vols. Philadelphia, PA: Muhlenberg Press, 1945.

*Proceedings of the Baptist Convention for Missionary Purposes*. Philadelphia, PA, 1814.

Pugh, Evan. *The Diaries of Evan Pugh (1762–1801)*. Transcribed by Horace Fraser Rudisill. Florence, SC: St. David's Society, 1993.

Rogers, William. *A Sermon Occasioned by the Death of the Rev. Oliver Hart*. Philadelphia, PA: Lang and Ustick, 1796.

*Second London Confession*. https://www.the1689confession.com.

Smith, Elias. *Five Letters, with Remarks*. Boston: J. Ball, 1804.

Spener, Philip Jacob. *Pia Desidera*. Translated by Theodore G. Tappert. Philadelphia, PA: Fortress Press, 1964.

Stiles, Ezra. *The Literary Diary of Ezra Stiles*. 3 vols. Edited by F. B. Dexter. New York, 1901.

Stillman, Samuel. *Good News from a Far Country*. Boston, 1766.

Stillman, Samuel. *Select Sermons on Doctrinal and Practical Subjects, by the Late Samuel Stillman, D.D., Comprising Several Sermons Never Before Published to Which Is Prefixed A Biographical Sketch of the Author's Life*. Boston: Manning & Loring, 1808.

320　BIBLIOGRAPHY

Taylor, John. *Baptists on the American Frontier: A History of Ten Baptist Churches*. Edited by Chester Raymond Young. Macon, GA: Mercer University Press, 1995.

Tennent, Gilbert. *The Danger of an Unconverted Ministry, Considered in a Sermon on Mark 6:34*. Philadelphia, PA: Benjamin Franklin, 1740.

Tennent, Gilbert. *A funeral sermon occasion'd by the death of the Reverend Mr. John Rowland*. Philadelphia, PA, 1745.

Tennent, Gilbert. *The Righteousness of the Scribes and Pharisees Considered*. Boston, MA, 1741.

Thomas, David. *The Virginian Baptist: or A view and defence of the Christian religion, as it is professed by the Baptists of Virginia*. Baltimore, MD: Enoch Story, 1774.

Washington, George. Letter to John Laurens, January 15, 1781. "The American Revolution, 1763–1783." Library of Congress. http://www.loc.gov/teachers/classroommaterials/presentationsandactivities/presentations/timeline/amrev/homefrnt/gwtojl.html.

Washington, George. "Thanksgiving Proclamation," October 3, 1789. George Washington Papers. Library of Congress. https://www.loc.gov/resource/mgw8a.124/?q=1789+Thanksgiving&sp=132&st=text.

Whitefield, George. *Journals*. Edinburgh: Banner of Truth, 1978.

Whitefield, George. *The Sermons of George Whitefield*. Edited by Lee Gattis. Wheaton, IL: Crossway, 2012.

Whitefield, George. *Works of the Reverend George Whitefield*. 4 vols. London: Edward and Charles Dilly, 1771.

Winchester, Elhanan. *The Reigning Abominations: Especially the Slave Trade, Considered as Causes of Lamentation; Being the Substance of a Discourse Delivered in Fairfax County, Virginia, December 30, 1774*. London: H. Trapp, 1788.

Winchester, Elhanan. *The Universal Restoration, Exhibited in Four Dialogues between a Minister and His Friend*. Worcester, MA, 1803.

Woodmason, Charles. *The Carolina Backcountry on the Eve of the Revolution: The Journal and Other Writings of Charles Woodmason, Anglican Itinerant*. Edited by Richard J. Hooker. Chapel Hill: University of North Carolina Press, 1953.

Zubly, John J. *The Journal of the Reverend John Joachim Zubly A.M., D.D., March 5, 1770 through June 22, 1781*. Edited by Lilla Mills Hawes. Savannah: Georgia Historical Society, 1989.

## Secondary Sources: Books

Ahlstrom, Sydney E. *A Religious History of the American People*. 2nd ed. New Haven, CT: Yale University Press, 2004.

Alexander, Archibald. *Biographical Sketches of the Founder, and Principal Alumni of the Log College*. Princeton, NJ: J. T. Robinson, 1845.

Ammerman, Nancy Tatom. *Baptist Battles: Social Change and Religious Conflict in the Southern Baptist Convention*. New Brunswick, NJ: Rutgers University Press, 1990.

Armistead, Wilson. *Journal of George Fox*. London, 1852.

Armitage, Thomas. *A History of the Baptists*. New York, 1890.

Asplund, John. *The Annual Register of the Baptist Denominations, in North America . . .* Southampton Co., VA: Thomas Dobson, 1792.

Bailyn, Bernard. *Atlantic History: Concept and Contours*. Cambridge, MA: Harvard University Press, 2005.

## BIBLIOGRAPHY 321

Baker, Frank. *From Wesley to Asbury: Studies in Early American Methodism*. Durham, NC: Duke University Press, 1976.

Baker, Robert A., Paul J. Craven, and Marshall A. Blalock. *History of the First Baptist Church of Charleston, South Carolina, 1682–2007*. Springfield, MO: Particular Baptist Press, 2007.

Bebbington, D. W. *Baptists through the Centuries: A History of a Global People*. Waco, TX: Baylor University Press, 2010.

Bebbington, D. W. *Evangelicalism in Modern Britain: A History from the 1730s to the 1980s*. New York: Routledge, 2005.

Beeman, Richard. *Plain, Honest Men: The Making of the American Constitution*. New York: Random House, 2009.

Benedict, David. *Fifty Years among the Baptists*. New York, 1860.

Benedict, David. *A General History of the Baptist Denomination in America, and Other Parts of the World*. 2 vols. Boston: Lincoln and Edmonds, 1813.

Boles, John B. *The Great Revival: Beginnings of the Bible Belt*. Lexington: University Press of Kentucky, 1996.

Bolton, S. Charles. *Southern Anglicanism: The Church of England in Colonial South Carolina*. Westport, CT: Greenwood Press, 1982.

Bonomi, Patricia U. *Under the Cope of Heaven: Religion, Society, and Politics in Colonial America*. New York: Oxford University Press, 2003.

Bowes, Frederick Patten. *The Culture of Early Charleston*. Chapel Hill: University of North Carolina Press, 1942.

Brekus, Catherine A. *Sarah Osborn's World: The Rise of Evangelical Christianity in Early America*. New Haven, CT: Yale University Press, 2013.

Brekus, Catherine A. *Strangers and Pilgrims: Female Preaching in America, 1740–1845*. Chapel Hill: University of North Carolina Press, 1998.

Broadus, John A. *Memoir of James Petigru Boyce*. Louisville, KY, 1893.

Bryant, Scott. *The Awakening of the Freewill Baptists: Benjamin Randall and the Founding of an American Religious Tradition*. Macon, GA: Mercer University Press, 2001.

Burrage, Champlin. *The Church Covenant Idea: Its Origin and Development*. Philadelphia, PA: American Baptist Publication Society, 1904.

Burrage, Henry S. *History of the Baptists in Maine*. Portland, ME: Marks, 1904.

Butler, Jon. *Awash in a Sea of Faith: Christianizing the American People*. Cambridge, MA: Harvard University Press, 1990.

Buzzell, John. *The Life of Elder Benjamin Randall Principally Taken from Documents Written by Himself*. Limerick, ME, 1827.

Caldwell, Robert W., III. *Theologies of the American Revivalists: From Whitefield to Finney*. Downer's Grove, IL: IVP Academic, 2017.

Carp, E. Wayne. *To Starve the Army at Pleasure: Continental Army Administration and Political Culture, 1775–1783*. Chapel Hill: University of North Carolina Press, 1990.

Carretta, Vincent, ed. *Unchained Voices: An Anthology of Black Authors in the English-Speaking World of the 18th Century*. Lexington: University Press of Kentucky, 1996.

Cohen, Charles. *God's Caress: The Psychology of Puritan Religious Experience*. New York: Oxford University Press, 1986.

Cohn, Norman. *The Pursuit of the Millennium: Revolutionary Millenarians and Mystical Anarchists of the Middle Ages*. Rev. ed. New York: Oxford University Press, 1970.

Collison, Patrick. *The Elizabethan Puritan Movement*. Oxford: Clarendon Press, 1967.

## 322 BIBLIOGRAPHY

Crisp, Oliver D., and Douglas A. Sweeney, eds. *After Jonathan Edwards: The Courses of the New England Theology.* New York: Oxford University Press, 2012.

Dalcho, Frederick. *An Historical Account of the Protestant Episcopal Church in South Carolina, from the first settlement of the province, to the war of the Revolution.* Charleston, SC: E. Thayer, 1820.

Davies, Hywel. *Transatlantic Brethren: Rev. Samuel Jones (1735–1814) and His Friends: Baptists in Wales, Pennsylvania, and Beyond.* Bethlehem, PA: Lehigh University Press, 1995.

Davis, W. W. H. *History of Bucks County, Pennsylvania, From the Discovery of the Delaware to the Present Time.* Doylestown, PA: Democrat Book and Job, 1876.

Davis, W. W. H. *History of the Hart Family of Warminster, Bucks County, Pennsylvania. To Which Is Added the Genealogy of the Family, from Its First Settlement in America.* Doylestown, PA: W. W. H. Davis, 1867.

Delbourgo, James. *Most Amazing Scene of Wonders.* Cambridge, MA: Harvard University Press, 2006.

Deweese, Charles W. *Baptist Church Covenants.* Nashville, TN: Broadman Press, 1990.

Dreisbach, Daniel. *Reading the Bible with the Founding Fathers.* New York: Oxford University Press, 2017.

Edelson, S. Max. *Plantation Enterprise in Colonial South Carolina.* Cambridge, MA: Harvard University Press, 2006.

Edgar, Walter B. *South Carolina: A History.* Columbia: University of South Carolina Press, 1998.

Elliot, Jonathan. *The Debates in the Several State Conventions . . .* Philadelphia, PA, 1876.

Fea, John. *Was America Founded as a Christian Nation? A Historical Introduction.* Louisville, KY: Westminster John Knox Press, 2016.

Fea, John. *The Way of Improvement Leads Home: Philip Vickers Fithian and the Rural Enlightenment in America.* Philadelphia: University of Pennsylvania Press, 2008.

Foote, William Henry. *Sketches of North Carolina, Historical and Biographical.* New York, 1846.

Fox-Genovese, Elizabeth. *Within the Plantation Household: Black and White Women of the Old South.* Chapel Hill: University of North Carolina Press, 1988.

Franklin, Benjamin. *Autobiography.* Boston: Houghton and Mifflin, 1906.

Fraser, Walter J. *Charleston! Charleston! The History of a Southern City.* Columbia: University of South Carolina Press, 1991.

Fraser, Walter J. *Patriots, Pistols and Petticoats: "Poor Sinful Charles Town" during the American Revolution.* Columbia: University of South Carolina Press, 1993.

Frey, Sylvia, R. *Water from the Rock: Black Resistance in a Revolutionary Age.* Princeton, NJ: Princeton University Press, 1991.

Frey, Sylvia R., and Betty Wood. *Come Shouting to Zion: African American Protestantism in the American South and the British Caribbean to 1830.* Chapel Hill: University of North Carolina Press, 1998.

Fuller, James A. *Chaplain to the Confederacy: Basil Manly and Baptist Life in the Old South.* Baton Rouge: Louisiana State University Press, 2000.

Furman, Wood. *History of the Charleston Association of Baptist Churches in the State of South-Carolina; with an appendix containing the principal circular letters to the churches.* Charleston, SC: J. Hoff, 1811.

Gardner, Robert. *Baptists of Early America: A Statistical Study.* Atlanta: Georgia Baptist Historical Society, 1983.

BIBLIOGRAPHY 323

Garrett, James Leo. *Baptist Church Discipline: A Historical Introduction to the Practices of Baptist Churches, with Particular Attention to the Summary of Church Discipline Adopted in 1773 by the Charleston Association.* Paris, AR: Baptist Standard Bearer, 2004.

Genovese, Eugene. *Roll, Jordan, Roll: The World the Slaves Made.* New York: Pantheon Books, 1974.

Gewehr, Wesley M. *The Great Awakening in Virginia, 1740–1790.* Durham, NC: Duke University Press, 1930.

Glasson, Travis. *Mastering Christianity: Missionary Anglicanism and Slavery in the Atlantic World.* New York: Oxford University Press, 2011.

Goen, C. C. *Broken Churches, Broken Nation: Denominational Schisms and the Coming of Civil War.* Macon, GA: Mercer University Press, 1985.

Goen, C. C. *Revivalism and Separatism in New England, 1740–1800.* Middletown, CT: Wesleyan University Press, 1987.

Graves, James Robinson. *Old Landmarkism: What Is It?* Memphis, TN: Baptist Book House, 1880.

Griffiths, Thomas Sharp. *A History of Baptists in New Jersey.* Hightstown, NJ, 1904.

Gronim, Sara S. *Everyday Nature: Knowledge of the Natural World in Colonial New York.* New Brunswick, NJ: Rutgers University Press, 2009.

Guild, Reuben Aldridge. *Early History of Brown University, Including the Life, Times, and Correspondence of President Manning.* Providence, RI, 1897.

Guthman, Joshua. *Strangers Below: Primitive Baptists and American Culture.* Chapel Hill: University of North Carolina Press, 2015.

Hambrick-Stowe, Charles E. *The Practice of Piety: Puritan Devotional Disciplines in Seventeenth-Century New England.* Chapel Hill: University of North Carolina Press, 1982.

Hankins, Barry. *The Second Great Awakening and the Transcendentalists.* Westport, CT: Greenwood Press, 2004.

Hankins, Barry. *Uneasy in Babylon: Southern Baptist Conservatives and American Culture.* Tuscaloosa: University of Alabama Press, 2002.

Hastings, Hugh, ed. *Ecclesiastical Records, State of New York.* Albany, NY, 1901.

Hatch, Nathan O. *The Democratization of American Christianity.* New Haven, CT: Yale University Press, 1989.

Hawkins, Ernest. *Historical Notices of the Missions of the Church of England.* London, 1845.

Heyrman, Christine Leigh. *Southern Cross: The Beginnings of the Bible Belt.* New York: Knopf, 1997.

Hill, Samuel S., ed. *Religion in the Southern States: A Historical Study.* Macon, GA: Mercer University Press, 1983.

Hindmarsh, D. Bruce. *The Evangelical Conversion Narrative: Spiritual Autobiography in the Eighteenth Century.* New York: Oxford University Press, 2005.

Hindmarsh, D. Bruce. *John Newton and the English Evangelical Tradition.* Grand Rapids, MI: Eerdmans, 1996.

Hindmarsh, D. Bruce. *The Spirit of Early Evangelicalism: True Religion in a Modern World.* New York: Oxford University Press, 2018.

Hinds, Hilary. *George Fox and Early Quaker Culture.* Manchester, England: Manchester University Press, 2011.

Hirsch, Arthur Henry. *The Huguenots of Colonia South Carolina.* Durham, NC: Duke University Press, 1928.

324 BIBLIOGRAPHY

Holifield, E. Brooks. *The Gentleman Theologians: American Theology in Southern Culture 1795–1860*. Durham, NC: Duke University Press, 1978.

Holifield, E. Brooks. *Theology in America: Christian Thought from the Age of the Puritans to the Civil War*. New Haven, CT: Yale University Press, 2003.

Holton, Woody. *Unruly Americans and the Origins of the Constitution*. New York: Hill and Wang, 2008.

Hovey, Alvah. *A Memoir of the Life and Times of Isaac Backus*. Boston, 1858.

Howe, Daniel Walker. *What God Hath Wrought: The Transformation of America, 1815–1848*. New York: Oxford University Press, 2009.

Howe, George. *History of the Presbyterian Church in South Carolina*. 2 vols. Columbia, SC: Duffie & Chapman, 1870.

Isaac, Rhys. *The Transformation of Virginia, 1740–1790*. Chapel Hill: University of North Carolina Press, 1982.

James, Charles F., ed. *Documentary History of the Struggle for Religious Liberty in Virginia*. Lynchburg, VA: J. P. Bell, 1900.

Jenkins, Geraint. *Literature, Religion, and Society in Wales, 1660–1773*. Cardiff: University of Wales Press, 1978.

Juster, Susan. *Disorderly Women: Sexual Politics and Evangelicalism in Revolutionary New England*. Ithaca, NY: Cornell University Press, 1994.

Kars, Marjorleine. *Breaking Loose Together: The Regulator Rebellion in Pre-Revolutionary North Carolina*. Chapel Hill: University of North Carolina Press, 2002.

Kidd, Thomas S. *Benjamin Franklin: The Religious Life of a Founding Father*. New Haven, CT: Yale University Press, 2017.

Kidd, Thomas S. *Colonial American History: Clashing Cultures and Faiths*. New Haven, CT: Yale University Press, 2016.

Kidd, Thomas S. *George Whitefield: America's Spiritual Founding Father*. New Haven, CT: Yale University Press, 2014.

Kidd, Thomas S. *God of Liberty: A Religious History of the American Revolution*. New York: Basic Books, 2010.

Kidd, Thomas S. *The Great Awakening: The Roots of Evangelical Christianity in America*. New Haven, CT: Yale University Press, 2007.

Kidd, Thomas S., and Barry G. Hankins. *Baptists in America: A History*. New York: Oxford University Press, 2015.

Krawczynski, Keith. *William Henry Drayton: South Carolina Revolutionary Patriot*. Baton Rouge: Louisiana State University, 2003.

Lambert, Frank. *Inventing the "Great Awakening."* Princeton, NJ: Princeton University Press, 1999.

Lambert, Frank. *"Peddlar in Divinity": George Whitefield and the Transatlantic Revivals, 1737–1770*. Princeton, NJ: Princeton University Press, 1994.

Lemay, J. A. Leo. *Ebenezer Kinnersley, Franklin's Friend*. Philadelphia: University of Pennsylvania Press, 1964.

Lemon, James T. *The Best Poor Man's Country: A Geographical Study of Early Southeastern Pennsylvania*. New York: Norton, 1976.

Lindberg, Carter, ed. *The Pietist Theologians*. New York: Blackwell, 2005.

Lindman, Janet Moore. *Bodies of Belief: Baptist Community in Early America*. Philadelphia: University of Pennsylvania Press, 2008.

Little, Thomas J. *Origins of Southern Evangelicalism: Religious Revivalism in the South Carolina Lowcountry, 1670–1760*. Columbia: University of South Carolina Press, 2013.

## BIBLIOGRAPHY 325

Lumpkin, William L. *Baptist Foundations in the South: Tracing through the Separates the Influence of the Great Awakening, 1754–1787*. Nashville, TN: Broadman Press, 1961.

Maier, Pauline. *Ratification: The People Debate the Constitution, 1787–1788*. New York: Simon and Schuster, 2010.

Manly, Basil. *Mercy and Judgment: A Discourse, Containing Some Fragments of the History of the Baptist Church in Charleston, S.C.* Providence, RI: Knowles, Vose, 1837.

Maring, Norman H. *Baptists in New Jersey: A Study in Transition*. Valley Forge, PA: Judson Press, 1964.

Marsden, George M. *Jonathan Edwards: A Life*. New Haven, CT: Yale University Press, 2003.

Matthews, Donald G. *Religion in the Old South*. Chicago: University of Chicago Press, 1977.

Maxson, Charles Hartshorn. *The Great Awakening in the Middle Colonies*. Chicago: University of Chicago Press, 1920.

McBeth, H. Leon. *The Baptist Heritage: Four Centuries of Baptist Witness*. Nashville, TN: Broadman Press, 1987.

McCurry, Stephanie. *Masters of Small Worlds: Yeoman Households, Gender Relations, and the Political Culture of the Antebellum South Carolina Low Country*. New York: Oxford University Press, 1995.

McKibbens, Thomas R., and Kenneth L. Smith. *The Life and Works of Morgan Edwards*. New York: Arno Press, 1980.

McLoughlin, William G. *Isaac Backus and the American Pietistic Tradition*. Boston: Little, Brown, 1967.

McLoughlin, William G. *New England Dissent, 1630–1833: The Baptists and the Separation of Church and State*. 2 vols. Cambridge, MA: Harvard University Press, 1971.

Miller, Randall M. *"A Warm and Zealous Spirit": John J. Zubly and the American Revolution. A Selection of His Writings*. Macon, GA: Mercer University Press, 1982.

Moore, Peter N. *Archibald Simpson's Unpeaceable Kingdom: The Ordeal of Evangelicalism in the Colonial South*. London: Lexington Books, 2018.

Mulder, Philip N. *A Controversial Spirit: Evangelical Awakenings in the South*. New York: Oxford University Press, 2002.

Music, David W., and Paul Akes Richardson. *"I Will Sing the Wondrous Story": A History of Baptist Hymnody in North America*. Macon, GA: Mercer University Press, 2008.

Myers, Robert Manson. *The Children of Pride: A True Story of Georgia and the Civil War*. New Haven, CT: Yale University Press, 1972.

Nash, Gary B. *Forging Freedom: The Formation of Philadelphia's Black Community, 1720–1840*. Cambridge, MA: Harvard University Press, 1988.

Nelson, John K. *A Blessed Company: Parishes, Parsons, and Parishioners in Anglican Virginia, 1690–1776*. Chapel Hill: University of North Carolina Press, 2003.

Nettles, Tom J. *The Baptists: Key People Involved in Forming a Baptist Identity. Beginnings in America*. Fearn, Scotland: Christian Focus, 2005.

Nettles, Tom J. *James Petigru Boyce: A Southern Baptist Statesman*. Philipsburg, NJ: Presbyterian & Reformed, 2009.

Noll, Mark. *America's God: From Jonathan Edwards to Abraham Lincoln*. New York: Oxford University Press, 2002.

Noll, Mark. *The Rise of Evangelicalism: The Age of Edwards, Whitefield, and the Wesleys*. Downers Grove, IL: IVP Academic, 2010.

## 326 BIBLIOGRAPHY

Olwell, Robert. *Masters, Slaves and Subjects: The Culture of Power in the South Carolina Lowcountry, 1740–1790*. Ithaca, NY: Cornell University Press, 1998.

Owens, Loulie Latimer. *Oliver Hart, 1723–1795: A Biography*. Greenville: South Carolina Baptist Historical Society, 1966.

Packer, J. I. *A Quest for Godliness: The Puritan Vision of the Christian Life*. Wheaton, IL: Crossway, 1991.

Pascoe, C. F. *Two Hundred Years of the S.P.G.: An Historical Account of the Society for the Propagation of the Gospel in Foreign Parts, 1701–1900*. London, 1901.

Patterson, James A. *James Robinson Graves: Staking the Boundaries of Baptist Identity*. Nashville, TN: B&H Academic, 2012.

Pinckney, Elise, ed. *The Letterbook of Eliza Lucas Pinckney, 1739–1762*. Columbia: University of South Carolina Press, 1997.

Queen, Edward L., II. *In the South Baptists Are the Center of Gravity*. Brooklyn, NY: Carlson, 1991.

Ragosta, John A. *Wellspring of Liberty: How Virginia's Religious Dissenters Helped Win the American Revolution and Secured Religious Liberty*. New York: Oxford University Press, 2010.

Ramsay, David. *The History of South Carolina, from its first settlement in 1670, to the year 1808*. Charleston, SC: David Longworth, 1809.

Ranck, George Washington. *"The Travelling Church": An Account of the Baptist Exodus from Virginia to Kentucky in 1781*. Louisville, KY, 1910.

Rogers, George C. *Charleston in the Age of the Pinckneys*. Columbia: University of South Carolina Press, 1980.

Rogers, James A. *Richard Furman: Life and Legacy*. Macon, GA: Mercer University Press, 2001.

Ryken, Leland. *Worldly Saints: The Puritans as They Really Were*. Grand Rapids, MI: Zondervan, 1986.

Salley, Samuel. *The History of Orange County, South Caroline*. Orangeburg, SC: R. L. Berry, 1898.

Schmidt, Leigh Eric. *Holy Fairs: Scotland and the Making of American Revivalism*. Grand Rapids, MI: Eerdmans, 2001.

Schwartz, Sally. *"A Mixed Multitude": The Struggle for Toleration in Colonial Pennsylvania*. New York: New York University Press, 1982.

Semple, Robert Baylor. *A History of the Rise and Progress of the Baptists in Virginia*. Richmond, VA: Pitt and Dickinson, 1894.

Shipp, Albert Micajah. *The History of Methodism in South Carolina*. Nashville, TN: Southern Methodist Publishing House, 1834.

Shurden, Walter B. *Not an Easy Journey: Some Transitions in Baptist Life*. Macon, GA: Mercer University Press, 2005.

Shurden, Walter B. *Not a Silent People: Controversies That Have Shaped Southern Baptists*. Macon, GA: Smyth & Helwys, 1972.

Simmons, William S., and Cheryl L. Simmons, eds. *Old Light on Separate Ways: The Narragansett Diary of Joseph Fish, 1765–1776*. Hanover, NH: University Press of New England, 1982.

Smith, Eric C. *Order and Ardor: The Revival Spirituality of Oliver Hart and the Regular Baptists of Eighteenth-Century South Carolina*. Columbia: University of South Carolina Press, 2018.

## BIBLIOGRAPHY 327

Smith, Merril D. *Breaking the Bonds: Marital Discord in Pennsylvania, 1730–1830.* New York: New York University Press, 1991.

Smith, Samuel C. *A Cautious Enthusiasm: Mystical Piety and Evangelicalism in Colonial South Carolina.* Columbia: University of South Carolina Press, 2013.

Sobel, Michael. *Trabelin' On: The Slave Journey to an Afro-Baptist Faith.* Westport, CT: Greenwood Press, 1979.

Spain, Rufus. *At Ease in Zion: A Social History of Southern Baptists, 1865–1900.* Tuscaloosa: University of Alabama Press, 2003.

Sparks, John. *The Roots of Appalachian Christianity: The Life and Legacy of Elder Shubal Stearns.* Lexington: University Press of Kentucky, 2005.

Spencer, David. *The Early Baptists of Philadelphia.* Philadelphia, PA, 1877.

Sprague, William B. *Annals of the American Baptist Pulpit.* New York: Robert Carter & Brothers, 1860.

Stein, Stephen. *The Shaker Experience in America.* New Haven, CT: Yale University Press, 1992.

Stewart, I. D. *The History of the Freewill Baptists.* Dover, NH, 1862.

Stout, Harry S. *The Divine Dramatist: George Whitefield and the Rise of Modern Evangelicalism.* Grand Rapids, MI: Eerdmans, 1991.

Stout, Harry S. *The New England Soul: Preaching and Religious Culture in Colonial New England.* New York: Oxford University Press, 1986.

Sutton, Robert P. *Communical Utopias and the American Experience: Religious Communities, 1732–2000.* Westport, CT: Praeger, 2003.

Sweeney, Douglas A., and Allen C. Guelzo, eds. *The New England Theology: From Jonathan Edwards to Edwards Amasa Park.* Grand Rapids, MI: Baker Academic, 2006.

Sweet, William Waren, ed. *Religion on the American Frontier: The Baptists, 1783–1830.* New York: Henry Holt, 1931.

Talbert, Roy, Jr., and Meggan A. Farish. *The Antipedo Baptists of Georgetown, South Carolina, 1710–2010.* Columbia: University of South Carolina Press, 2013.

Thom, William Taylor. *The Struggle for Religious Freedom in Virginia: The Baptists.* Baltimore, MD, 1900.

Thomas, George. *The Founders and the Idea of a National University: Constituting the American Mind.* New York: Cambridge University Press, 2015.

Torbet, Robert G. *A History of the Baptists.* Rev. ed. Valley Forge, PA: Judson Press, 1963.

Townsend, Leah. *South Carolina Baptists, 1670–1805.* Baltimore, MD: Clearfield, 2003.

Tupper, H. A., ed. *Two Centuries of the First Baptist Church of South Carolina, 1683–1883.* Baltimore, MD: R. H. Woodward, 1889.

Turner, Edward Raymond. *The Negro in Pennsylvania: Slavery—Servitude—Freedom 1639–1861.* Washington, DC, 1911.

Tyler, Moses Coit. *The Literary History of the American Revolution, 1763–1783.* New York, 1897.

Ward, William R. *Early Evangelicalism: A Global Intellectual History, 1670–1789.* New York: Cambridge University Press, 2006.

Ward, William R. *The Protestant Evangelical Awakening.* New York: Cambridge University Press, 1992.

Weir, Robert M. *Colonial South Carolina: A History.* Columbia: University of South Carolina Press, 2007.

Wigger, John H. *American Saint: Francis Asbury and the Methodists.* New York: Oxford University Press, 2009.

328 BIBLIOGRAPHY

Wigger, John H. *Taking Heaven by Storm: Methodism and the Rise of Popular Christianity in America*. New York: Oxford University Press, 1998.

Wills, Gregory A. *Democratic Religion: Freedom, Authority, and Church Discipline in the Baptist South, 1785–1900*. New York: Oxford University Press, 1998.

Wills, Gregory A. *Southern Baptist Theological Seminary, 1859–2009*. New York: Oxford University Press, 2009.

Winiarski, Douglas L. *Darkness Falls on the Land of Light: Experiencing Religious Awakenings in Eighteenth-Century New England*. Chapel Hill: University of North Carolina Press, 2017.

Witzig, Fred E. *Sanctifying Slavery and Politics in South Carolina: The Life of the Reverend Alexander Garden*. Columbia: University of South Carolina Press, 2018.

Wolever, Terry. *The Life and Ministry of John Gano, 1727–1804*. Springfield, MO: Particular Baptist Press, 1998.

Wood, Gordon S. *The Creation of the American Republic, 1776–1787*. Chapel Hill: University of North Carolina Press, 1998.

Wood, Peter H. *Black Majority: Negroes in Colonial South Carolina from 1670 through the Stono Rebellion*. New York: Norton, 1996.

Yeager, Jonathan M., ed. *Early Evangelicalism: A Reader*. New York: Oxford University Press, 2013.

Young, Charles Raymond, ed. *Westward into Kentucky: The Narrative of Daniel Trabue*. Lexington: University Press of Kentucky, 2004.

Young, Jeffrey Robert. *Domesticating Slavery: The Master Class in Georgia and South Carolina, 1670–1837*. Chapel Hill: University of North Carolina Press, 2005.

## Secondary Sources: Articles and Book Chapters

Allen, Wm. Loyd. "The Peculiar Welsh Piety of *The Customs of Primitive Churches*." In *Distinctively Baptist: A Festschrift in Honor of Walter B. Shurden*, edited by Marc A. Jolley, 171–92. Macon, GA: Mercer University Press, 2005.

*The Baptist Magazine for 1815*. Vol. 7. London, 1815.

Brackney, William H. "James Manning (1738–1791)." In vol. 3 of *A Noble Company: Biographical Essays on Notable Particular-Regular Baptists in America*, edited by Terry Wolever, 511–38. Springfield, MO: Particular Baptist Press, 2013.

Burrage, Henry S. "The Baptist Church in Kittery." *Collections and Proceedings of the Maine Historical Society*, 2nd ser., 9 (1898): 382–91.

Burrage, Henry S. "Memoir of William Screven." *Collections and Proceedings of the Maine Historical Society*, 2nd ser., 1 (1889): 45–56.

Burrage, Henry S. "Some Added Facts concerning William Screven." *Collections and Proceedings of the Maine Historical Society*, 2nd ser., 5 (1894): 275–84.

Butler, Jon. "Enthusiasm Described and Decried: The Great Awakening as Interpretative Fiction." *Journal of American History* 69, no. 2 (September 1982): 305–25.

Butler, Jon. "Gospel Order Improved: The Keithian Schism and the Exercise of Quaker Ministerial Authority." *William & Mary Quarterly* 31, no. 3 (July 1974): 431–52.

Butterfield, L. H. "Elder John Leland, Jeffersonian Itinerant." *American Antiquarian Society Proceedings* 62 (1952): 155–242.

## BIBLIOGRAPHY 329

Clayton, J. Glenwood, and Loulie Latimer Owens, eds. "Oliver Hart's Diary of the Journey to the Backcountry." *Journal of the South Carolina Baptist Historical Society* 1 (November 1975): 2–17.

Dowling, John. "Rev. Thomas Paul and the Colored Baptist Churches." *Baptist Memorial and Monthly Record* 8 (1849): 295–99.

Dunaway, Wayland F. "Early Welsh Settlers of Pennsylvania." *Pennsylvania History* 12, no. 4 (October 1945): 251–69.

Fea, John. "Samuel Finley versus Abel Morgan: Revivalism, Denominational Identity, and an Eighteenth-Century Sacramental Debate in Cape May, New Jersey." *New Jersey History* 117, nos. 3–4 (Fall–Winter 1999): 24–45.

Feight, Andrew Lee. "Edmund Botsford and Richard Furman: Slavery in the South Carolina Lowcountry, 1766–1825." *Journal of the South Carolina Baptist Historical Society* 19 (November 1993): 2–22.

Finn, Nathan A. "The Making of a Baptist Universalist: The Curious Case of Elhanan Winchester." Paper presented to the Baptist Studies Group at the Evangelical Theological Society, San Francisco, 2011.

Harkness, R. E. E. "Early Relations of Baptists and Quakers." *Church History* 2 (December 1933): 227–42.

Haykin, Michael A. G. "'His Soul-Refreshing Presence': The Lord's Supper in Baptist Thought and Experience in the 'Long' Eighteenth Century." In *Baptist Sacramentalism*, edited by Anthony R. Cross, 177–93. Waynesboro, GA: Paternoster Press, 2003.

Jackson, Harvey H. "Hugh Bryan and the Evangelical Movement in Colonial South Carolina." *William and Mary Quarterly* 43, no. 4 (1986): 594–614.

Johnson, Theodore, ed. "Biographical Account of the Life, Character, & Ministry of Father Joseph Meacham . . . by Calvin Green, 1827." *Shaker Quarterly* 10 (1970): 20–32.

Johnson, Walter E. "Isaac Eaton (1725?–1772)." In vol. 3 of *A Noble Company: Biographical Essays on Notable Particular-Regular Baptists in America*, edited by Terry Wolever, 217–33. Springfield, MO: Particular Baptist Press, 2013.

Kegley, Sarah E., and Thomas J. Little, "The Records of the Ashley River Baptist Church, 1736–1769." *Journal of the South Carolina Baptist Historical Society* 27 (November 2001): 3–32.

Landsman, Ned. "Revivalism and Nativism in the Middle Colonies: The Great Awakening and the Scots Community in East New Jersey." *American Quarterly* 34 (1982): 149–64.

Lebeau, Bryan F. "The Acrimonious, Controversial Spirit among Baptists and Presbyterians in the Middle Colonies during the Great Awakening." *American Baptist Quarterly* 9 (September 1990): 167–83.

Levy, Barry. "'Tender Plants': Quaker Families and Children in the Delaware Valley, 1681–1735." *Journal of Family History* 3 (Summer 1978): 116–35.

Lockley, Tim. "David Margrett: A Black Missionary in the Revolutionary Atlantic." *Journal of American Studies* 46, no. 3 (2012): 729–45.

Lodge, Martin E. "The Crisis of the Churches in the Middle Colonies, 1720–1750." *PMHB* 95 (April 1971): 195–220.

May, Cedrick. "John Marrant and the Narrative Construction of an Early Black Methodist Evangelist." *African American Review* 38, no. 4 (Winter 2004): 553–70.

McKibbens, Thomas R. "Over Troubled Waters: Baptist Preachers Who Were Bridge Builders." *Baptist History and Heritage* 40, no. 2 (Spring 2005): 58–63.

Owens, Loulie Latimer. "Oliver Hart and the American Revolution." *Journal of the South Carolina Baptist Historical Society* 1 (November 1975): 2–17.

## 330 BIBLIOGRAPHY

Owens, Loulie Latimer "South Carolina Baptists and the American Revolution." *Journal of the South Carolina Baptist Historical Society* 1 (November 1975): 31–45.

Pennsylvania Historical and Museum Commission. "Southeastern Pennsylvania Historic Agricultural Region, c. 1750–1960." http://www.phmc.state.pa.us/portal/communities/agriculture/files/context/southeastern_pennsylvania.pdf.

Ray, Thomas. "Jenkin Jones (c. 1686–1760)." In vol. 2 of *A Noble Company: Biographical Essays on Notable Particular-Regular Baptists in America*, edited by Terry Wolever, 179–212. Springfield, MO: Particular Baptist Press, 2006.

Salliant, John. "'Wipe Away All Tears from Their Eyes': John Marrant's Theology in the Black Atlantic, 1785–1808." *Journal of Millennial Studies* 1, no. 2 (Winter 1999): 1–23. http://www.mille.org/publications/winter98/saillant.PDF.

Scarberry. Mark S. "John Leland and James Madison: Religious Influence on the Ratification of the Constitution and on the Proposal of the Bill of Rights." *Penn State Law Review* 113, no. 3 (April 2009): 733–800. https://ssrn.com/abstract=1262520.

Shurden, Walter B. "The Southern Baptist Synthesis: Is It Cracking?" *Baptist History and Heritage* 16, no. 2 (April 1981): 2–11.

Smith, Preserved. "Chronicles of a New England Family." *New England Quarterly* 9 (September 1936): 417–46.

"South Carolina Just before the Revolution." *Southern Literary Messenger* 11 (1845): 139.

Stout, Harry S. "Religion, Communications, and the Ideological Origins of the American Revolution." *William & Mary Quarterly* 3rd ser., 34, no. 4 (October 1977): 519–44.

Tully, Alan. "Patterns of Slaveholding in Colonial Pennsylvania: Chester and Lancaster Counties 1729–1758." *Journal of Social History* 6, no. 3 (Spring 1973): 284–305.

Walsh, John. "Religious Societies: Methodist and Evangelical 1738–1800." In *Voluntary Religion*, edited by W. J. Sheils and Dianna Wood, Studies in Church History, 279–302. New York: Oxford University Press, 1986.

Wills, Gregory A. "From Congregationalist to Baptist: Judson and Baptism." In *Adoniram Judson: A Bicentennial Appreciation of the Pioneer American Missionary*, edited by Jason G. Duesing, 149–66. Nashville, TN: B&H Academic, 2012.

Wood, Peter H. "'Jesus Christ Has Got Thee at Last': Afro-American Conversion as a Forgotten Chapter in Eighteenth-Century Southern Intellectual History." *Bulletin of the Center for the Study of Southern Culture and Religion* 3, no. 3 (November 1979): 1–7.

Wood, Peter H. "Slave Labor Camps in Early America: Overcoming Denial and Discovering the Gulag." In *Inequality in Early America*, edited by Carla Gardina Pestana and Sharon V. Salinger, 222–38. Hanover, NH: University Presses of New England, 1999.

Zuckerman Michael. "Introduction: Puritans, Cavaliers, and the Motley Middle." In *Friends and Neighbors: Group Life in America's First Plural Society*, edited by Michael Zuckerman, 3–25. Philadelphia, PA: Temple University Press, 1982.

# Index

*For the benefit of digital users, indexed terms that span two pages (e.g., 52–53) may, on occasion, appear on only one of those pages.*

African American Baptists
  and the Great Awakening, 46–48
  and church membership,
    177–78, 179–80
  conversion testimony of, 46–48,
    133–37, 274
  growth of, 304–5
  leadership of, 97–100, 274, 285–86
  reciprocal effect on white Baptists,
    118, 274
  separation from white Baptist churches,
    168–69, 179–80, 264, 285–86
  *See also* African American Baptists;
    George, David; Hart, Oliver; Liele,
    George; Mageay, Margaret; Margarett,
    David; Marrant, John; paternalism;
    Southern Baptist Convention
American exceptionalism, 239–40, 280–84
American Revolution
  and Baptists in middle
    colonies, 225–26
  and Baptist wartime ministry, 240–42
  Carolina Back Country
    mission, 228–34
  and evangelical language, 230–32
  hardships of, 243–44, 252–59
  invasion of Charleston, 1–3, 244–47
  and New England Baptists, 223–25, 235
  and religious liberty, 223–25, 235–39
  and South Carolina Baptists, 228–48
  and union of Regular and Separate
    Baptists, 237–39
  and Virginia Baptists, 226–28
Anglicans, 11–12, 28, 40–42, 45–46, 78–79,
    90–91, 93–95, 100–1, 106, 114, 191–92,
    207–8, 226–27, 235–36
Arminianism, 50–51, 74–75, 89–90, 217–18.
  *See also* General Baptists

Ashley Ferry Baptist Church (South
    Carolina), 44–45, 74–75, 80, 118
assurance of salvation, 24–25,
    83–84, 136–38
atonement. *See* death of Christ
awakenings. *See* conversion; Evangelicalism;
    First Great Awakening; Hart, Oliver;
    Second Great Awakening; visions;
    Whitefield, George

Backcountry (South Carolina), 110, 113–
    20, 188, 190–98, 214–15, 228–34
Backus, Isaac, 2–3, 35, 49–50, 58, 223–25,
    235, 237–38, 261–62, 264, 267–68,
    279, 290, 293–94
Baker, Desolate. *See* Loveall, Henry
Baldwin, Thomas, 168–70
baptism. *See* believer's baptism; infant
    baptism
Baptist growth and sophistication 3–5,
    11–12, 32, 57–58, 123–24, 145–48,
    167–71, 184–90, 287–88, 304–6
Bedgegood, Nicholas, 149, 154, 160–64
Beissel, Conrad 28–29, 35–36
believer's baptism
  conversion and, 85, 99, 116–17, 130–31,
    170–71, 174–75, 215, 219
  as defining practice of Baptists, 11,
    17–18, 28, 30–31, 56, 58, 59–60, 146,
    191–92, 246–47, 295
  descriptions of the practice, 55–56, 143,
    170, 246–47, 301–2
  despite ice in the river, 298
  as difficult choice, 11, 208, 211–12, 307–8
  mockery of, 22–23, 26–27,
    191–92, 304–5
  regulation of, 30–31, 59–60, 62–63,
    142–43, 215, 275

332 INDEX

Bible
authority of, 58, 216
impulsive verses, 134–36, 195
preaching of, 23–25, 68–70, 80–83, 133
private reading of, 83–84, 132
Blair, James, 106
Boston, Massachusetts
First Baptist Church of, 50–51, 71–72, 161–62, 167–71, 223
Second Baptist Church of, 50–51
and Stamp Act, 222–23
Botsford, Edmund, 101–2, 163–67, 171, 179, 205–6, 211–12, 246–48, 274–75, 277–78, 286–87, 293–94, 300–2
Boyce, James P., 82n8, 313
Bryan, Hugh, 88–89, 93–94, 100–1
Butler, Jon, 106, 123–24, 127–28n8, 231–32n31

Callender, Elisha, 50–51
Calvinism
Baptist commitment to, 7–8, 23, 89–90, 173–74, 178–79, 193–94, 217–18, 268–69, 306–7, 313
challenges to, 12–13, 74–75, 167–68, 263–69
covenant of grace, 24–25, 156–57, 163, 268–69
New Divinity modifications of, 268, 290–91
and original sin, 14–15, 24–25, 33–34, 139, 211–12, 215, 240
See also Particular Baptists; Regular Baptists; Separate Baptists
Cashaway Church (South Carolina), 152, 154–55, 176, 181, 182
catholicity. See ecumenism
Chanler, Isaac, 44–45, 53–54, 56, 74–75, 79, 108–9, 110, 183–84
Charleston Association of Baptists
and Charleston Confession, 122–23, 173–74, 184, 306–7, 313
correspondence with other associations, 121–22, 215–16, 235
disciplinary actions of, 162, 232–33, 237
and education, 122–23, 151–52, 187–88
founding of, 9, 105–13

growth and development of, 120, 121–24, 173, 198, 237–39, 286–87, 307
and missions, 113–20
and Summary of Church Discipline, 173, 174–84
Charleston (First) Baptist Church
attempts to recall Hart after war, 271–74
effort to supplant Hart as pastor, 160–62
founding of, 70–74
Hart's weekly ministry in, 80–87
years of decline preceding Hart's arrival, 74–76, 79
Charleston Confession. See Charleston Association of Baptists
Charleston, South Carolina, 1–2, 44–45, 77–79, 86–87, 88–98, 102–3, 106, 199–200, 202, 244–46
"Charleston Tradition," 52, 104
Church Covenant, 18–19, 55, 58–59, 175–76, 178, 180, 209
church discipline, 18–20, 22–23, 49, 59–60, 61, 177–84, 209, 313–14
Church of England. See Anglicans
Clarke, Richard, 90
College of Rhode Island (Brown University), 2–3, 122–23, 169, 184–90, 205, 212–13, 247–48, 283–84, 290–91
communion. See Lord's Supper
Condy, Jeremiah, 50–51, 53, 104, 162, 167–68, 170–71, 184–85, 186, 187
confessions of faith. See Charleston Confession; London Baptist Confession(1689); Regular Baptists; Separate Baptists
Congaree Church (South Carolina), 121–22, 197–98, 214–16, 230–31
Congregationalists, 11–12, 33–34, 51, 61, 68, 72–73, 80–81, 128–29, 130, 134–35, 146, 150, 170, 184–87, 223–25, 226, 288–89, 302–3
Constitution of the United States, 169, 235, 278–80, 281–82
conversion
and assurance of salvation, 136–37
doctrine of, 18, 33–34, 47, 51–52, 68–69, 217–18, 259–60

experiences of, 37, 39, 43–45, 85, 119, 139–40, 163–65, 195–96, 199–200, 219–20, 264–65, 266, 298

testimonies of, 46–47, 51–52, 117–18, 134–38, 206–7

*See also* revivals

Cox, Nicholas, 291–92

Cross of Christ. *See* death of Christ

dancing, 95, 177–78, 183, 194–95, 241–42, 267–68, 313–14

Davies, Samuel, 157–58

deacon and deaconess, 22–23, 61–62, 66–67, 154–55, 252–53, 298

death of Christ, 21–22, 24–26, 37, 52, 53–54, 85–86, 163, 178–79, 195, 268–69, 290–91

devil and demons, 28–29, 141–42, 195–96, 199–200, 255–56, 289–90

diary keeping, 83–84, 125–27, 165, 190–91, 230, 233, 251–52, 255–56

disestablishment. *See* religious liberty

Drayton, William Henry, 229–34

Eaton, Isaac, 67–68, 69–70, 153, 249–50, 274–75

ecumenism, 5–6, 26–28, 41–42, 49–50, 56–57, 88–92, 186, 294–95

Edisto Baptist Church (South Carolina), 75, 144, 153–54

education, 32, 65, 75–76, 122–23, 151–52, 167, 184–90, 211, 212–14, 287–88, 306–7, 313. *See also specific institutions and organizations*

Edwards, Jonathan, 33–34, 130–31, 133–37, 141–42, 288–91, 302–3

Edwards, Morgan, 16–17, 25, 59–60, 61–62, 68, 73–74, 144, 145, 147, 185–88, 193–94, 205–6, 209, 214–16, 225–26, 232–33

egalitarianism, 13–14, 46–48, 49, 60–62, 133–38, 177–80, 202–11, 266–68, 313–14

election. *See* Calvinism

enlightenment, 58–59, 136–37, 155–56, 230–31, 240

enthusiasm. *See* First Great Awakening; visions

Ephrata Cloister, 28–29, 35–36

Euhaw Baptist Church (South Carolina), 75, 105, 108–9, 110, 144, 211–12, 221, 287–88

evangelicalism and Baptist movement, 33–54, 56–64, 87–92, 136–37, 143–48, 157–58, 199–201, 246–47, 294–95. *See also* conversion; revivals

evangelism, 36–37, 40–45, 88, 100–1, 113–21, 153–54, 190–96, 199–201, 211–12, 259–61, 274, 307

excommunication. *See* church discipline

faith. *See* conversion

Federalists, 278–82

Finley, Samuel, 37–38, 57, 91–92

First Great Awakening

and 1754 Charleston Baptist youth revival, 125–48

and birth of Separate Baptists, 35, 51, 53

effects on American Baptists, 53–54

origins in middle colonies, 35–44

persistence of throughout eighteenth century, 127–28, 143–48, 274

spectrum of participation, 3–6, 47–48, 51, 53, 61–62, 64, 93–95, 104, 146–48, 266–68

*See also* conversion; evangelicalism; revivals; Hart, Oliver; Whitefield, George

Fleetwood, William, 100–1

Fletchall, Col. Thomas, 233–34

foot washing, 25–26, 219, 263

foreign missions. *See* missions; Triennial Convention

Fox, George, 12–13, 47, 50–51

Free Will Baptists, 3–4, 7–8, 266

Frelinghuysen, Theodorus, 36–38, 42–43

friendship, 9, 66, 157, 159–60, 167, 207, 214, 219, 220–21, 299–303

Furman, Richard, 1, 8, 11, 35, 64–65, 95–96, 102–4, 121–22, 166–67, 188–89, 214–16, 228, 236, 237–39, 272–74, 286–88, 294, 299–303, 306–13

Gano, John, 91, 116–22, 151–52, 153, 188, 205–6, 217–18, 242, 257–58, 275–76, 285–86, 306–7

gender. *See* women

334  INDEX

General Baptists, 30, 73–75, 116–17
George, David, 99
Georgia, colonial Baptist activity in, 98–100,
    121, 149, 162–63, 177–78, 188–89,
    212–13, 217–18, 309–10
Gill, John, 50–51, 68, 173–74n3, 174,
    185–86, 187–88
Great Awakening. *See* First Great
    Awakening; Second Great
    Awakening

Hart, Ann ("Nancy") Marie Sealy
    Grimball (Oliver's second wife),
    219–20, 230, 244–46, 252–58
Hart, John (Oliver's grandfather), 12–17
Hart, John (signer of Declaration of
    Independence), 250–51
Hart, John (Oliver's son), 230, 243–44
Hart, Oliver
    and 1754 Charleston youth
        revival, 125–48
    baptism of, 55–56
    Baptist precisionism of, 173–84, 294–95
    bridge-building with Separate Baptists,
        197–98, 214–21, 237–39
    call to ministry of, 66–77
    conversion of, 51–52
    death of, 303–4
    description of, 64–66
    ecumenism of, 88–92, 294–95
    flight from Charleston, 1–3, 245–48
    itinerant ministry of, 87–88, 150,
        166, 190–98
    leadership in Charleston Association,
        105–6, 108–24
    legacy of, 5–8, 313–15
    mentoring of young leaders, 149–71
    ministry in New York City, 275–76
    old age of, 276–78
    participation in American Revolution,
        1–2, 222–48
    pastoral ministry of, 80–87,
        125–48, 259–61
    piety of, 8, 23–26, 83–84, 125–48
    poetry of, 51–52, 65–66, 277
    politics of, 230–40, 278–84
    preaching of, 68–70, 80–83, 132–33,
        192, 230–31, 259–60, 284

and slavery, 9–22, 95–103, 166–67, 204,
    295–98, 309–14
    theology of, 23–26, 68, 89–90,
        155–57, 288–95
Hart, Sarah Brees (Oliver's first wife), 70,
    76–77, 201–11
Heyrman, Christina Leigh, 63–64n24, 95–96,
    102–3, 209
Holy Spirit. *See* conversion; revivals;
    visions
Hopewell Academy (New Jersey), 153–55,
    157, 185, 249–52, 259–63, 271–72,
    274–75, 299–300
Hopewell Baptist Church (New Jersey),
    30–31, 116–18
Hutson, William, 88–89

immersion. *See* baptism
Indians. *See* Native Americans
individualism, 58–60, 62–63
infant baptism, 18, 28, 56, 130–31, 146,
    149, 246–47, 294–95, 307–8
Ireland, James, 277

James, Philip, 105, 108–9, 144–45
Jones, Jenkin, 23–26, 39, 41–42, 43–44,
    48–49, 55–56, 57–58, 66–67, 87–88,
    150, 201
Jones, Samuel, 153–57, 158–59, 160, 162,
    171, 186–87, 201, 277–78, 305–6
Judson, Adoniram and Ann, 307–9

Keach, Elias, 16, 31–32, 174
Keithianism, 14–17, 20–22
Kentucky, Baptists in, 217–18, 275, 284–86,
    302–3, 313
Ketocton Association of Baptists
    (Virginia), 215–16, 237, 309–10
Kidd, Thomas, 47–48
Kinnersley, Ebenezer, 48–49, 53,
    104, 184–85

Landmark Baptists, 91–92,
    174–75, 313–14
laying on of hands, 25, 30, 74, 173–74,
    196, 263n50
Leland, John 2–3, 64, 194, 216, 247, 261,
    279, 309–10

INDEX 335

letter writing, 158–60, 299–300
Liele, George, 98–100, 261
London Baptist Confession of Faith
    (1689), 23–25, 30, 73–74, 156–57,
    173–74, 216, 290–91
Lord's Supper, 25–26, 45–46, 49, 50–51,
    56, 57–58, 85–86, 128–30, 142–43,
    196, 211–12, 214, 217, 260–61, 263,
    291–92, 298, 299–300, 302–3
love feasts, 25–26, 196
Loveall, Henry, 31–32, 119
Lumpkin, William, 104, 127–28n9

Mageay, Margaret, 101–2, 133–39,
    142–43, 206–7
Maine, Baptist origins in, 70–72
Manly, Basil Jr., 313
Manly, Basil Sr., 74, 75, 79, 95–96, 102–4,
    307, 311–13
Manning, James, 157–59, 161, 171,
    185–89, 201, 212–14, 267–68,
    290–91, 295–96
Margarett, David, 99–100
Marrant, John 199–201
Marshall, Daniel, 61–62, 147,
    193–94, 217–19
Marshall, Martha, 61–62, 147
Massachusetts, Baptists in, 2–3, 58, 70–73,
    146, 154, 167–71, 222–25, 235, 261–62,
    267–68, 279, 284–85
Maxcy, Jonathan, 283–84, 290–91, 307
McAden, Hugh, 114–15, 120
McCoy, Isaac, 309
Methodists, 40, 53, 62–63, 89–90,
    91–92, 120, 124, 174–75, 183–84,
    191–92, 200–1, 207–8, 293–94,
    295, 305–6, 309–10. See also Joseph
    Pilmoor
missions, 87–88, 113–20, 145–46,
    190–98, 307–9, 313. See also Judson,
    Adoniram and Ann; McCoy, Isaac;
    Southern Baptist Convention;
    Triennial Convention
moderate evangelicalism, 5–6, 47–48,
    64, 80–104, 110, 135–36, 140–42,
    147–48, 167, 171, 189, 211, 217, 241,
    296–97, 307–8, 310–11
Morgan, Abel, Jr., 46–48, 57

Mulkey, Philip, 193–96, 215–16, 217–18,
    232–33, 237
mysticism. See Ephrata Cloister; visions

Native Americans, 31–32, 71–72, 99,
    113–16, 196–97, 200–1,
    243, 309
new birth. See conversion
New Divinity theology, 268, 290–91
New Testament. See Bible
Noll, Mark, 6–7, 301
North Carolina, Baptist activity in, 117–20,
    145–46, 147, 184, 193–98, 215–16, 228

Particular Baptists
    basic beliefs and practices, 17–27, 55–56,
        80–84, 217
    and the Great Awakening, 41–54, 56–61
    "regular call" to ministry, 62–64, 66–70,
        76, 149–50
    See also Philadelphia Association of
        Baptists; Regular Baptists; specific
        individuals and churches
paternalism, 101–2, 204, 311
Paul (apostle), 33, 60, 61–62, 82–83, 117–18,
    151–52, 303–4
Pedobaptism. See infant baptism
Pelot, Francis, 101–2, 105, 108–9, 110, 144,
    150, 151, 174, 184–85, 188, 211–12,
    220–21, 244–45
Penn, William, 13–15, 26–27
Pennepek Baptist Church (Pennsylvania),
    15–20, 22–26, 29–30, 39, 41–42, 43–
    44, 48–49, 55–56, 154–55, 162
Pennsylvania Baptists. See Keithianism;
    Penn, William; Pennepek Baptist
    Church (Pennsylvania); Philadelphia
    Association of Baptists
Persecution of Baptists. See religious liberty
Philadelphia Association of Baptists
    and American Revolution (see
        American Revolution)
    and education (see College of Rhode
        Island)
    founding, 29–32, 108
    and the Great Awakening, 41–54, 56–64
    influence on the South (see Charleston
        Association of Baptists)

336   INDEX

Philadelphia Confession. *See* London
  Baptist Confession (1689)
Pilmoor, Joseph, 8, 89–90, 293
Pinckney, Eliza Lucas, 77–78, 94–95,
  203–4, 205
Presbyterians, 27–28
Protestant Reformation. *See* reformation
Pugh, Evan, 121–22, 151–52, 154, 158–59,
  166, 172–74, 190–92, 197–98, 205–6,
  215, 219, 246, 294
Puritans, 33–34, 68–69, 71–72,
  80–84, 136–37, 163–64, 241,
  253–54, 280–81

Quakers, 20–22

race. *See* African American Baptists;
  paternalism; slavery
Randall, Benjamin, 3–4, 266
Reese, Joseph, 230–31
Reformed Baptists. *See* Particular
  Baptists
Regular Baptists
  distinctions from and union with
    Separate Baptists, 52–53, 147–48,
    197–98, 215–19, 237–39, 273–
    74, 306–7 (*see also* "Charleston
    Tradition;" Particular Baptists;
    *specific individuals, churches, and
    associations*)
religious liberty. *See* American Revolution;
  Backus, Isaac
revivals. *See* conversion; evangelicalism;
  First Great Awakening; Hart, Oliver;
  Second Great Awakening; visions;
  Whitefield, George
Revolutionary War. *See* American
  Revolution
Rhode Island, Baptists in, 71. *See also*
  College of Rhode Island
Richardson, William, 116, 120, 192–93
Rogers, William, 82, 101–2, 188–89, 225,
  247–48, 249, 257–58, 262–63, 268–69,
  289–90, 296–97, 303
Roman Catholic Church, 25–26, 45–46,
  85–86, 126
Rowland, James "Hellfire," 37–39,
  43–44, 48

sacraments. *See* baptism; Lord's Supper
Sandy Creek Association of Baptists
  (North Carolina). *See* Marshall,
  Daniel; Separate Baptists
Second Great Awakening, 299–303
Screven, William, 70–74
Scripture. *See* Bible
self-examination, spiritual discipline of,
  83–84, 125–27
Separate Baptists, distinctions from and
  union with Regular Baptists, 51, 52–53,
  147–48, 197–98, 215–19, 237–39,
  273–74, 306–7. *See also* First Great
  Awakening *specific individuals*
Separation of Church and State. *See*
  American Revolution; Backus, Isaac
Shakers, 266–68
Shurden, Walter, 104
Silver Bluff Church (South Carolina), 99
Simmons, Thomas, 73–75
slavery
  antebellum Baptist defense of, 310–13
  and Baptist antislavery movement,
    295–98, 309–10
  and early Pennsylvania Baptists, 20–22
  evangelical sanctifying of, 100–3
  fear of slave revolts, 97, 243, 310–11
  *See also* African American Baptists;
    George, David; Hart, Oliver;
    Liele, George; Mageay, Margaret;
    Margarett, David; Marrant, John;
    paternalism; Southern Baptist
    Convention
Smith, Elias, 169–70
Smith, Hezekiah, 153–54, 157, 169–70,
  184–85, 188, 225, 242, 295–96
Southampton Baptist Church
  (Pennsylvania), 22–23, 66–70, 76,
  153, 154–55, 162
Southern Baptist Convention,
  91–92, 312–15
Southern Baptist Theological
  Seminary, 313
Stamp Act (1765), 222–23
Stearns, Shubal, 7–8, 61–62, 147–48, 193–94,
  299. *See also* Separate Baptists
Stephens, John, 105, 109–10, 118, 128, 145,
  151, 154

INDEX 337

Stiles, Ezra, 185–87, 224–25, 226
Stillman, Samuel, 133–34, 137–39, 149–50, 167–71, 201, 222–23, 242, 297–98

Tennent, Gilbert, 37–39, 42–43, 48
Tennent, William III, 229–34, 235–37
Tilly, William, 45–46
total depravity. *See* Calvinism
Triennial Convention, 307–13
Trinity, 23–25, 155–56, 268–69, 298

Universalism, 263–65, 291–92

Virginia Baptists. *See* American Revolution
visions, 48, 144–45, 195–96

war. *See* American Revolution
Warren Association (New England), 187, 224–25, 235–36, 237–38, 265, 283–84

Washington, George, 151–52, 250–51, 254–55, 257–59, 279–82
Welsh Baptists, 15–16, 23–26, 30, 108–9
Welsh Neck Church (South Carolina), 105, 108–9, 144, 149, 162, 172–74, 177–82, 264
Whitefield, George, 40–47, 74–75, 87–88, 91, 101–2, 131, 133, 149, 165, 199–201
Williams, David, 101–2, 121–23, 165–67
Winchester, Elhanan, 263–65
women
    and "domesticated piety," 201–11
    and role in early Baptist churches, 46–49, 60–62
    *See also specific people*
Woodmason, Charles, 95, 114–15, 191–94, 196–97, 232–33

Zubly, John, 88–89, 141–42, 196